SHIBARI SUSPENSIONS

A STEP BY STEP GUIDE

GESTALTA

kahboom

First published in the United Kingdom in 2019
by Kahboom Ltd.
The Mount Business Park,
Horseheath,
Cambridge CB21 4QX
UK

www.kahboom.com

www.gestalta.co.uk

www.shibaristudio.com

ISBN: 978-0-9576275-4-3

Text, editing and layout design by Gestalta
Proofread by Cad
Printed by KOPA in Lithuania

NOTICE

Whilst it is hoped that the information contained in this book will be helpful to people at many different levels, it is primarily intended as supplementary material and should not be seen as a substitute for working with a real life teacher, or with other experienced practitioners in a peer learning environment.

The techniques shown in this book are not suitable for beginners. Following these directions safely requires a base level of knowledge that this book is unable to cover effectively. In addition to this, proficiency in rope bondage comes only with dedicated, regular practice. Understanding a technique in theory is no substitute for real life experience.

It cannot be emphasised enough that you should avoid practicing rope bondage unsupervised if you do not have sufficient training and experience.

Rope bondage, like any other adult activity, carries an inherent risk of injury. The safety information contained within this guide cannot comprehensively cover every possible eventuality. By choosing to engage in these activities you are accepting personal responsibility for your own actions, and you agree that those involved with the creation, publication and distribution of this book cannot be held responsible for any physical or emotional injury sustained.

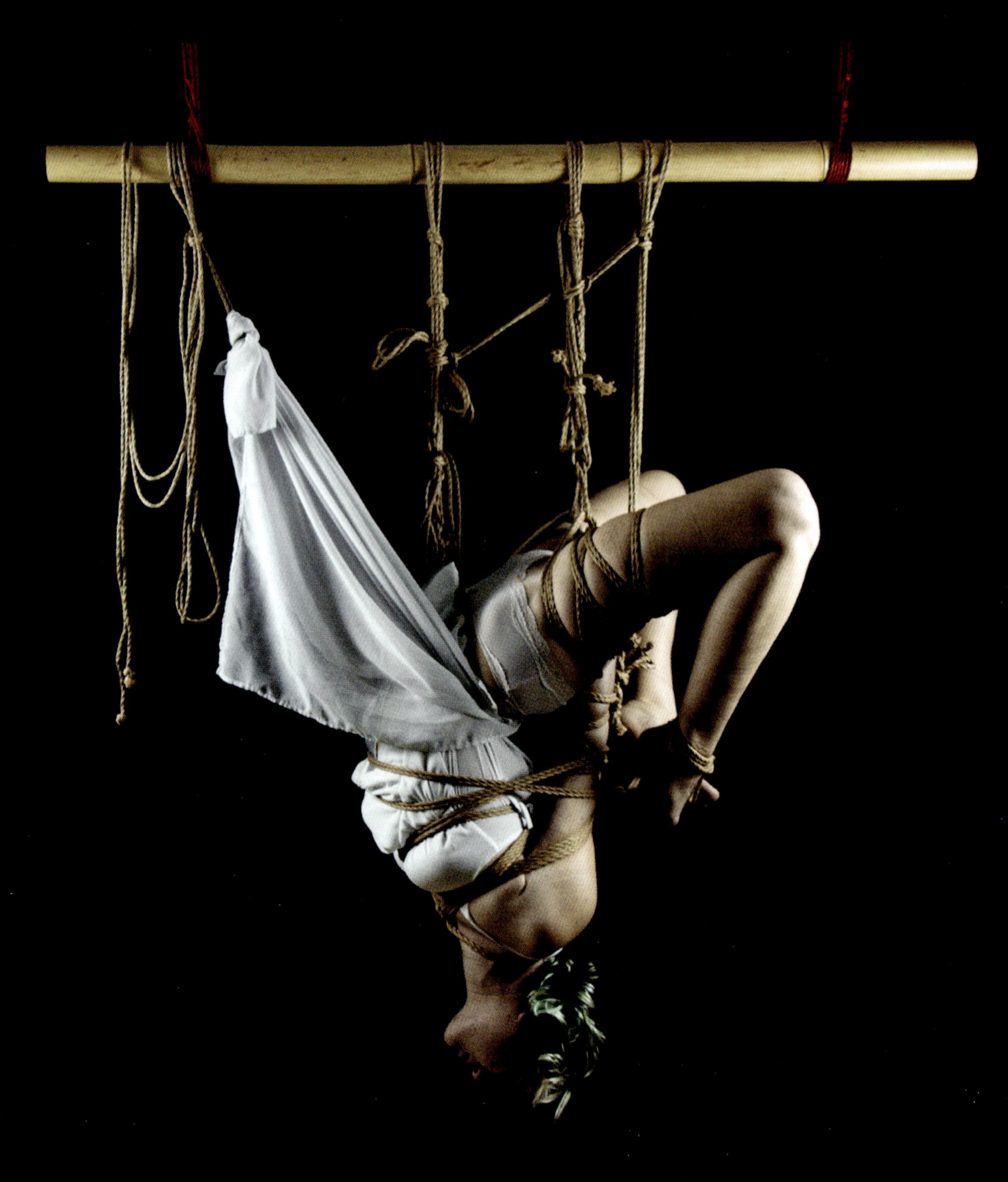

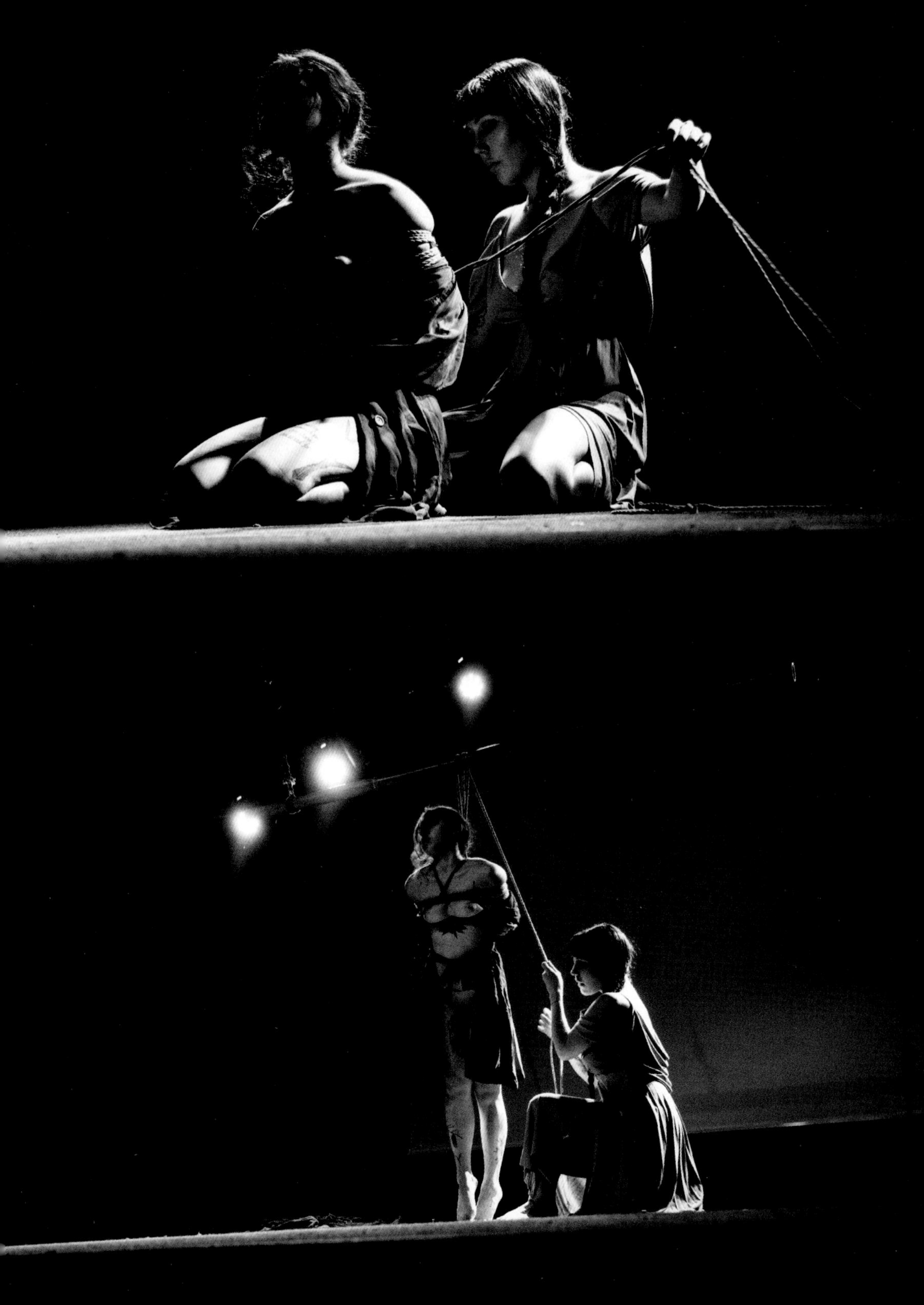

About the Book

The popularity of shibari in the west has been growing exponentially in recent years. With this the accessibility and quality of rope education has expanded to a point that was unimaginable when I first started practicing in 2007. Then, unless you had the means to travel to Japan, the most common way of learning was from one of the few books available, or by trying to reverse-engineer ties from photos, which (perhaps understandably in the latter case) seems to horrify some people today.

However with the wider availability of in-person teaching, it's often forgotten that attending classes is a privilege many people don't have – either because they don't live in a city with an established community, or because the cost is prohibitive. Whilst there are advantages to having a teacher, if that option isn't available it's far better to have some affordable, accessible information out there than none at all. It's my hope that this book can go some way to providing that information.

Shibari is a broad subject, and deciding what needed to be left out of this book was a difficult task. I've opted to keep its scope limited in order to give more in-depth explanations. Whilst I've included all the information necessary to create the suspensions demonstrated, I have presented it as a very direct pathway. To my mind, this is not an accurate representation of the process of learning shibari at beginner level. I have assumed readers to have a base level of knowledge of rope handling, tensioning, fundamental frictions, and preferably some basic familiarity with body movement. For a book providing a more comprehensive overview of rope practice right from the beginning I would recommend reading 'Essence of Shibari' by Shin Nawakiri. 'Miumi-U Teaches Japanese Shibari' also gives some alternative variations on the patterns shown here.

This book is intended to provide a 'bare bones' framework upon which you can base your own independent research and practice. I recommend taking time to explore each part slowly, experimenting with what works and feels fun for you, looking for different options, and becoming deeply familiar with each idea. Where possible, I believe this book will be most useful as a 'study guide' within a peer learning environment. If you are able to take lessons, you might consider using this book as supplementary material to give yourself a broader exposure to different styles of tying, or as a reminder to help you solidify what you've learnt between classes.

I also hope it can give you an idea of the directions it's possible to go in when you start experimenting – both with tying creatively and with modifying the ties to suit your needs. The various alternatives suggested (such as hands free chest harnesses, alternative hand positioning etc.) won't be a solution to everyone's problems, but I hope they will give you an idea of how to think when you're trying to come up with your own solutions.

All of the content is aimed at both riggers and models. Even if you see yourself as fitting only one of those roles, I recommend that you read all parts of the book. For me (as someone who is both) the two roles are so interlinked that I find it hard to explain them separately. Understanding as much as possible from both viewpoints can help you to empathise with each other, and also to better evaluate a situation and make informed decisions.

Notes on the Language Used in This Book

JAPANESE TERMINOLOGY

If it is already in common usage, I have generally chosen to use the Japanese terminology along with a literal translation and, in some cases, its most common English translation. I believe that it's worth being familiar with these terms even if you choose not to use them yourself.

Being aware of the Japanese terms can be interesting in informing the way that you think about rope. Mostly they describe the position of the body rather than of how the rope is tied and I think that having this in the back of your mind helps to keep your focus on the body, and away from obsessing too much about what the 'correct' rope pattern for a particular tie is.

Some people, myself included, also find it useful to have a common terminology that is specific to rope practice as it can make discussion of a particular topic easier – and I like the fact that this has largely been kept to the Japanese words as it pays homage to where the practice has come from, even though it has started to diverge and evolve separately in some ways.

GLOSSARY

For ease of reference, I have included a glossary at the back of the book (pg. 166) which includes English and Japanese terminology. The first usage of a new English glossary term is written in **bold**.

TECHNICAL LANGUAGE

I will sometimes use words like up, down, left, and right to refer to what you can see in the accompanying photos. In real life this doesn't matter – you can work in whichever direction you like as long as you modify the directions as required at every step.

I have also used words such as '**U-turn**' or '**full turn**' to describe the path that the rope follows. I hope that for the most part, these terms will be self explanatory when seen in context, but I have listed them in the glossary nonetheless.

OTHER LANGUAGE

I am using the terms 'rigger' and 'model' to refer to the one who ties and the one who is tied. Although I have never really been happy with these words they are the most neutral currently in common parlance. I wished to avoid anything that indicated an unequal power dynamic between partners, partly because rope is not *necessarily* a D/s activity and many people (myself included) don't practice it as such – and partly because I feel it's important to stress that the model is not an unequal contributor to the process of learning shibari. Where possible I prefer to use the term 'tying partner' although this doesn't work when it is necessary to specify which one.

I use gender neutral language when describing the human body so you will come across terms such as 'bodies with breasts', 'bodies with broader shoulders', 'bodies with bottom heavy weight distribution'. This is done with the intention of being as inclusive as possible – but it also provides you with a more helpful and accurate way of looking at the human body when you are tying. In my experience, I have tied far more people with some element to their physicality that doesn't fit within the stereotypical gender binary, than those who fit it completely.

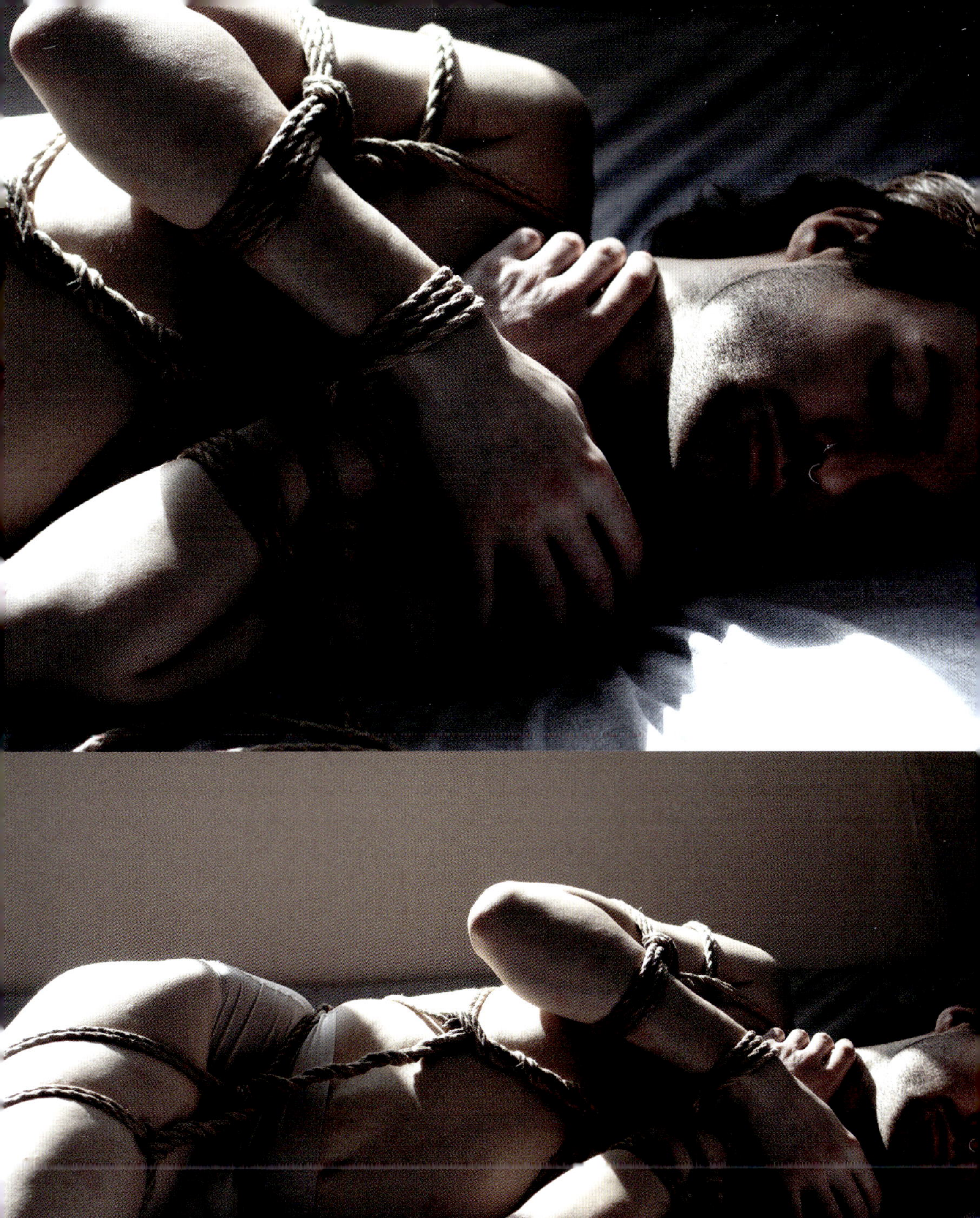

Am I Ready to Suspend?

There is no definitive way to decide when someone is ready to begin learning suspension. Although shibari is a relatively new practice there are already many different teachers with their own ideas on how to make the assessment.

Some teachers mandate that students practice **floor work** for at least a year before adding suspension lines, regardless of how quickly an individual picks techniques up. Others introduce small exercises involving suspension lines right from the beginning and gradually move towards full suspension over time. Some judge based on how fast you can tie common harnesses – for example, a suspension worthy takatekote in X minutes. There is no single way that works for everyone.

However, there are a number of things that seem to be almost universally considered that you might find a useful guide. The *fluency* with which a rigger is able to tie common harnesses such as the takatekote (pg. 50) is important – if you're still finding yourself stopping to think about the next step, or aren't consistently getting the tension right every time, it's probably not safe to begin suspension. The only way to achieve this kind of fluency is to practise frequently, until it becomes muscle memory. You can time yourself if you wish. Anything from about five to seven minutes for a three rope takatekote (pg. 59) is adequate when working at a steady pace and stopping to check tensions and **dress the wraps** – if this still feels like a rush you might need more practice.

Remember that untying with a similar level of fluency is just as important.

Before attempting to suspend a model you should be well practiced in working with suspension lines (pg. 106-119) quickly and safely. I recommend first practising by attaching the lines to inanimate objects and repeating the process of lifting, locking, unlocking and lowering as frequently as possible.

When you feel ready, both riggers and models can begin by trying **partial suspensions** (pg. 125). Although not entirely without risk, this removes many of the potential complications that could lead to critical situations, giving the rigger more time to think about the next step as they tie, and helping both rigger and model explore how the body moves and reacts when in rope.

You should have considered the process of taking a suspension down before going up. This might sound obvious but it's easily overlooked. All the suspensions in this book can be untied in the exact reverse of the order they were tied – but this won't always be the case as you progress onto more advanced work. If something goes wrong and you can't get down as planned there is some information on getting out of an emergency situation on page 123.

Models can prepare by reading about some of the common problems encountered in suspension, and spending time getting to know your body within common harnesses. Sit on the floor and ask a rigger to attach and lock a suspension line at various different points on the harness so that you can lean your weight into it, testing how it feels at different angles. This can help you understand your wrap placements and the effects of pressure on the body.

I also recommend that you and your partner (particularly if you are regularly tying with the same person) build good ways of communicating right from the beginning. Learning rope can at times be frustrating and it's useful if you are willing to take the time to learn how to talk to each other productively even if something has just gone wrong.

Thinking About Rope

Different Bodies

The idea that being tied is reserved for a very narrow range of body types – small, flexible, cis women – is a pervasive one, despite the fact that there are many shibari models who don't fit this description at all. A visit to most shibari events will quickly demonstrate that it is suitable for a wide range of body sizes, shapes, and types.

However, all bodies are different and often need to be tied differently as a result. There really is no such thing as 'one size fits all' bondage: even between two people with seemingly similar bodies there will often need to be modifications made to tailor a tie to them. It can seem very frustrating when you try something and it doesn't work for you – but there is also a great potential for tying partners to have fun together working to find inventive ways to overcome the problems they encounter.

Within the book I have given some suggestions for potential adaptations. They are not comprehensive, but rather are included with the intention of illustrating the way that you might need to think in order to find your own solutions, and to help you keep in mind that if something doesn't work for you the first step should be to look for a way to change the rope, and not for a way to change your body.

Remember that no matter how you might think it looks from the outside, *everyone* has something that they struggle with in ropes.

Whilst some models do choose to work on increasing their strength or flexibility for shibari it's not a necessity. Rope is first and foremost about the effect that it has on the people doing it: many people who practise rope do enjoy being pushed to physical limits, but that limit is completely personal, and the psychological effect will be similar whether your limit is putting your feet on the back of your head or lying tied up on the floor.

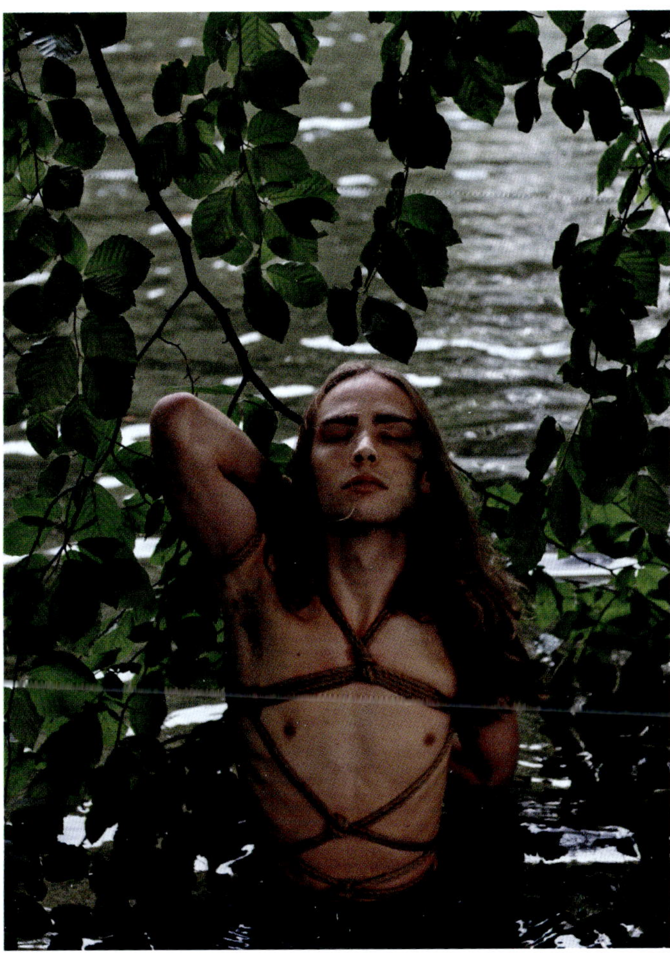

Please also bear in mind that this book has a focus on suspension and whilst this is fun for many people, it is far from the only reason to practice rope bondage. Trying it and deciding that it's not for you doesn't mean that bondage isn't for you – in fact there are many great riggers who are not interested in suspending models at all, preferring to focus on the intimacy and connection involved with floor work. There is such a huge range of enjoyable things you can be doing with ropes that it's likely that you can find something that feels right for you.

Different Tying Styles

The idea that there is only one 'correct' way to tie makes no sense. There are many different ways of tying **single column ties** and harnesses, of locking suspension lines etc. I would tend to be wary of anyone who tries to tell you theirs is the only right way. This doesn't mean that there's no such thing as a wrong way to do something – and when you are first learning it is safest to stick to the methods that a teacher has given you – but eventually you will hopefully get to a point where you can work out for yourself why something does or doesn't work. Although, even at an advanced level if you are taking a class with a particular teacher, they may ask you to stick to their way of doing things for the duration of the class, and it's both helpful and respectful to do so.

The methods taught in this book are there to give you a consistent technique that I know will work within the context that I've given it – but that doesn't necessarily mean that it's the 'best' way, or even the only way that I do things myself. I personally find it useful to learn as wide a variety of different techniques as possible so I can mix and match elements from each and remain adaptable to different situations.

In addition to there being many different ways to achieve the same thing technically, there are also many different styles of suspension bondage that you might wish to explore after you have become a bit more confident with the basics. Knowing what you're looking for can help you to find the right teacher for you later on. Some common styles include:

- ◊ Dynamic **transitions**, where the model is moved around between different positions in the air. This style can look quite impressive from a performative point of view. The advantage of tying like this is that you can prolong the time you are able to keep a session going, even if the model is in relatively tough positions, as they don't have to sustain them for very long, and you can also rapidly move the stressful areas from one part of the body to the other. The repeated build-up and release of different tensions can also create a headspace which some models enjoy. Tying like this requires a lot of practice in fluid movements, and in planning several steps ahead.
- ◊ Some people like to focus on creating solid, comfortable harnesses and positions so that the model can be left in a suspension for a relatively long time. This is perhaps most advantageous if you wish to engage in other forms of play whilst the model is suspended.
- ◊ Semenawa – torture rope – is not the only way of practicing sadomasochistic shibari, but what sets it apart is that the rope and body positions themselves are often the primary cause of pain, rather than any additional elements. It can of course be practiced on the floor as well as in suspension. When it is used in suspension it is often fairly slow

moving in comparison with other styles, giving time for the stress/pain to build in intensity.

Many people also practice a fusion of these styles.

Making Decisions

My thought process when I'm tying often seems to revolve around finding a good balance between safety, efficiency, and aesthetic. Sometimes it's inevitable that I have to sacrifice a degree of one, in order to gain a degree of another. It is a gradual process to train your brain to be able to make these decisions quickly and naturally – especially under pressure.

Sometimes there might be a technically safer option, but it would take a long time meaning the model might be left in a stressful position for longer than strictly necessary. Sometimes there might be a more efficient option that you dislike the aesthetic of etc.

As a beginner, it is advisable that you make the majority of your decisions based around safety, with efficiency as a second, and worry about aesthetic last. As you become more skilled you can slowly re-adjust this ratio.

You and Your Tying Partner

It is the shared responsibility of both model and rigger to choose carefully who they tie with and communicate openly and honestly with each other. The following information is relevant to both tying partners and should be a good starting point, but there are many other resources available if you want to learn more. You can also talk to other people within the rope community and find out how they approach interactions between tying partners.

Choosing Who To Tie With

If you're planning to tie with a new person for the first time it's a good idea to ask around for feedback from people they have tied with before. Useful questions to ask might include:

- When negotiating, did they listen well?
- Did they respect your limits?
- Did they listen to you during the session?
- Were they open to hearing any feedback you gave them after the session? Would you tie with them again? Why?

Remember that these are questions that both models and riggers should be asking. It is just as possible for a rigger to have a negative experience because a model didn't give feedback on the tie, as it is for a model to have a negative experience because the rigger didn't listen to their feedback.

Where possible, I would also suggest that you take the opportunity to watch a potential new partner tie with other people. Ask yourself if this looks like the kind of bondage that you would enjoy. Does it look sadistic, sensual, sexual, challenging, soft, dominant, submissive, comical, humiliating? Bear in mind that the dynamic they have with that person may not be the be the dynamic that the two of you would have together, but it will be worth bringing up in any pre-rope negotiation with them. For example "I saw that the rope you did with person X involved humiliation play. I don't think I would be comfortable with this. Is this something that's a deal-breaker for you, or are there other things that you would enjoy doing together?" Or on the flip-side: "I'm approaching you to see if you'd like to tie because I saw the scene you did with X the other day and that seems like the kind of thing I'm really into."

As an inexperienced model it can be difficult to assess the skill/safety of a rigger. "I've been doing this for 10 years" doesn't necessarily mean that they're safe or knowledgeable – which is why I always suggest that your first step should be to ask the community – but another useful tool is to increase your understanding of rope bondage so you're better able to make your own judgements. Familiarising yourself with the information contained in this book can help you get a rough idea of what to look out for – but as there are many different ways to tie the fact that something looks unfamiliar, doesn't necessarily mean it's unsafe or wrong. If you see something you're unsure of don't be afraid to ask the rigger.

Asking loaded questions such as "Is this dangerous?" can make some riggers feel defensive. Approaching with curiosity can make them more receptive: "How does this suspension line lock off work?" or "How does this piece of equipment work?" I would personally be wary about tying with someone who had a problem with being asked this kind of question, and if they didn't have all the answers I would respect them a lot more for being honest about it so that we could look for the solution together.

Likewise, it's important for models to be honest about their level of experience. If you tell a rigger that you are very experienced they will probably assume that you know your own body well and are confident in their ability to gauge and communicate problems. As a result they may check in with you slightly less, or be inclined to try something more advanced than they would with someone they knew didn't have much experience.

Trust is a two way thing, and honesty is the basis of that.

When you tie together for the first time, it's also worth thinking carefully about the situation in which you wish it to take place. Many people prefer to meet and tie at public rope events initially, and if this isn't possible, perhaps invite some friends to be present at home.

Communicating and Negotiating with Your Partner

Communication and negotiation are things that should be an ongoing process before, during, and after you tie, but how you choose to negotiate is highly individual. Some people like to specify everything in detail upfront to avoid the possibility of misunderstandings, whilst others feel this kills spontaneity and prefer to keep the negotiation process open as the session unfolds. For many people some combination of the two works well.

Negotiation is not only about discussing your limitations, but also your desires and interests, and finding common ground between tying partners.

BEFORE

At an absolute minimum, inform each other of any conditions, either physical or mental/emotional, that might have an impact on the session. Breathing or heart conditions, circulation, nerve or mobility issues, old injuries, epilepsy, anxiety triggers: however irrelevant it might seem it's probably better to mention than not. This goes for riggers as well as models.

It's also a good idea discuss your risk profile (pg. 18) and let each other know of any hard limits (i.e. things that you absolutely would not consent to under any circumstance). Some people find it useful to agree on a specific safe word: something you can say at any point which brings the whole scene to an immediate close.

People sometimes overlook the need to discuss their expectations of each other once the tie has finished. Whilst some are able to continue with their day as normal the second it's over, others will need time to readjust, and might wish to know they have someone there for support.

If you're confident in your ability to communicate effectively whilst doing rope you might choose to leave your pre-tie negotiation there. You should explicitly discuss this with any new partner as it's not uncommon to struggle with verbal communication whilst tying.

Others may wish to have more in-depth discussions, and talk about what they would like to experience in the session.

DURING

Even if you have had a detailed pre-tie talk, you can still negotiate throughout. Whether there's something you forgot to mention or you've suddenly realised that you're not enjoying something that you thought you would, there is no such thing as a bad moment to make your needs or wants known.

If you do decide you're happy to continue negotiating mid-scene it's helpful to discuss beforehand how this is going to take place. For example, some riggers will just ask outright "are you ok with hair rope?" whereas others might just pull gently on the hair and wait to see how the model reacts before going further. Whilst this latter style of communication is fine in theory, remember that it requires a certain amount of familiarity and skill to be able to read a person non-verbally and there is always going to be a degree of ambiguity which you need to have mutually decided you are comfortable with. It's also not uncommon to have trouble expressing yourself as you normally would when

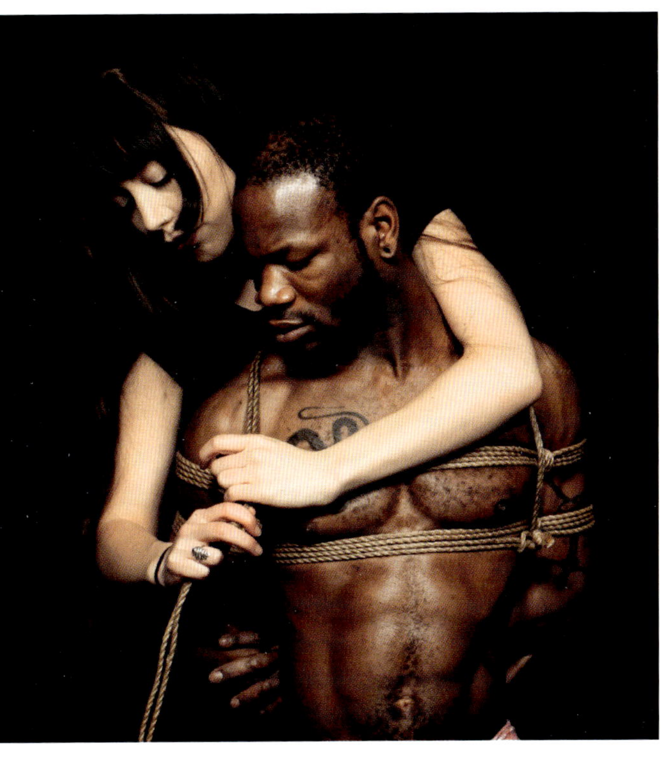

in a rope headspace, so I would advise familiarising yourselves with your reactions so you are confident you have some method of communicating with each other.

The model can also let the rigger know about pinches or discomfort that might need fixing, or any tingling or numbness that is causing concern (pg. 43-46). As you become more experienced you might find it becomes easier to be quite direct with this. Saying things like "move my left thigh wrap" or "I have five minutes left in this position" is very helpful for riggers and can make a tie far more relaxed.

AFTER

It's useful to give each other feedback on how you feel both physically and emotionally afterwards as this can help you both improve your skills, and get to know each other better if you decide to tie again. Some people also find it useful to check in with each other a few days after tying, once they've had time to process everything.

Remember that a successful negotiation of one tie with a partner doesn't necessarily cover all future ties together. Someone who agreed to being blindfolded during a play session may not wish this to happen in a workshop context. Someone who was comfortable with nudity in private may not be comfortable with this in public. Sometimes you just feel a bit different from one day to the next for no definable reason. It is ok for partners to have different guidelines for different situations.

Defining Your Risk Profile

In order to be able to negotiate effectively it's essential to have a clear idea of what you consider to be acceptable and unacceptable risks.

Potential risks involved in shibari include:

- ◊ Marks left on the skin, which could take anything from an hour to a week to disappear (in some rare cases they may last months) but are otherwise superficial injuries that shouldn't cause discomfort.
- ◊ A rope pulled quickly across the body with too much friction can cause rope burns. In some cases this can be painful and take a few weeks to fully heal, but are otherwise unlikely to have any long term negative effects.
- ◊ Nerve damage (discussed in detail on pg. 43-47) can cause a loss of sensation in the skin or loss of motor control. The effects can last minutes, to months. Sensory loss generally won't have much effect on your day to day life, but loss of motor function can have a big impact.
- ◊ Pulled muscles, damaged joints etc. can cause pain or discomfort for a while after the session – in more severe cases you may need to look into physiotherapy.

With these risk factors in mind, you should think about any individual life circumstances that might affect how much risk you're willing to take.

- ◊ Some people have jobs or personal life situations where it might be inappropriate to have rope marks in visible areas, such as the neck or the wrists, and so might decide that they don't want any rope in these areas.
- ◊ Whilst no one particularly wants to encounter nerve damage there are some people for whom it would cause much bigger problems than others and they may consider factoring that into their risk profile accordingly – for example anyone who has a job which requires arm strength or a steady

hand. Many people are ok to accept sensation loss, whereas others find all forms of nerve damage unacceptable, and might wish to untie as soon as they feel anything odd in the hands, rather than asking the rigger to move the wraps or switch positions and wait to see if the feeling goes away.

- ◊ If you have a very physically demanding job, or play a lot of sports, then damage to the joints or muscles may have more effect on you than if you have a desk job.
- ◊ If you have young children or other dependants then even a relatively temporary incapacitation could be hard to manage.

Whilst it's generally models who are more likely to sustain physical injuries, the rigger must consider their risk profile also. For example, a model might consider nerve damage to be an acceptable risk for them – but that doesn't necessarily mean that the rigger is ok with the idea that they might cause someone a nerve damage and so you should also communicate this with the model.

Safety

For the most part, I have addressed any safety issues where they are most relevant so they can be understood in context.

The information here relates to more general safety concerns to keep in your mind at all times. Reading about safety in ropes can leave you with the impression that rope is an unreasonably dangerous activity where an accident is imminent and inevitable. Thankfully, serious accidents within shibari are incredibly rare – but they stay rare precisely because people take the time to educate themselves and behave responsibly. However overwhelming it might seem at first, after a while awareness will become second nature and your safety checks will be built in as habits, making the whole process far more relaxing.

Safety Cutters

Most people will tell you that safety cutters are an essential part of your rope bag – but it's less common to hear anyone talking about how and when to use them. Although it's rare that they're needed you should still have thought through the process. I would strongly recommend doing a trial run in a nonemergency situation to familiarise yourself with the feeling. This could also help to stop you being hesitant about sacrificing a set of ropes you've become sentimentally attached to; rope is a consumable item and you should never be afraid to cut it.

You can carry **[A]** EMT shears, which are great for sliding in close to skin (try to keep these only for emergencies as they can become blunt with repeated use). A safety knife might be an easier option should you ever need to cut something under tension.

For the most part you should only cut rope from people who are already on the floor

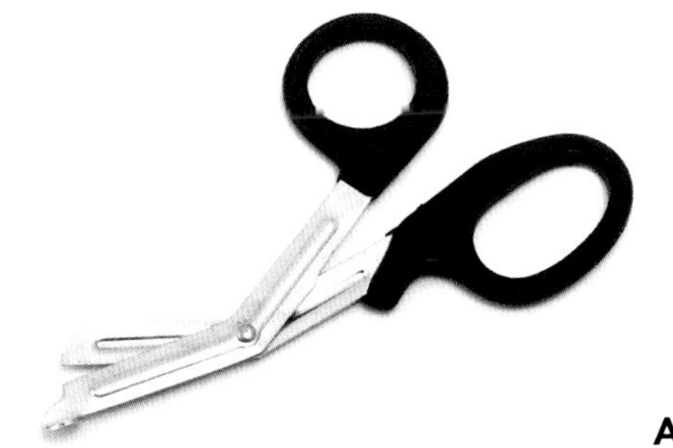

A

as cutting down a suspension can create a whole set of additional dangers – but in very rare circumstances this might be the best course of action; I've briefly explained the process of this on pg. 123.

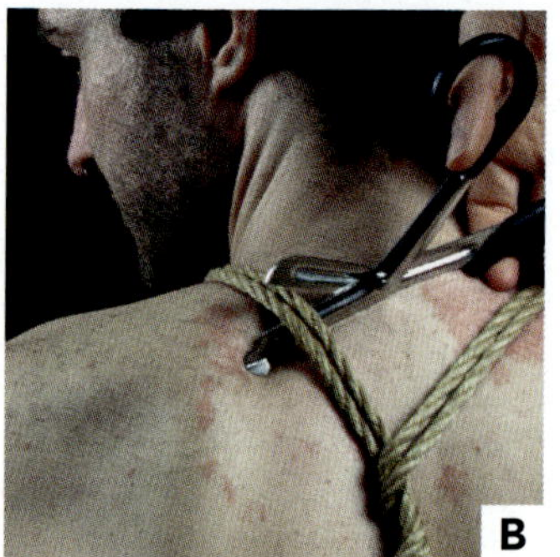

[B] It goes without saying that you should never put rope anywhere near the neck unless you have first double checked your shears are to hand – and this includes the third ropes on a takatekote (pg. 59-65). When cutting, slide your shears in towards the back where there is most space.

The Role of a Spotter

When learning shibari it is essential that you practice where there is someone around to help if you get into difficulties. It is preferable, at least initially, that they are more experienced than you, but as you progress you can take it in turns to practice with people of a similar level so you can all watch out for each other.

As a beginner, it's easy to miss seemingly 'obvious' steps if you are feeling nervous or pressured, so the spotter can act as a second pair of eyes. They can also make sure that other people stay out of your space if you are in a public environment, and keep an eye on the situation around you whilst you are focussed on tying.

Should the model need to come down from suspension in a hurry, an extra pair of hands is invaluable, as one person can hold and support the model's weight whilst the other person concentrates on the suspension lines. I've given a little more information on getting down from suspension in an emergency on pg. 123. They can also help you in a similar way if one of your lines becomes caught or jammed, and you need help to take the weight off it to release it.

Even when you are experienced it's a good idea to ask a spotter to watch you if you are trying something new that you're unsure of.

The Head and Neck

The head and neck are by far the most important body parts to protect, as any damage to them can really be catastrophic. For this reason I have chosen not to cover inverted suspensions, or any ties involving the hair, face, or neck in this book, and strongly discourage you from attempting them without proper supervision and instruction.

You will probably see people tying rope around the hair or the face and using it to pull the head, which can be damaging to the neck if not practiced carefully. Although the neck is reasonably strong when pulled backwards, it is quite weak when pulled to the side, and easy to strain, or even break in this way. If you do attempt this kind of tie, remember to pull slowly and gently, leave the rope on a quick release where it is easy to undo, and ensure that it is the *first* thing you untie before attempting to move any other part of the body. Avoid swinging, or spinning the person in suspension whilst the head is tied.

Pulling the neck too far back can also restrict the breathing so it must be monitored very carefully.

POSITIONAL ASPHYXIA

Positional asphyxia, as the name suggests, occurs when the body is left in a position that hinders breathing, and within shibari there are various potential ways this could happen.

Positions in which the mouth or nose are blocked (e.g. with a gag), or in which the neck is restrained in such a way that the airways are obstructed (e.g. with a hair tie) are both obvious examples to watch out for, but a restriction of movement in the respiratory muscles can also be a cause.

The primary muscle used in respiration is the diaphragm* which lies between the chest cavity and the abdominal cavity. When you inhale the diaphragm contracts, simultaneously compressing the abdominal cavity and expanding the chest cavity which draws air into the lungs. In a relaxed, healthy state it is only inhalation that requires muscular effort – exhalation occurs passively as the muscles relax. However, if this process is disrupted in some way it may be necessary to also *exhale* actively by contracting the muscles of the abdominal wall* which reduces the volume of the chest cavity by pushing the abdominal organs upwards against the diaphragm.

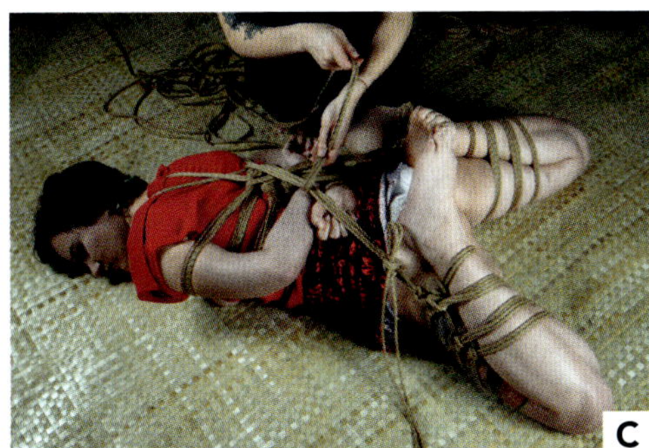
C

If the amount of effort it takes to breathe either in or out becomes greater than the muscles are capable of sustaining they may simply cease to function, causing respiratory failure. The amount of time this takes is hugely dependent upon the person and the situation, which is why it is necessary to monitor a tied person constantly, even if everything seems fine at first.

The following is a non-exhaustive list of positions that could pose a risk:

- ◊ Being restrained face down (for example in **[C]** a **hogtie**/gyaku-ebi). This is more likely to carry a risk for people with larger abdomens because the abdominal organs can be pushed upwards, restricting the diaphragm. Hanging upside down can carry this risk for the same reason.
- ◊ Being forced forward when in a seated position (for example in the traditional **[D]** 'ebi' torture position).

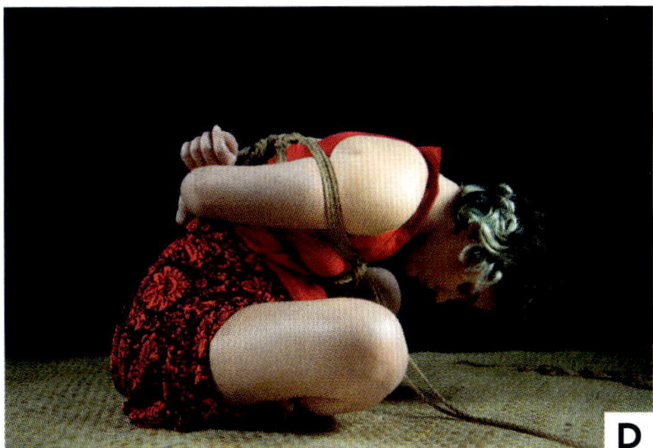
D

- ◊ A face down suspension can limit the expansion of the chest cavity due to the pressure from the ropes of the chest harness.
- ◊ Crucifixion position, if there is too much weight on the arms and not enough supporting the torso.

---

* The external intercostal muscles are also used in inhalation and the internal intercostal muscles also play a role in active exhalation.

Positional asphyxia tends to occur quite slowly and the model is likely to be aware of it and able to say something early on. There are also some general warning signs you can look out for:

- A blockage of the airways might be indicated by a gurgling or gasping sound.
- The lips or face may turn blue due to lack of oxygen.
- In some cases the model may have difficulty speaking.
- Low oxygen levels often induce a panic response.

If you witness any of these things, you should untie immediately.

As a model, you should disclose to the rigger before you tie if you have any pre-existing breathing condition (for example asthma, emphysema, heart disease etc.) as this will put you at higher risk – as will being tied if you have taken drugs or alcohol.

It is possible that excessive struggling may decrease the time taken to succumb to positional asphyxia. You should exercise additional caution if you are involved in 'take down' scenarios.

Although this might sound very scary, it isn't something that you need to be worried about. When bondage is practiced responsibly, by people who are informed and conscious of the risks, serious incidents of this nature are completely preventable.

Tying Whilst Intoxicated

It goes without saying that you should avoid anything that could impair your judgement prior to tying. However you should also remember that it isn't just slowed response times that could pose a risk: the combination of certain drugs or alcohol and rope could also put the model at increased risk of cardiac arrest, asphyxia, or other issues.

The Rope Itself

In this book I am using a loose lay, single ply, natural fibre jute rope of around 6mm in diameter. This works well for shibari as it compacts tightly enough to hold knots and frictions but not so tightly that they become difficult to undo, it doesn't have too much stretch making it easy to work with in suspension, it tends to become smoother and less 'fluffy' with use, and it's a fairly light rope, making it easy to move if you're tying with some speed.

Although this seems to be the most popular shibari rope it's by far not the only option – hemp, cotton, and linen are all common choices, and certain types of synthetic rope might also be suitable. It's worth noting that if you decide to use a different type of rope some of the information in this book may need to be adjusted to compensate for its different properties. If possible, I would suggest contacting a practitioner who has experience with the rope you want to use to ask for advice. If this is impossible, thoroughly test the rope on inanimate objects before you attempt a suspension on a person.

Most people use ropes of 7 to 8 meters in length, with a few shorter pieces (1 to 4 meters) on hand should they be needed. I also like to keep a few ropes cut to specific lengths to fit the bodies of the models I tie most frequently – for example I like to have a rope cut especially for the upper wrap of the takatekote (pg. 50) so that the join ends up at the back where it won't cause problems.

The **[E]** ends of the rope (nawajiri) are finished with a simple **overhand knot**. All the ties in this book use the rope folded in half, and start from **[F]** the middle point, or **bight** (nawagashira), of the rope. The term **working end** refers to the remainder of the rope from the last knot or friction that you made, up to the rope ends (i.e. the part of the rope you are still working with).

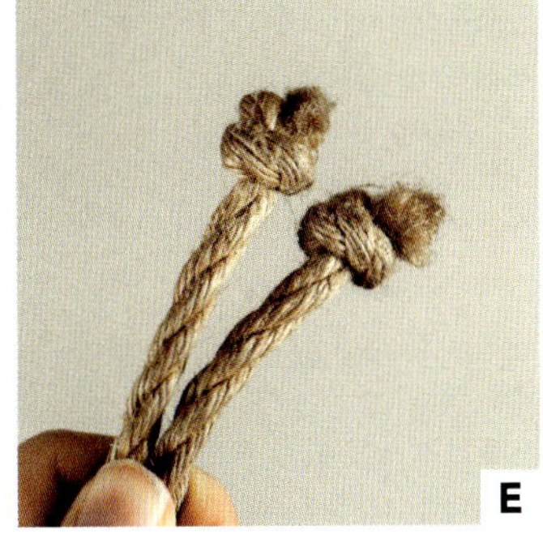
E

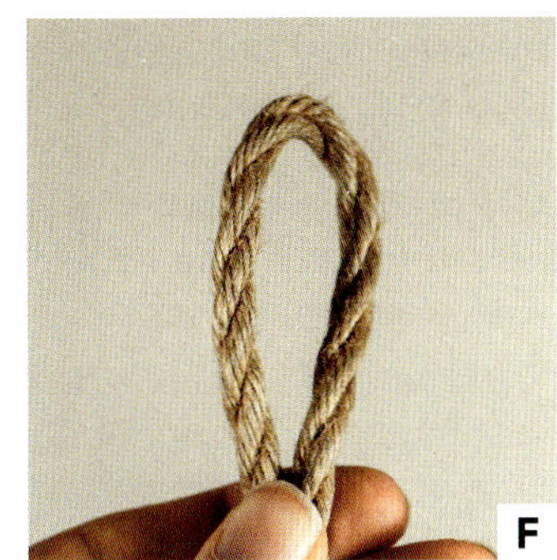
F

Rope Maintenance

The initial treatment process for new rope will vary a lot depending on what kind you buy; if you wish to learn how to do it there are many online resources that can teach you. You can also buy pre-treated rope from many different suppliers. The following is general advice on how to maintain your pre-treated natural fibre rope and ensure that it stays suspension worthy.

It's especially important that your **main line** (pg. 106) is in good condition. I replace main lines frequently, moving them into my regular kit once they start to wear in. As my regular ropes become too worn I retire them to be used for floor work. Exactly how long this cycle takes will depend on how well you look after your rope, how frequently you tie, and what type of rope you are using – but a good measure is to examine the rope and look for any **[G]** fraying in the yarns, or signs that the strands are separating.

Jute that gets too dry can become brittle, so it's important to treat it regularly with oil or wax. Common choices for oil include camellia and jojoba oil – although any oil that does not go rancid over time could be used. You can also make a treatment paste by combining one of the oils with a wax such as bees wax or soya wax – many suppliers also sell these pastes pre-made. To treat your rope just rub a little oil or wax into the palms of your hands and run the rope through them a few times – paying particular attention to the bight. Avoid saturating the rope as it may become heavy or sticky, making it difficult to use – a light coating on a regular basis is all you need.

Washing or dying jute rope can weaken the strands and mess up the tension – I personally avoid it, but if this is something you wish to do then make sure you've thoroughly researched the process first.

If rope begins to **[H]** highstrand it could

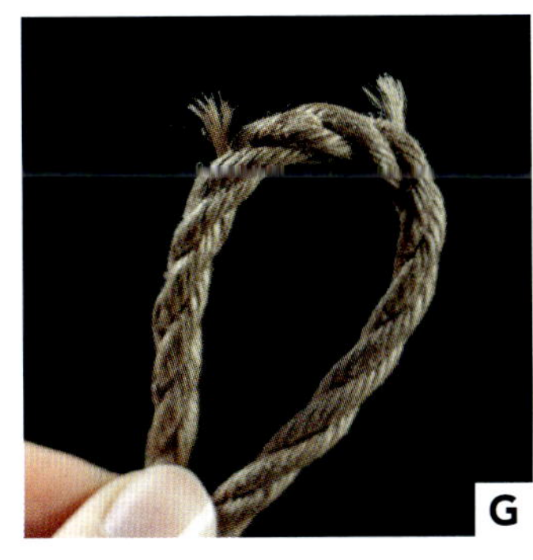
G

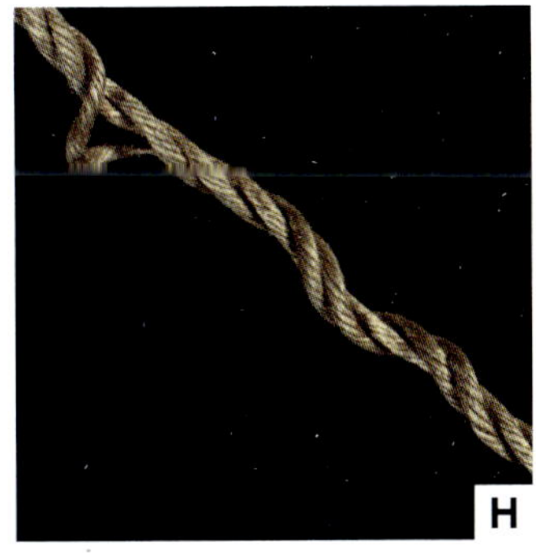
H

be weakened because the strands will not load evenly – once again, there are plenty of online resources to help you deal with this problem should it arise, but you can help to prevent the problem by storing it well when it's not in use.

If you have the space to do so, then leaving your rope **[K]** hung up over a bamboo, ring, or even over a clothes rail is the ideal way to store it to avoid kinks forming in the rope. Otherwise, **[J]** loosely coiling it in a bag is a good alternative (ensuring the bag is made of breathable material).

Although you will often see rope **[L]** hanked like this when it is about to be used it's not a good option for long term storage as kinks will form around the bight.

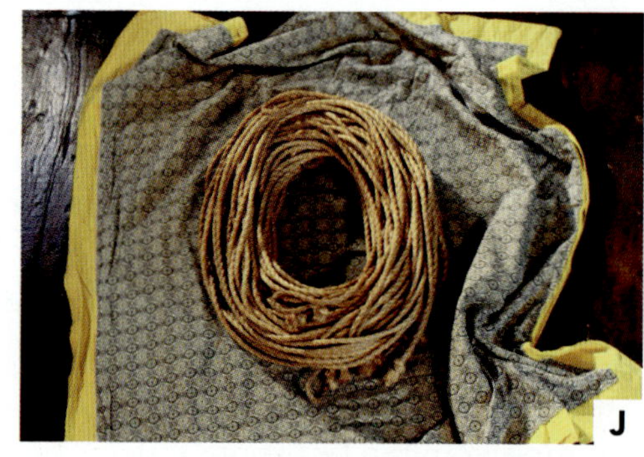
J

You can also keep your rope **[M]** folded in 4 with a loose knot in the middle; if you keep the bight slightly longer than the other strands you'll still be able to find it when you want to tie, but there won't be so much risk of damage.

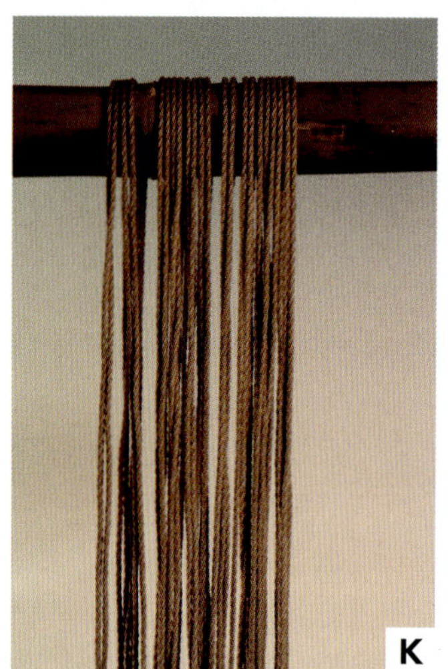
K

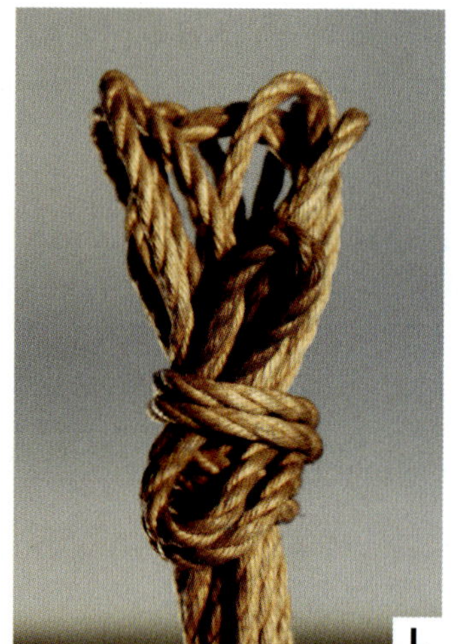
L

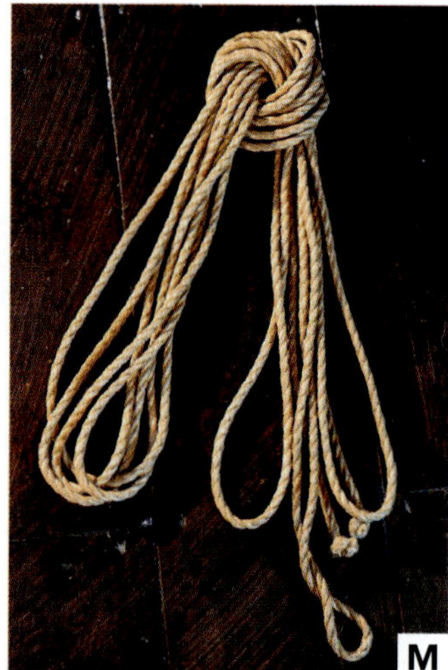
M

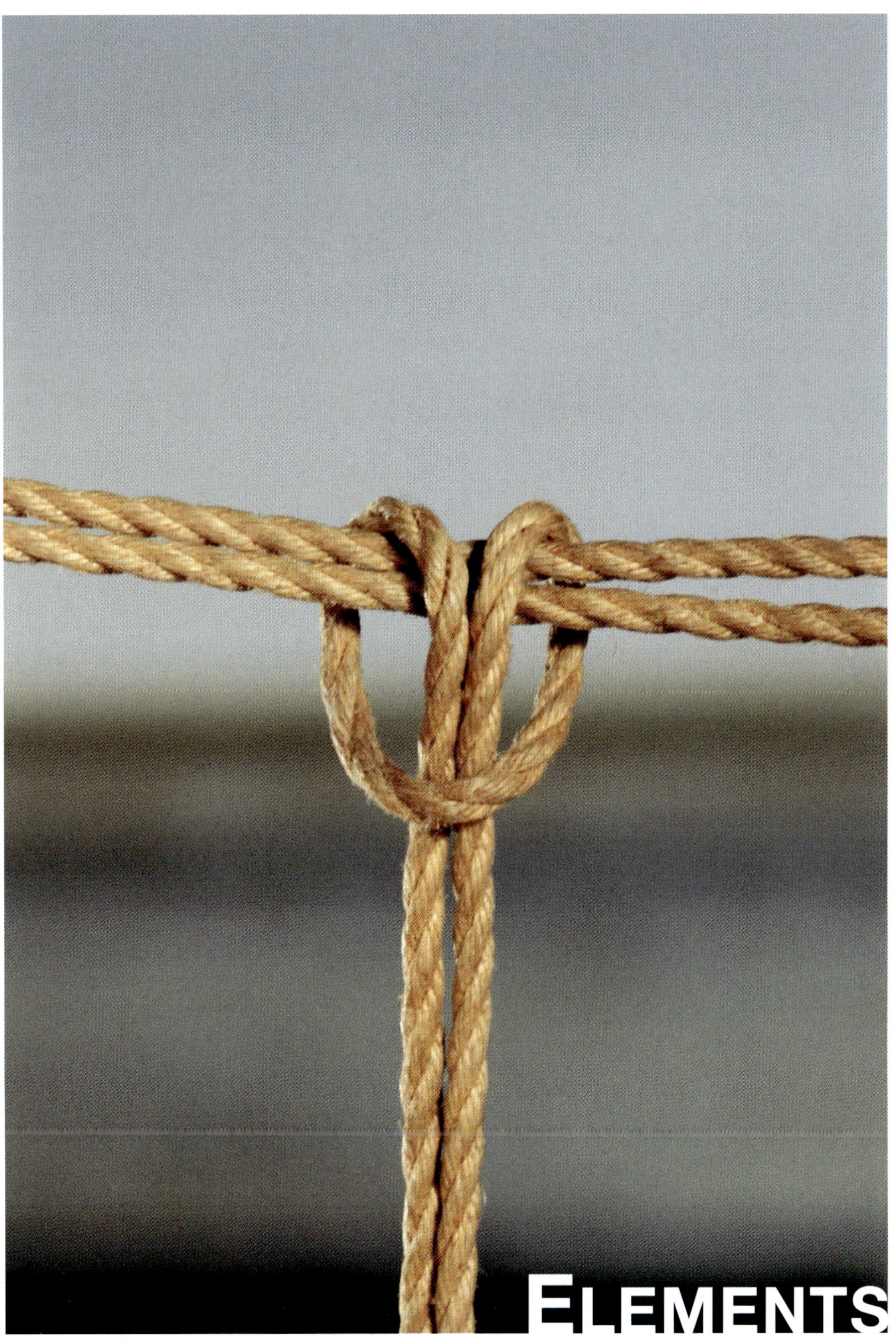

ELEMENTS

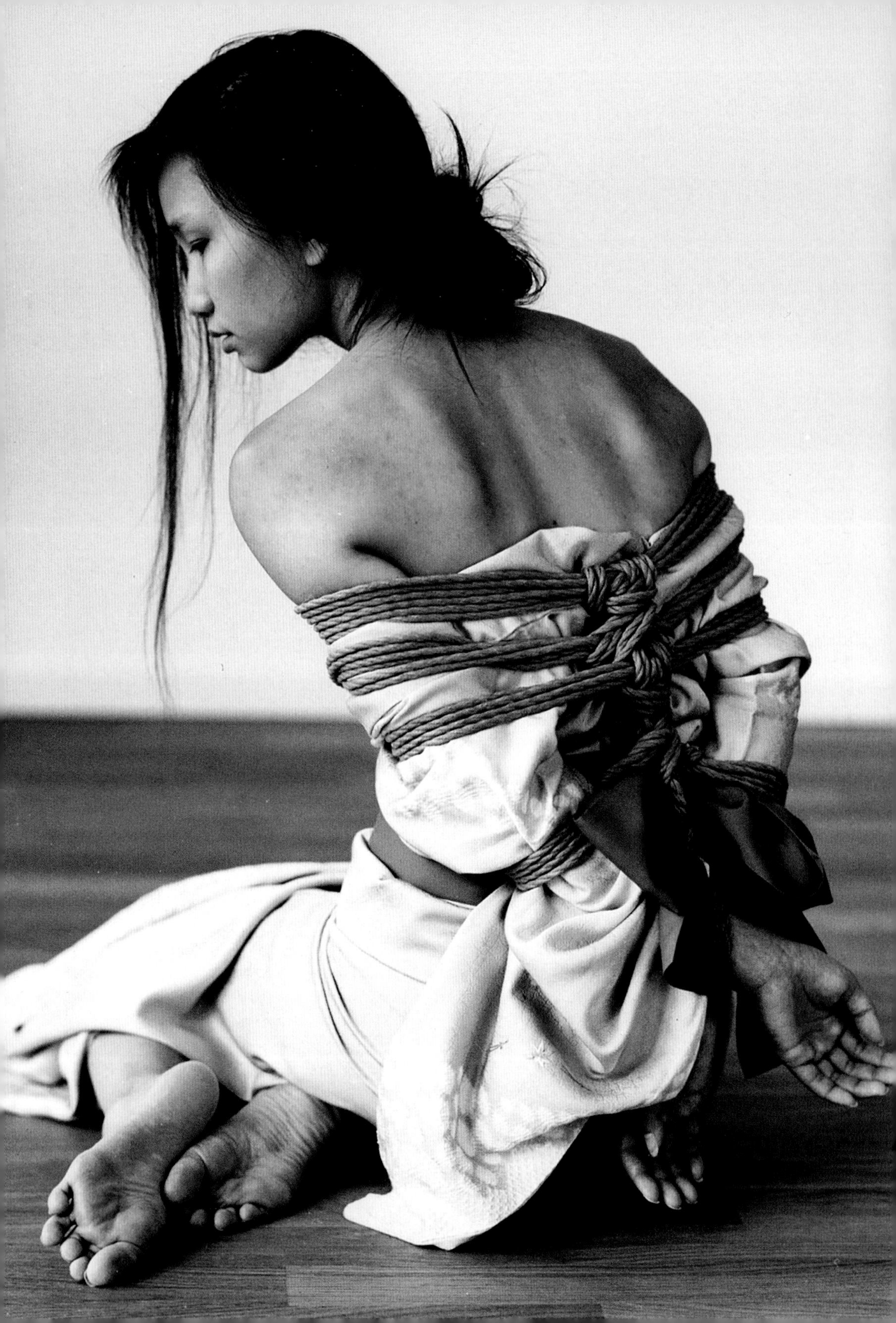

Elements

This chapter is a breakdown of the various elements used in creating the other ties throughout the book.

They are presented here primarily for consistency as I am writing with the assumption that some readers may already have learnt a different way of doing things. Feel free to apply your own methods if you are more comfortable with them, and refer back here for guidance if you find something isn't working quite as expected. The tutorial function of this chapter is secondary, as this book is not aimed at complete beginners and although I have gone into a little detail, I have kept my explanations brief.

How the Single Column Tie Is Used in This Book

The single column is the starting point of most ties in this book. This section demonstrates how I am using it within those ties (though there are many other ways to tie it and other uses for it).

The tension you use will be addressed at the relevant part of the book.

Basic Single Column Tie

This form of single column uses a **reef knot** – also referred to as a square knot or honmusubi. It is not the strongest knot so if you are planning to use this at a critical point in a suspension you should reinforce it with an extra knot or two over the top, or locking the bight (pg. 29). Alternatively, you could use a stronger knot such as a somerville bowline (aka myrtle loop).

[1] Begin with two flat, evenly tensioned wraps around the part of the body you wish to tie.

[2] Cross the bight over both wraps.

[3] Use your index finger to hook it underneath the wraps.

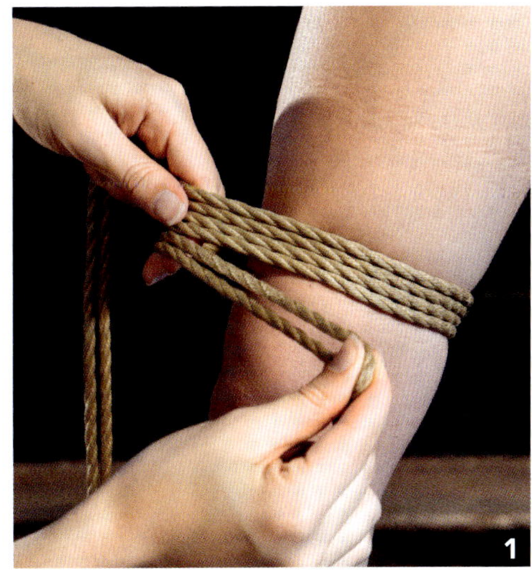

1

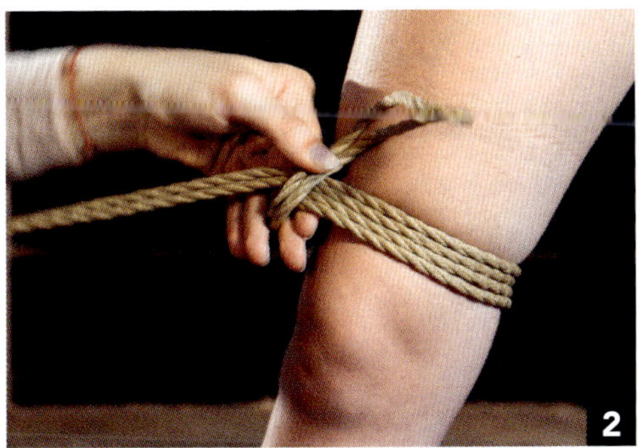

2

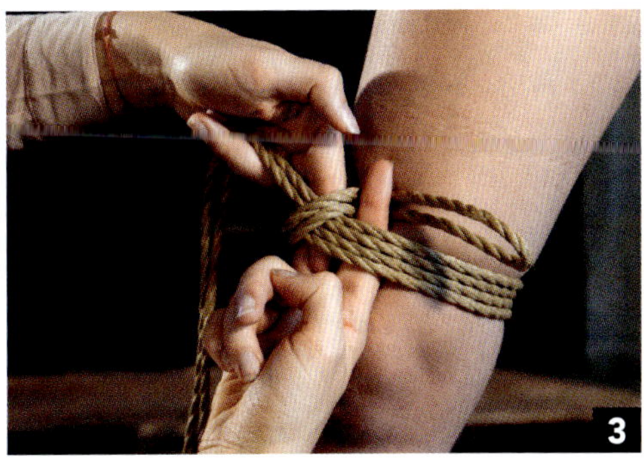

3

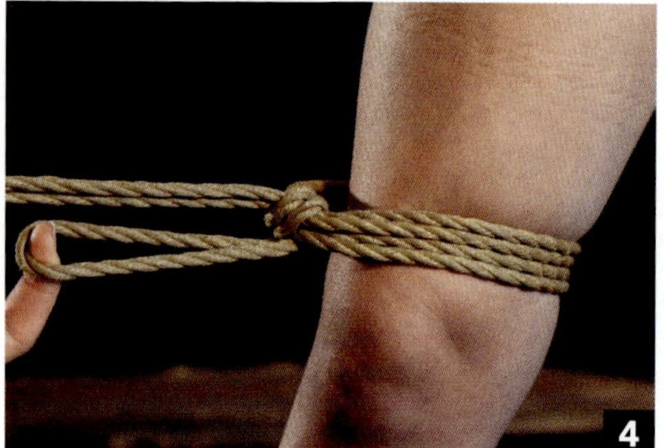
4

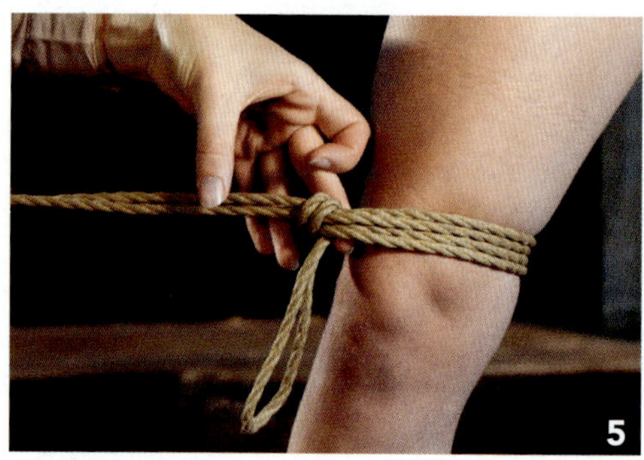
5

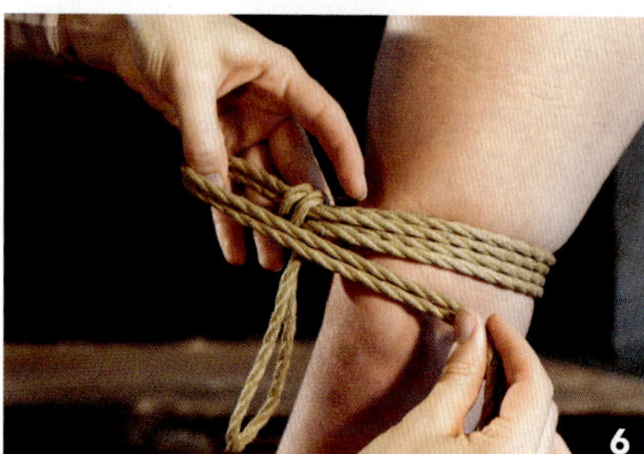
6

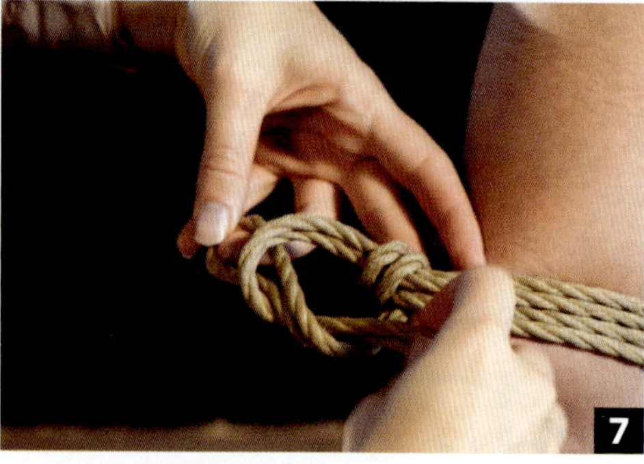
7

[4] Hold the bight and the working end together with equal tension, and take a moment to check the size of the wrap – make any minor adjustments as necessary.

[5] Place your middle finger at the point where the bight crosses underneath the wraps and hold firmly. This should allow you to let go with your other fingers, freeing them to complete the knot.

[6] Wrap the working end around your thumb so that it makes a 'U-turn'.

[7] Pass your bight through the centre of the loop you have just made with your thumb.

[8] Tighten by pulling the bight and working end out sideways, so both lines have a bend in them. Compact as firmly as possible.

To make it more secure you can add additional knots on top by repeating steps 6-8 once or twice.

[A] If the knots are not secure, you run the risk of the single column tie collapsing and tightening down around the body.

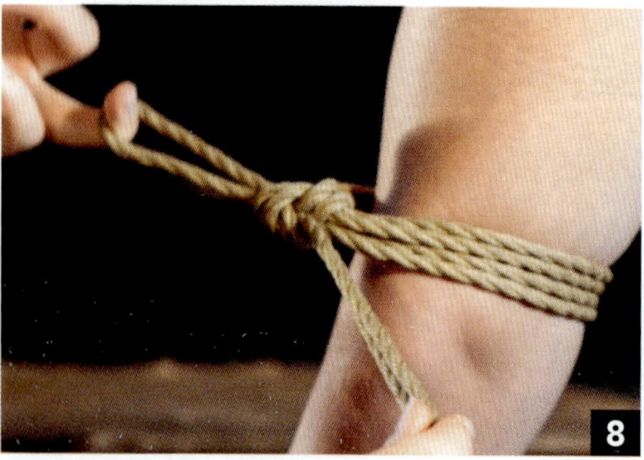
8

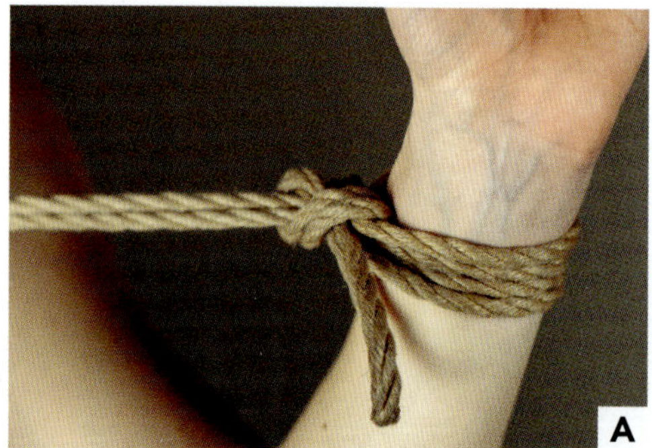
A

Placement on the Body

Broadly, there are two ways of placing a single column on the body. The tension you need to use will vary depending on the situation.

[B] Both wraps are kept evenly tensioned and the working end is pulled outwards, perpendicular to the body. This can be used as the starting point for the takatekote or futomomo, and for most suspension lines.

[C] The wraps are tied with a slight unevenness in tension so they lie flat to the body in a 'V' shape. This can be used when tying around the waist to pull downwards for a **hip harness** or **gunslinger**, or around the ankle for a suspension line where the foot is pointed upwards. Make the two wraps then shuffle them into the required position before you complete steps 2-8 (pg. 27-28) to lock the tie *N.B.: the placement of this type of single column tie when used on an ankle is discussed in the notes for models on pg. 164.*

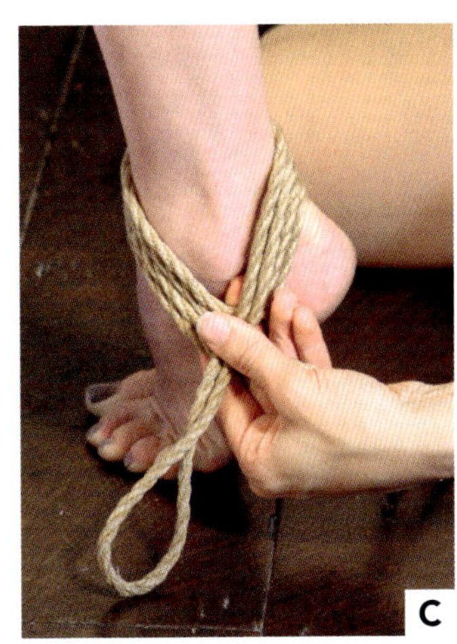

C

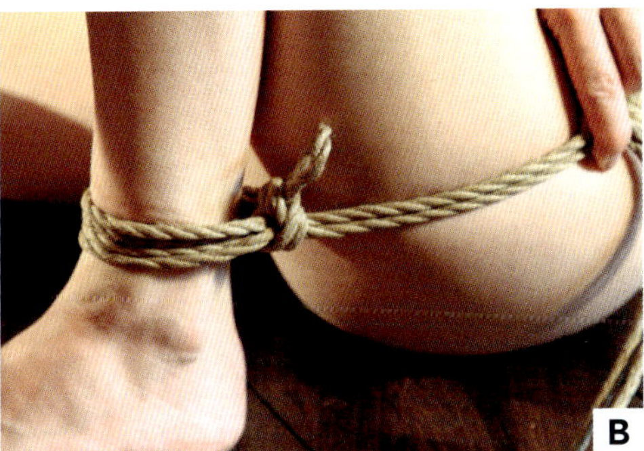

B

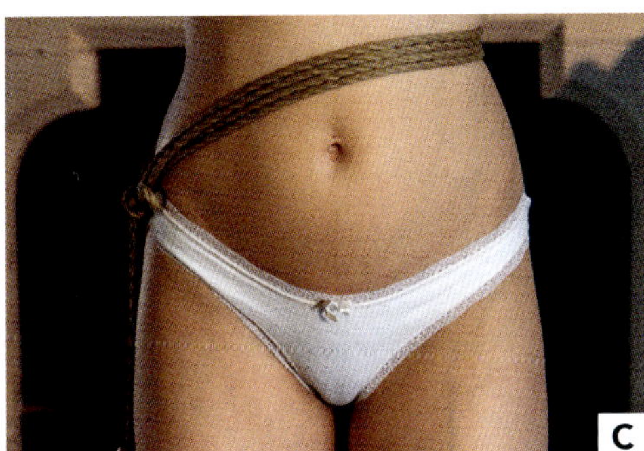

C

Locking the Bight

For extra security, you might wish to lock the bight of your harnesses to ensure it doesn't come undone unexpectedly.

To do this, you can either **[D]** thread the working end through the bight before you start tying or **[E]** trap the bight by wrapping it into the rest of the tie at some point during the tying process.

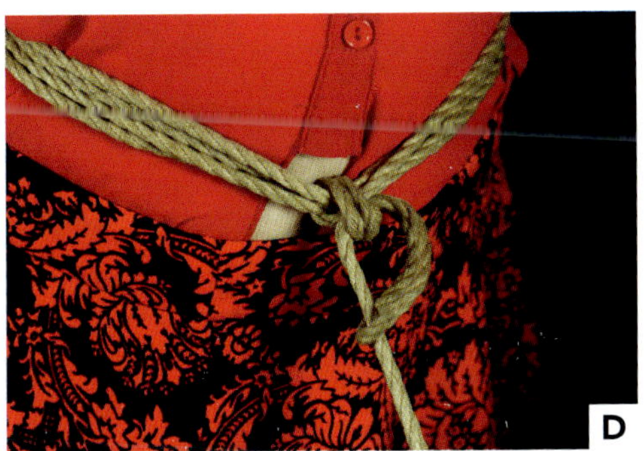

D

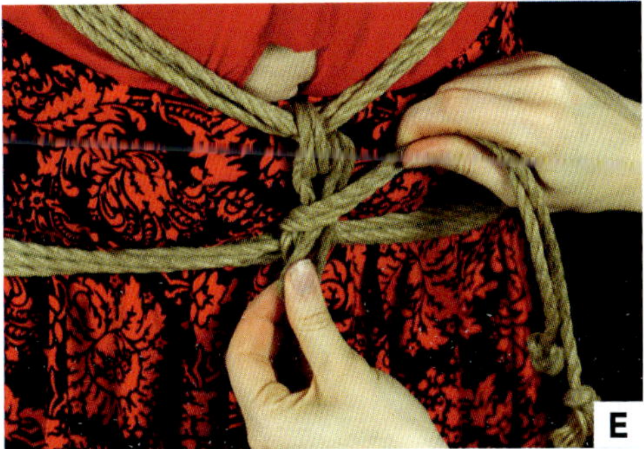

E

Quick Release Single Column

The takatekote (pg. 50) begins with this type of single column so the hands can be released quickly if necessary. You can collapse the knot by pulling on the bight. This can be done even under tension, although I advise against doing this if your main line (pg. 106) is attached near the quick release for obvious reasons.

This knot has the additional advantage of being stronger than a basic single column (pg. 27) when the working end is pulled.

This is NOT suitable for use on suspension lines.

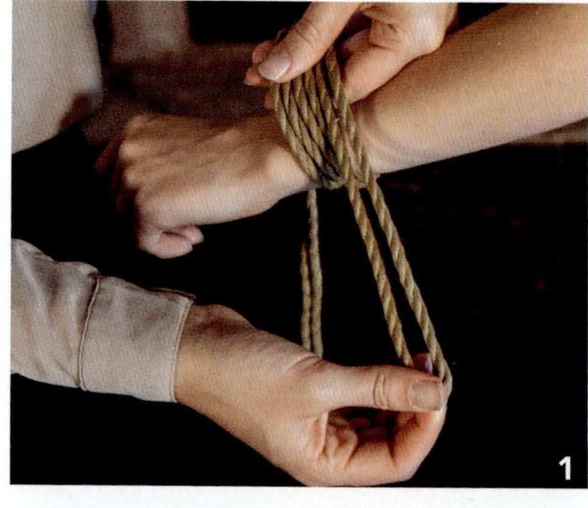

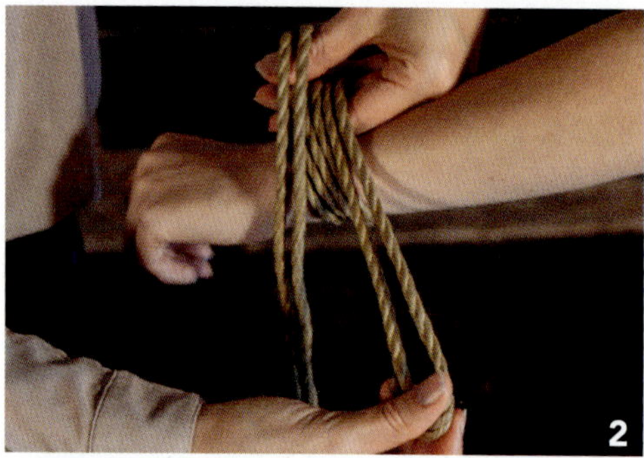

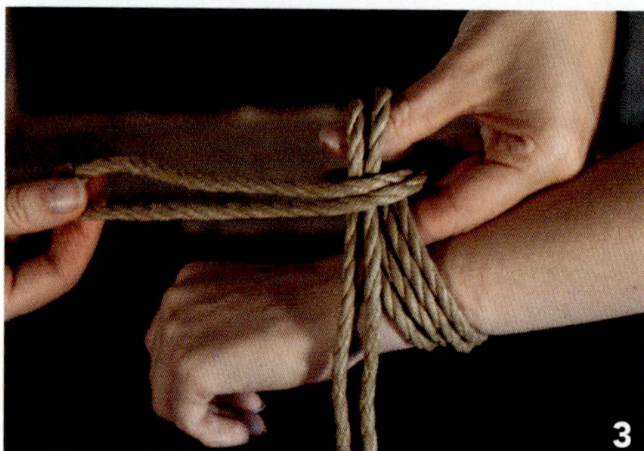

[1] Start with two evenly tensioned wraps, and leave a longer bight than usual – the length shown here is about the minimum you need.

[2] Fold the working end back on itself in a 'U-turn' to form a loop. I find this easiest to do by draping it over my thumb.

[3] Pass the bight over both wraps and the folded working end, keeping your thumb in place to maintain the space in the loop.

[4] Pass the bight under everything.

[5] Then pass it half way through the loop you made with the working end in step 2.

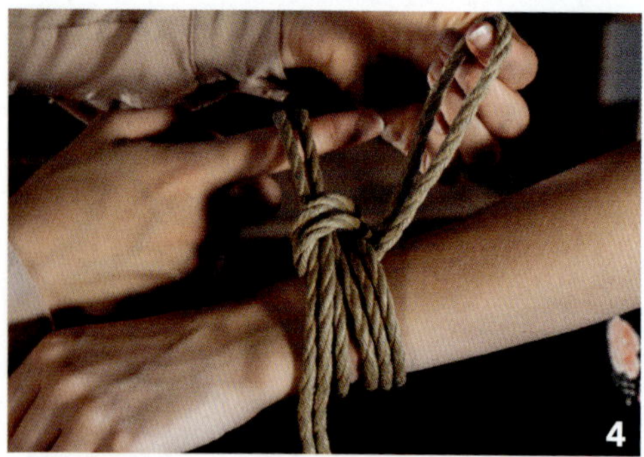

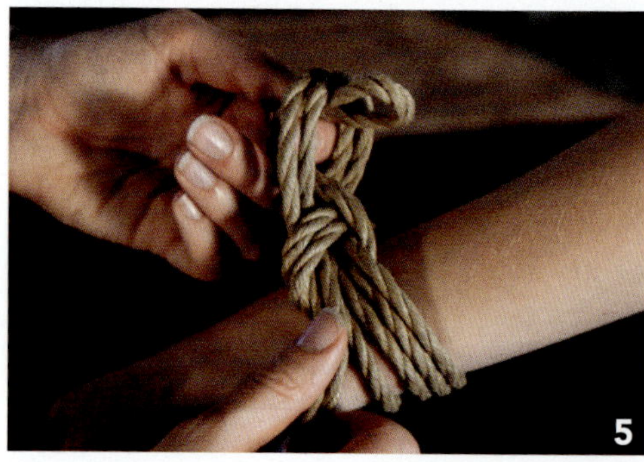

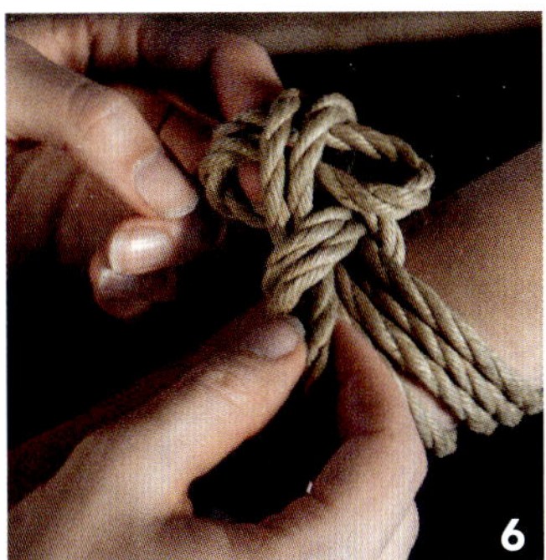

[6, 7] Pull on the working end so it tightens down over the bight.

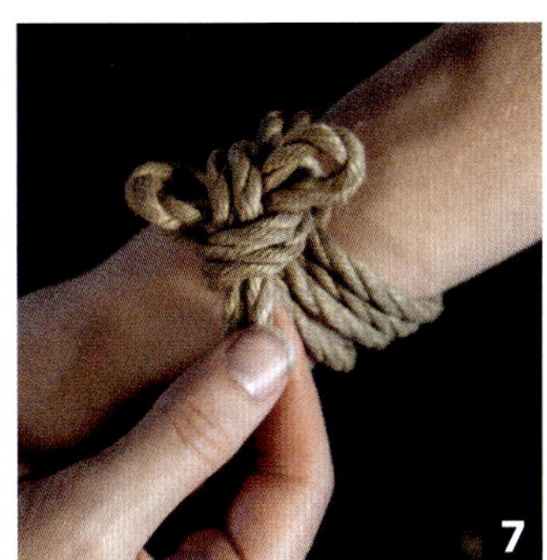

Hojo Cuff

A **hojo cuff** is a way of making a single column tie in the middle of the rope, when you have already started the tie somewhere else and so don't have access to the bight. Unlike the single column, it won't hold unless there is an equal tension kept on the ropes leading both to and from the cuff itself. In this example I have kept the tension by taking the rope back to the bight of the initial single column and securing it there, however you can secure this anywhere that makes sense within the context of the tie you are making.

Here I am demonstrating on the wrists.

[1] Start with single column on one wrist.

[2] Wrap the working end twice around the other wrist at the desired distance.

[3] Hook your finger under the central wrist wrap and ease it outwards to the required size. Cross the working end over the top of the two wraps.

[4] Then hook the working end back underneath the two wraps and pull it all the way though.

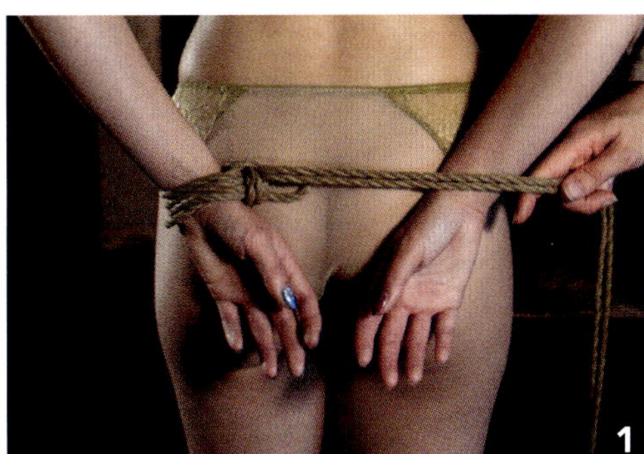

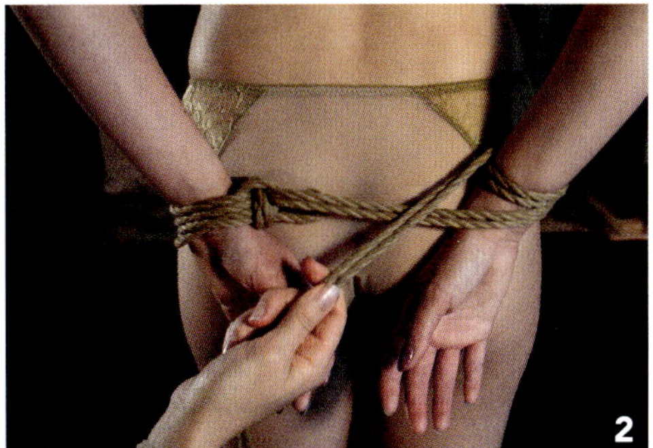

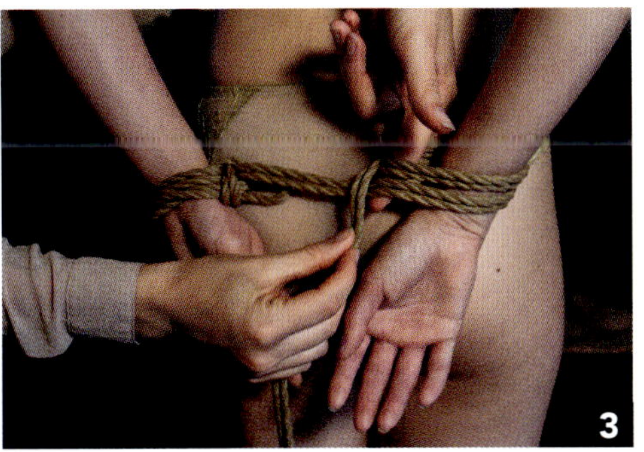

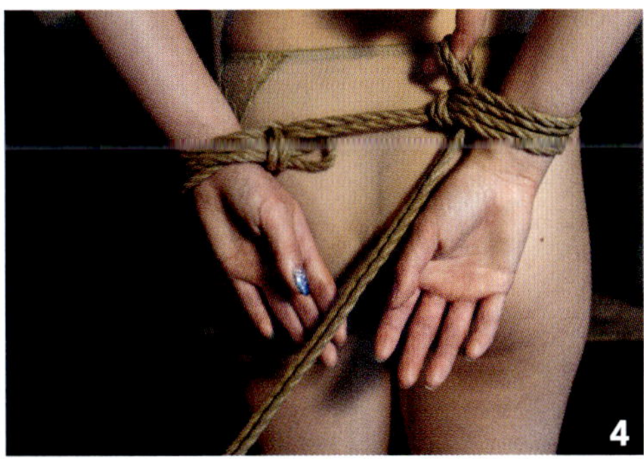

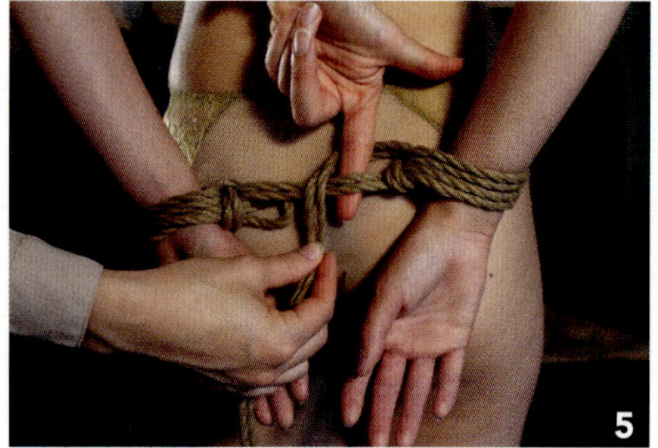
5

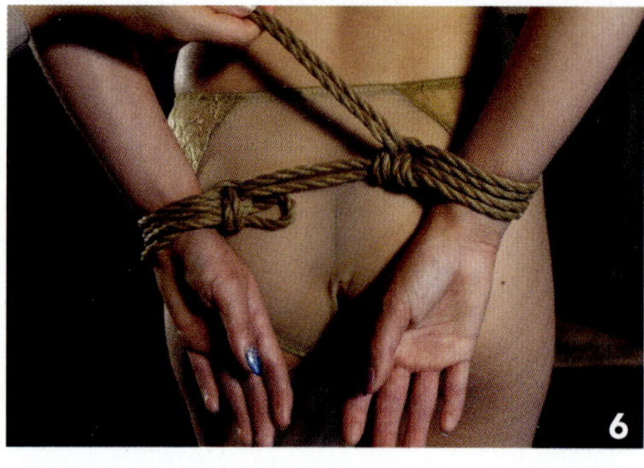
6

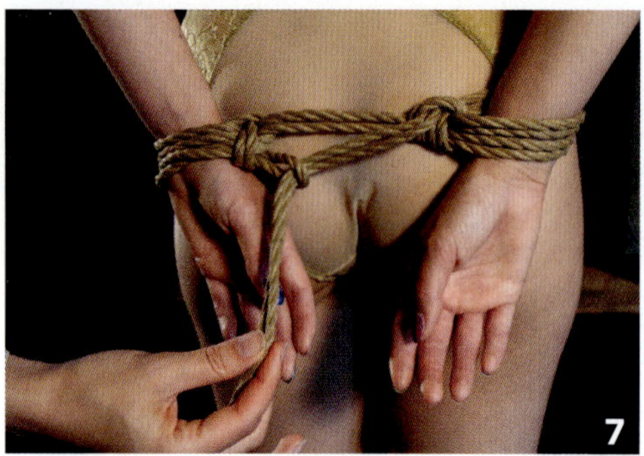
7

[5, 6] If you wish, use a **half hitch** (pg. 39) to help secure the cuff.

[7] In this case, I will maintain the tension by threading the working end through the bight of the first single column.

Here you are finished, how you secure it will depend on what you are planning to do next – if you are unsure, a half hitch around both ropes of the **stem** between the cuffs should work fine.

Kannuki

[F-H] When you have a single wrap going around any two body parts with a gap between them (in this example, the ankles) it can be difficult to stop the wrap slipping without tying it crushingly tight.

The function of a kannuki (a.k.a. cinch) is to keep the wrap in place allowing you to tie with a more gentle tension. You should take care to apply it in such a way that the wrap remains flat to the skin, as shown.

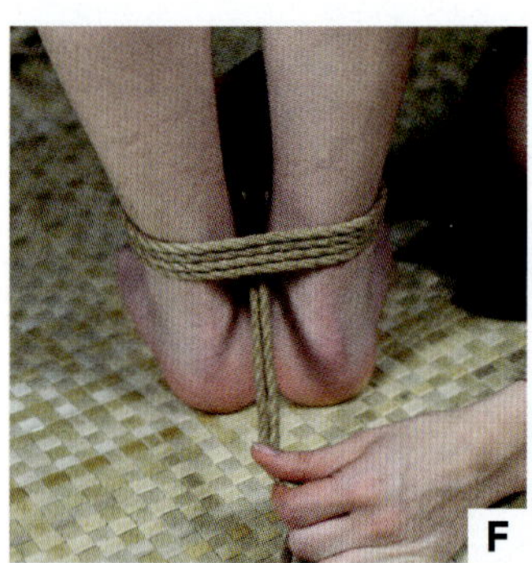
F

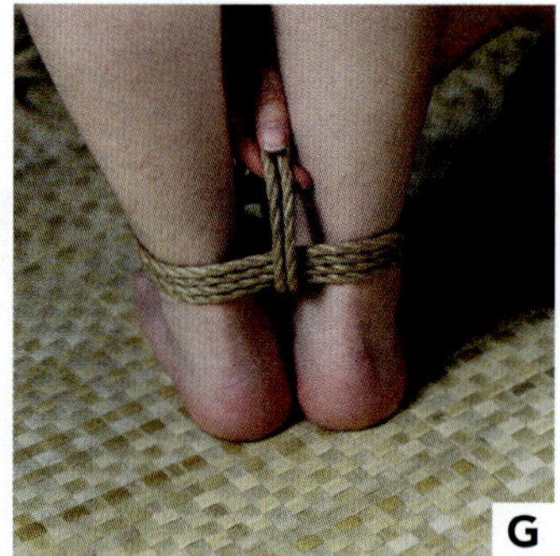
G

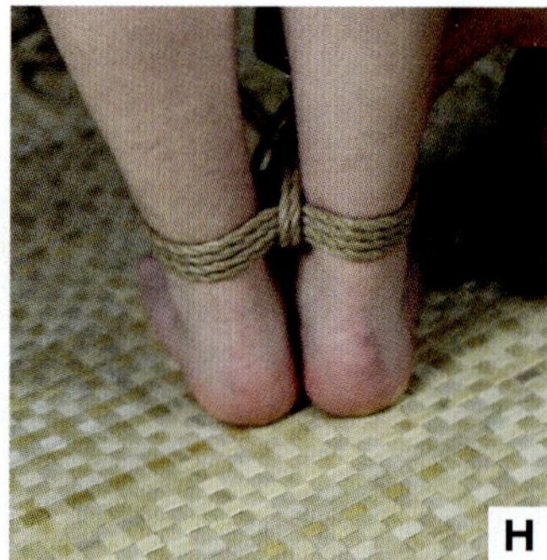
H

Joining New Ropes

Two methods of attaching new ropes to your tie are used in this book. Many people stick to using only one or the other for stylistic reasons, but I personally find both useful.

Using the **lark's head** means you don't have to worry too much about the length of your ropes as you can just continue adding new ones until the tie is complete. It is often a little faster to tie like this as you don't need to find ways to lock and finish the old rope before you begin the new one. The downsides are that you need to be very aware of where the joins in the rope end up on the body, as some placements could be unsafe or uncomfortable (see pg. 44). The joins are also not so beautiful, so I try to find discreet places to hide them.

Using the overhand knot gives you the freedom to attach a new rope anywhere you like, regardless of how the rest of the tie is structured.

Lark's head

[1] Place your thumb, and two fingers into the bight of the new rope.

[2] Flip your hand over to create two loops, then put your thumb and fingers together to catch the working ends inside the bight.

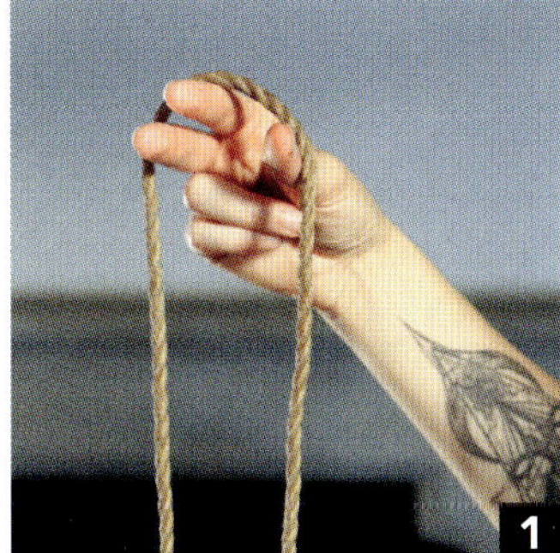

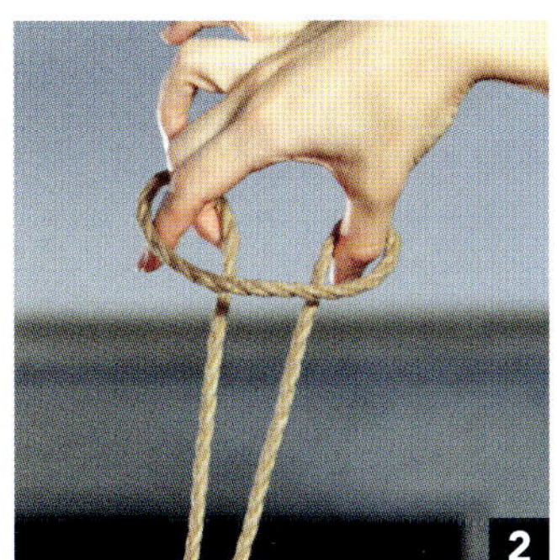

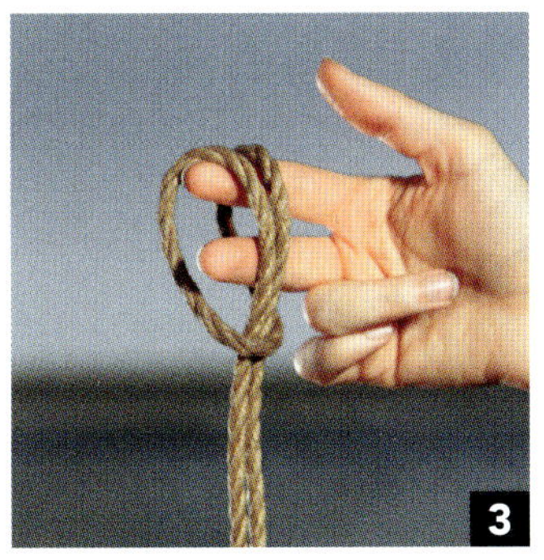

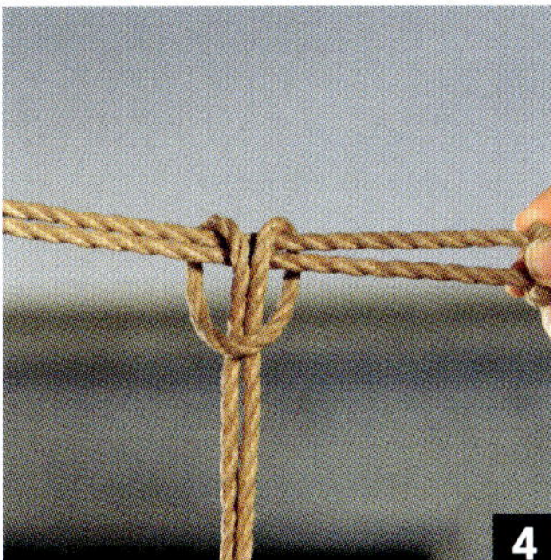

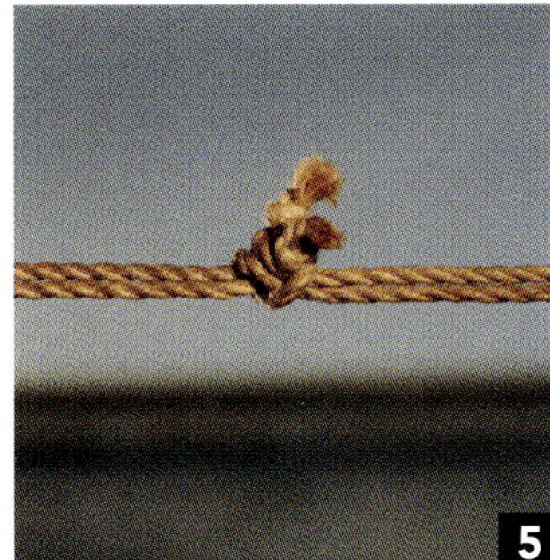

[3] Slide both loops onto one hand, to create a doubled loop.

[4] Place this over the end of the old rope.

[5] Pull it tight, then to then pull it to the knots at the end of the rope so that it can jam there.

Overhand Knot

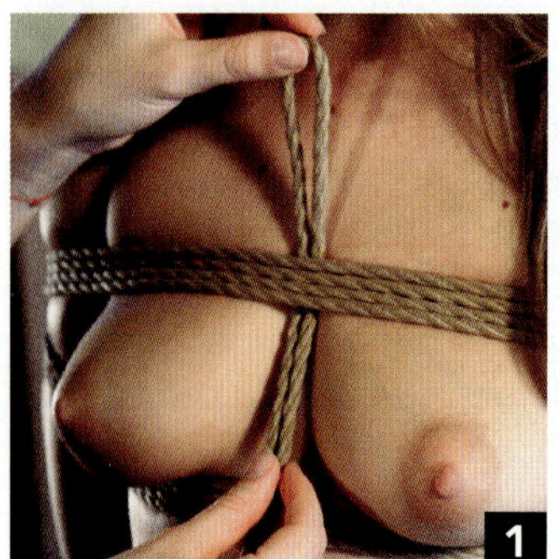

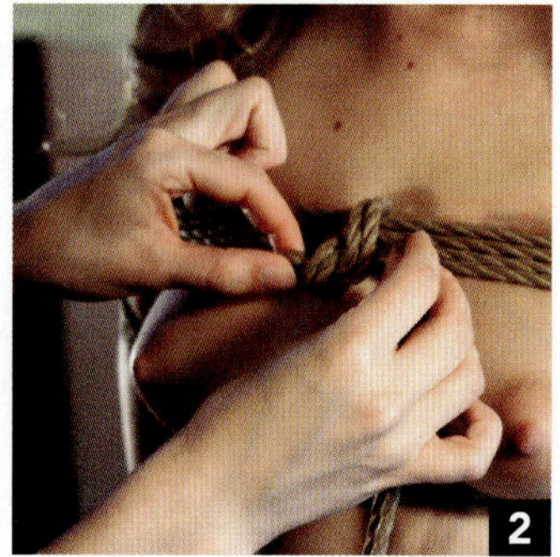

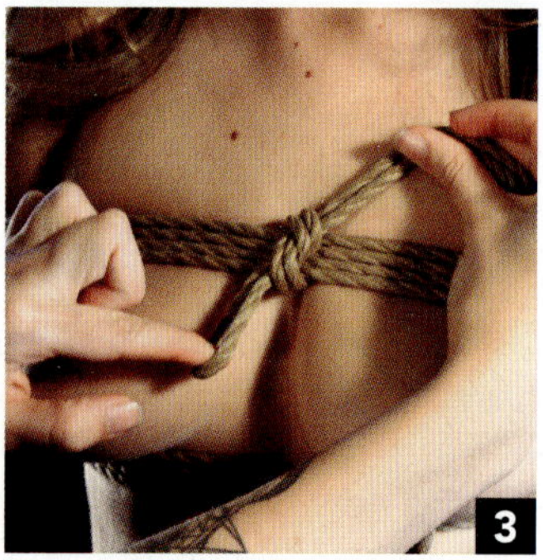

[1] Thread the new rope under the existing tie with the bight pointing in the direction you are going to tie (here I have threaded my bight from bottom to top, so my new rope will travel up towards the shoulder).

[2] Make an overhand knot be crossing the bight over and then under the working end.

[3, 4] Pull tight and compact the bight down on top of the working end so that it's tightly wedged, as shown.

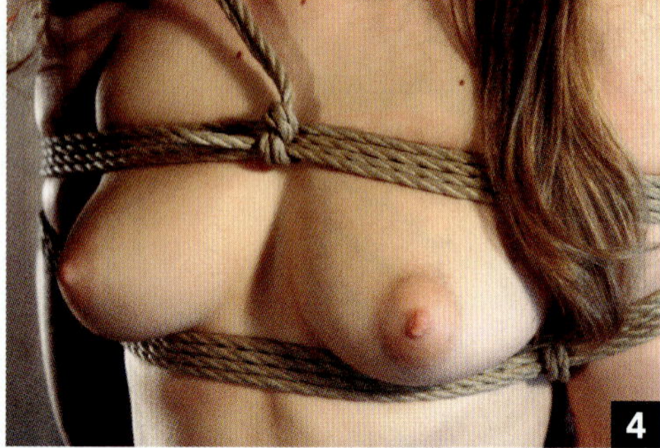

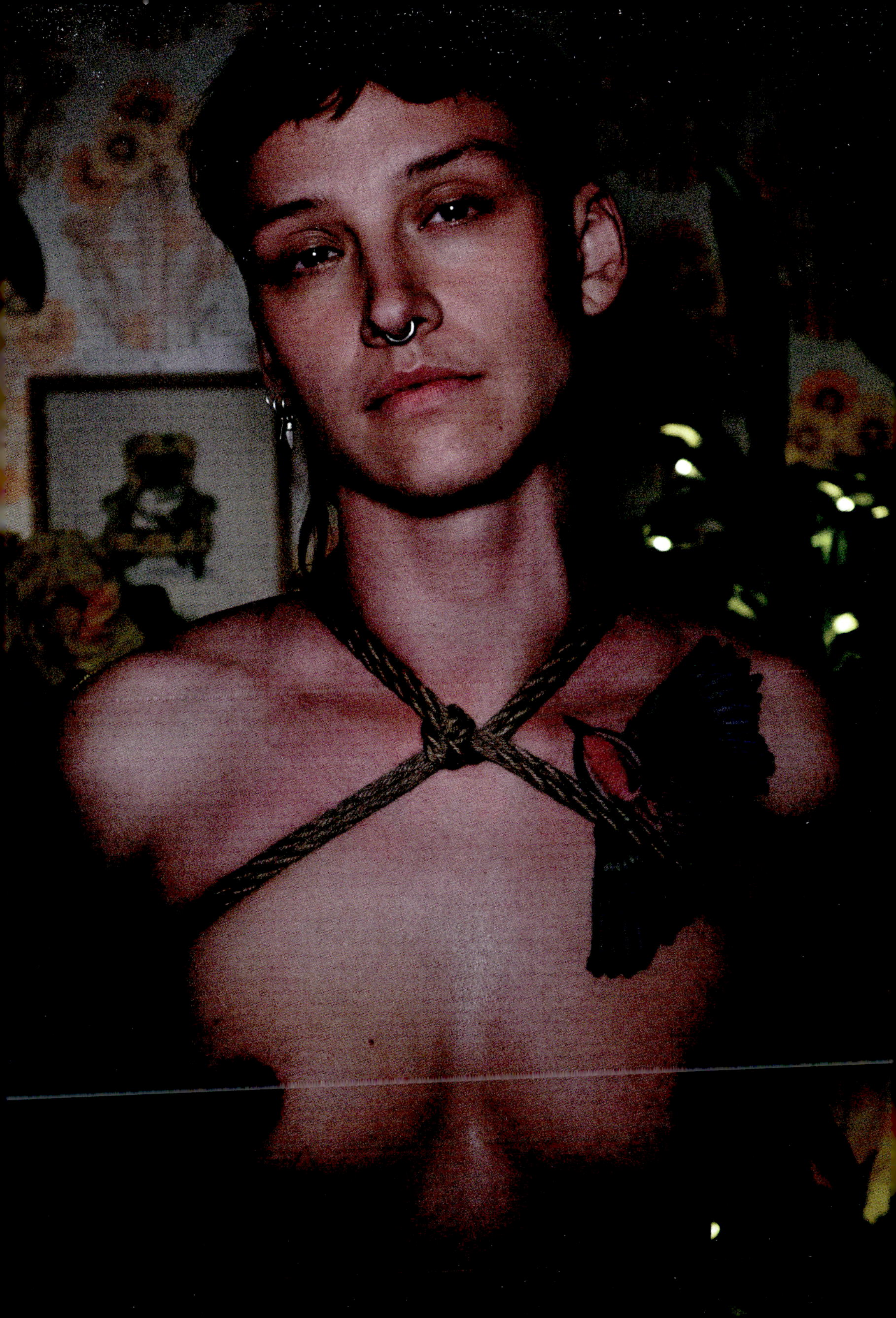

No-dome

A no-dome is a simple friction used to secure together two or more crossing ropes, or to change the direction the working end is travelling in. It takes its name from its shape, which is similar to the the phonetic character 'no' in Japanese writing – with 'dome' simply meaning lock or stop. You might also hear it called a Munter hitch.

It is more secure if it is tied so the working end travels towards the inside of the friction to close it, as shown below.

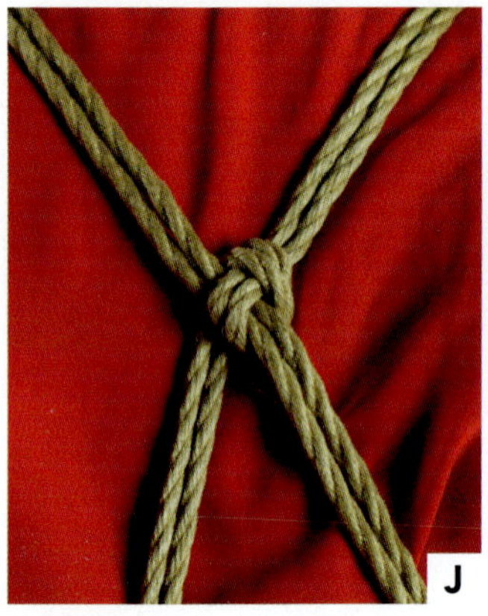

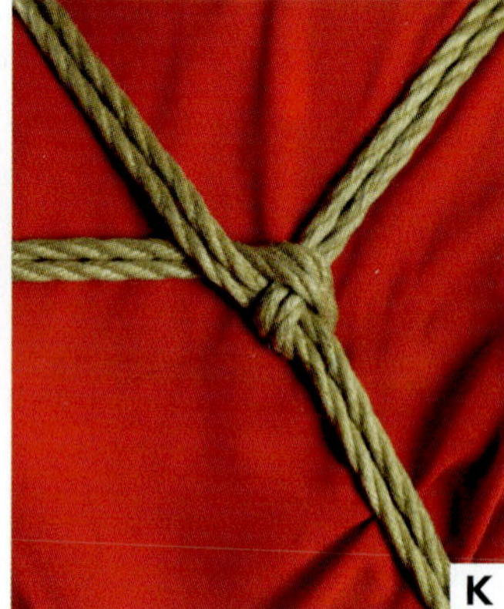

[J] A closed no-dome. To create this, start the friction (steps 1-2) in the same direction you want to take the working end in next, then complete the friction on the other side so it pulls against itself (steps 3-4). i.e. "If you want to go left, go left first". If you have something that crosses at an exact 90° angle this may not be so obvious or important.

[K] An open no-dome, which is less stable.

[1, 2] Hook your working end over and under the ropes you are crossing, and pull it gently to take in some of the tension.

[3, 4] Pass the working end over the top of itself, and back underneath the rope you are crossing.

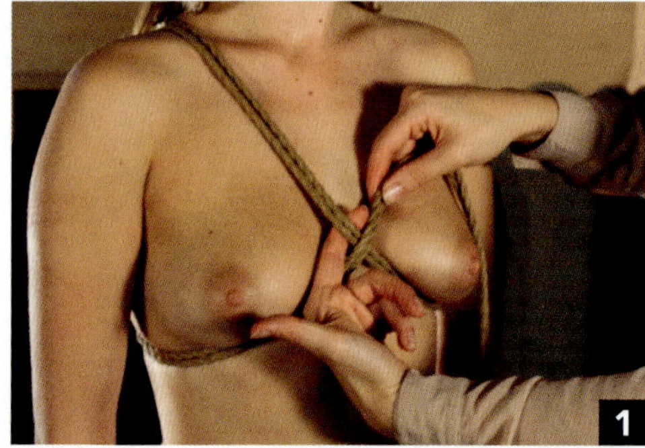

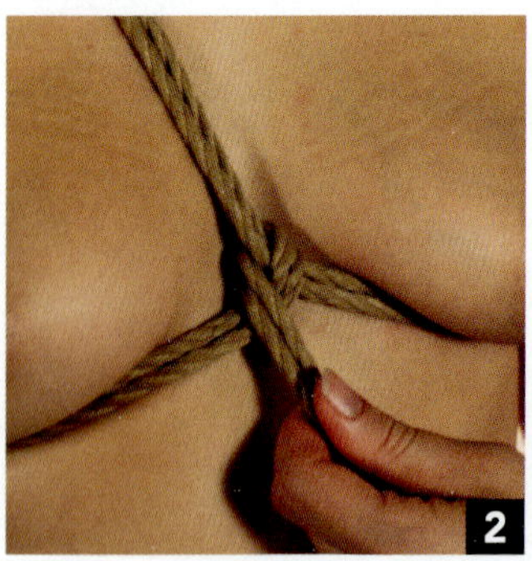

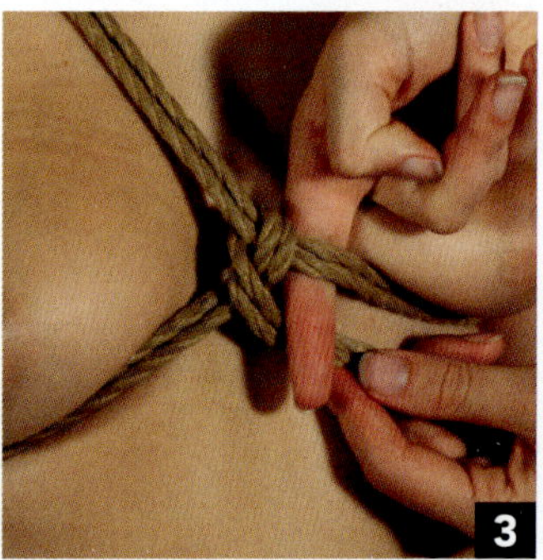

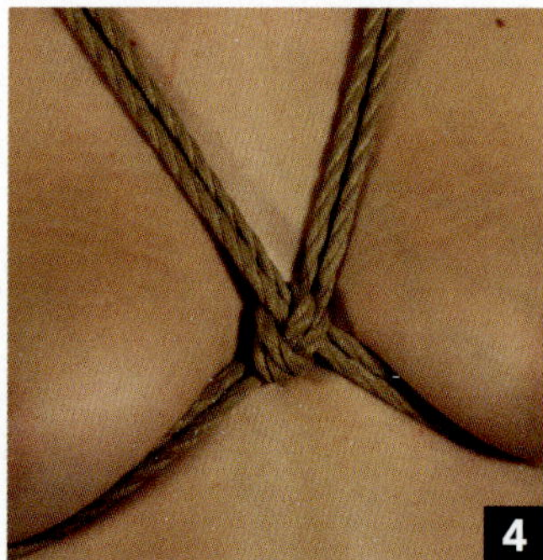

Yuki Knot

The **yuki knot** is incredibly versatile. It can be used to make a **double bight** for suspension (pg. 109), lock a suspension line (pg. 115), or create **[L]** an additional attachment point on a tie (pg. 65). Because you don't need to pull through many meters of rope it's a fast option to tie/untie if you wish to lock off when your working end is still very long.

It is made by partially pulling the working end under another part of your tie to make a loop, then securing with a half hitch. The initial loop can be made under whatever you like; various uses will be addressed in more detail as and when they are relevant.

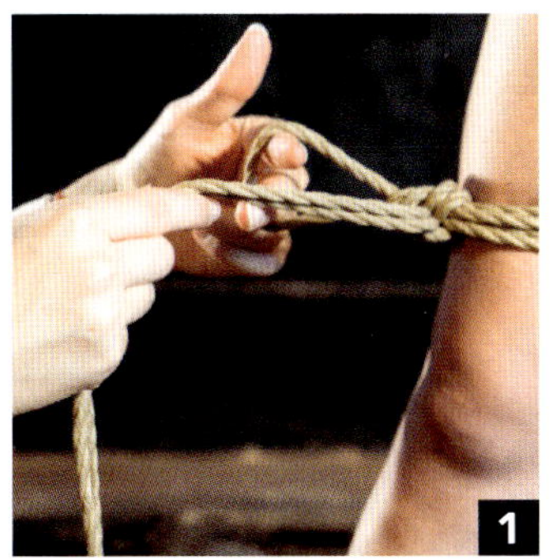

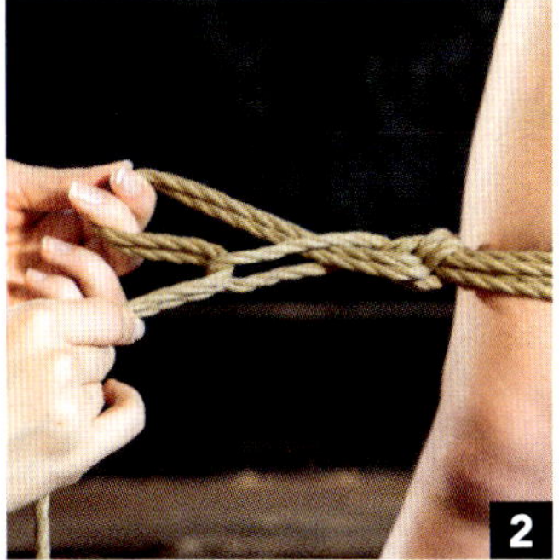

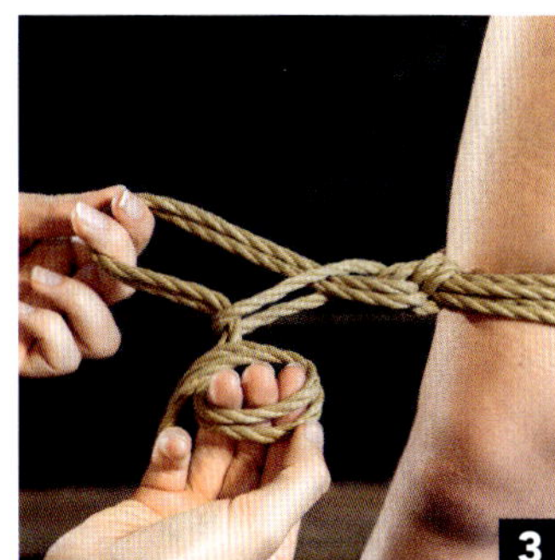

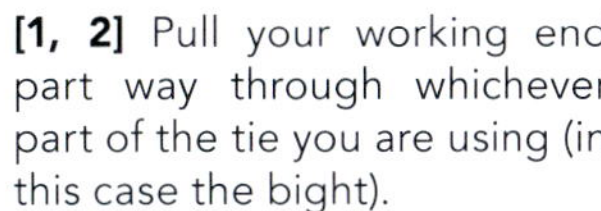

[1, 2] Pull your working end part way through whichever part of the tie you are using (in this case the bight).

[3] Twist the rope so that the working end hangs down in the middle, between the two loops.

[4] Place the second loop over the first loop so the working end is trapped inside.

[5] Pull it down so that it is snug.

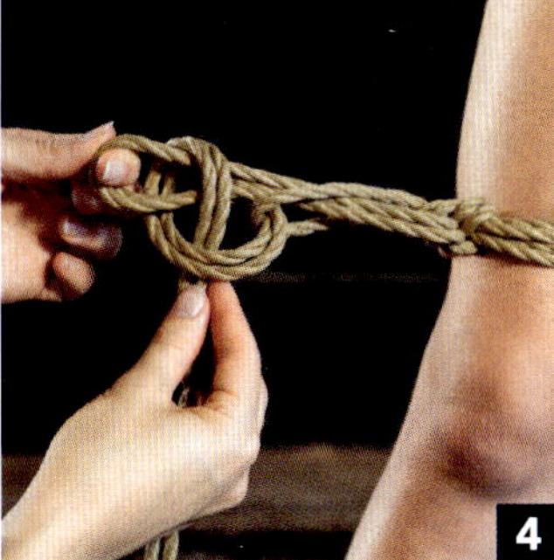

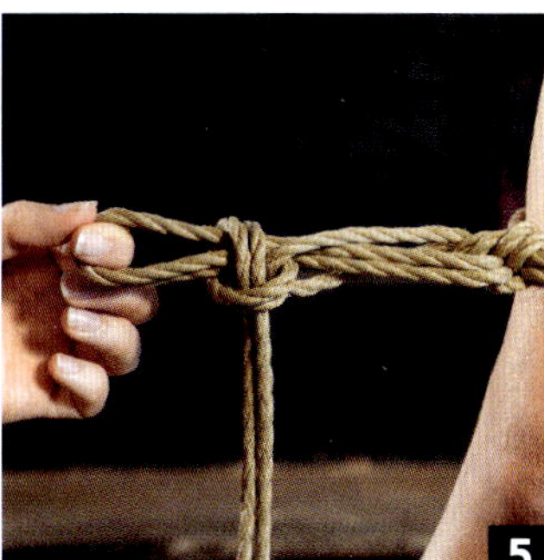

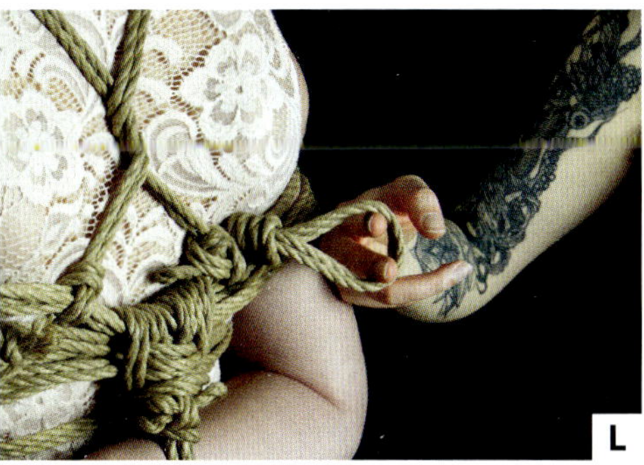

Reverse Tension

There are many uses for reverse tensioning, but in the context of this book it is used as an alternative way to create wraps around the body when achieving a good tension would be difficult in the 'normal' way (eg. pg. 51 steps 6-7). This could be because there is a long distance between the starting point and the wrap (as shown below) or because you want to give extra support by creating 3 or more wraps.

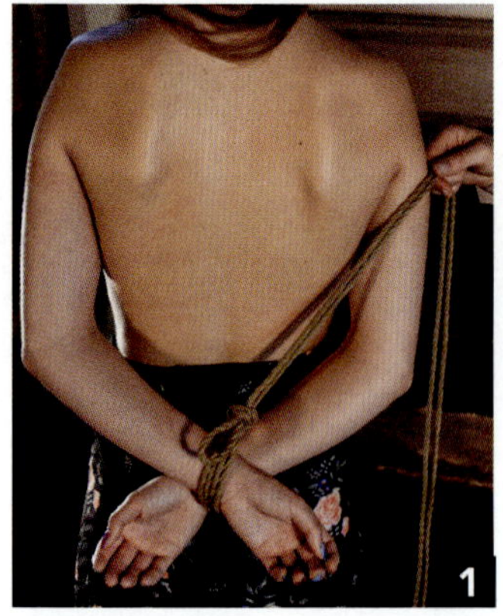
1

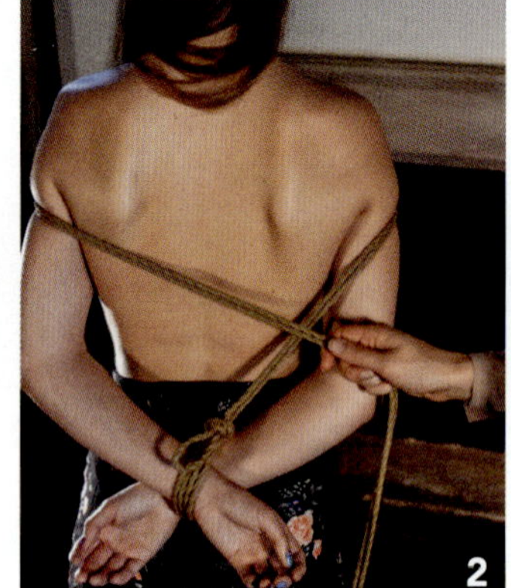
2

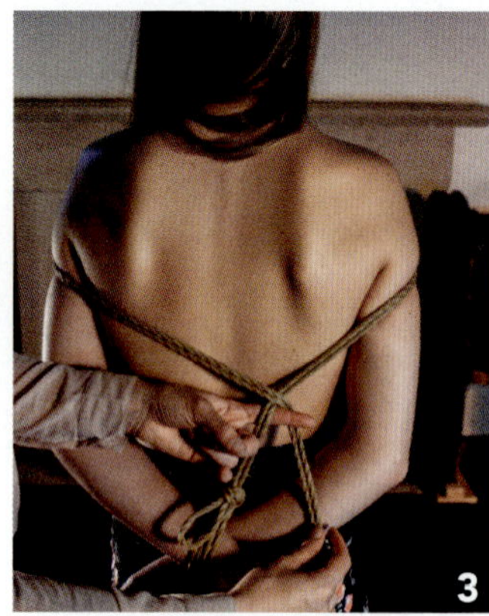
3

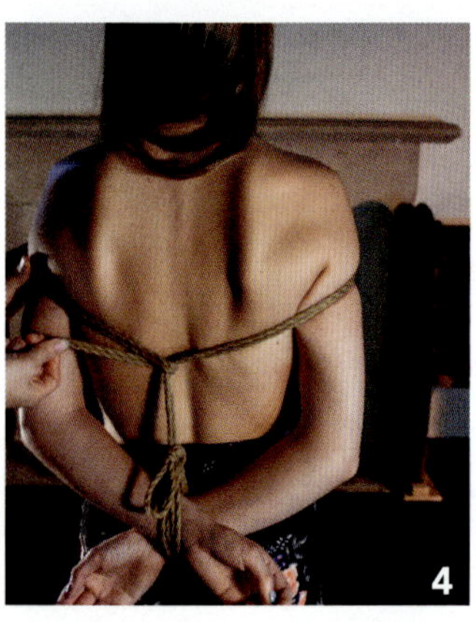
4

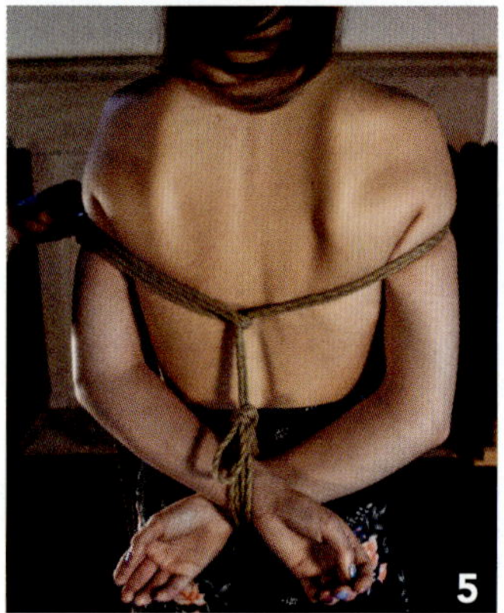
5

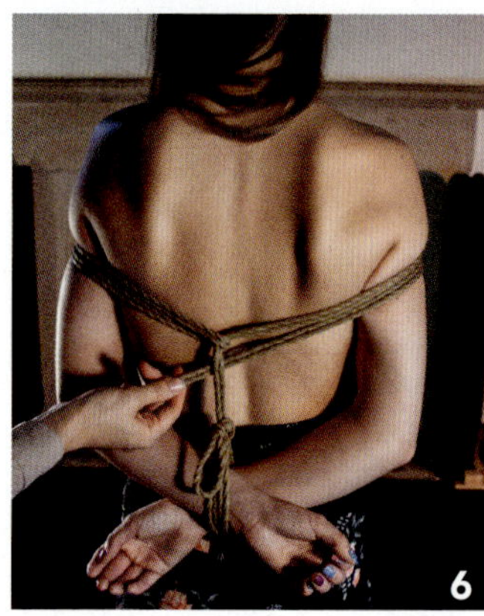
6

[1, 2] Make the first wrap just slightly looser than you want it to end up.

[3] Hook your working end under at the point where the ropes cross.

[4] Pull it to centre. Before you move onto the next step take a moment to check that the tension on both the wrap *and* the central stem are as you want them.

[5] Make the second wrap, taking care to match the tension of the first wrap.

[6] When you reach the central stem again you can either use a friction (such as an **L-friction** – pg. 54, steps 22-25) to isolate the tensions, or you can add additional wraps by making another U-turn around the stem and repeating the process.

Finishing Your Ties

Once you reach the end of your tie you will need to lock off your rope. It's useful to have a few different options to hand for different situations. Below are the three methods I use most frequently.

If you have a lot of rope left over then you might need to find a creative way to use up the excess, such as making extra wraps or decorative elements. If you are using a half hitch to lock then you can use up the excess rope either before or after you make the lock. For the other methods, it is preferable to use up the excess rope first.

Half Hitch

In order to lock with a half hitch, you need to have something to hitch against – in this example, I am using the point at which the wraps and stem intersect.

[1, 2] Place the working end behind your index finger and your index finger behind the wrap.

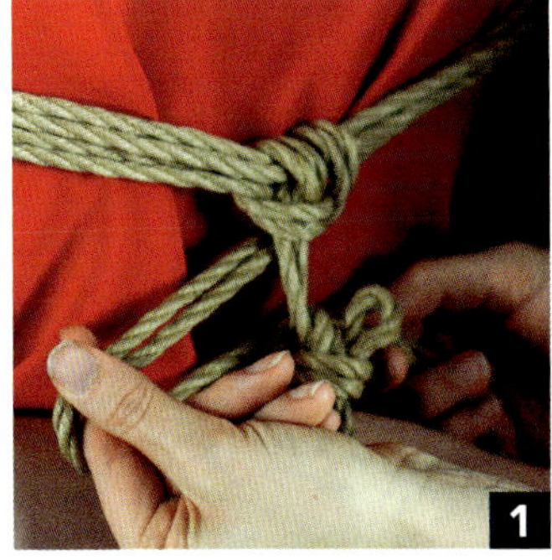

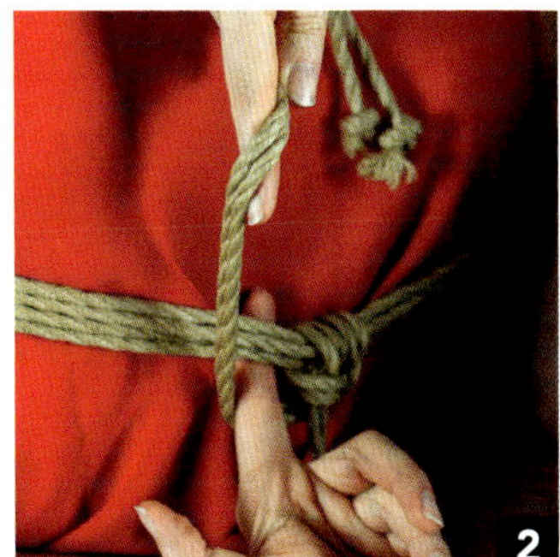

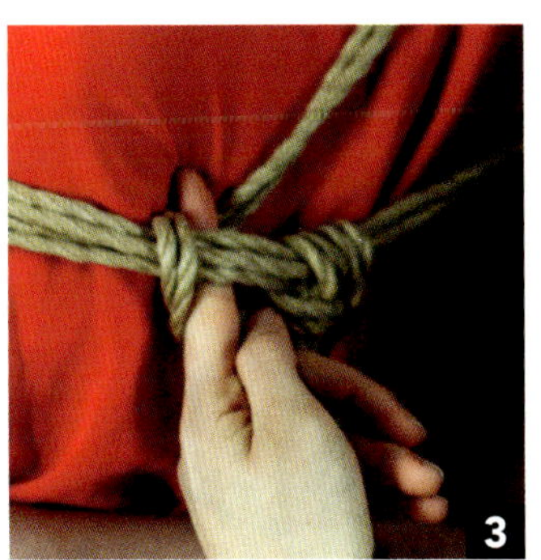

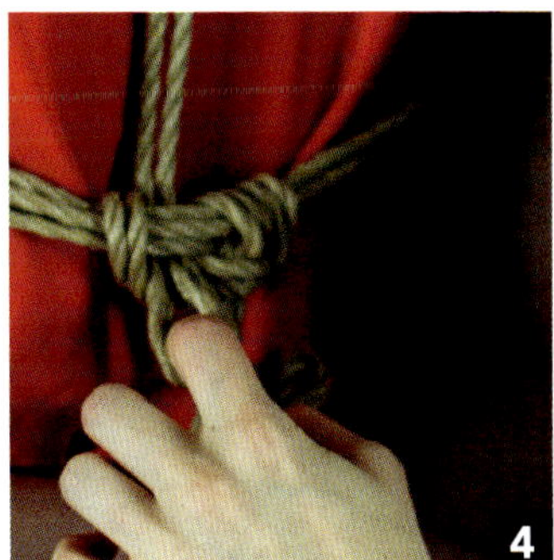

[3, 4] Pass the working end over the wrap and hook it behind your index finger, then pull your index finger backwards taking the working end with it so it becomes trapped between itself and the wrap.

[5, 6] Pull it tight against the stem.

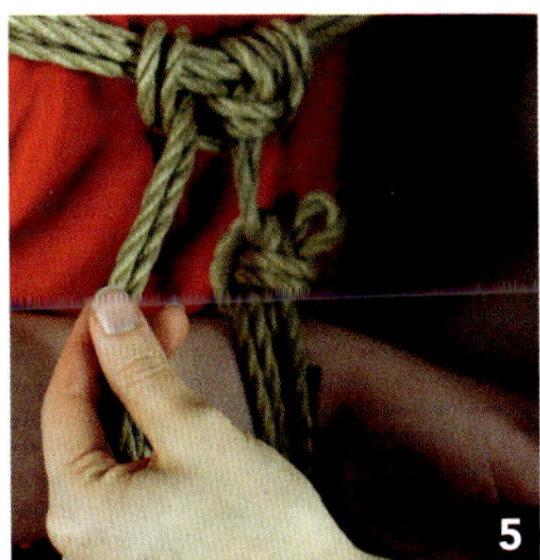

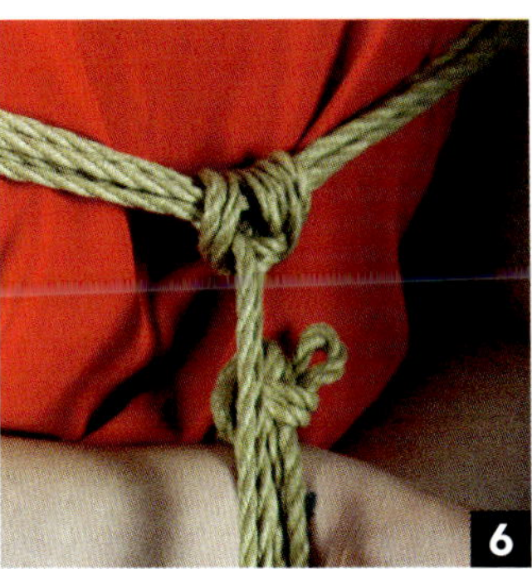

Splitting the Rope

[1] When you reach the end of your rope, take the two strands and separate them.

[2] Pass one of the strands underneath another part of your tie – in this case I'm using the stem of a takatekote.

[3, 4] Tie the strands together using a reef knot pulled down tight to the tie. To do this, pass the left strand over and then under the right strand, and pull tight, then repeat passing the right strand over and under the left strand.

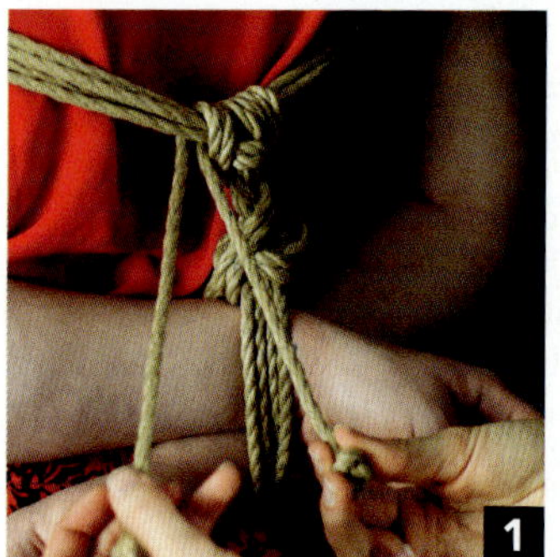

1

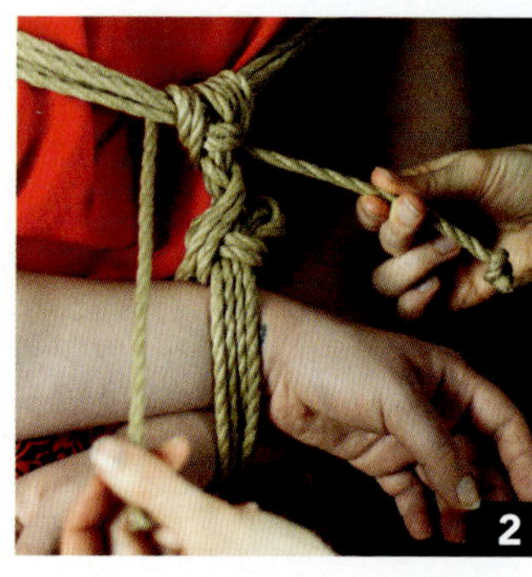

2

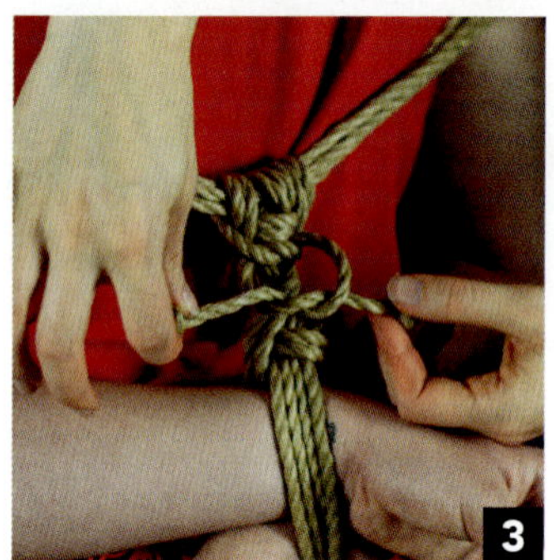

3

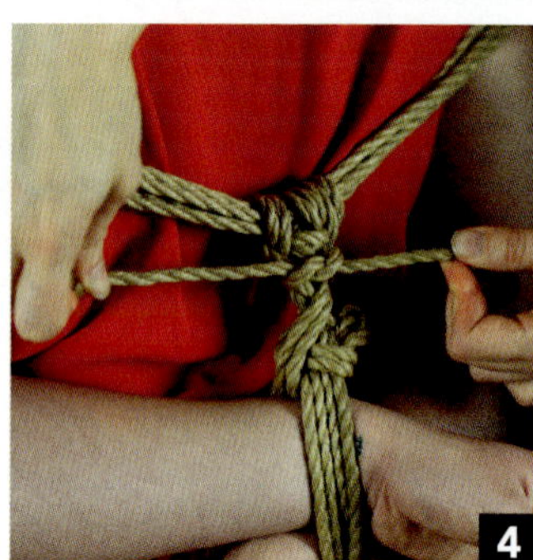

4

Overhand Lock

This is the same as an overhand knot but with the working end pulled only half way through to form a loop, so that it is easy to release just by pulling on the rope ends. In some cases pulling the working end all the way through might make the rope difficult to undo, which could be dangerous in some cases (e.g. **[2]** if used on a suspension line).

This lock is used on **[1]** the wrist cuff of the takatekote (pg. 56) and **[2]** to tidy up the rope on your suspension lines (pg. 118). For context, it is explained there in more detail – but the same method can also be used in many other places.

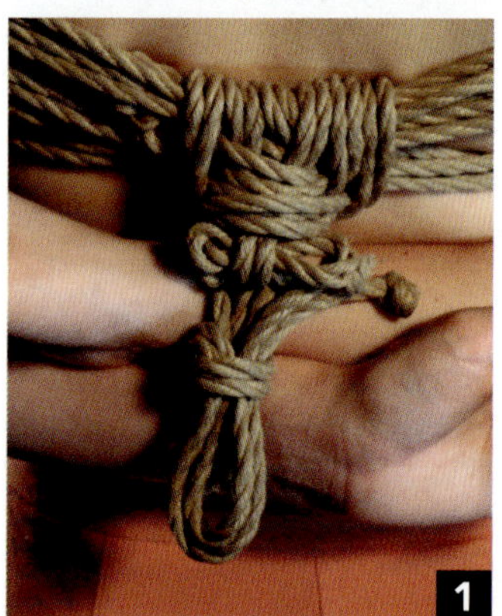

1

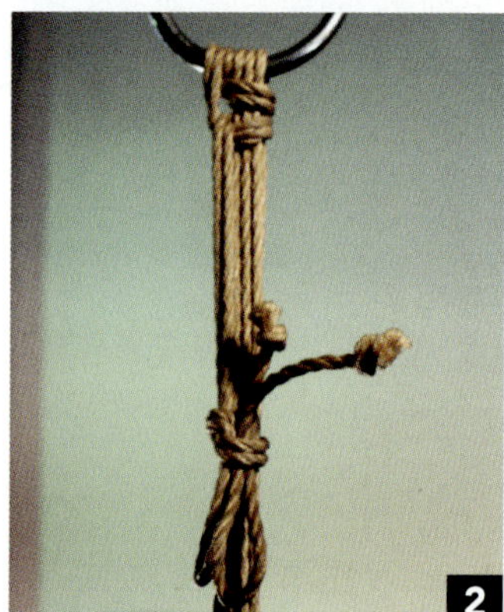

2

The advantage of this type of lock is that it can be used anywhere (even in the middle of a stem or wrap) and it uses up your rope ends nice and neatly.

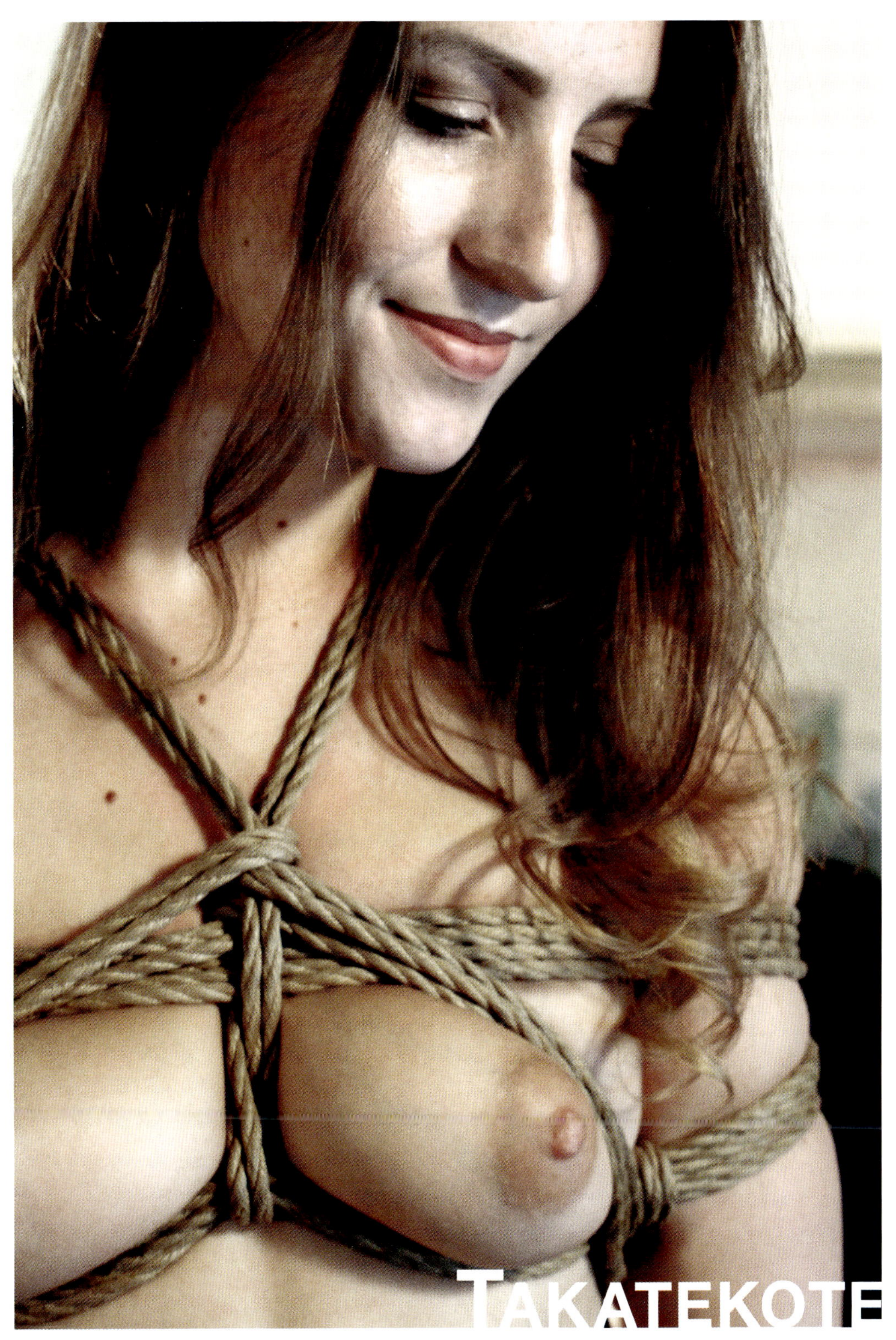

TAKATEKOTE

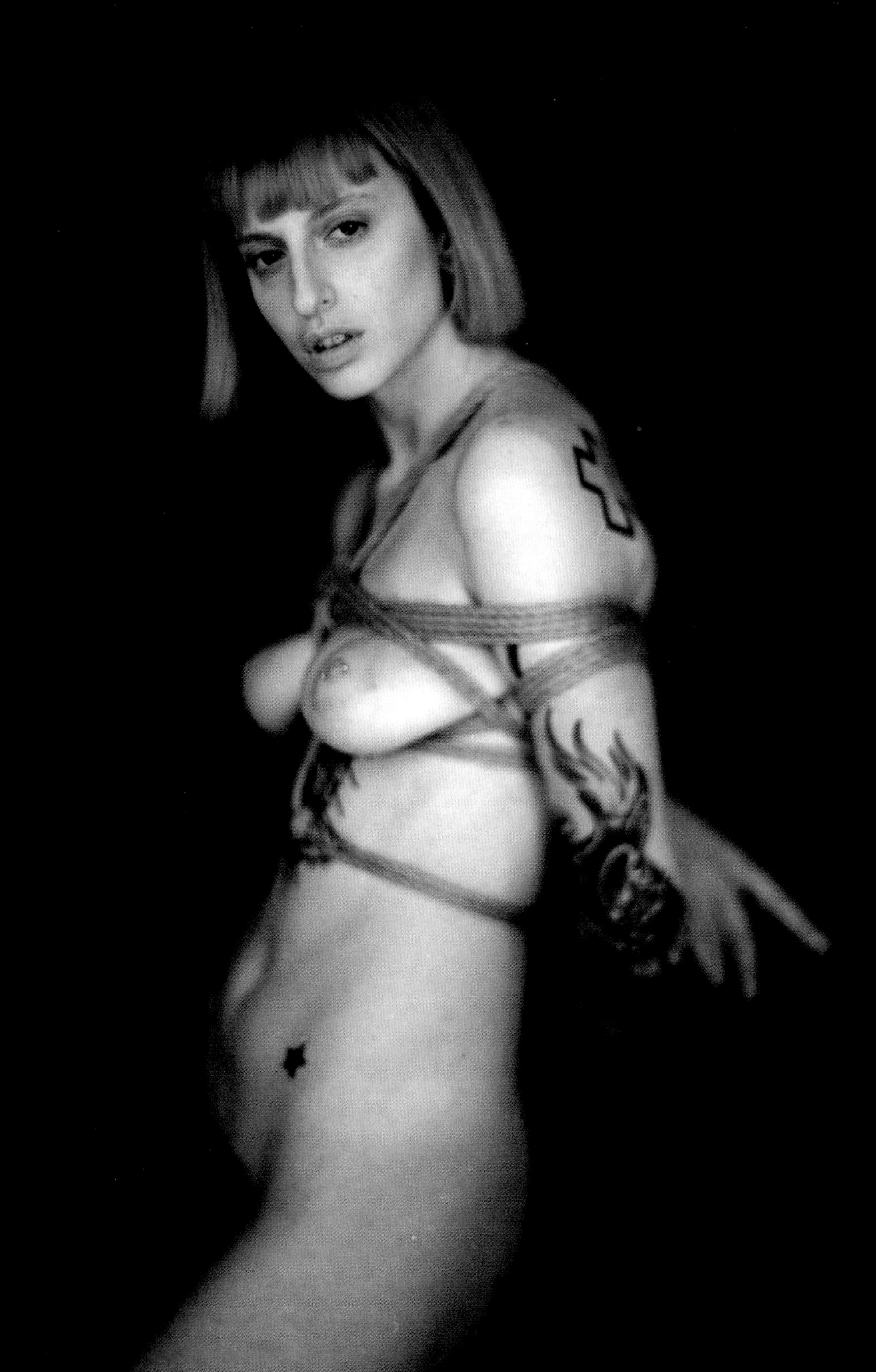

Takatekote

A takatekote is any tie where the model's arms are secured in a folded position behind their back. I have devoted a whole chapter to this because it's so frequently used as a starting point when learning to suspend. It forms a good basis for understanding other ties later on, and a solidly structured takatekote is a little more forgiving of beginner mistakes than some of the more severe positions.

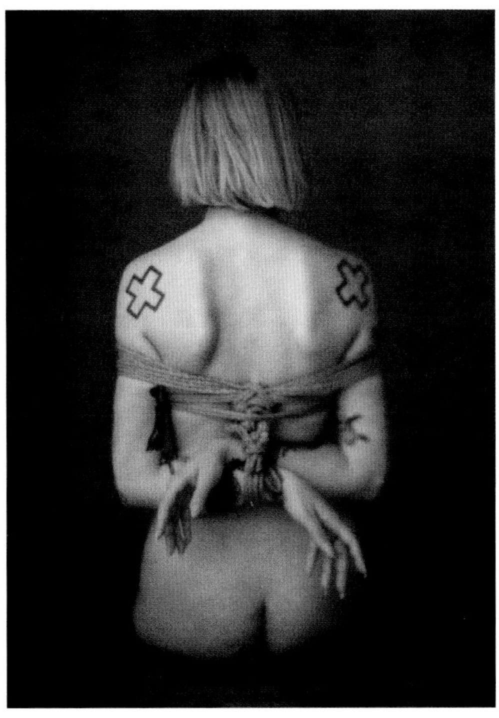

Although this harness is popular and versatile, it's by no means the only option for use in suspension, even for those just starting out – if it doesn't seem to work for your body then look around to see if you can find a better option.

I have used the term takatekote (often abbreviated to TK) as it seems to be the most commonly understood name, but you will also frequently hear gote, ushiro-takatekote, munenawa, and box tie. As with most shibari terms, takatekote refers only to the position that the body is in and says nothing about how the rope should be tied.

This chapter demonstrates one basic structure, or 'two rope' takatekote – and a few variations on 'third rope' patterns for different situations. I've also included a modification on page 68 for people who struggle to touch their hands together at the back.

The Body in a Takatekote

The information included here has been reviewed by a medical professional for accuracy. I strongly recommend both riggers and models read this to understand how you can use a basic knowledge of anatomy to mitigate the risks involved in this tie. Much of this information can be modified to apply to other situations where rope is applied on the arms and upper body.

Nerves

The nerve fibres in your body are insulated by a fatty substance called myelin. A severe or prolonged compression can cause a lesion or swelling in this protective layer resulting in loss of sensory and/or motor function. Loss of motor function is generally considered to be the more severe outcome but it is worth noting that it is not caused by a more severe damage; the outcome depends purely on whether the damage is to a motor nerve, sensory nerve, or combined motor-sensory nerve.

More severe cases of nerve damage are caused by a disruption of the nerve fibre itself.

In shibari, nerve issues most frequently occur as the result of rope pressure on the skin, although it is also possible that they are caused by the position of the body or by a restriction in blood supply to the nerve. In the majority of cases recovery comes very quickly once the rope is removed, however it can take up to six months, and in very severe cases there may be a permanent impairment.

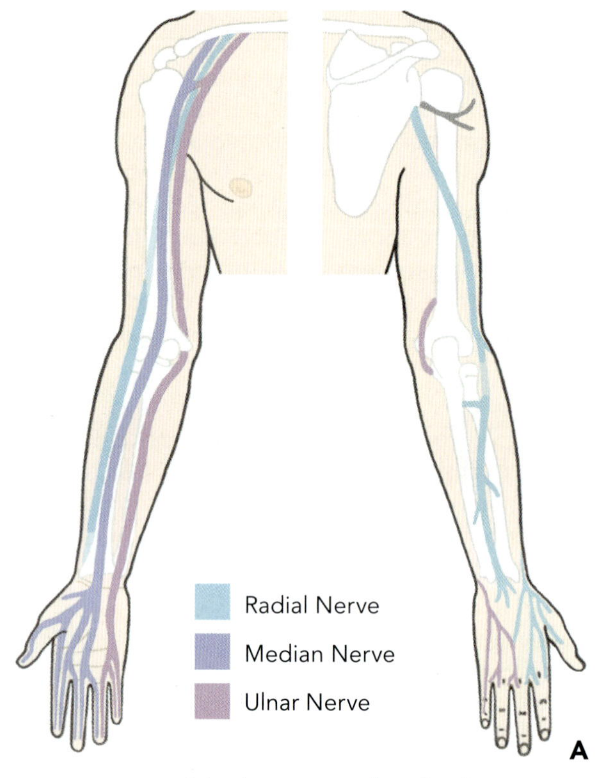

The nerves controlling your hands run from the spinal cord at the back of the neck (the brachial plexus) across the shoulder, under the collar bone, and all the way down to your fingers **[A]** Any point along this path where the nerves run close to the surface is a potential risk area. In a takatekote problems are most commonly caused by **[F]** the lower wrap, any rope going under the arm or the armpit, and the shoulder straps of a third rope. However the nerve path and depth will vary person to person. It is important that you take the time to learn where rope is best placed on your body before you jump into doing complex suspensions.

[B, C] These photos show the variety in potential placements for the lower wrap on a takatekote – a **[B]** high placement seems to be slightly more common. You can also minimise the risk of nerve damage by ensuring the wraps are flat and evenly tensioned. **[D]** Here the upper wrap is twisted, there is a gap between the lines, whilst the lower wrap has a join in the rope right over a potential risk area – all of which should be avoided.

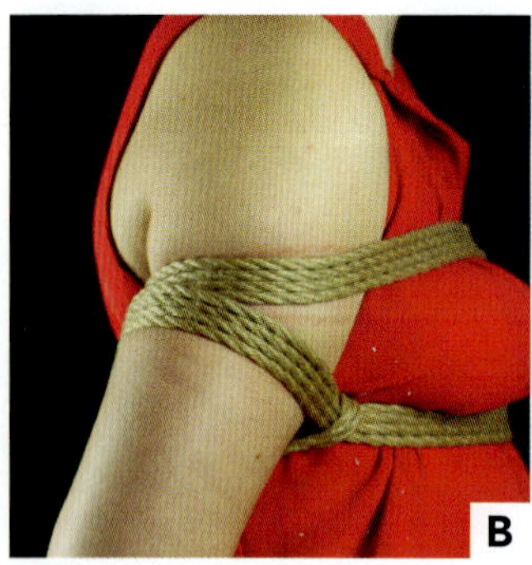

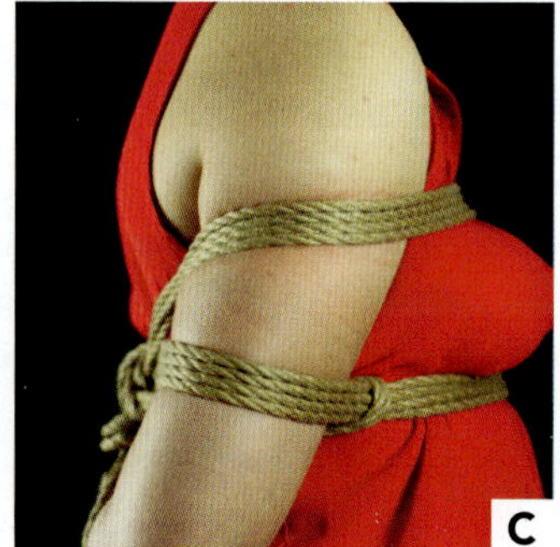

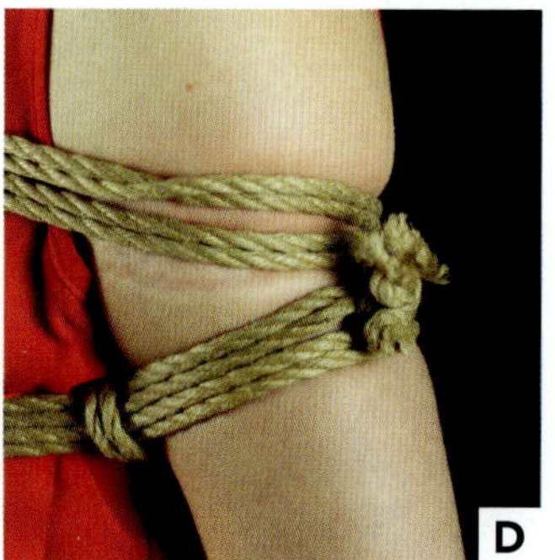

MOTOR ISSUES IN A TAKATEKOTE

You are most likely to experience motor function issues in your hands; recognisable as a feeling of weakness either in grip, in the case of median/ulnar issues, or in keeping the hand held up straight ('**wrist drop**') in the case of a radial nerve issue. You may also experience diminished fine motor control in the fingers. In rare cases it is possible that the whole arm could be affected ('arm drop').

SENSORY ISSUES IN A TAKATEKOTE

Sensory damage is usually experienced as patches of numbness on the skin of the hands, arms, or the area around the neck and shoulders. In a few cases it can manifest as permanent pins and needles, or even constant pain.

[E, F] Paying attention to which part of the body is affected can help you establish which nerve, and therefore which part of the tie, is the most likely cause. In the case of sensory loss in the hands, models can test this themselves whilst tied (steps 1-2, pg. 46) but note that there can be some considerable overlap between these areas which may be confusing in a stressful time such as suspension.

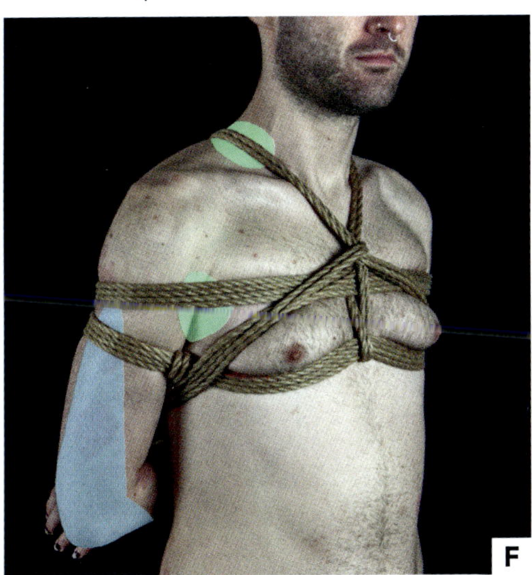

Radial Nerve Brachial Plexus

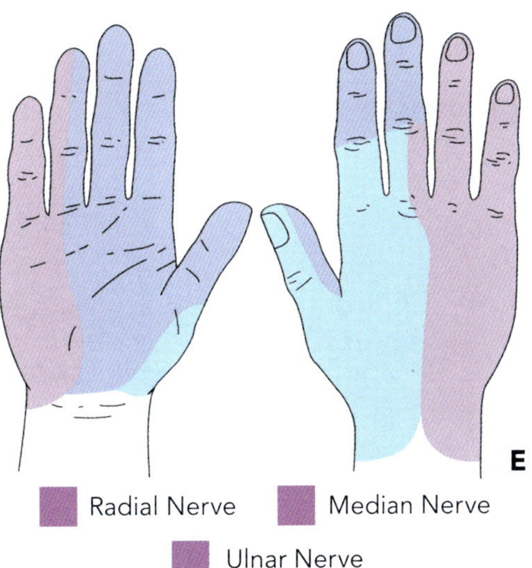

Radial Nerve Median Nerve
Ulnar Nerve

CIRCULATION

A feeling of numbness caused by diminished circulation is very common when being tied. This isn't something to be overly worried about per se, as it is unlikely to do any damage unless left unrectified for an excessive amount of time (just think how often you might wake up with a 'dead arm' after a period of several hours asleep). The main danger is that it can be difficult to distinguish between circulation and nerve issues.

As a general rule, circulation loss will cause the whole limb to become numb, whereas a sensory nerve issue will be localised in one patch depending on which nerve has been compressed **[E, F]**. Although it is possible that a whole limb could become numb through a nerve issue, it is quite unlikely during 'normal' practice of shibari.

Note that numbness is caused mostly by arterial obstruction, whereas a change of skin colour (specifically purpling) is caused by venous obstruction. Whilst this is also not something you should worry about in itself, you should also avoid using skin colour as an indicator that it's 'just circulation', as this is not reliable.

The following are tests which can help you to identify a nerve issue whilst in ropes.

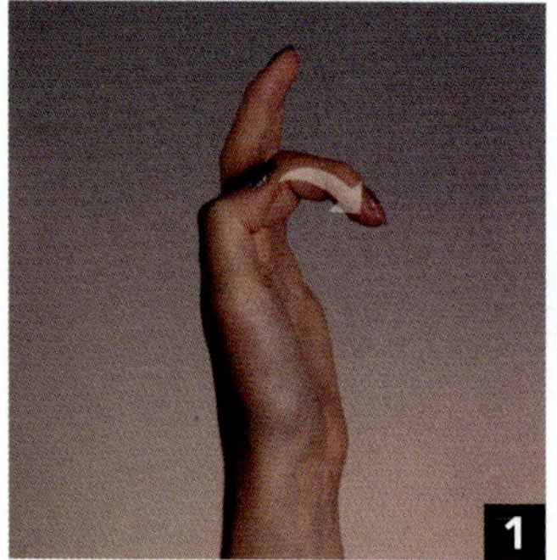

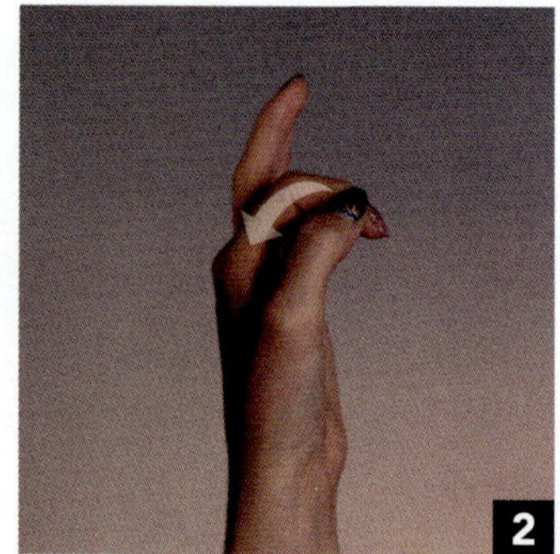

[1, 2] You can check for sensory issues by running your thumb gently forward and back along the side of each of your fingers in turn – this can also help you check which nerve has been the probable cause (see E, pg. 45)

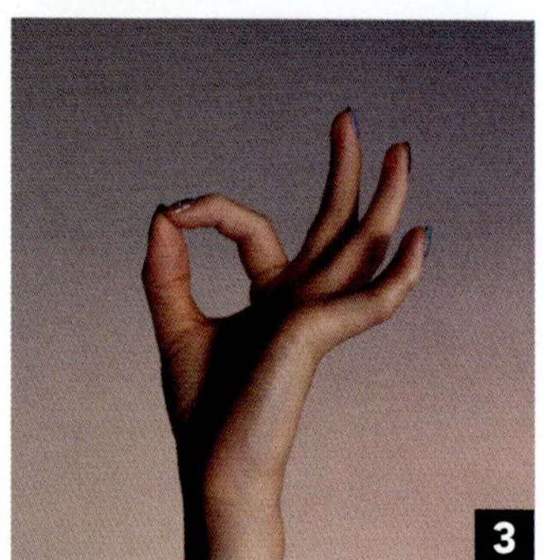

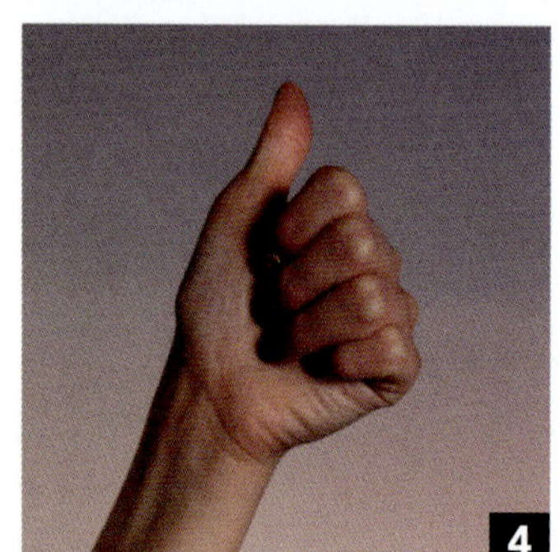

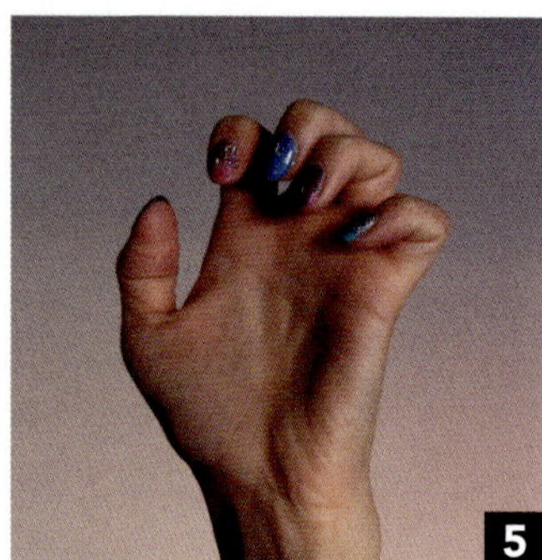

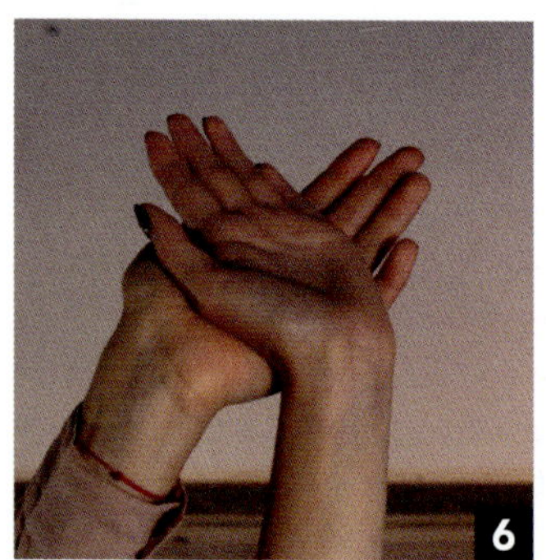

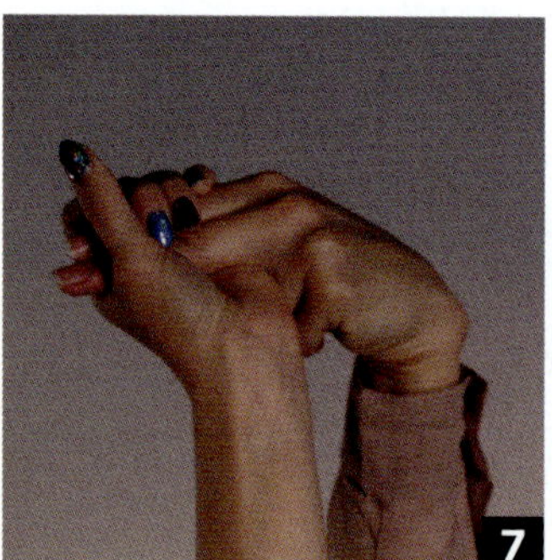

[3, 4, 5] Making these hand symbols firmly, and with strength can help you test your own motor function.

As a rigger, you can also check in with your partner using the following methods.

[6] Place your hand behind your model's and ask them to push backwards against it. A weakness in upward strength indicates a radial issue.

[7] Ask the model to squeeze your fingers. The muscles used to grip are high up on the arm and innervated by the median and ulnar nerves.

IN THE EVENT OF ENCOUNTERING A NERVE ISSUE:

- Untie gently to avoid further aggravating the area.
- Give the damaged limb time to rest and recover – in particular, you should avoid further compressing the area with bandages, with more rope, or by massaging it.
- Consult a doctor. A professional can provide physical therapy to help you strike a good balance between activity and rest. In the case of a wrist drop they can provide splints for protection.
- Taking an anti-inflammatory (such as ibuprofen) is often proposed as a matter of course. Although the evidence that this will help is not concrete at the time of writing, some medical professionals do still err towards recommending them.

THINGS THAT *MIGHT* HELP

- Vitamin B (especially B12) is known to have a role in nerve duplication and, although it isn't concretely proven to help, it likely won't harm you to try it.

THINGS THAT PROBABLY WON'T HELP

- Application of ice to the area should be avoided as it causes blood vessels to constrict, reducing blood flow. If any nerve or myelin cells are in critical condition, this could finish them off.

SOME THINGS TO NOTE

- Nerves can suffer from cumulative damage that starts manifesting once it passes a certain threshold. It's easy to become complacent when you have performed a certain tie many times with no apparent issue, but minor injuries might still have been sustained so you should try and be vigilant of small changes in your body over time.
- You are at risk of nerve compression during both suspension and floor bondage. If you are lying down with ropes pressed between the floor and your body this is practically not much different to being in full suspension.
- Pay attention that the ropes don't slip during dynamic rope play – that is, moving around either in the air (transitions) or on the floor. This is in part because the rope might unintentionally end up in an problem area, and in part because the force from a sliding (or 'shearing') rope may be more dangerous than that of a static compression.

ALTERNATIVES

If you find that you are very sensitive in the arms, or the potential for a nerve damage is completely outside of your risk profile you may wish to experiment with alternative ties. One option cold be to use a hands free chest harness (pg. 89), although some people find that because these ties load directly onto the chest/ribs they can be more restrictive on the breathing than a standard takatekote.

AND FINALLY, DON'T WORRY

Nerve issues are a frequent topic of discussion for anyone who practices rope – so much so that I've occasionally seen it scare some people away altogether. Although you should be aware of the possibility, serious nerve injuries are quite rare. You can mitigate a lot of the risk by being careful, sensible, and taking time to get to know your own body and/or the bodies of the people you tie.

Arm Placement

Protecting the shoulder area from injury is just as important as protecting the nerves. Small damages have a tendency to build up over time when repeatedly practising suspension. Whilst some degree of wear and tear might be unavoidable, you can still take steps to minimise these risks.

There are several different positions you can hold your arms in when in a takatekote. The most common are **[G]** high hands and **[H]** parallel hands, though a **[J]** low handed position is also widely used, particularly by those with less flexibility – though it can also be a choice of comfort or aesthetic.

Personally, I tend to favour whichever option makes maximum use of the model's flexibility, without becoming stressful, painful or unsustainable. The intention here is to protect the shoulder area by limiting mobility (see 'Locking the Shoulder').

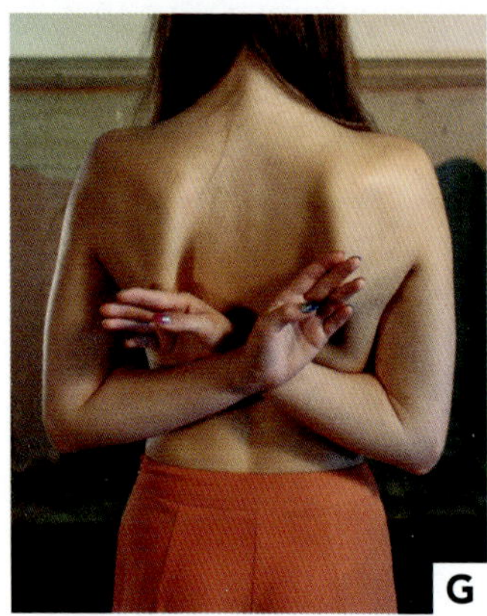

G

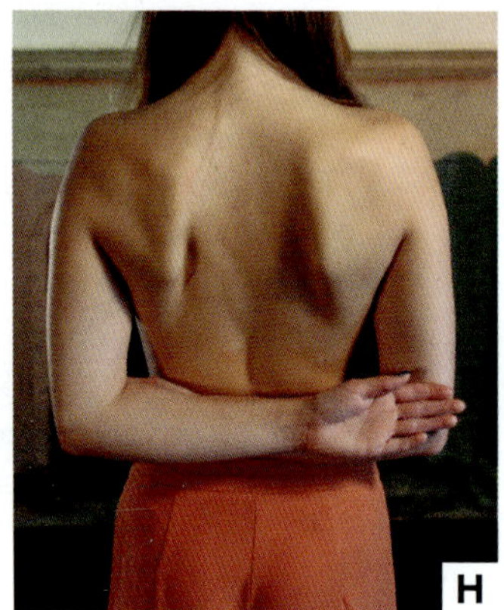

H

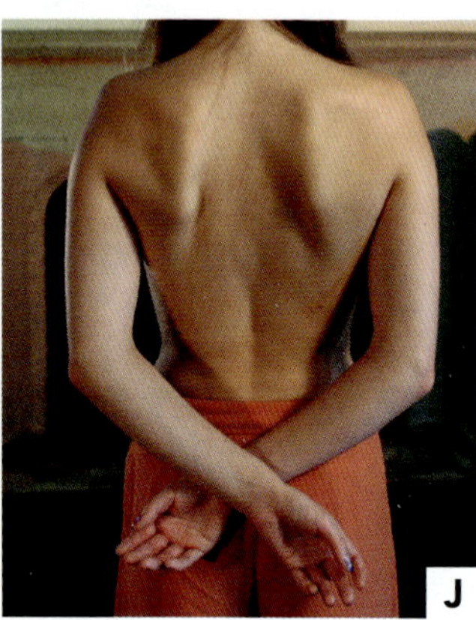

J

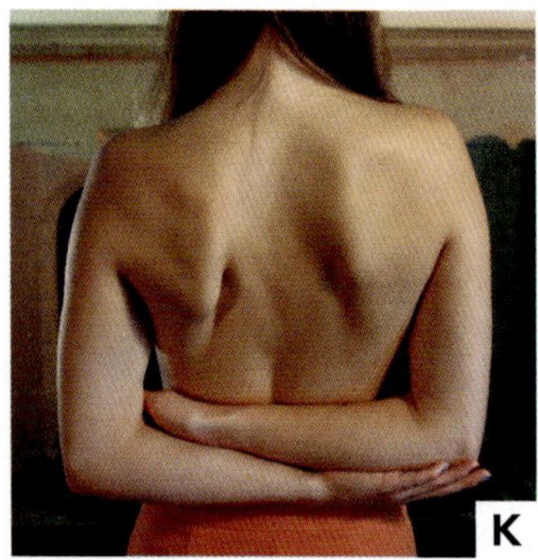

K

[K] When you are in parallel position you can choose to stack the hands one on top of the other, rather than **[H]** placing one behind the other. Some models find this stacked position more comfortable, however be aware that the imbalance in the shoulders, both in height and in scapula placement (as seen in the image) could become problematic in some cases.

Locking the Shoulder

The shoulder area is very complex; it includes the scapula (shoulder blade), clavicle (collar bone) and glenohumeral joint (shoulder joint) – all of which contribute to the overall mobility of the shoulder, particularly the scapula in relation to the ribs. This means that when the wraps of the takatekote are put under pressure in suspension they can easily move the whole shoulder, sometimes in an unhealthy direction. Even if this doesn't result in an immediate injury it can cause cumulative stress over time. There is some debate over the best way to handle this – some models prefer to keep their arms folded loosely so they have the ability to adjust as they wish, whilst others prefer to 'lock' the joint tightly to minimise the amount of movement possible.

Below I have shown one possible method for locking the shoulder area, including the shoulder blade. I use this for parallel and low handed positions, as well as high handed ones, to help keep the arm in a good position even if you are not using the maximum flexibility possible.

[1] Pull the arm downwards, firmly but not sharply.

[2] Twist the arm from above the elbow counter clockwise on the right arm or clockwise on the left. Make sure that you are gripping firmly enough that the you are actually manipulating the joint and not just moving the skin. Gently rotate the hand so that it follows in the same direction.

[3] Lift the hand up as far as it is comfortable to go. Once again, do not lift sharply; you need to allow the model enough time for their body to adjust to the position and enough time to react if there is any pain.

Repeat steps 1 to 3 on the other side.

[4] Once both arms are in position, place your hands on the outside of the elbows and press them gently inwards to push the hands in further.

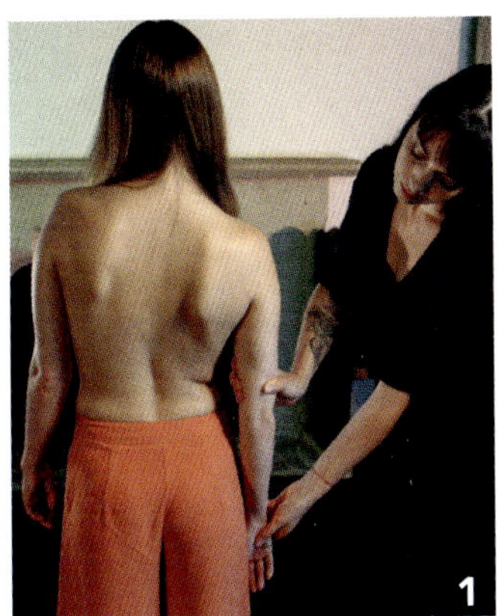
1

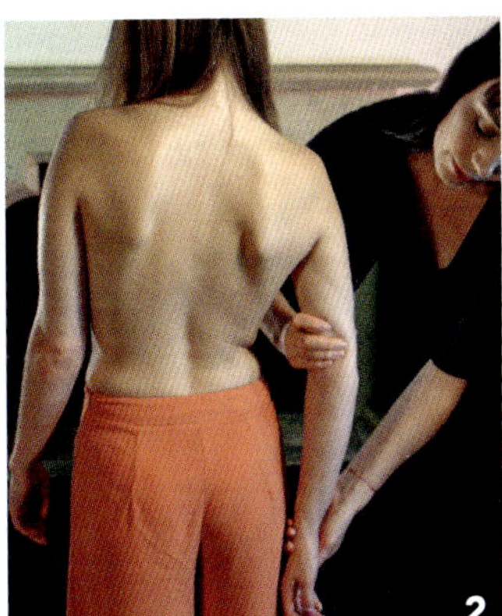
2

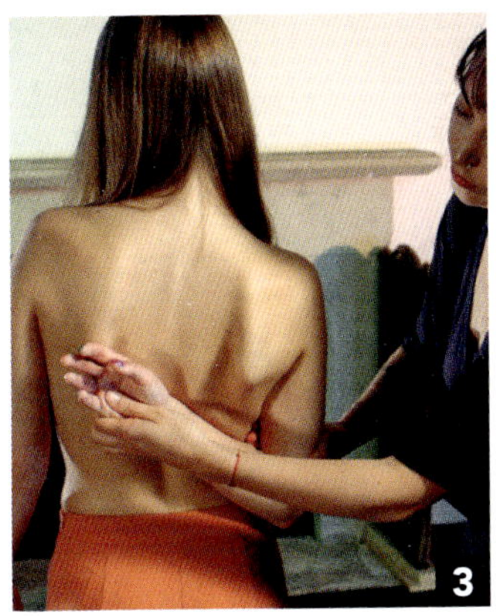
3

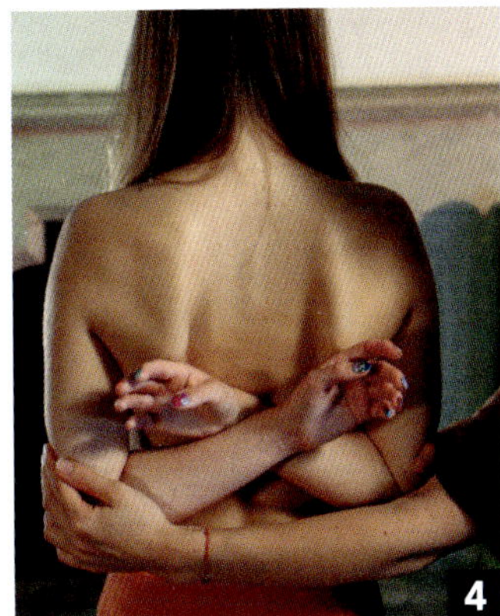
4

Exercise

You may wish to look into shoulder exercises to warm up/down before and after rope.

Although altering your body is in no way a necessary prerequisite for rope, some people find it helpful to work on building the muscles in the shoulder and upper back to further protect their joints – you may find this particularly useful if you have a high level of flexibility.

Two Rope Takatekote

One of the hardest parts of writing this book was deciding which form of takatekote to show, as there are innumerable ways to tie it. I've personally found it useful to familiarise myself with several different versions so that I can be adaptable to different situations, such as the type of tie I'm doing, the body type and personal preferences of the model, and perhaps the particular aesthetic I want to achieve.

In the end the harness I decided to use was based on that of Kazami Ranki, with two minor modifications*. This is a fairly strong and versatile structure that is also simple to tie and relatively easy to tension well as the rope is firmly locked off after every step.

In most cases I tie this with quite gentle tension; applying the rope as if 'drawing on the skin' and leaving enough space to easily run my fingers under the wraps. Although this slightly increases the likelihood of rope slipping, it also feels much more comfortable and sustainable for the model. Many people prefer to have the upper wrap a bit firmer than the lower so it moves the pressure onto the stronger area around the shoulder and top of the chest, and away from the sensitive lower arms and sternum/ribs.

One of the drawbacks with this type of takatekote is that the relative bulk of the **stem** doesn't necessarily suit everyone, and can be 'overkill' in some situations.

As ever, if you find this tie isn't working for you, there are many other options out there for you to experiment with.

The term 'two rope takatekote' refers to any form that has an upper and lower wrap as shown here. Whether or not it actually uses two ropes will of course depend on the length of the ropes in relation to size of the model.

The Upper Wrap

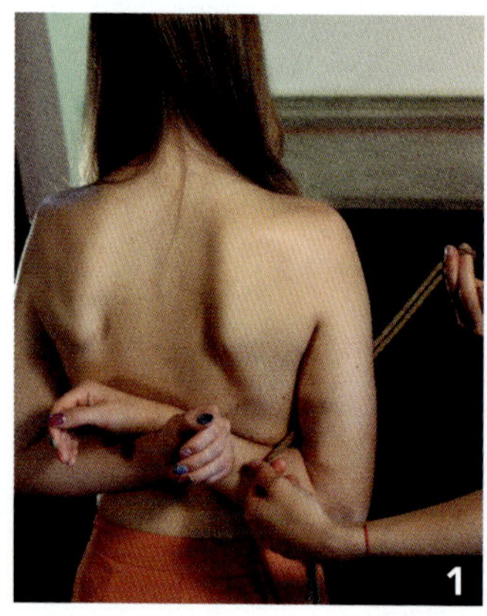

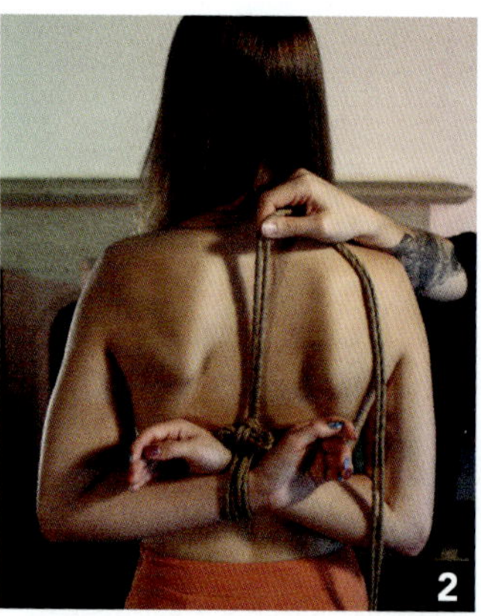

[1] Place the bight through the gap in the crook of the elbow and slide it along to the centre of the back - this is much smoother than forcing the rope directly under the wrists.

[2] Tie the quick release single column (pg. 30) around the wrists. Adjust so the knot is at the highest point, closest to the body.

* The first being the combination of reinforced stem with quick release wrist cuff *(steps 12 - 17)* which is something that I find a useful addition to many forms of takatekote, and was inspired by Macphisto and Miumi-U. The second is the omission of the upper kannukis. Whilst I have found the original Kazami structure to be more stable and comfortable with the upper kannukis left in, a reasonable number of models seem to dislike them. In this case locking the two wraps together *(steps 24, 32, 36)* is one commonly used way of preventing the structure from becoming unbalanced. Gorgone has another version of this structure, which has the further modification of locking only the wraps into the 'L' friction and leaving out the lines from the kannukis - you may find this a good solution if you are struggling to tension the lower wraps.

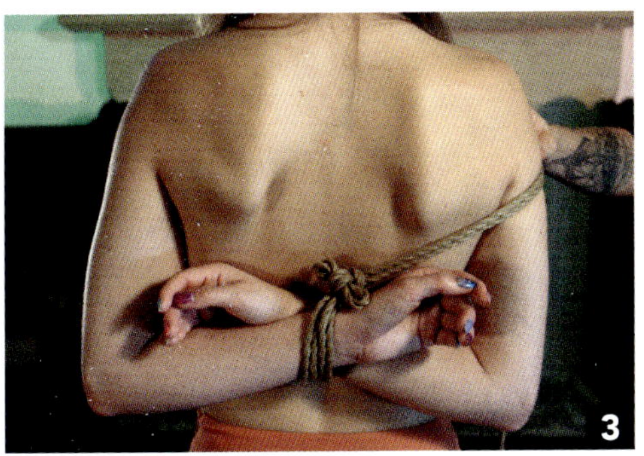
3

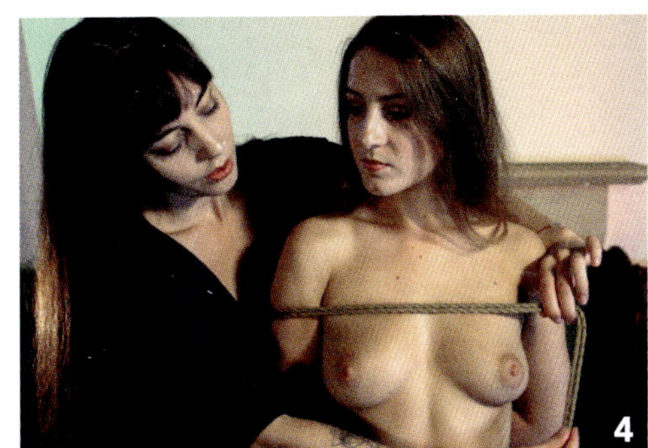
4

[3, 4] Make a wrap around the shoulder and across the front of the chest. Aim for the placement to be on the shoulder muscle and below the crook of the armpit. Placing the wrap too high can stress the shoulder and, in some people, restrict breathing.

[5] Continue the wrap across the back, letting the rope curve gently under the shoulder blades. Cross over the first wrap as you pass at the shoulder and make a second wrap following the line of the first.

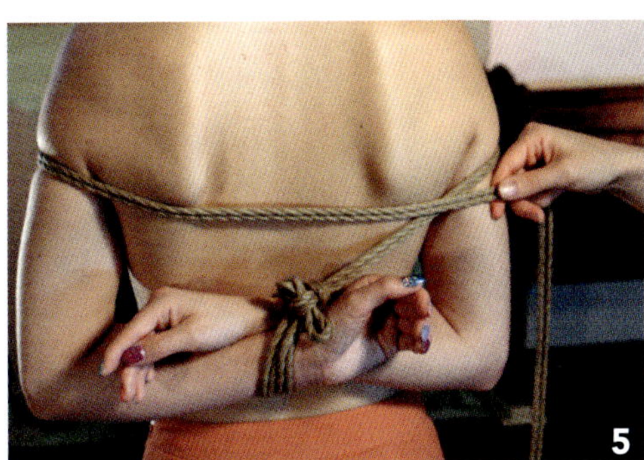
5

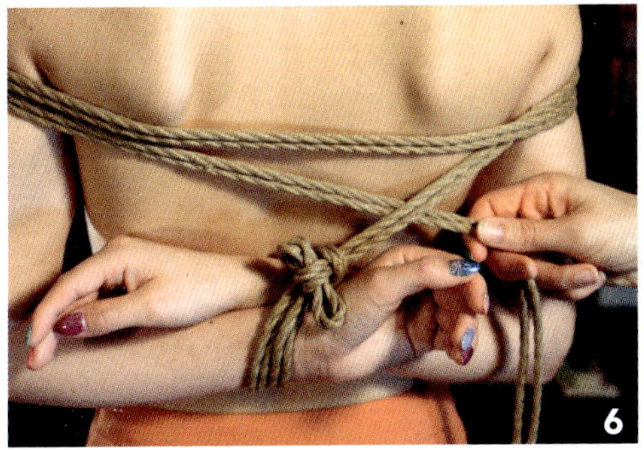
6

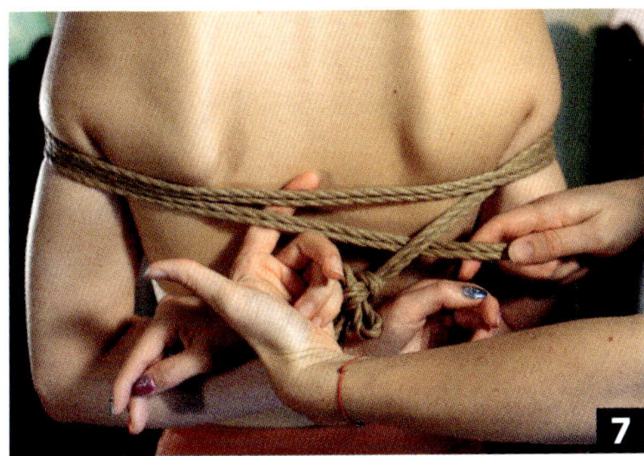
7

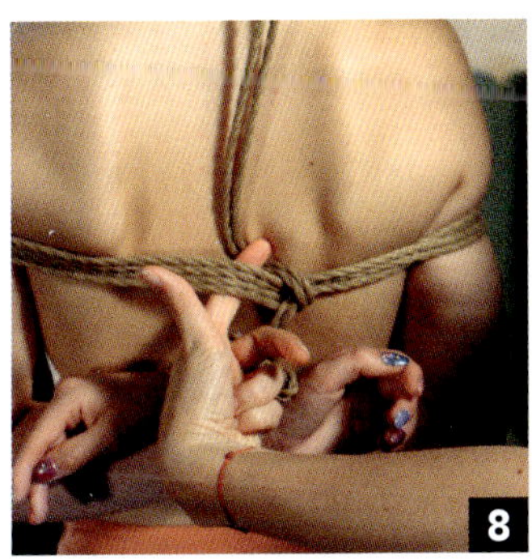
8

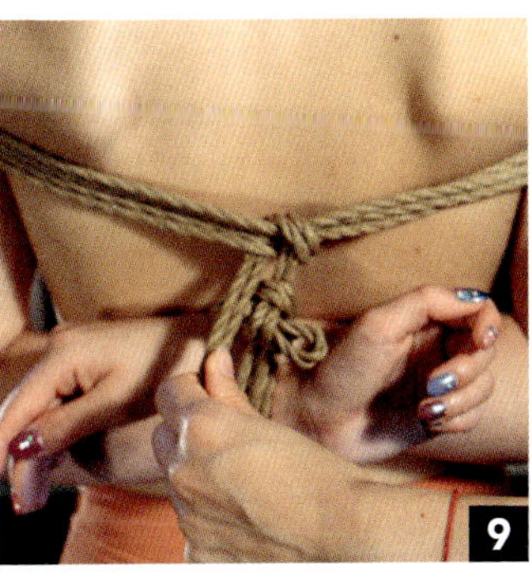
9

[6] Pass the working end underneath the line connecting the wrist and chest wraps.

[7] Place your index finger underneath both wraps and pull down slightly.

[8, 9] Hook the working end under your index finger and draw it through underneath the wraps. This forms the 'stem' of the takatekote.

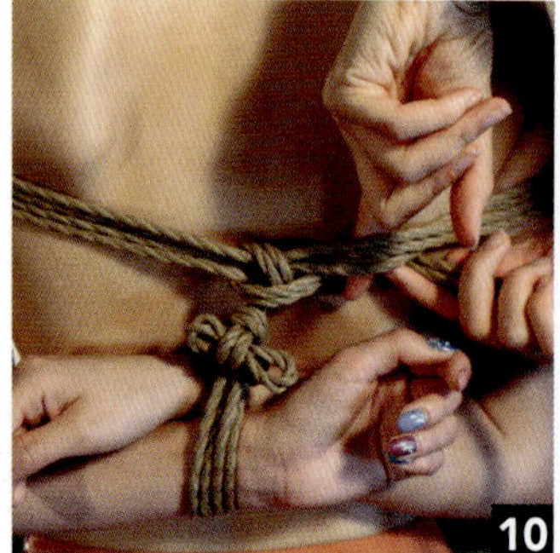

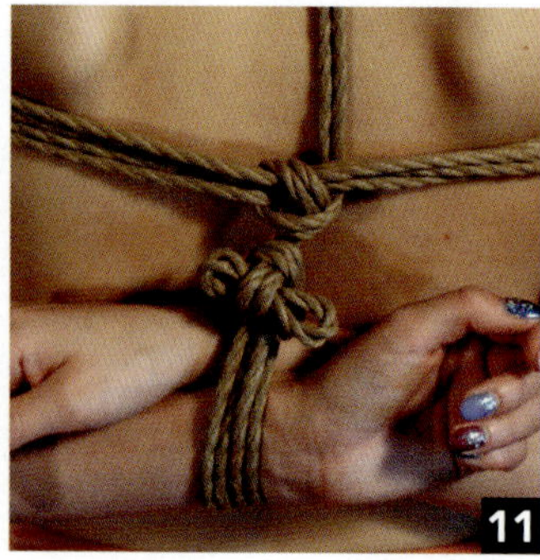

Steps 10-17 finish the upper wrap by reinforcing the stem.

[10, 11] Pass the working end horizontally across the top of the stem, and vertically up underneath the wrap.

[12, 13] Then pass it down over the wrap and underneath the wrist cuff. Ensure that it sits behind the quick release knot so you can release the hands.

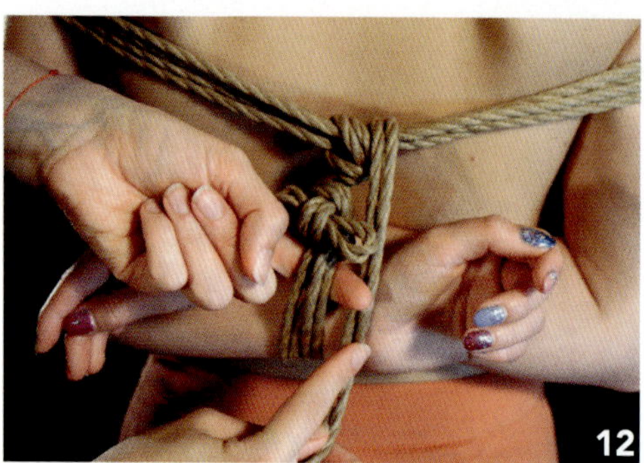

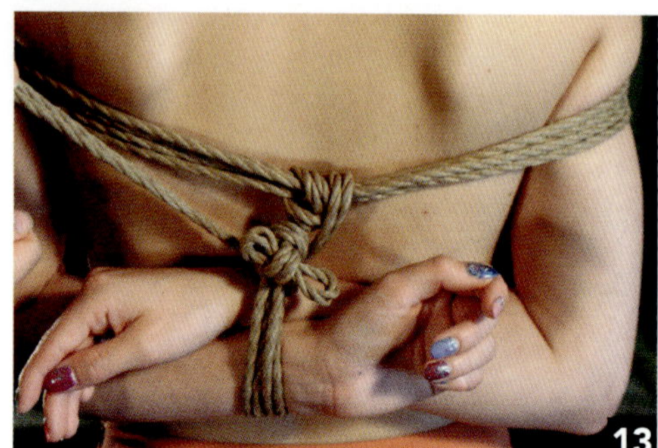

[14, 15] Pass the working end back over the wrap on the opposite side of the stem, creating equal reinforcement on both sides. Try to roughly match the tension of the central rope.

[16, 17] To close, wrap once around the stem, first over, then under.

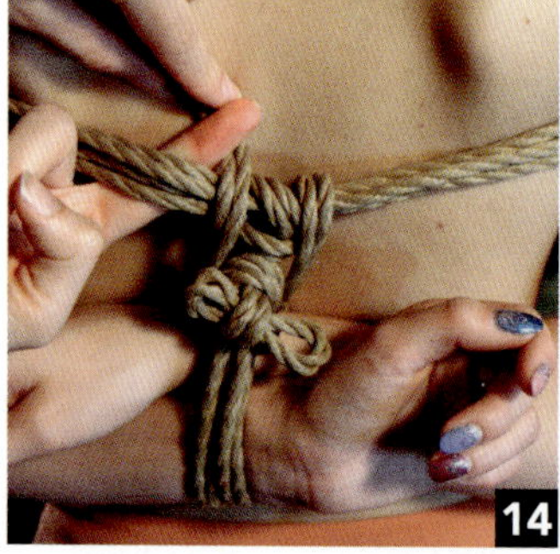

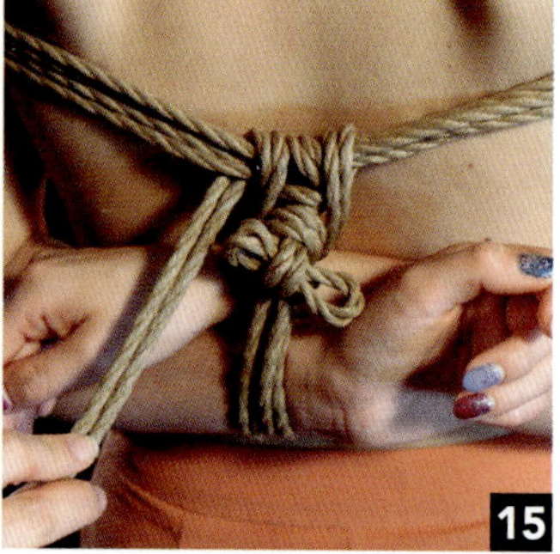

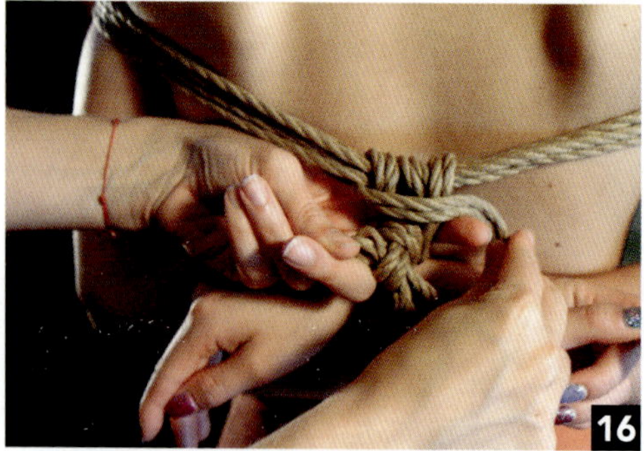

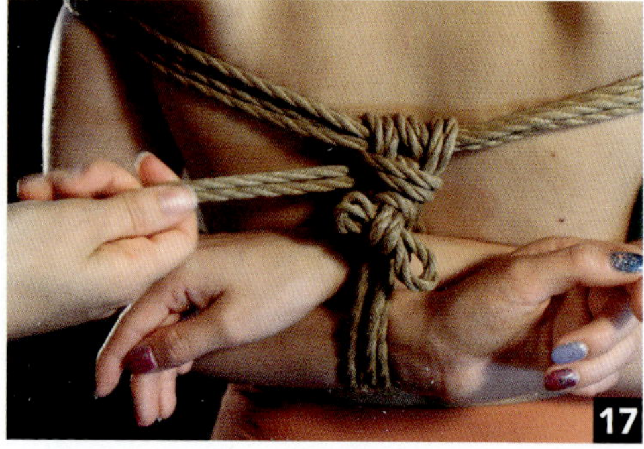

This completes the structure of the upper wrap. Before starting the lower wrap take a moment to check the tension – in most cases it should be firm, but not so tight that you struggle to run your finger around under the wrap.

You should also check that your stem is central, in line with the wrist cuff and the spine. You can slide it round to adjust it now if necessary (if moving the wrap is difficult it might be a sign that it's too tight).

The tension you choose will vary depending on the type of tie you plan to use it for. I've also sometimes found that more muscular bodies benefit from tighter rope, and some models just seem to have a preference for the feeling of being tied tighter or looser.

The stem reinforcement (steps 10-17) serves the dual purpose of preventing the hands from dropping, and giving the tie a strong stem for suspension whilst still allowing the wrists to be easily released. I find it a useful addition to many types of takatekote including the commonly used Akechi and Kazami styles.

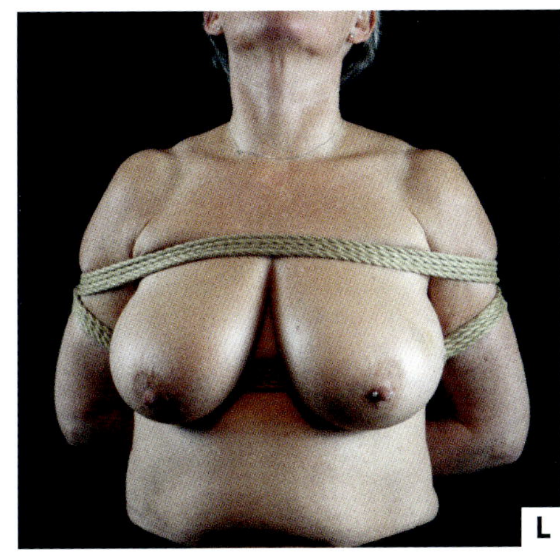

L

Tip

[L] It is easy to accidentally place the upper wrap too high, particularly on models with larger breasts. **[M]** It is usually more comfortable to place the rope in a straight line over the fat surrounding the breast tissue.

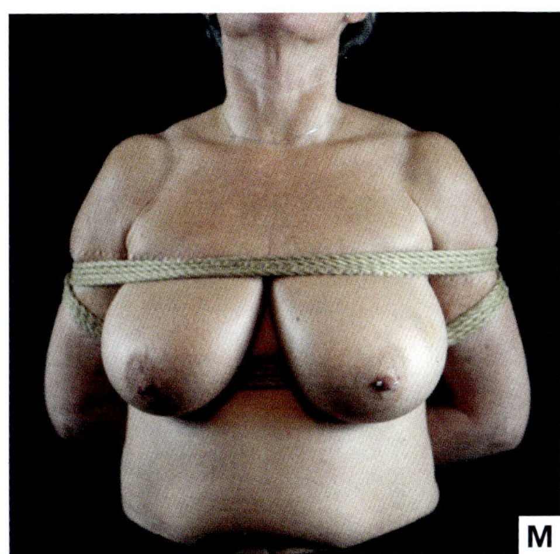

M

The Lower Wrap

[18] I have joined a second rope onto the first one using a lark's head (pg. 33) to begin the lower wrap.

I like to keep a selection of ropes cut to the right length for the upper wraps so that any joins fall at the back where they won't cause problems.

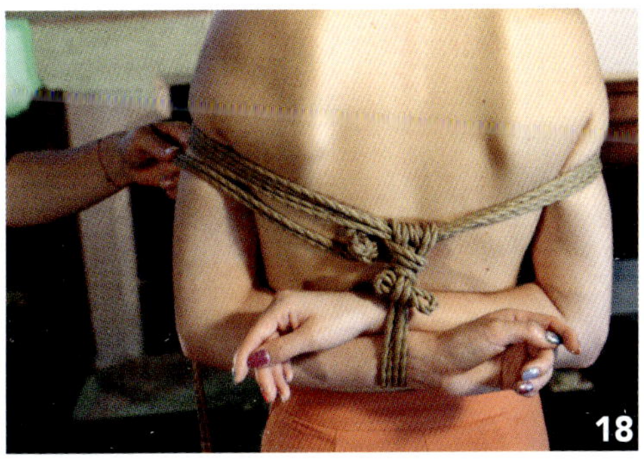

18

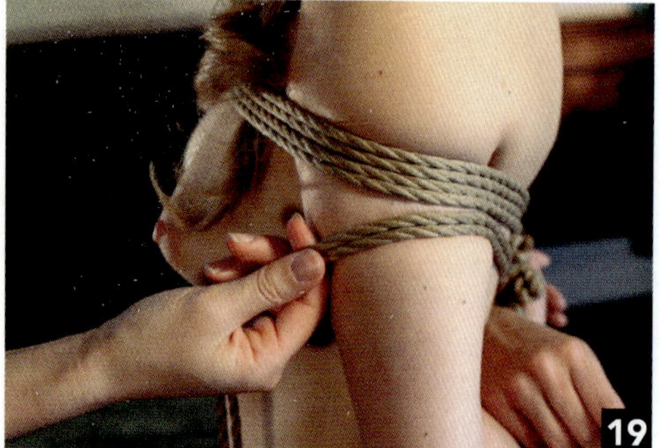
19

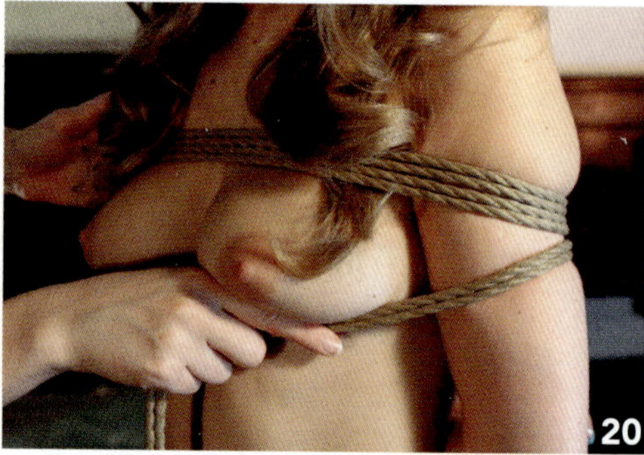
20

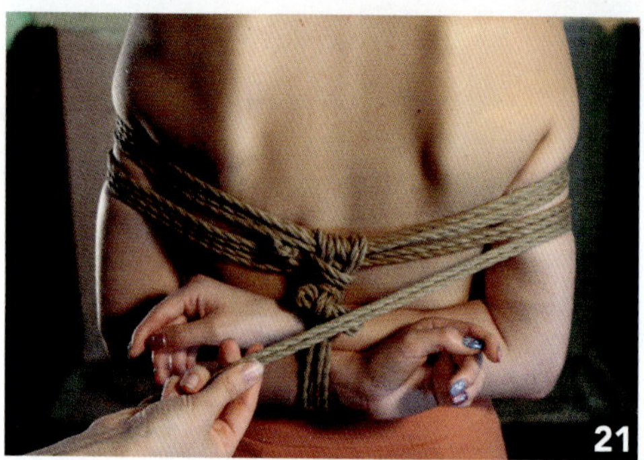
21

[19, 20] Wrap the working end over the arm at the model's preferred placement, and then across the chest.

[21] Continue around the body, making two wraps, passing the working end underneath the stem as you pass it.

TIP

If you are tying bodies with breasts it is generally more comfortable to lift the breasts up as you place the rope underneath.

If you are tying bodies without breasts it's easy to assume that the gap underneath the pectoral muscle is the equivalent placement to this, however it's often more comfortable to let the rope rest on the muscle itself where the ribs have more padding.

Steps 22-25 will create your first 'L' friction.

[22, 23] As you finish the second wrap, pass the working end under the stem and make a U-turn to come back over the stem, then up and underneath both wraps.

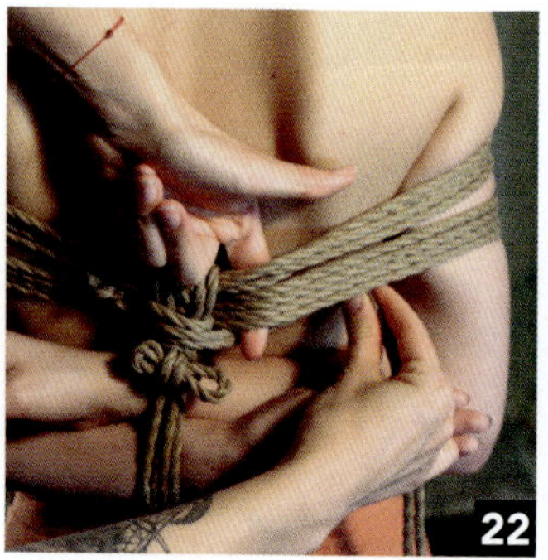
22

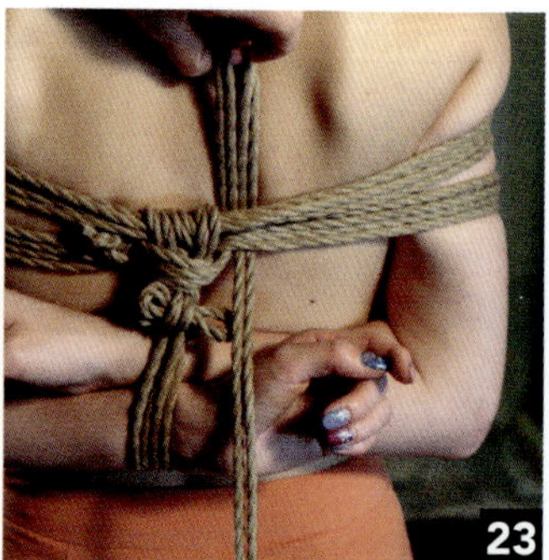
23

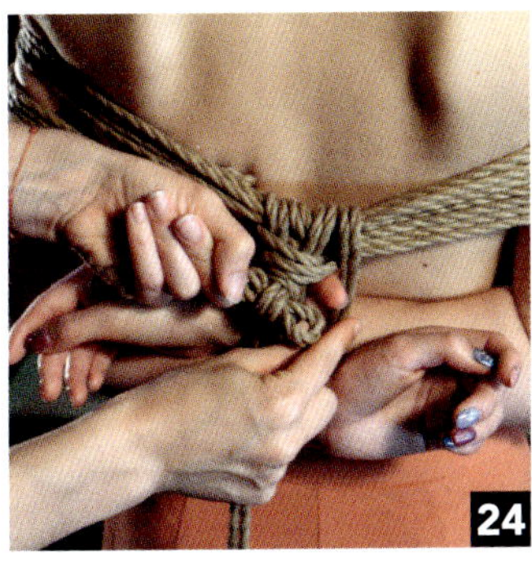

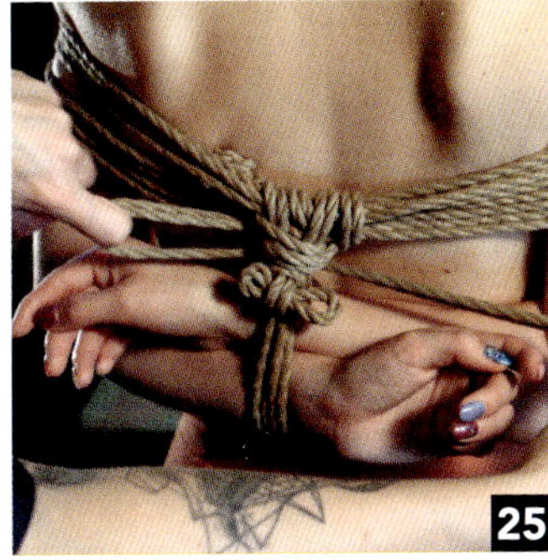

[24, 25] Take the working end back down over the wraps and back underneath the stem.

Take care not to make this too tight. The 'L' friction should rest over the wraps, rather than compacting them together.

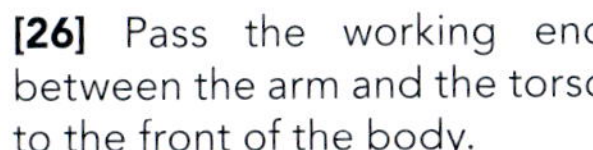

[26] Pass the working end between the arm and the torso to the front of the body.

[27] Pass the working end in between the upper and lower wraps at the front of the body.

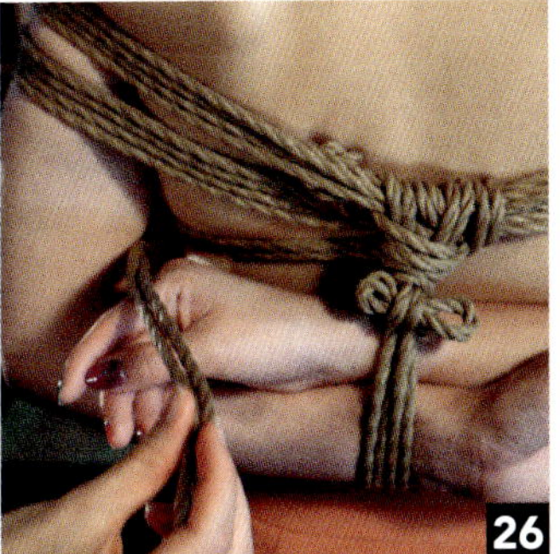

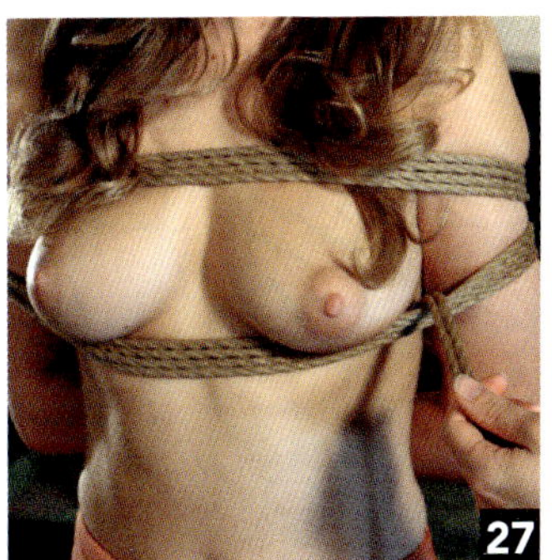

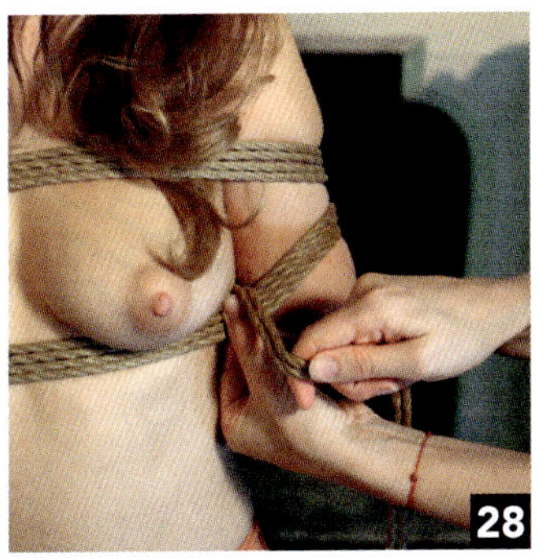

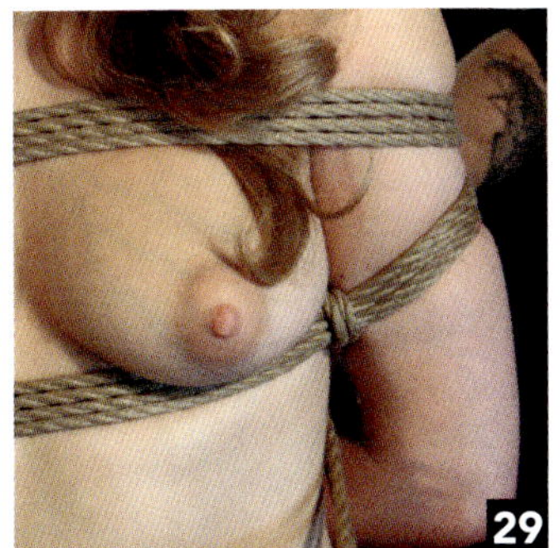

[28] Gently press the lower wrap against the body with your thumb to keep it flat. Lay the working end over to make a kannuki (pg. 32).

[29] Pass back underneath the arm. Try not to tighten the kannuki as you do so; the tension you set with your thumb should be about the right amount.

Steps 30-32 will create the second 'L' friction.

[30] Pass the working end back under the stem.

[31] Make a U-turn over the stem and then pass upwards behind the kannuki lines and both wraps.

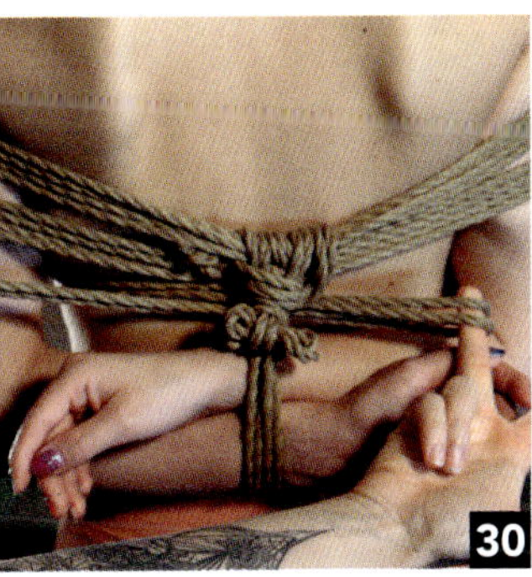

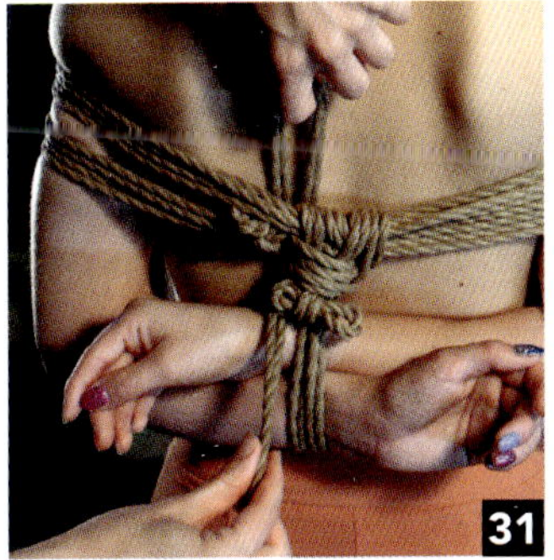

[32] Pass the working end back over the top of everything and underneath the stem.

[33] Repeat steps 26-29 to create the kannuki on the other side.

[34 - 36] Create the third 'L' friction by repeating steps 30 to 32 this time in a mirror image.

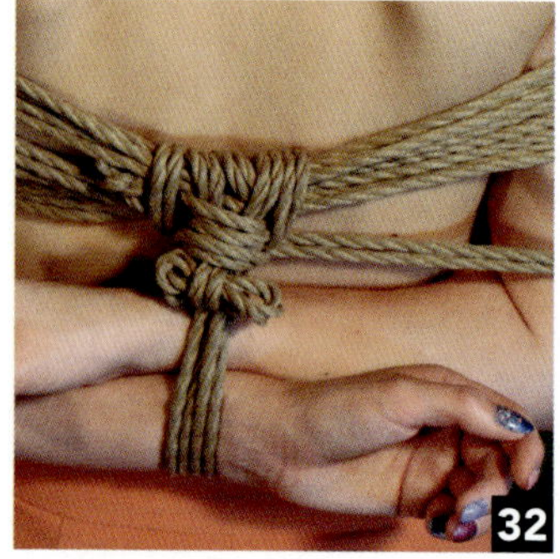

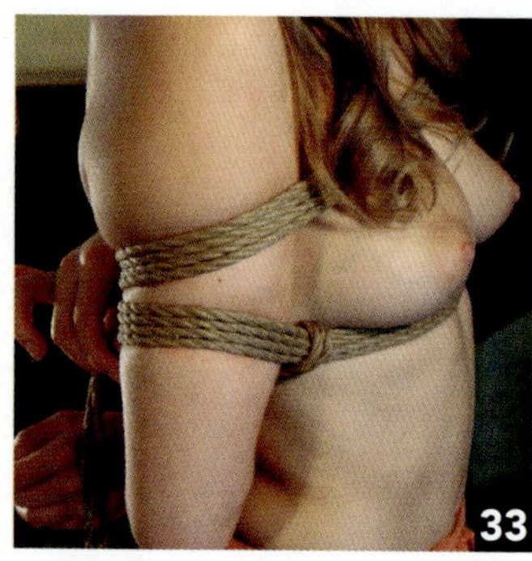

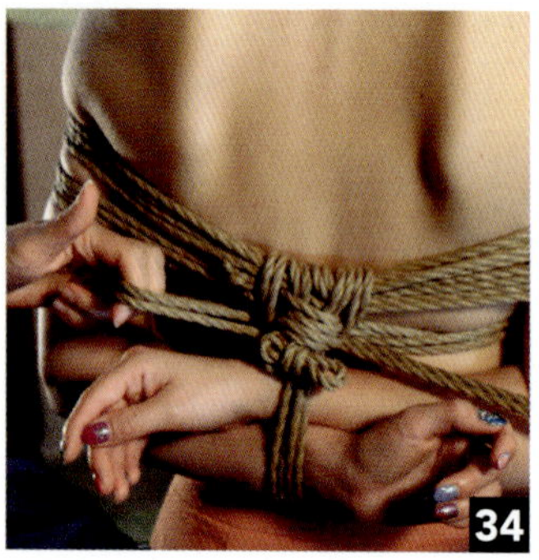

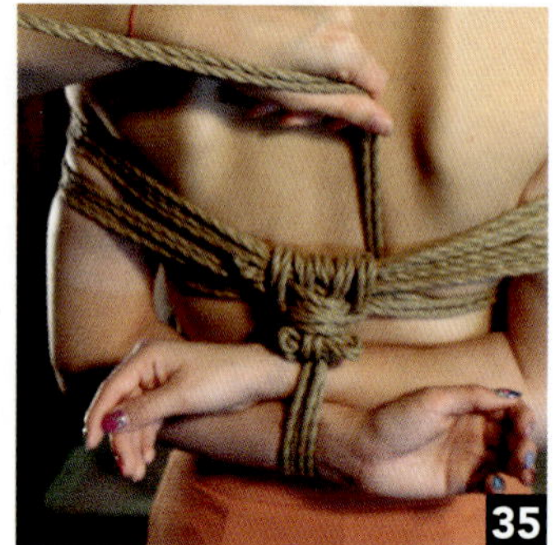

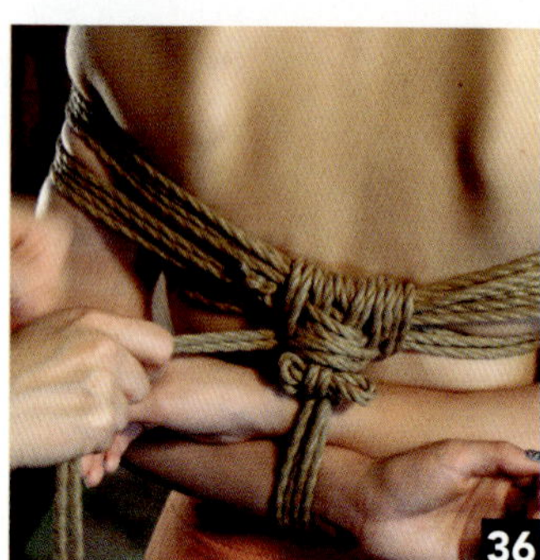

The basic structure is now finished.

To lock off, I normally make an overhand lock (pg. 40) on the wrist cuff.

[37] Take the working end and wrap it over and under the cuff.

[38] Make space in this wrap with your index finger.

[39, 40] Pass the working end over the wrap and pull it half way through the space made with your finger so that it forms a loop, then tighten securely.

If you have considerably more rope left over you can experiment with alternative ways to use up the rope and lock off.

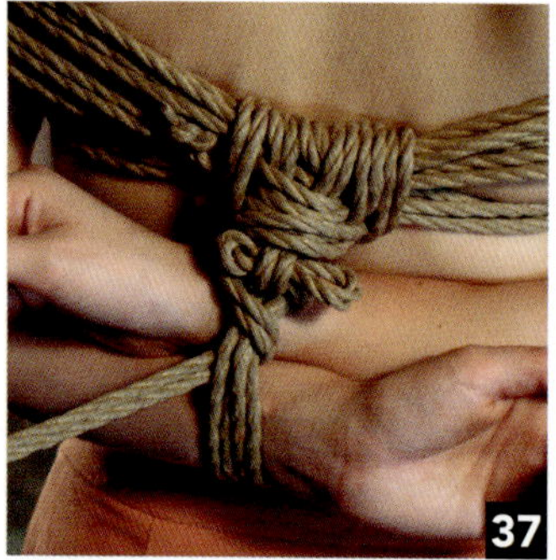

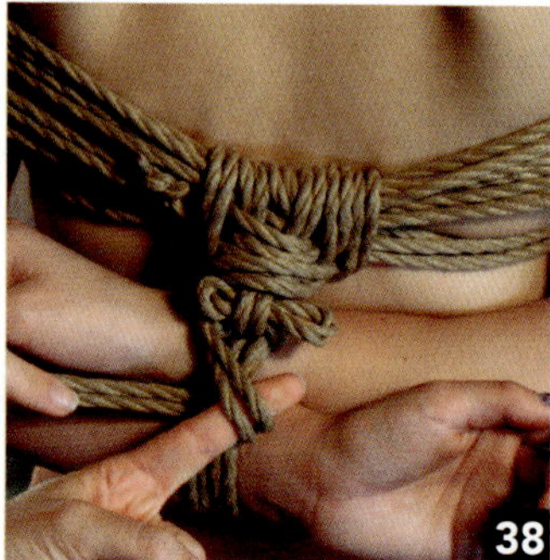

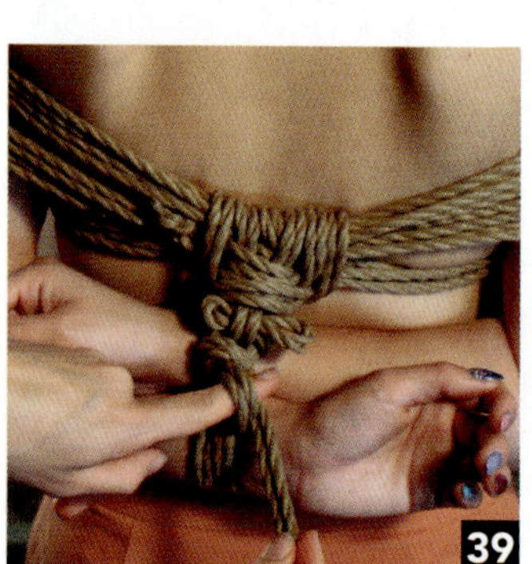

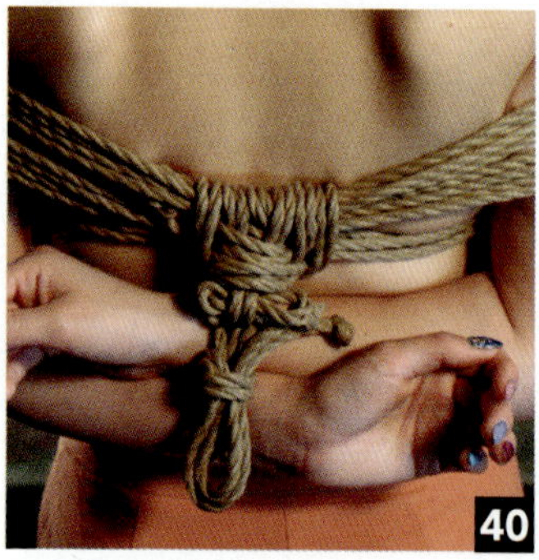

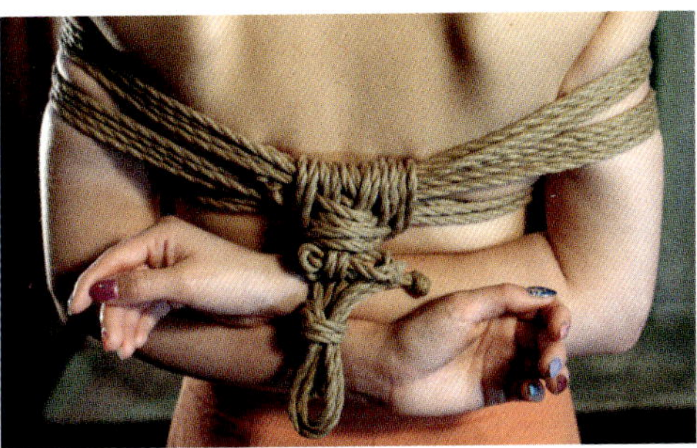

Once you've completed the structure you can dress the wraps over the arms by running your finger underneath from front to back. This will help the rope lie better on the skin and also to move any slight unevenness in tension to the back of the harness where it will not cause discomfort.

On the lower wrap you can loosen the tension on the arms by pushing the kannuki slightly towards the chest and pulling the wrap outwards a little as you run your finger back to dress the wrap.

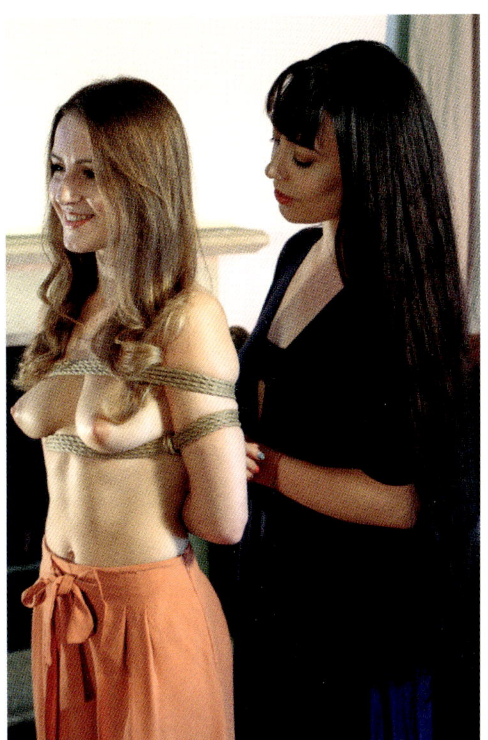

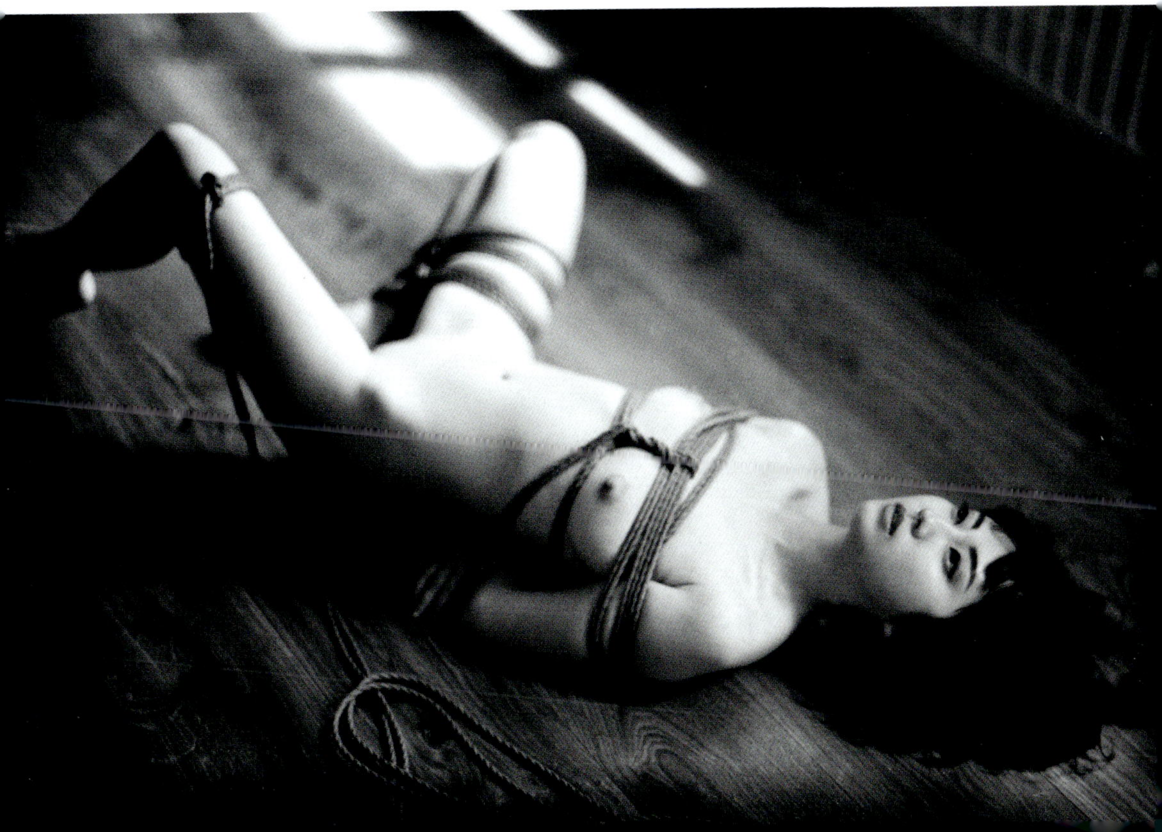

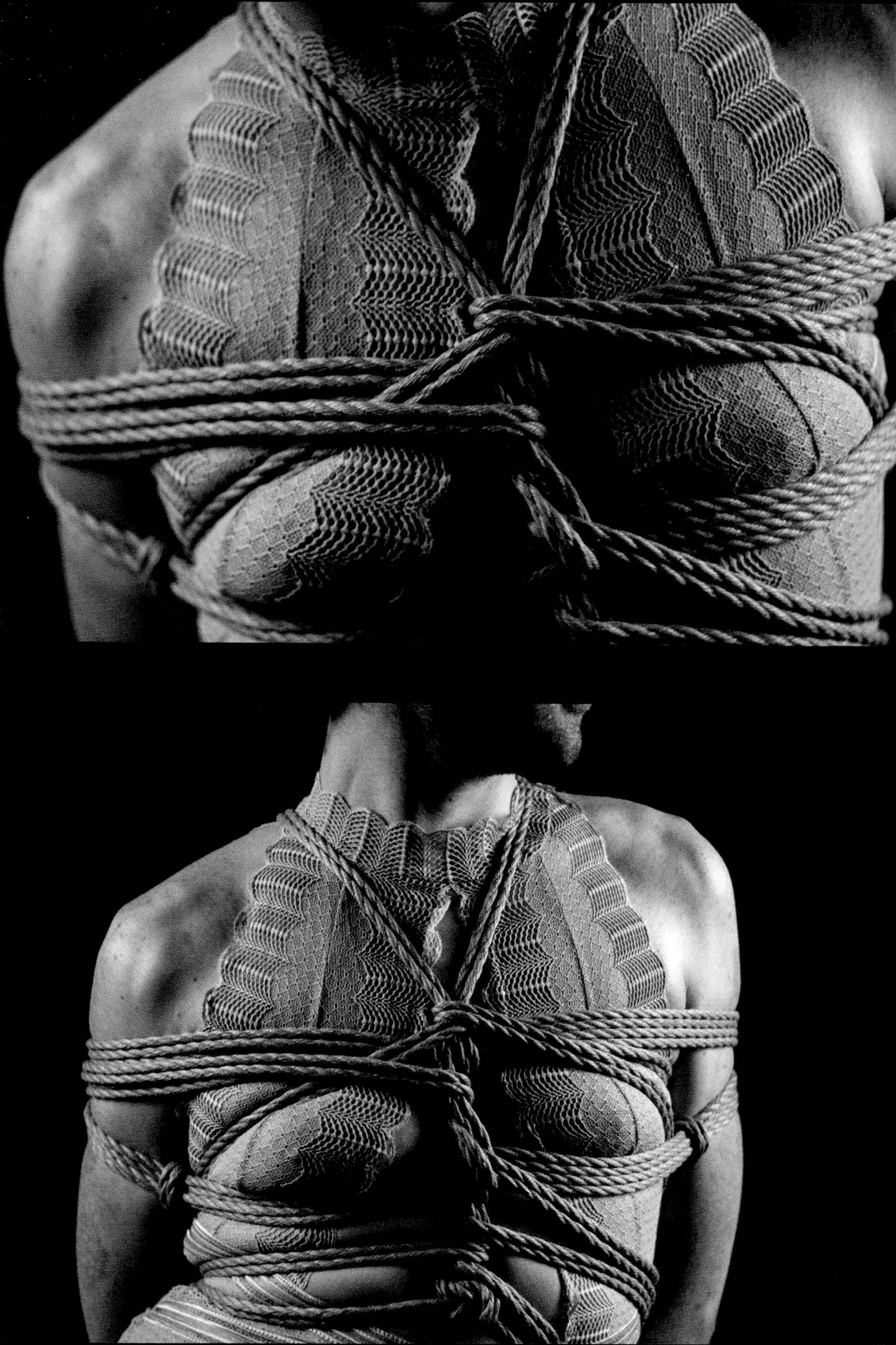

The Third Rope

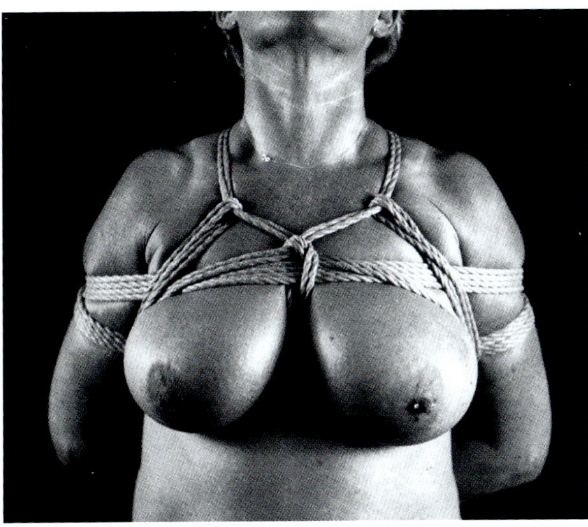

A 'third rope' is added to the basic structure of the two rope takatekote to increase stability and support in suspension.

I often alter the design of the third rope to better fit the type of suspension I'm planning to do. To make this process simple, I have shown one basic option for a third rope pattern, that can be easily adapted for a range of different situations with only minor modifications.

Although I recommend you start by suspending using a set pattern (such as one offered here) the third rope is often one of the first places that people begin to think about tying creatively – whether by experimenting with the way it feels for the model, or in the different ways of using up excess rope aesthetically.

Basic Pattern

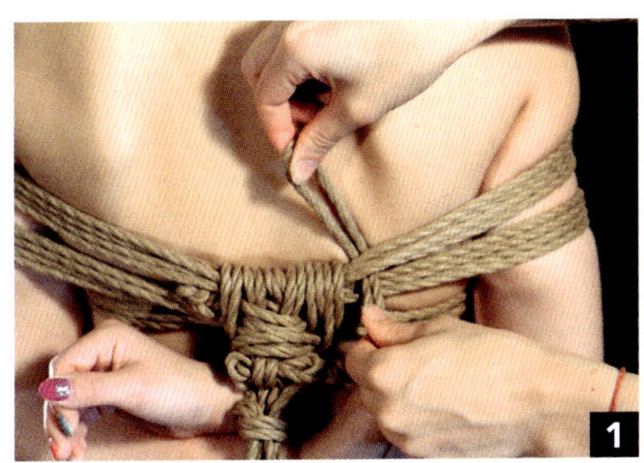

1

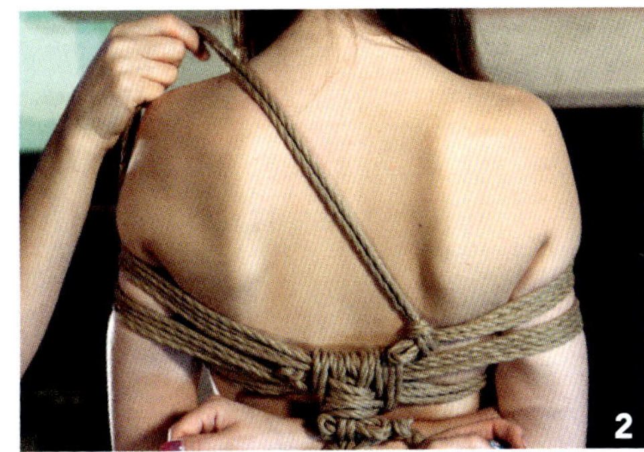

2

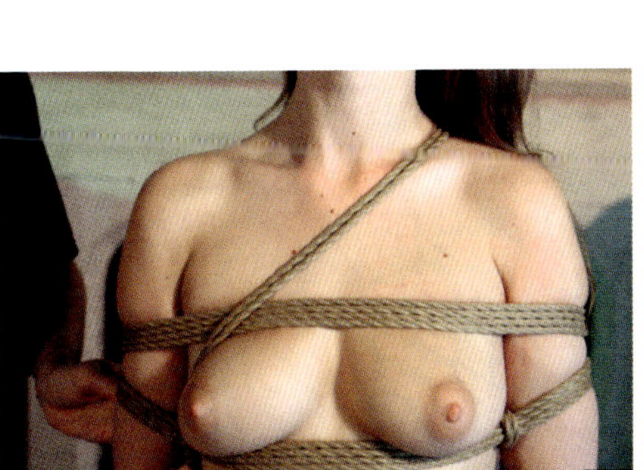

3

[1] Attach a new rope to the back of the harness, on the upper wrap to one side of the stem (using an overhand knot pg. 34).

[2] Pull a little tension on the rope so the upper wrap just begins to deform. Take the working end diagonally across the back and over the shoulder.

[3] And then across the chest and underneath the opposite arm, below the lower wrap.

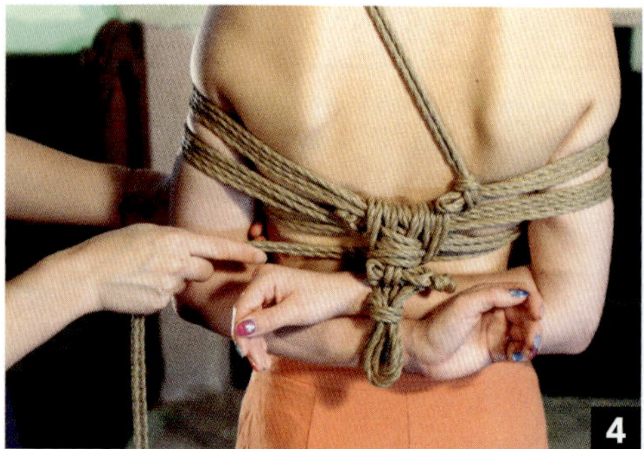
4

[4] Pass the working end under the stem and back out under the arm on the opposite side. If you wish, you may do a turn around the stem to isolate the tension here; this can also alter the feeling, which some models find preferable.

[5] Pass the working end upwards across the body to the centre of the chest. Hook your finger underneath the upper wrap and first diagonal rope and **[6]** pass under both wraps from top to bottom so that all 3 ropes are drawn together.

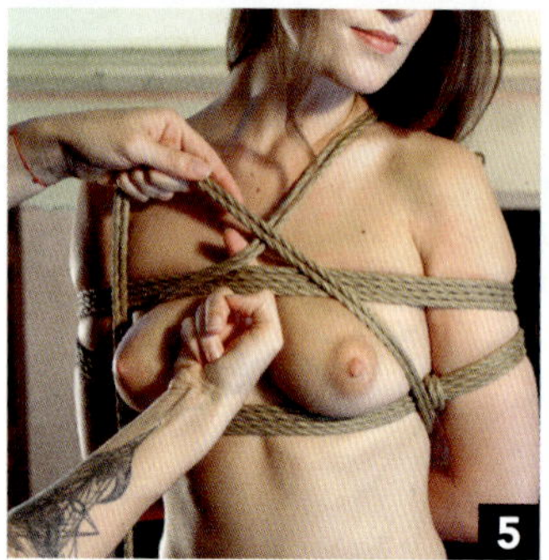
5

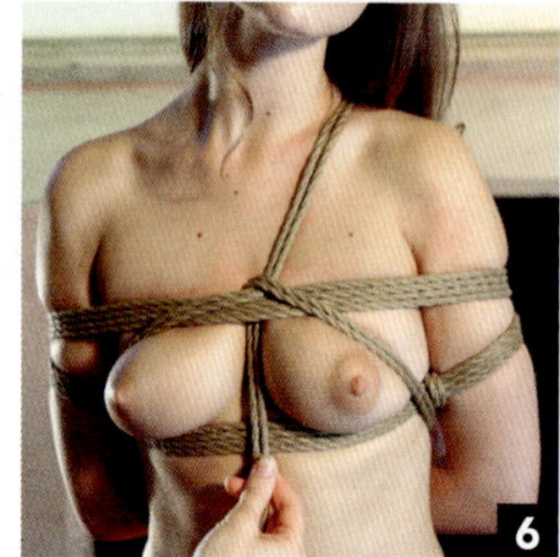
6

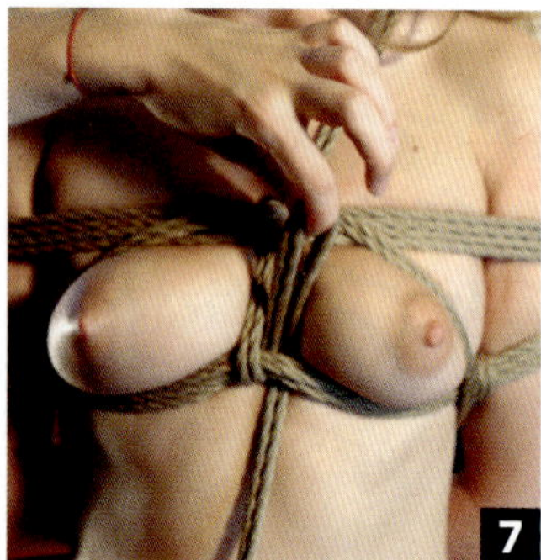
7

[7] Pass the working end over and under the lower wrap. This will help prevent the wrap slipping down and causing discomfort around the ribs.

[8] Take the working end back over the shoulder, ensuring that you have equal tension in both shoulder wraps.

[9] Pass diagonally across the back **[10]** as the two ropes cross you may lock them together using a twist or a no-dome (pg. 36) if you wish.

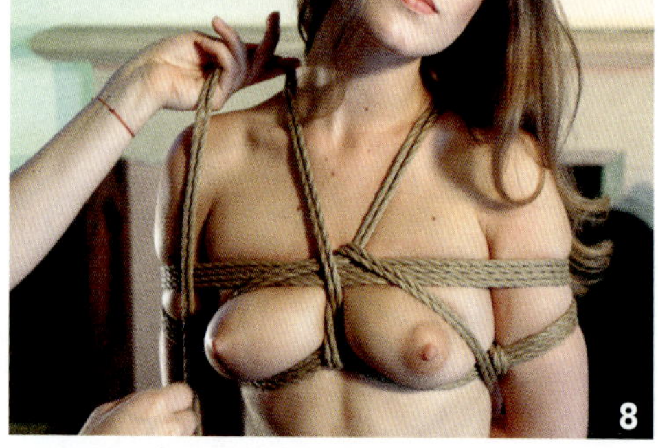
8

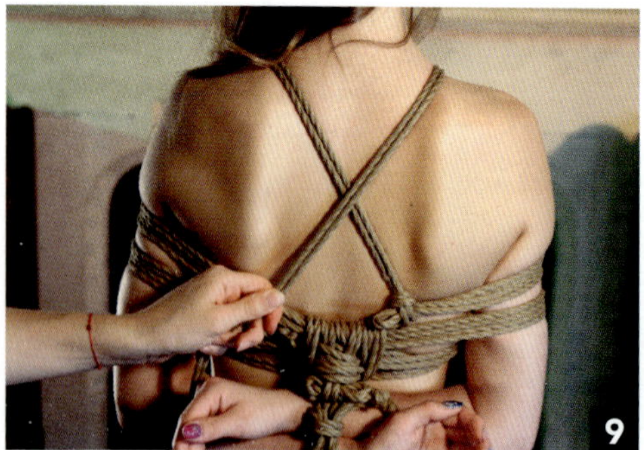
9

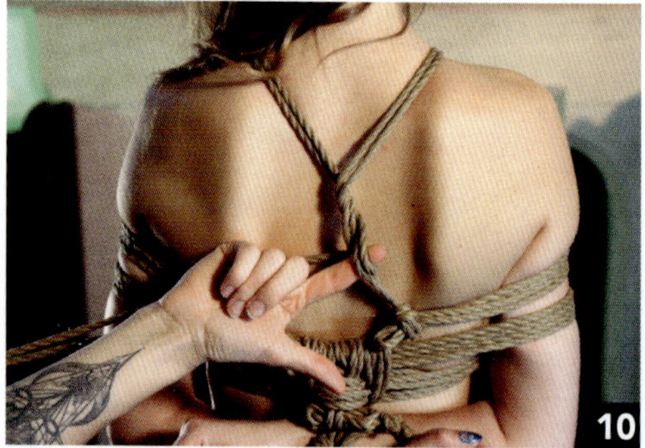
10

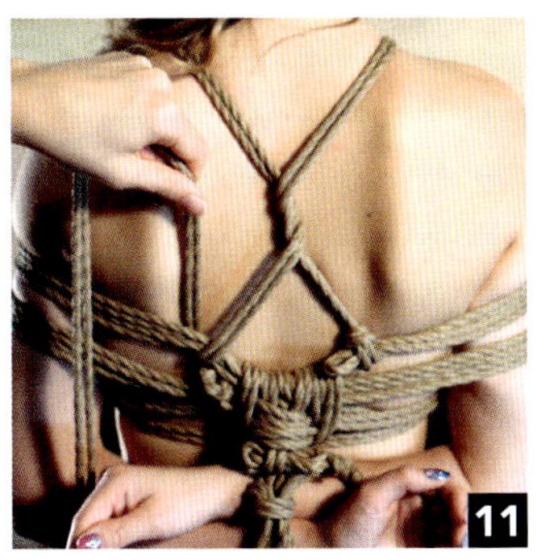

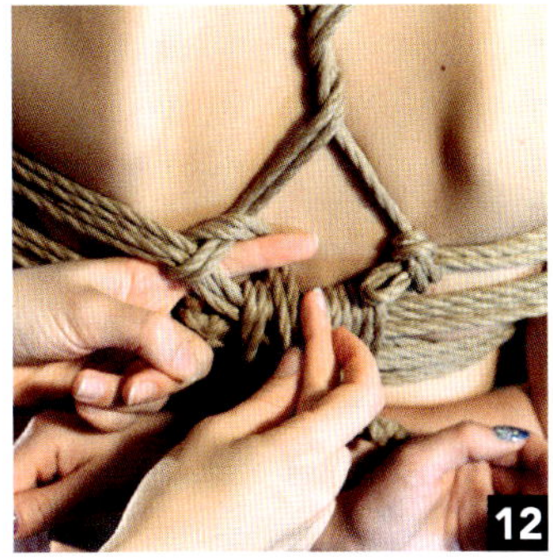

[11] Hook over and under the upper wrap and pull up a little to match the tension you created on the opposite side in step 2.

[12] Create a no-dome (pg. 36) to isolate the tension.

[13] Take the working end underneath the lower wrap and then back under the arm to the front of the body.

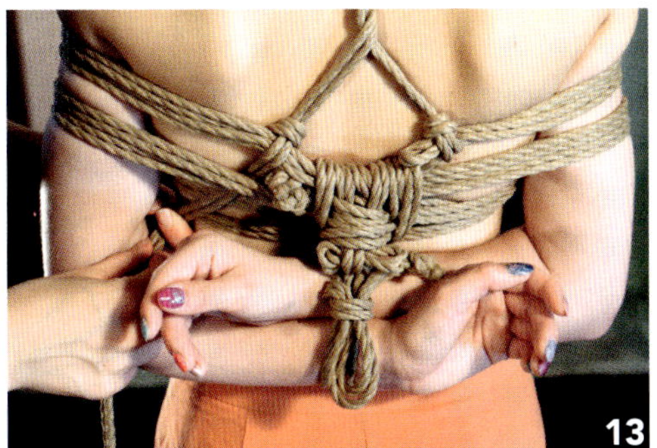

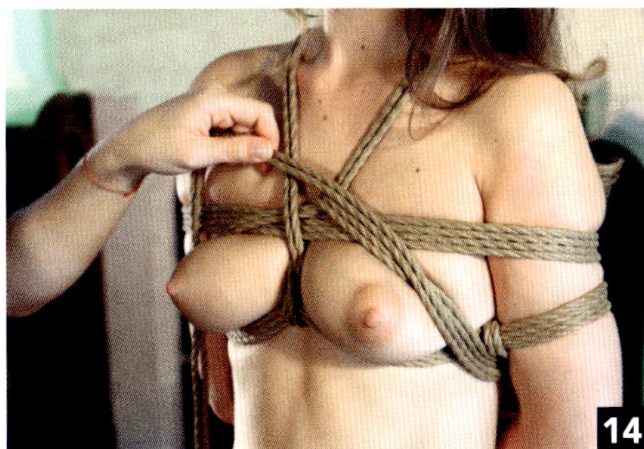

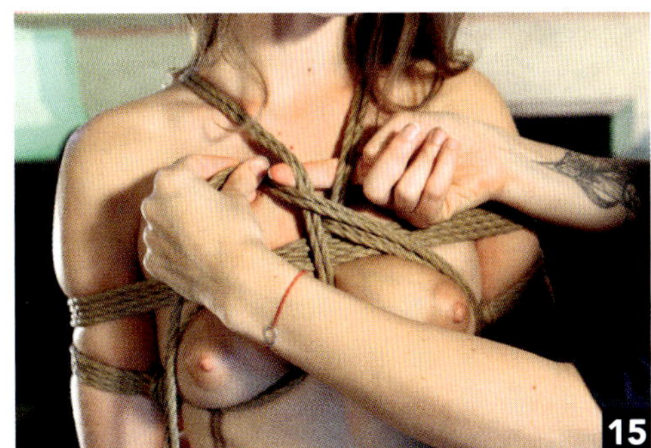

[14] Pass the working end diagonally across the chest, following the line of the rope already there.

[15, 16] Make a full turn around the two shoulder lines in the centre then pass back under the arm on the opposite side.

[17] Pull the working end out between the two wraps at the back.

[18] Pass over the upper wrap and behind the diagonal shoulder line from left to right.

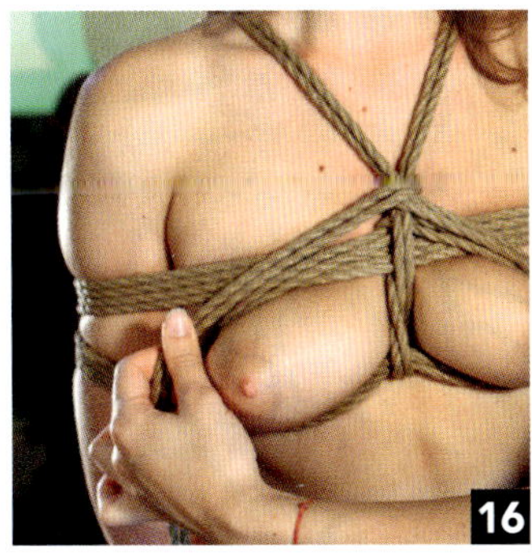

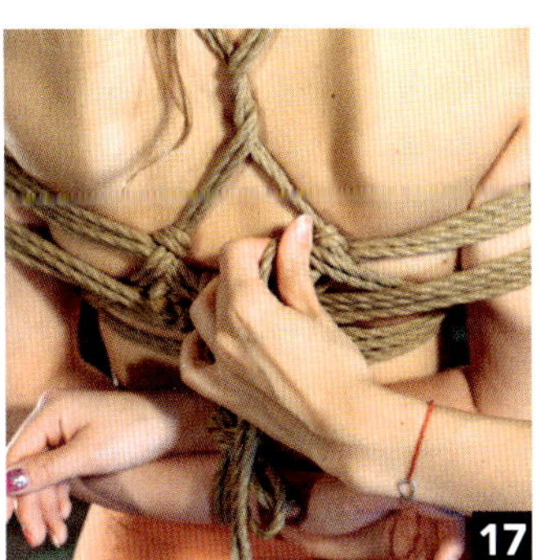

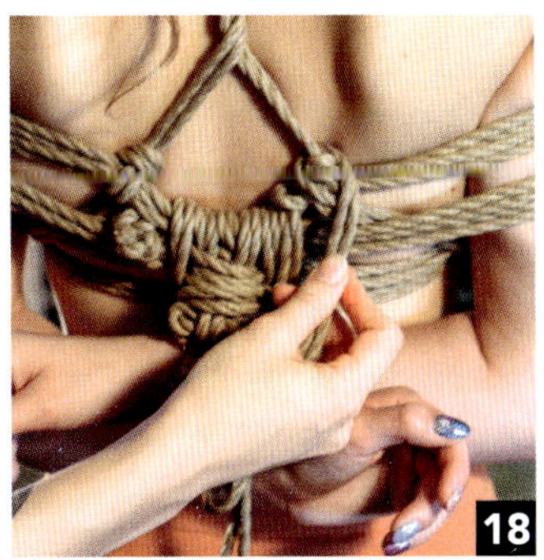

[19] and then wrap around the rope leading up to the friction, over and under.

[20] Finish the third rope by locking it in place with a half hitch (pg. 39), an overhand lock (pg. 40), or whatever other decoration you wish depending on the amount of rope you have left over.

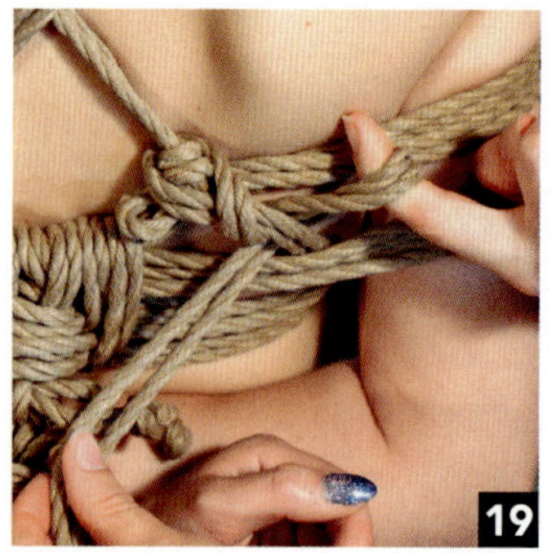

19

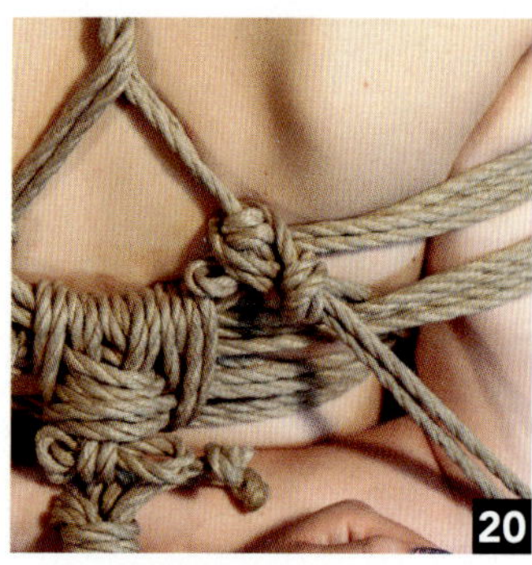

20

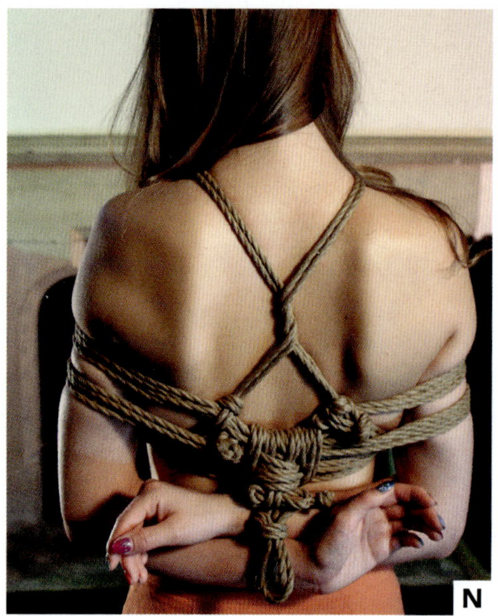

N

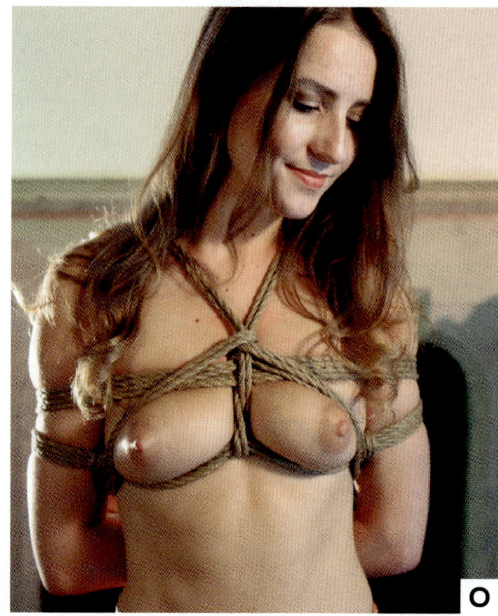

O

Tip

Once you've finished, it's a good idea to run your finger underneath the neck wraps to ensure that they are sitting flat and are not too close to the neck, or pressing/pulling on any sensitive part.

Pattern for Face Down

Some models find this pattern preferable, particularly in a face down suspension, or any suspension where the head is lower than the rest of the body. It helps keep rope away from the neck and slightly reduces the bulk on the sternum.

Repeat steps 1-8 of the basic pattern.

[1] Cross the working end under the shoulder line before you go back over the opposite shoulder. This will stop the ropes from separating.

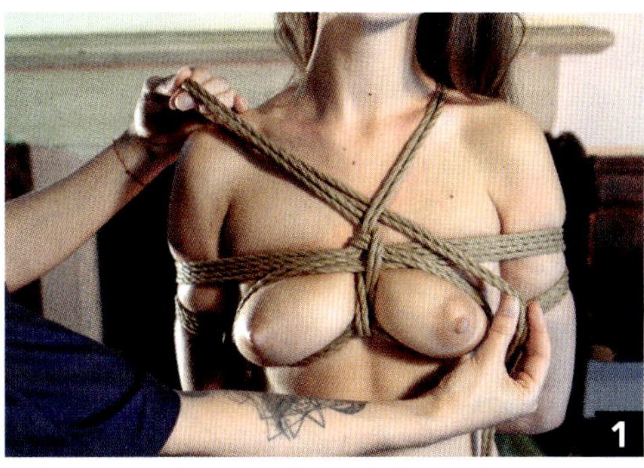

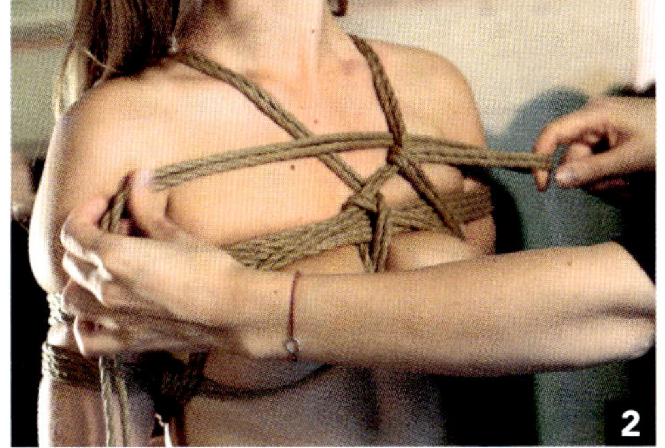

Repeat steps 9-13 of the basic pattern.

[2] As you return to the front hook around the shoulder line and pull outwards to move the line away from the neck. I find it useful to run a finger under the neck line as I do this to help the rope sit well.

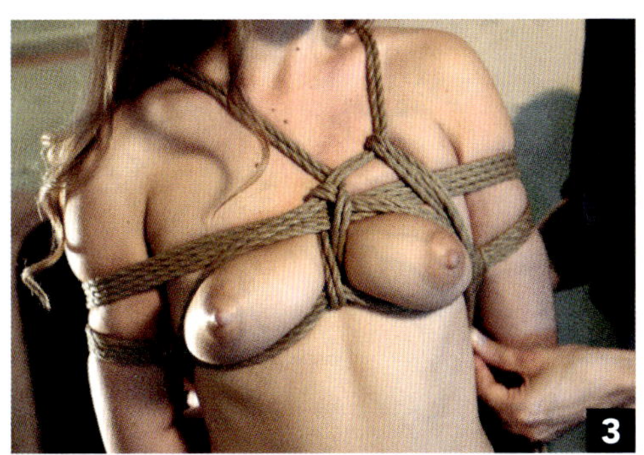

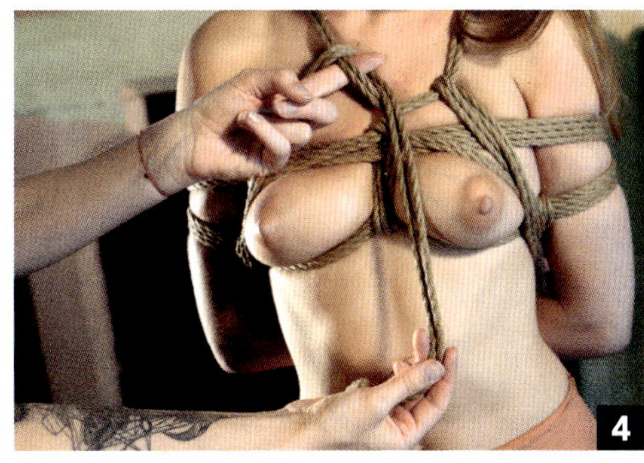

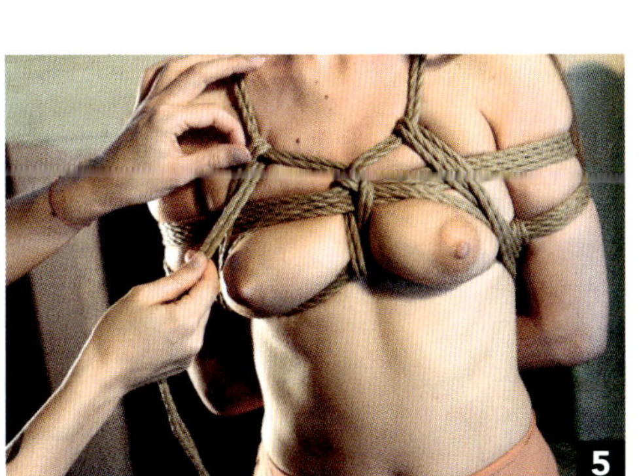

[3] Pass the working end back under the arm and across the back, underneath the stem.

[4, 5] Come back up under the other arm, and hook around the neck line as you did in step 2.

[6] Take the working end back under the arm and finish in the same way you did for the first rope in steps 17-20.

Take a moment to dress the wraps and check that they're not sitting in a place that causes discomfort on the model's clavicle.

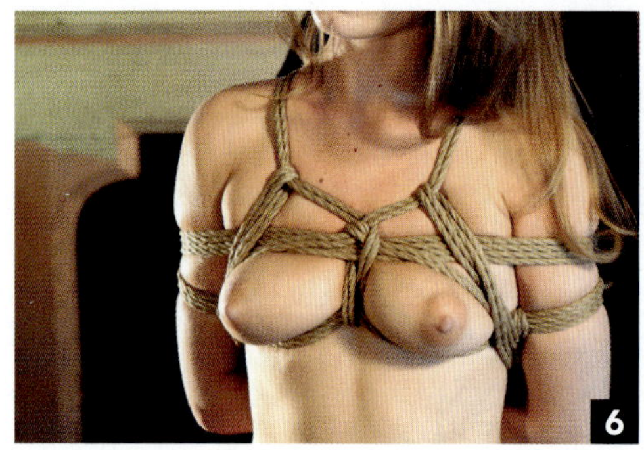

Pattern for Face Up

Here the pattern is modified for ties where the suspension line is attached to the front of the harness, and is particularly useful when the body is suspended vertically (such as the hikyaku-zuri on pg. 151) as it stops the lower wrap from pulling upwards. The wrap lying across the middle of the back can also offer a little extra support. When using this, I tend to tie the upper wrap of the two rope takatekote tighter than normal to ensure it doesn't slip.

[1] The process is identical to the basic pattern but you can skip step 7 and go straight back over the shoulder. **[2]** Then complete the rest of the basic pattern from step 8 onwards.

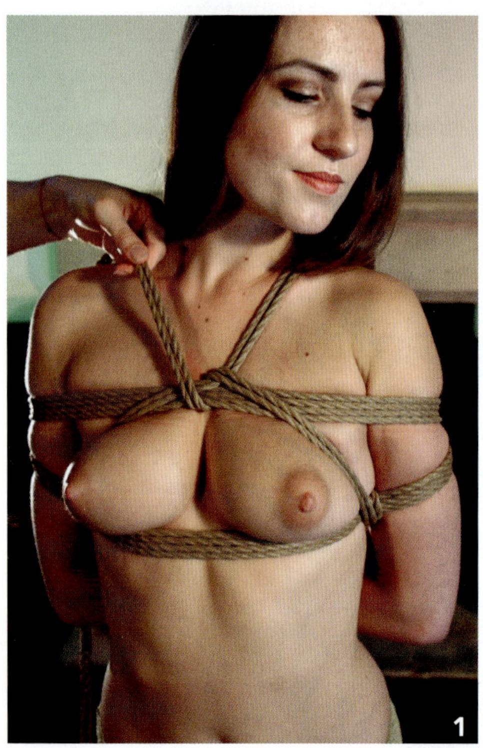

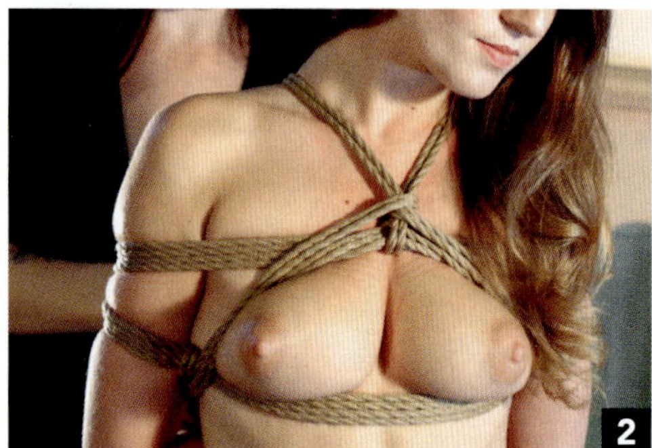

Yuki Knot Finishing

This is an alternative way of finishing a third rope that I find really useful when I want to attach **secondary lines** to the back of the takatekote (as I have done on pages 148, 153 and 157) and don't want the difficulty of trying to pass the working end under the wraps. This is especially helpful if the takatekote is under load, as getting ropes in and out can become difficult.

Complete everything up to step 18 on the basic pattern (or whichever pattern you are tying).

[1] Pass the working end over the top of the friction, then hook it back underneath the upper wrap *and* the rope leading diagonally up to the friction.

[2] Partially pull it through so it creates a loop of around 4 inches in length.

[3, 4] Secure by making a twist in the working end and placing it over the loop.

[5, 6] Repeat steps 3 and 4 to reinforce.

Hide away or secure the remaining rope however you wish.

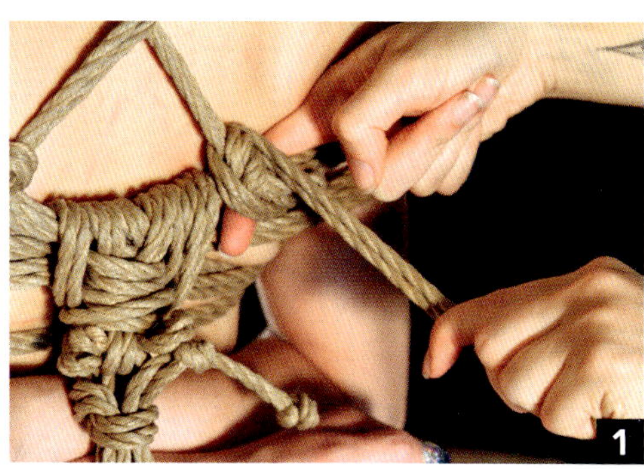
1

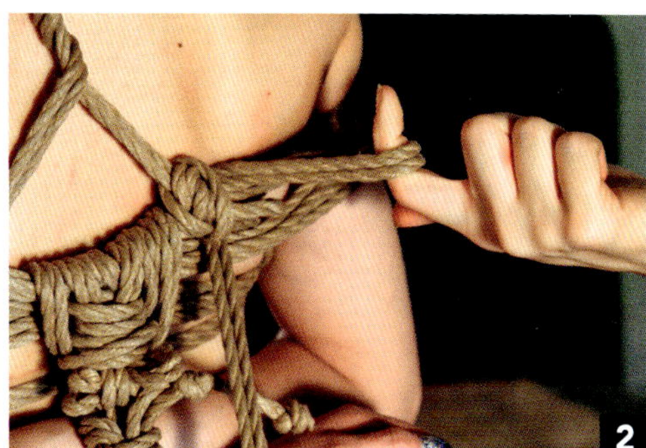
2

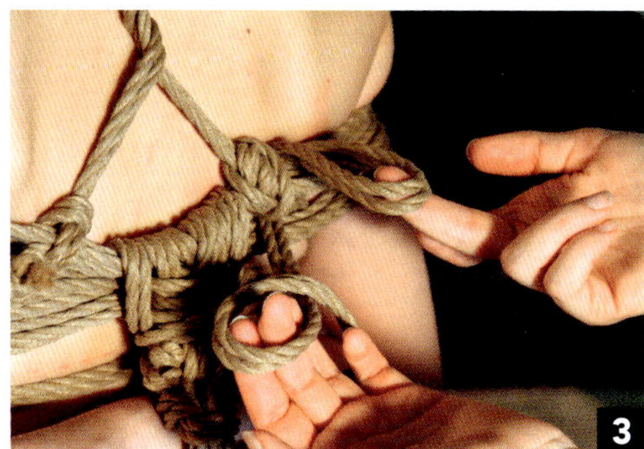
3

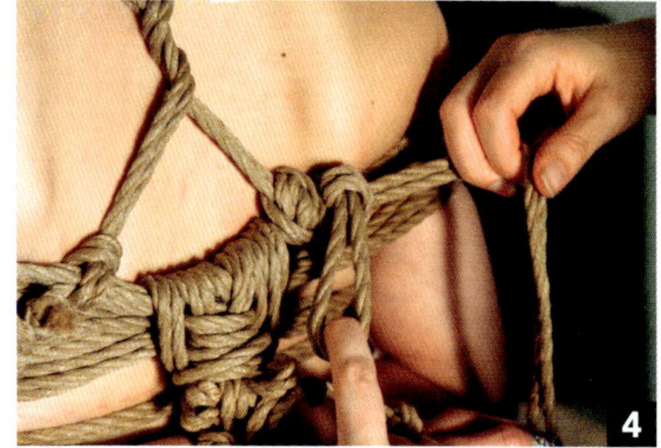
4

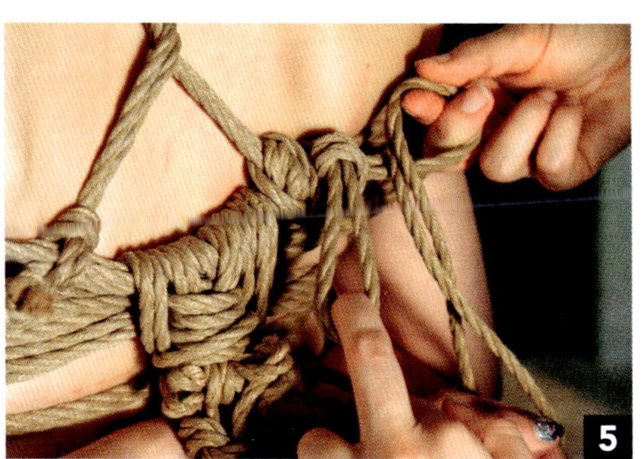
5

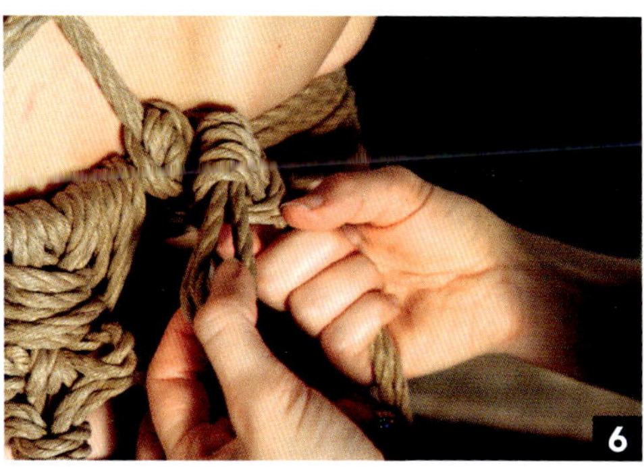
6

Takatekote Suspension Line Attachment Points

This section shows the three places suspension lines are most commonly attached on this type of takatekote. The methods I use for attaching suspension lines are shown on pages 107-109 so you will need to read that part first to fully understand this.

Back Attachment

[1, 2] If attaching to the back I generally use a single column tie (pg. 107) around the stem, between the upper and lower wraps. I leave some space in the single column to make it easier to use up excess rope (steps 7-8 pg. 119).

If the model has very sensitive lower arm nerves you can also attach to the upper wrap alone using an **ypsilon** *(spiral – pg. 108).*

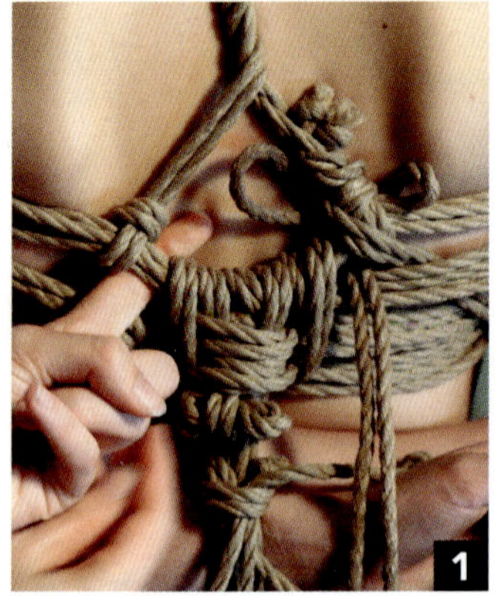
1

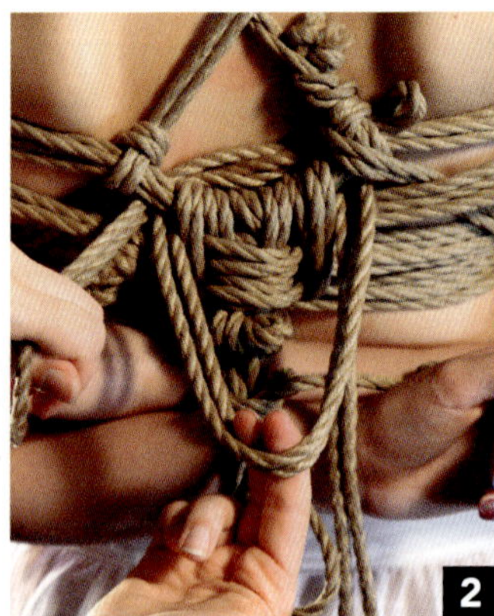
2

Front Attachment

[1-4] When using a takatekote with the face up third rope, you can attach at the front of the harness using an ypsilon (spiral – pg. 108) over the top of the central friction, which takes in all of the ropes of both the upper wrap and the third rope.

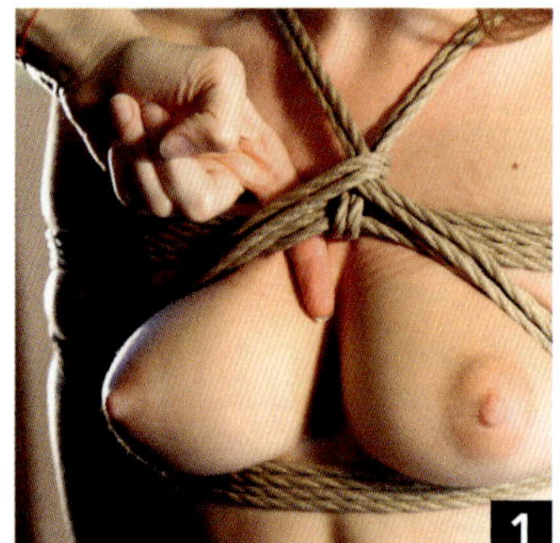
1

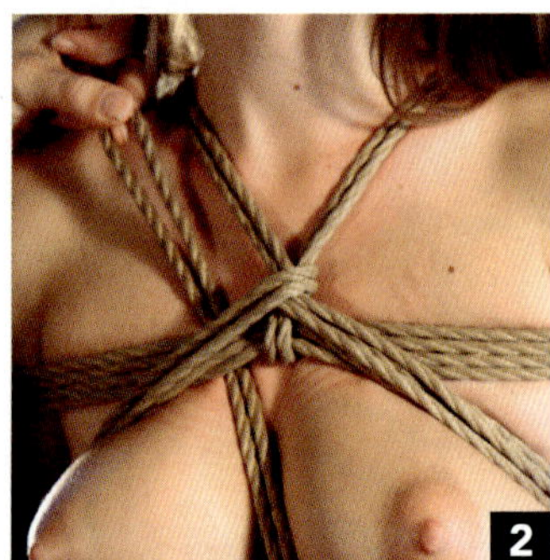
2

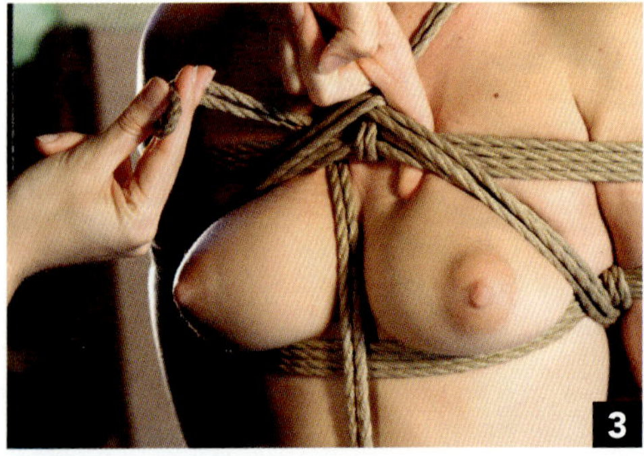
3

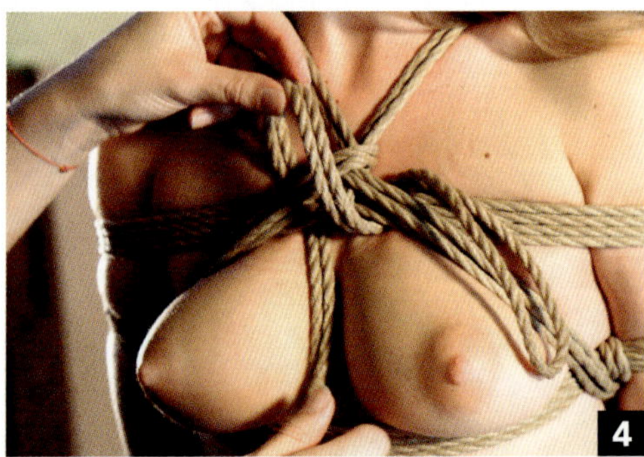
4

Side Attachment

When attaching at the side of the harness **[1, 2]** use an ypsilon (pg. 107) on the arm wraps. It's easiest to tie this at the back of the harness, in the space between the arm and the body.

[3] Then slide it around to the side of the arm. To avoid pinching the skin, you can create space between the wraps and the arm by pushing the shoulder with one hand whilst pulling the suspension line towards you with the other as it slides.

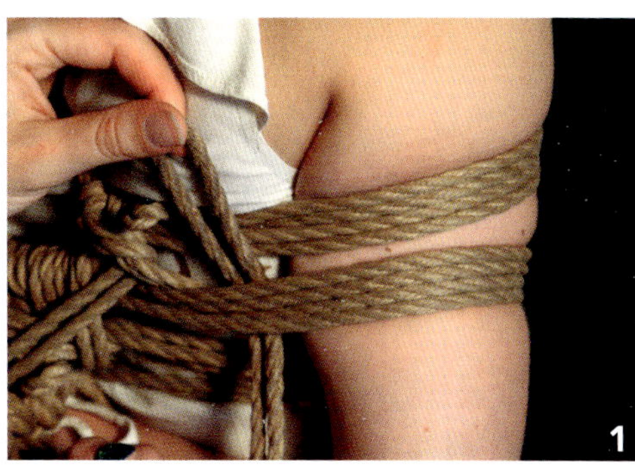

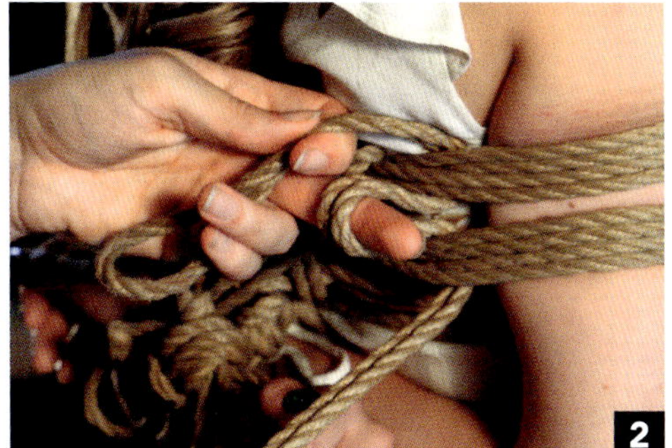

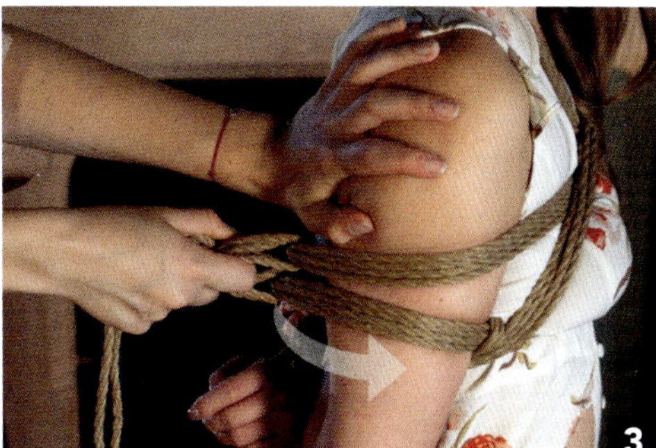

Alternative Hand Position

This is a possible alternative way of beginning a takatekote that those who struggle to touch their hands together behind their backs might consider.

I've seen similar structures used by several people. Often students in my workshops have come up with this modification themselves and I think it serves as a great example of the sort of solutions you can find when you start thinking outside the box. I hope it will inspire you to look around to find other alternative solutions to tailor rope to your individual needs.

I have only included the wrist tie, upper wrap, and stem – from there you can complete the lower wrap in the same way as before (or you can continue with any other takatekote structure that works for you).

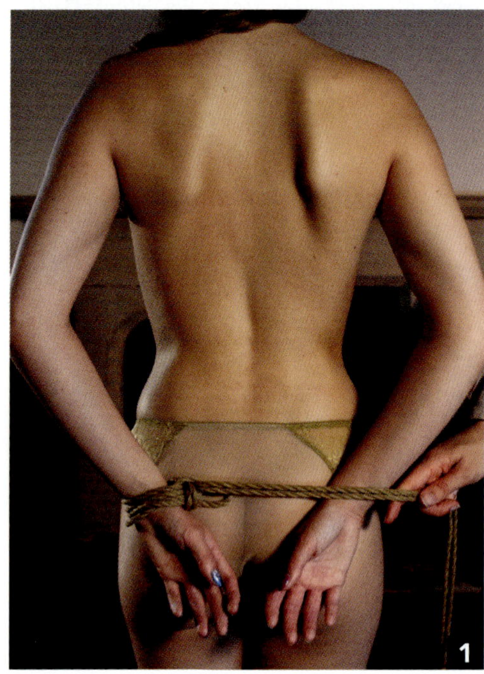

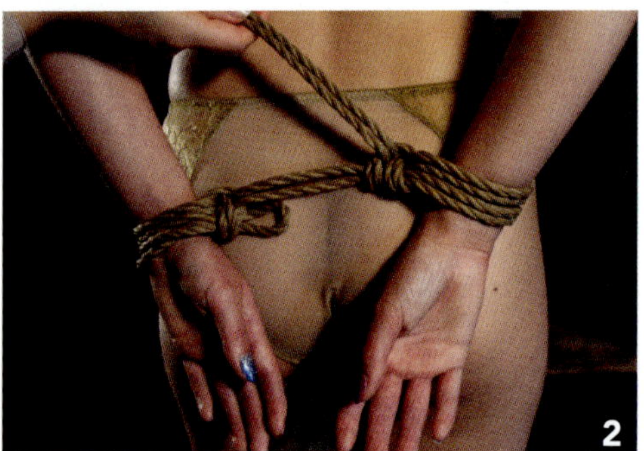

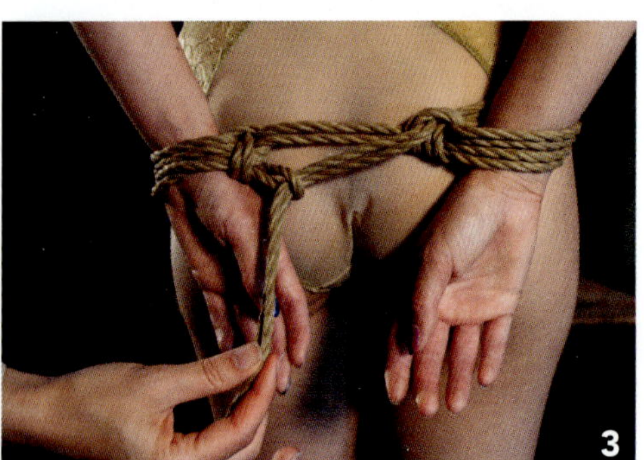

[1] Tie a single column around one wrist, keeping the bight short.

[2] Bring both wrists together at whatever distance feels comfortable and create a hojo cuff (pg. 31) on the other wrist.

[3] Go back through the bight of the first single column. (if your bight is too long, this won't work.)

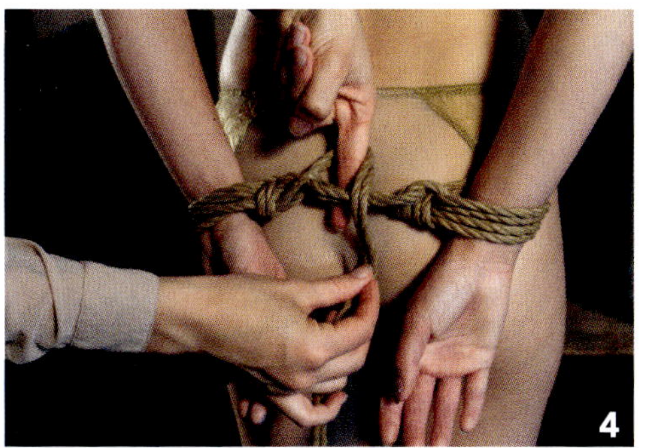

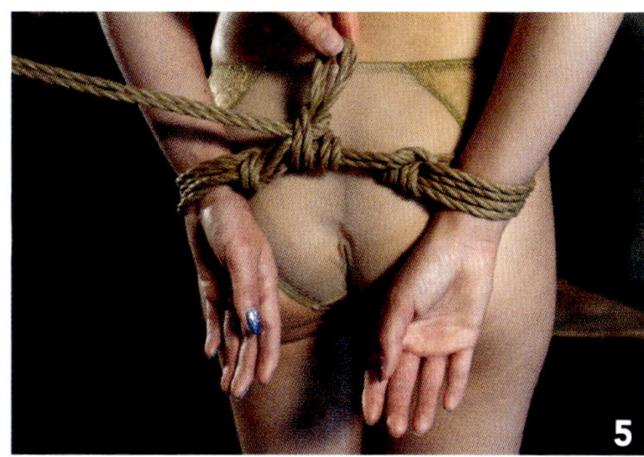

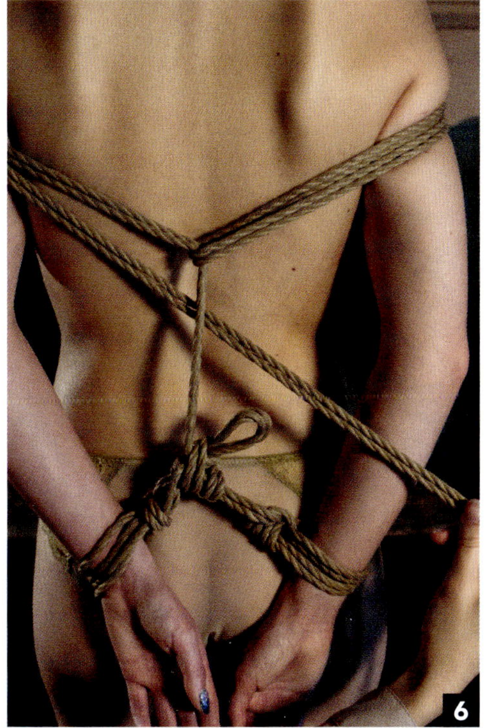

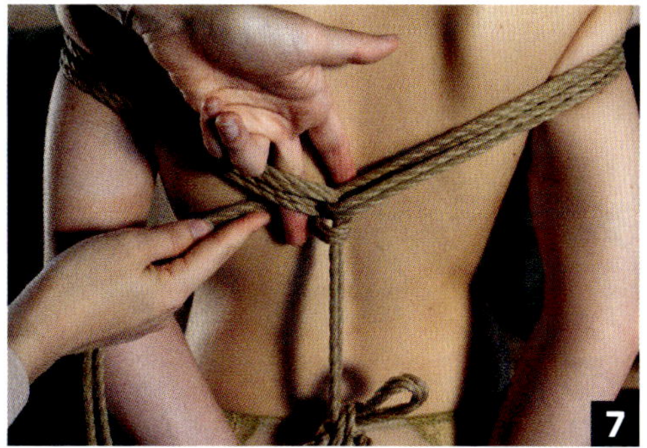

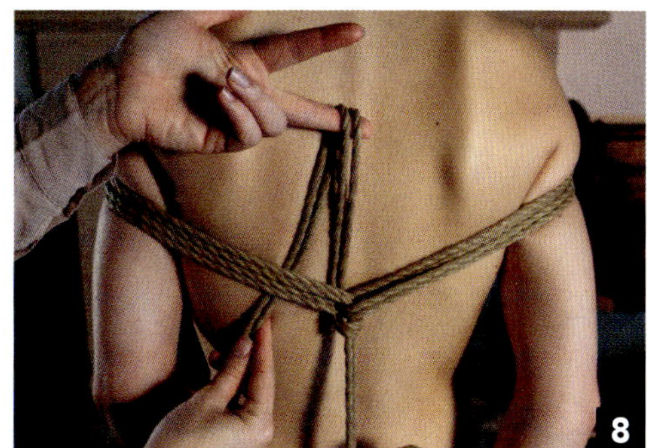

[4, 5] Lock with a yuki knot (pg. 37) around both ropes of the stem. It should be roughly central between the wrists.

[6] Make two wraps around the shoulders using reverse tension (pg. 38) (you may do three wraps for extra support if you prefer).

[7, 8] Make a U-turn around the stem and hook the working end under the wrap.

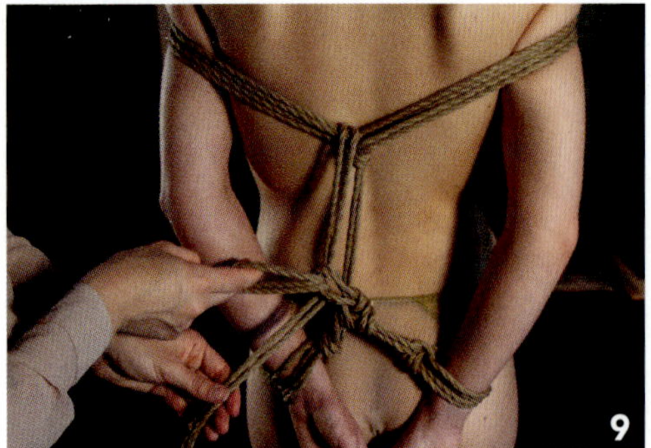
9

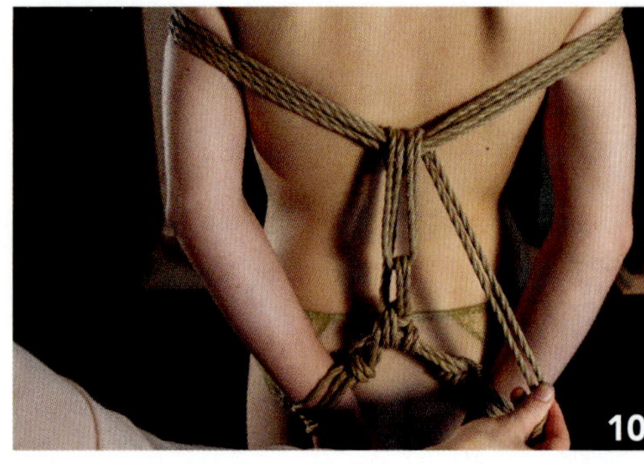
10

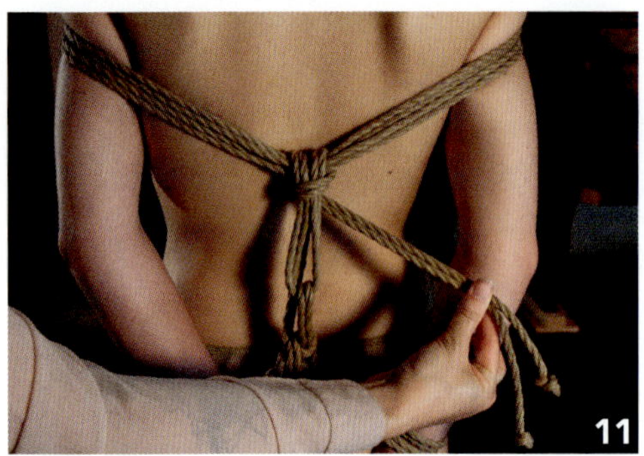
11

[9] Pass the working end down, and through the loop of the yuki knot.

[10] Pass back up and over the upper wrap from front to back then **[11]** wrap around the stem – over, then under.

At this point, you can continue to tie the rest of the takatekote as normal, starting from step 18 on pg. 53.

Finishing the Tie

[Q] Picture of the finished tie, using the lower wrap pattern on pg. 53.

[P] Picture of the finished tie with the face up third rope (pg. 64) from the front and **[R]** from the back. In addition I have used two more hojo cuffs to fill up the space on the lower arms. Whilst this is mostly for aesthetic, some models like the feeling of having extra rope on the body.

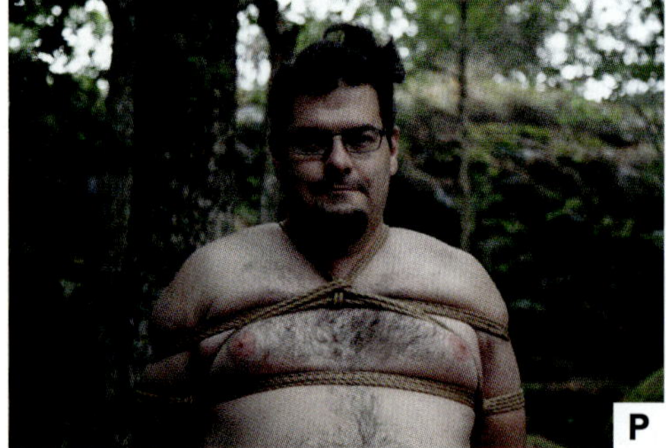
P

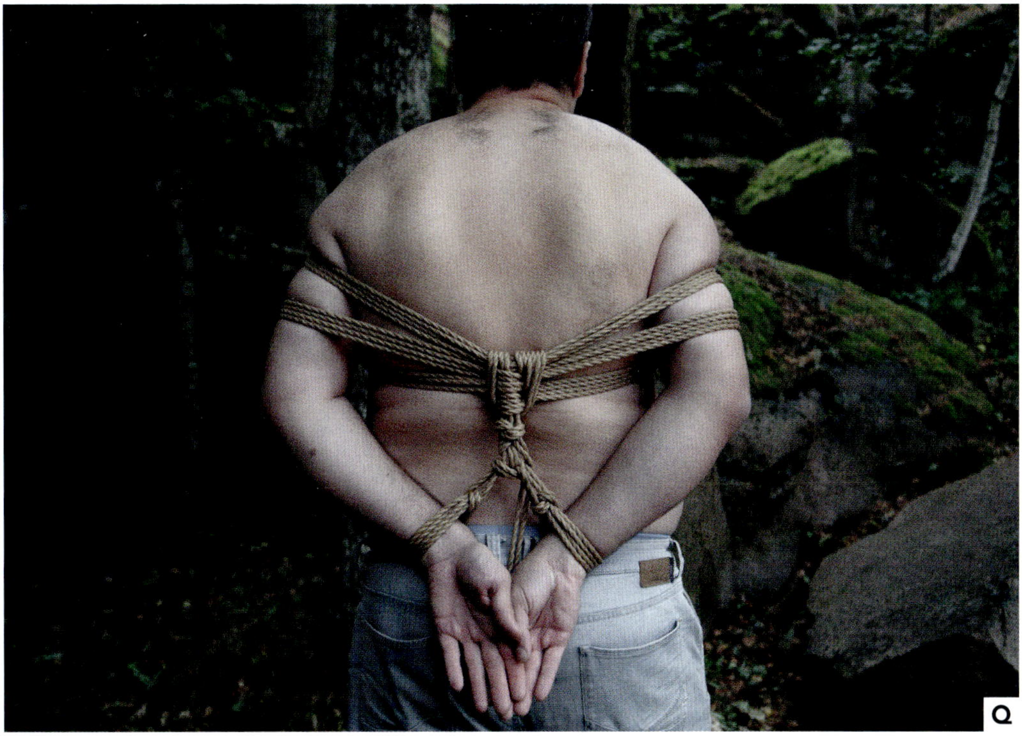

Q

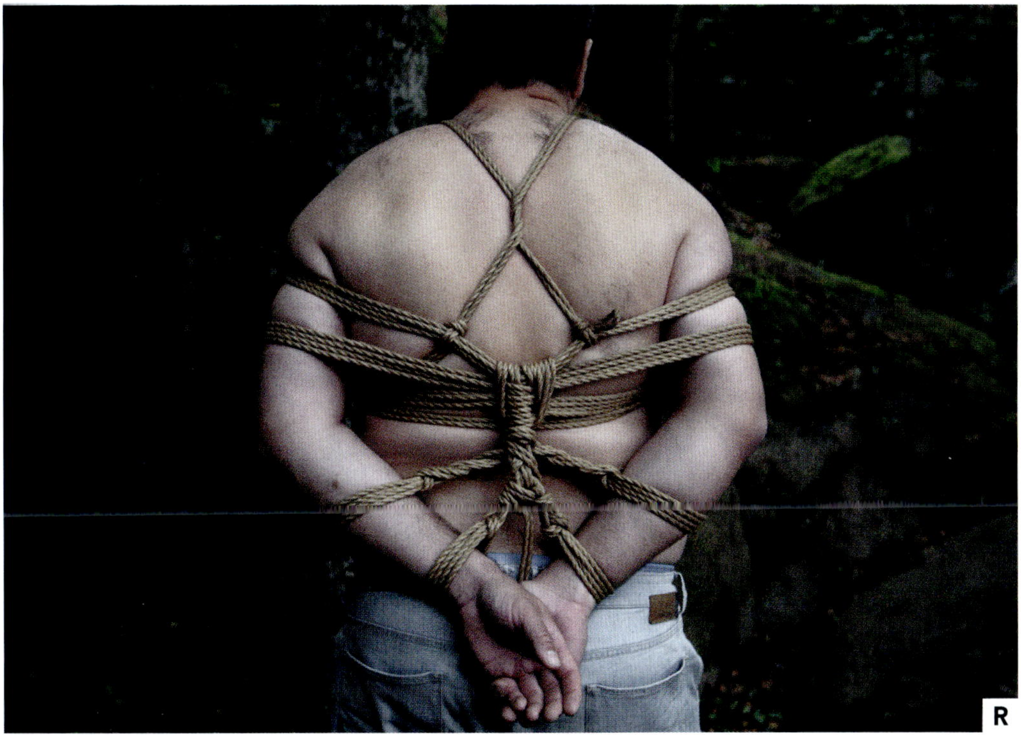

R

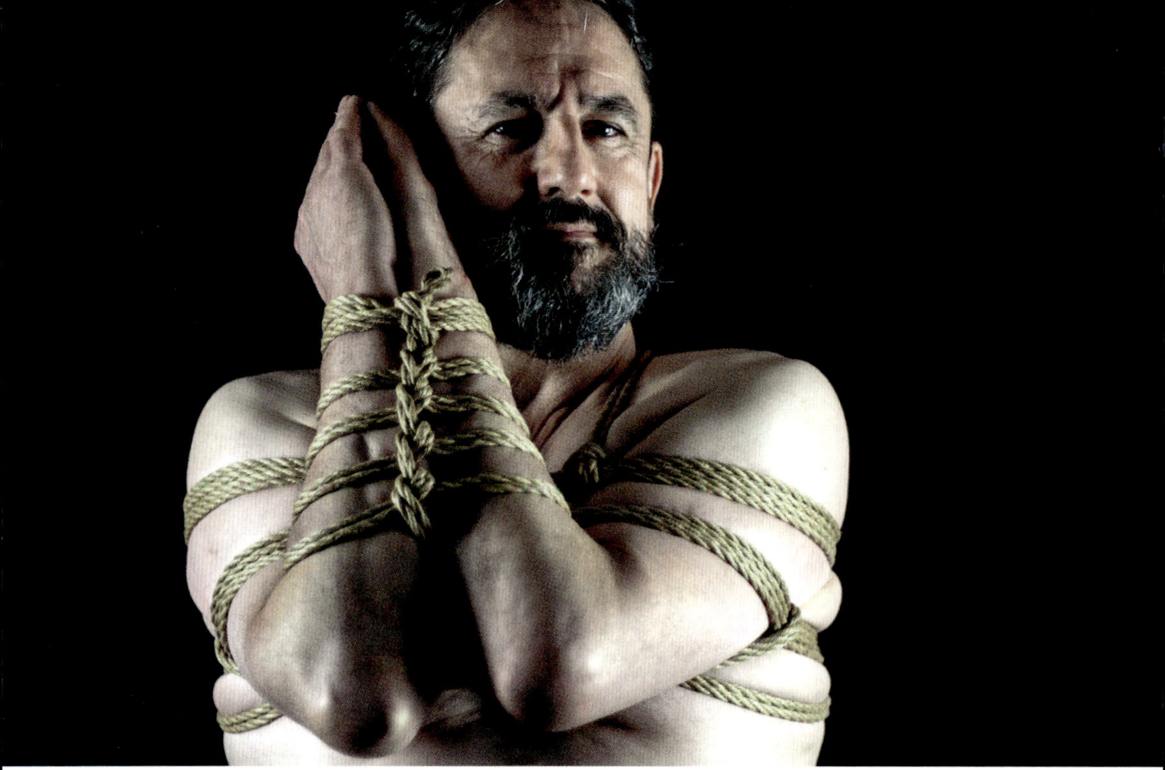

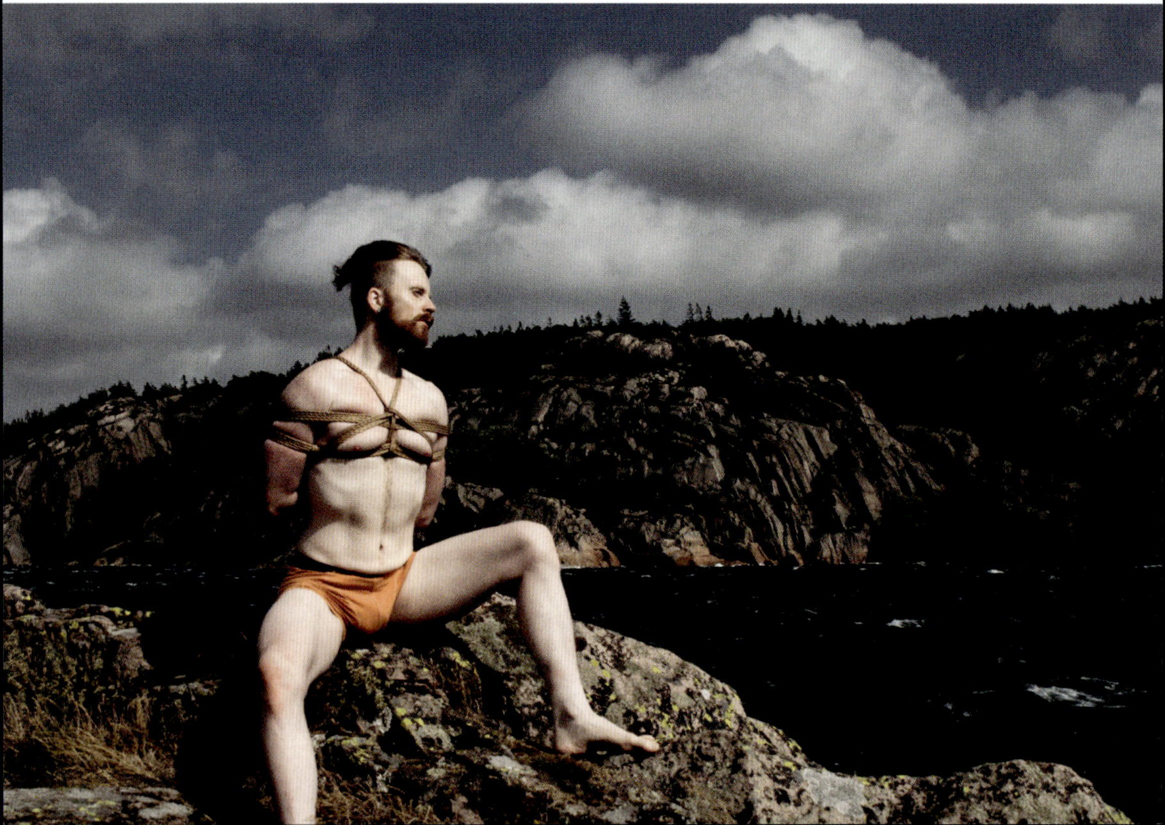

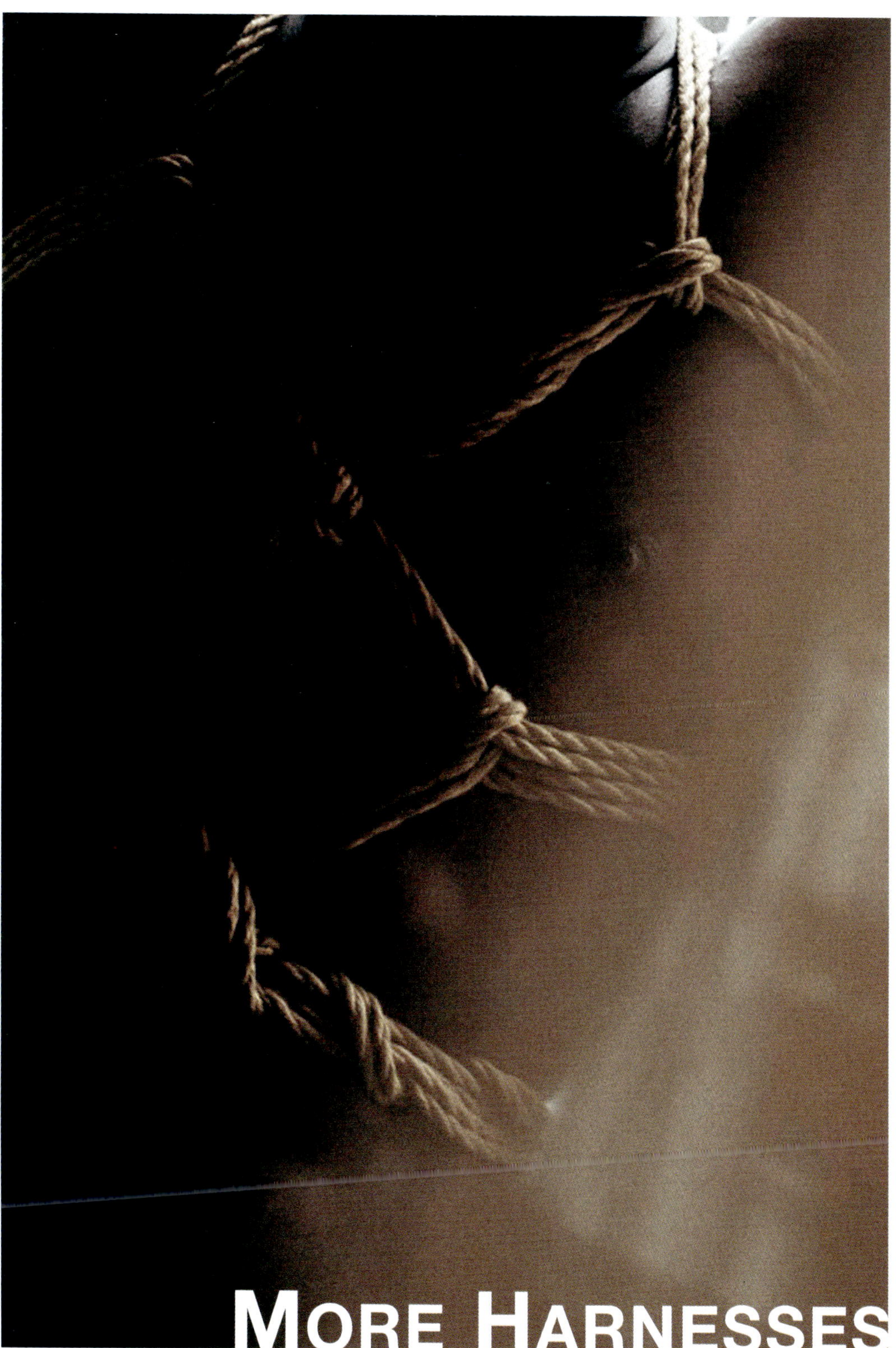

More Harnesses

Nerves Relating to Leg and Hip Ties

Please read pages 43 - 47 first to fully understand this section.

The nerves of the lower body are discussed far less frequently than the nerves of the upper body, likely because the majority of lower body nerve issues encountered in shibari are sensory, which some people consider less serious.

Although less frequent, injuries that affect movement do still occur so you should be aware of the possibility.

The patches highlighted in **[A]** this photo indicate where people commonly suffer from sensory loss and the nerve that was the likely cause of this, which should help you to work out which part of a leg or hip tie was the likely cause.

It is possible to suffer from 'foot drop' in much the same way you can suffer from wrist drop – although it does seem to be comparatively rare. In the cases I am personally aware of, an injury to the common peroneal nerve (highlighted in red) has been the likely cause.

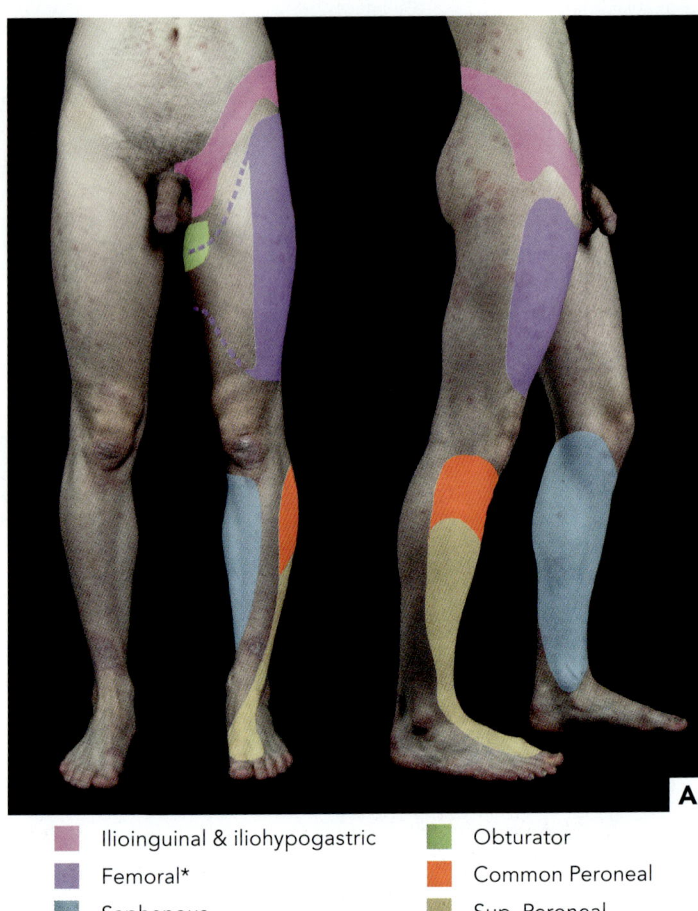

- Ilioinguinal & iliohypogastric
- Femoral*
- Saphenous
- Obturator
- Common Peroneal
- Sup. Peroneal

* There are several cutaneous femoral nerves (anterior, lateral and medial), that all serve a sensory function and that can all be easily compressed when in a hip harness. This region of the body is perhaps the most common place to sustain sensory nerve damage whilst in rope.

Gunslinger

A gunslinger is most often used to add a secondary support when in a side suspension (pg. 146). You can start this tie with either **[1i]** a loose single column around the waist pulled down into a 'V' shape (pg. 29) or **[1ii]** a tight single column around the hips according to the model's preference. Tying around the hips avoids putting pressure on the soft area of the stomach and on the floating ribs, however many models find it uncomfortable to have their joints blocked by rope around the hips, limiting their flexibility. It is best to experiment to find your ideal placement. In this example I have tied around the waist, as I personally find it more comfortable, and also prefer the aesthetic of it.

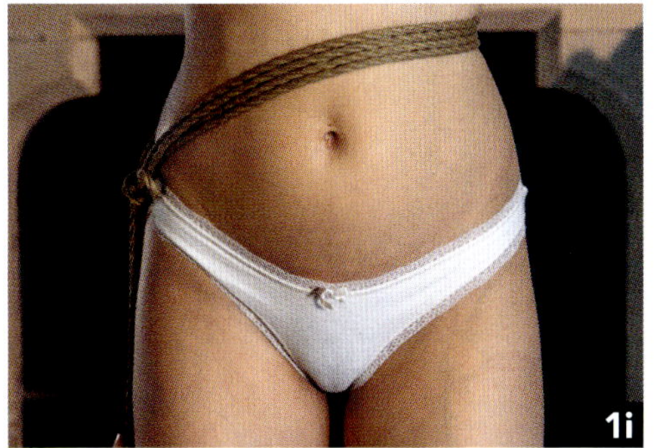
1i

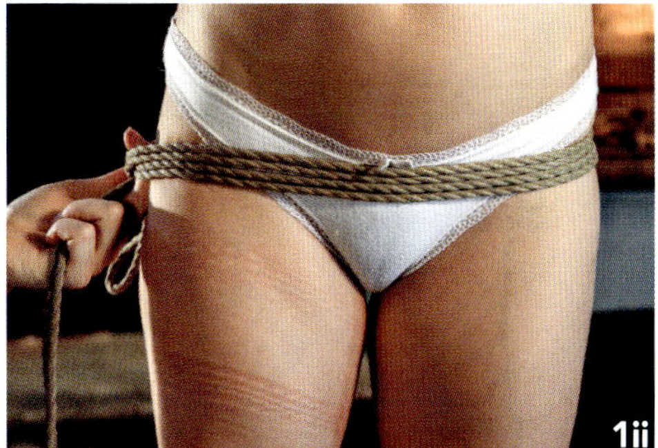
1ii

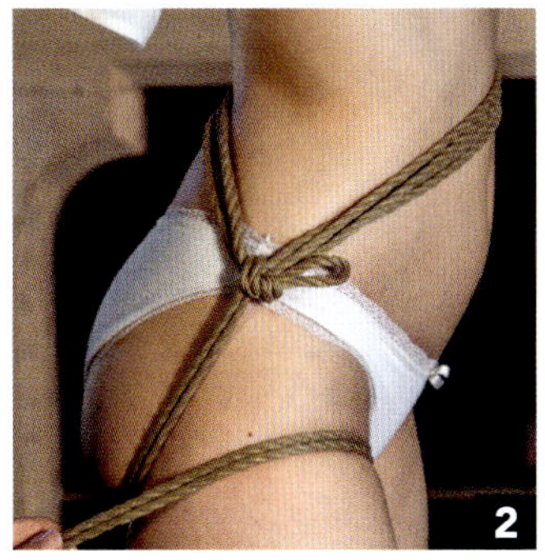
2

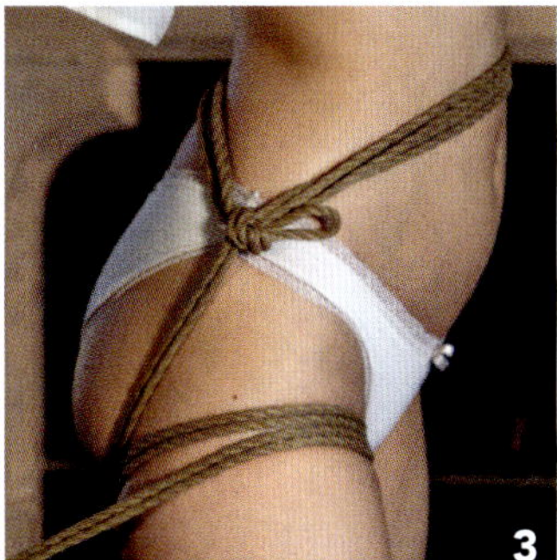
3

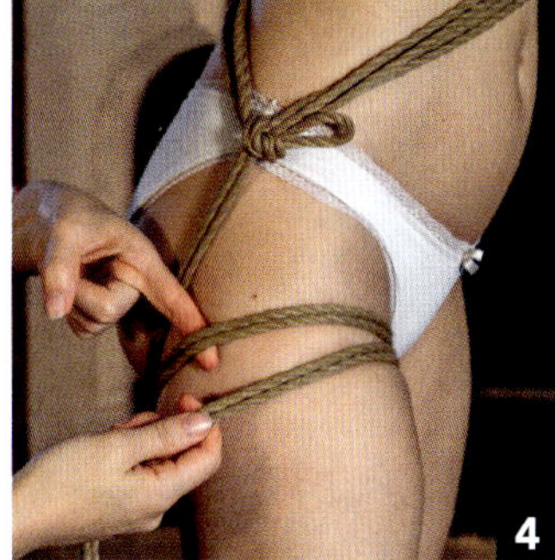
4

[2+3] Wrap the working end twice around the leg. Some models will prefer to keep the wraps as close to the top of the inside leg as possible, whilst others might prefer a small gap.

[4] Gently loosen the middle of these two wraps, pulling it upwards into a 'V' shape to meet the rope travelling from the waist.

[5] Pass the working end over the top of the stem, and hook underneath both leg wraps.

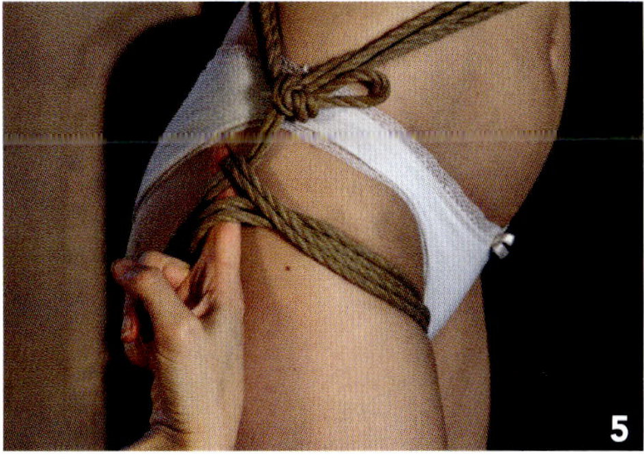
5

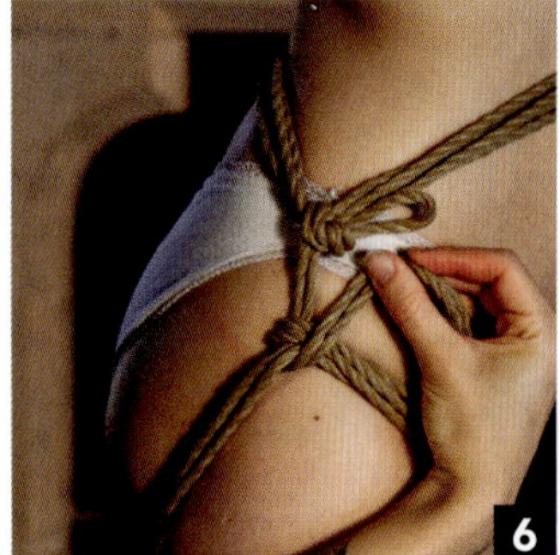

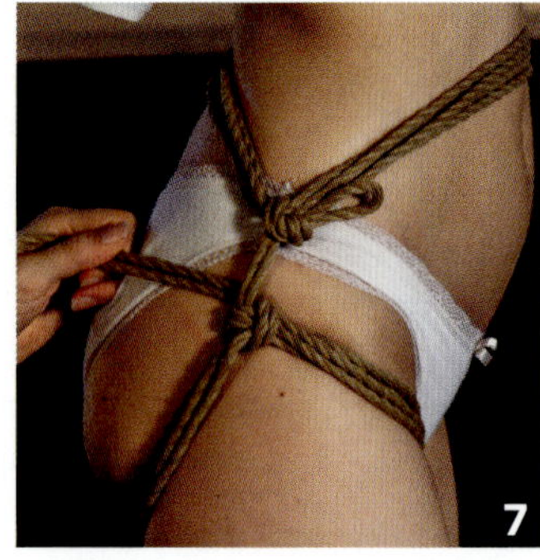

[6, 7] Pass the working end up and over both leg wraps and under the stem to make a no-dome (pg. 36).

[8] Then twist upwards, over the stem and under the waist wrap.

[9, 10] Pass the working end down over the waist wrap, and back underneath the stem.

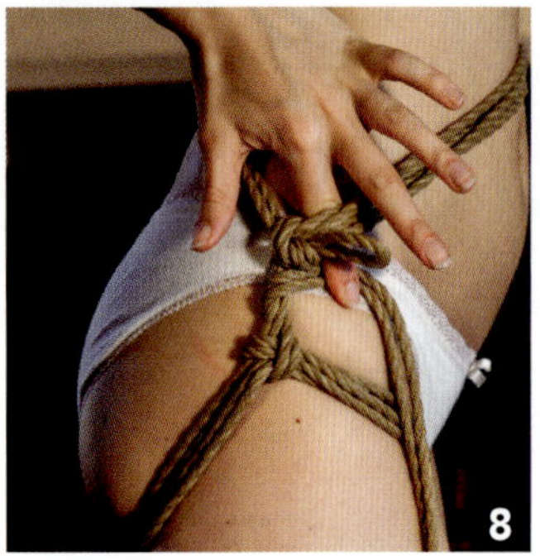

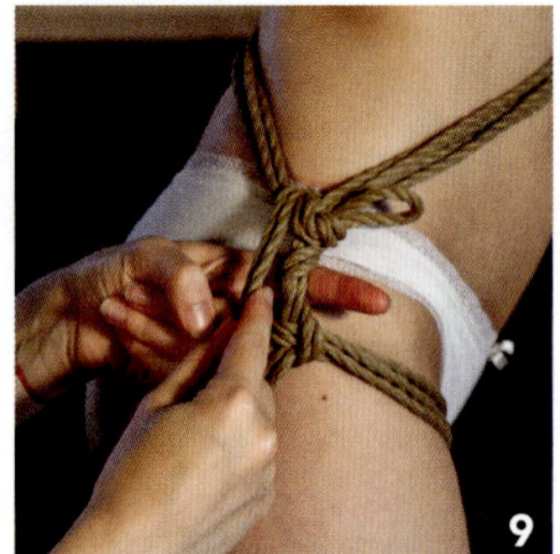

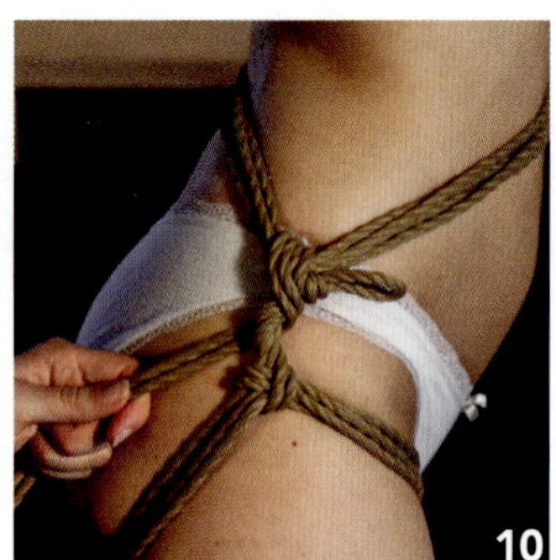

[11, 12, 13] Hook your finger under the last pass you made over the stem and open it up to make space, then close with a half hitch (pg. 39) or overhand lock (pg. 40).

Suspension Line Attachment Point

When using this harness in suspension you can attach the line using a tightly compacted single column tie on the stem between the waist and thigh wraps.

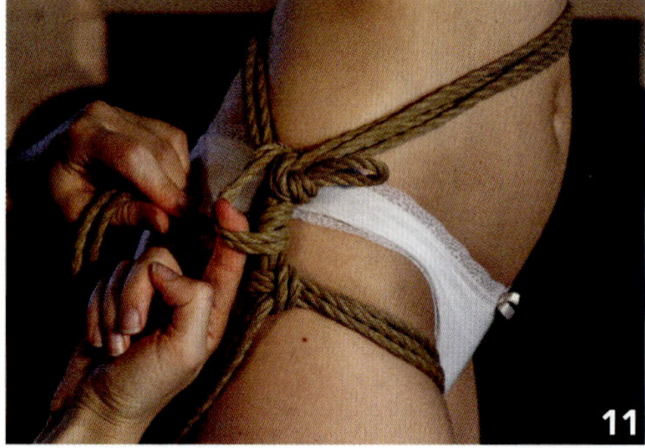

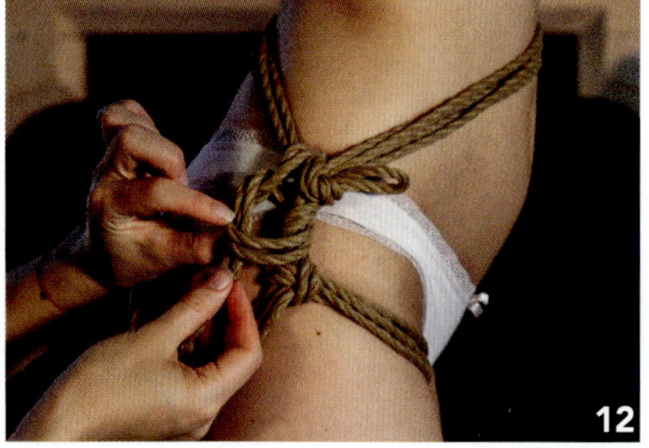

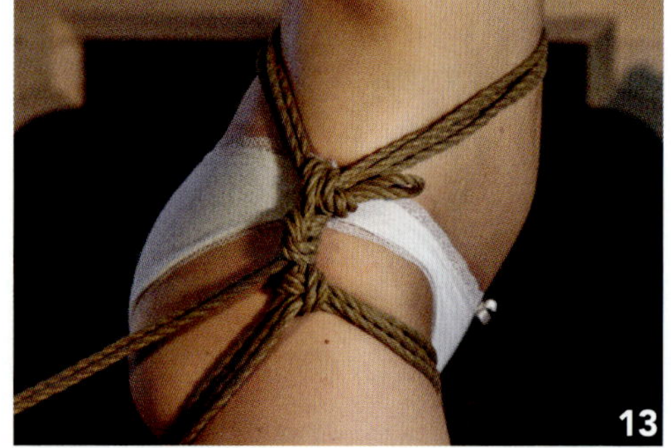

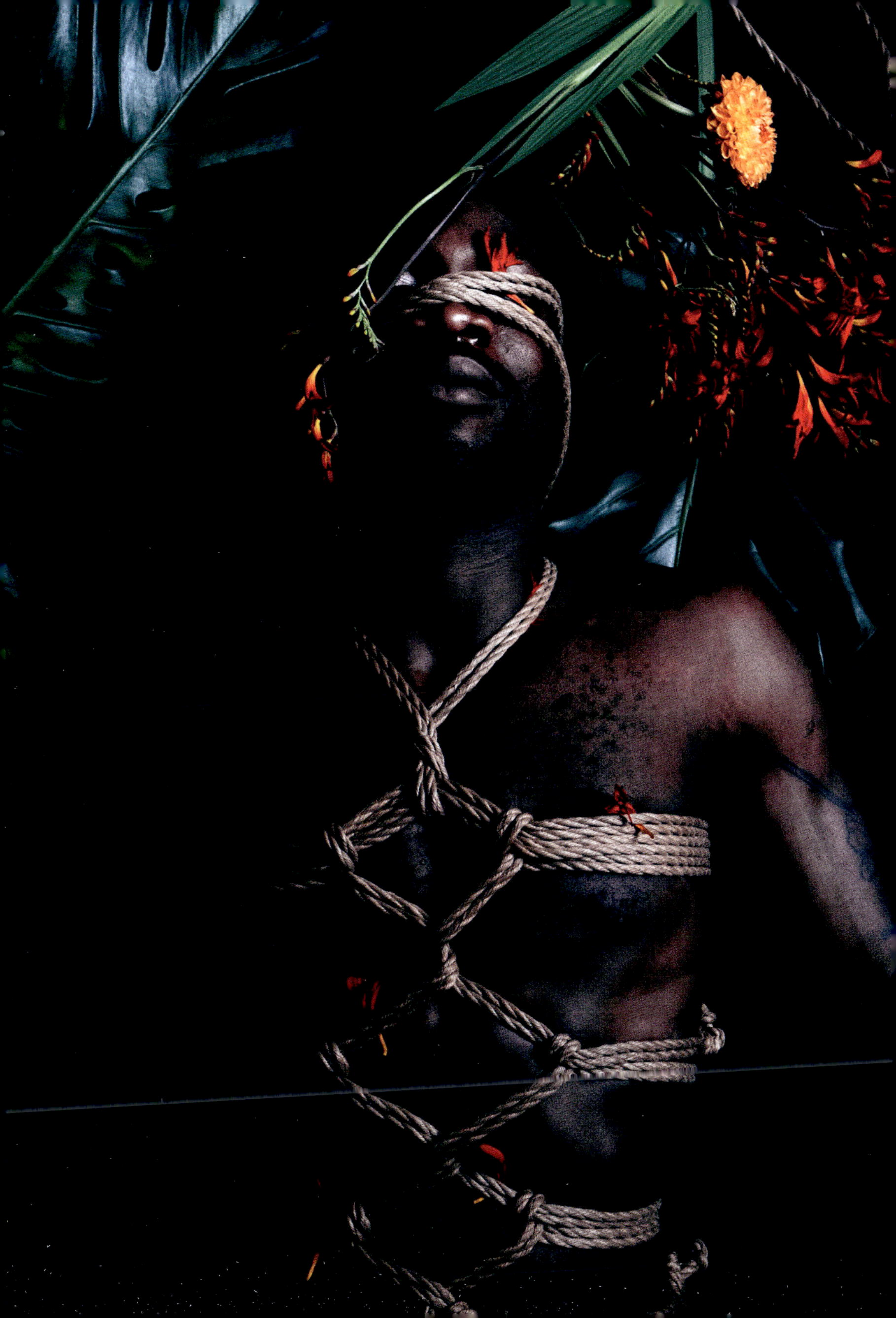

Futomomo

'Futomomo' (translating simply as 'thigh') is used to refer to a harness where the leg is tied into position whilst bent.

Don't worry if you don't have the flexibility to fold your leg in this way as there are plenty of alternative ties.

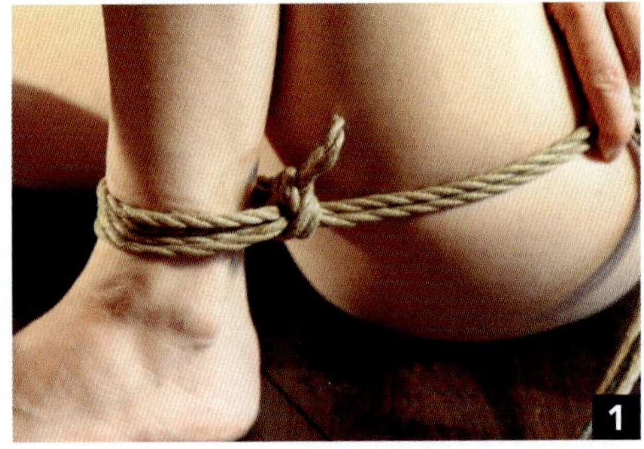

[1] Create a single column tie around the ankle. You should make it fairly snug, leaving around two fingers of space. If you find yourself frequently running out of rope for completing the rest of the tie you can also create this using only one wrap.

[2] Fold the leg in reasonably tight and make two wraps around the thigh and calf as shown.

Note that whichever direction you start making this wrap (towards the outside vs. inside of the leg) will be the side of the leg the central stem ends up on, and therefore the side of the tie you attach a suspension line to. Some other futomomo patterns make it possible to attach from either side – this is a very simple version.

[3] Make a no-dome (pg. 36) by going over and under both wraps **[4, 5]** then going through the gap between the wraps and the stem.

[6] Pass the working end through to the other side of the leg to make a kannuki (pg. 32), then pass it back.

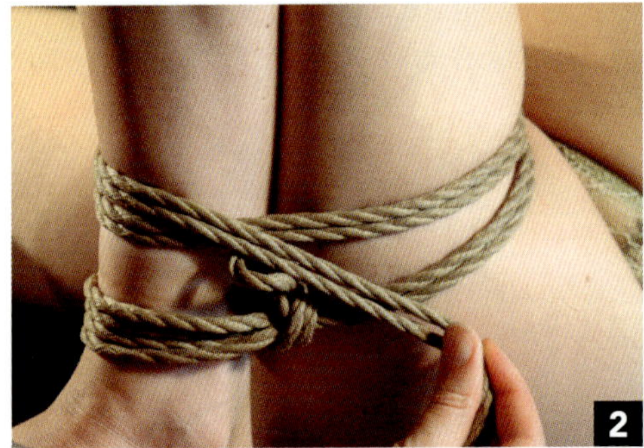

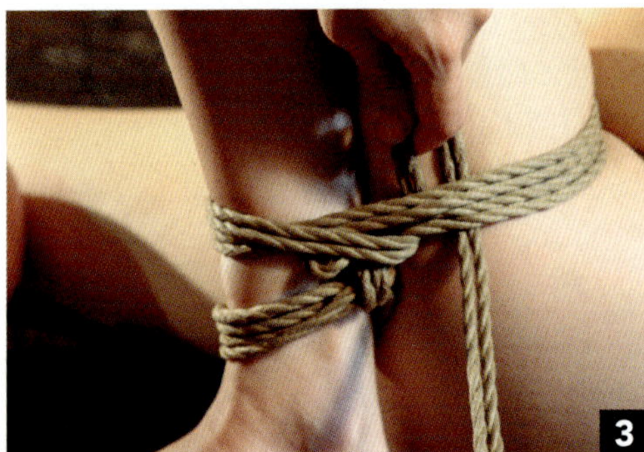

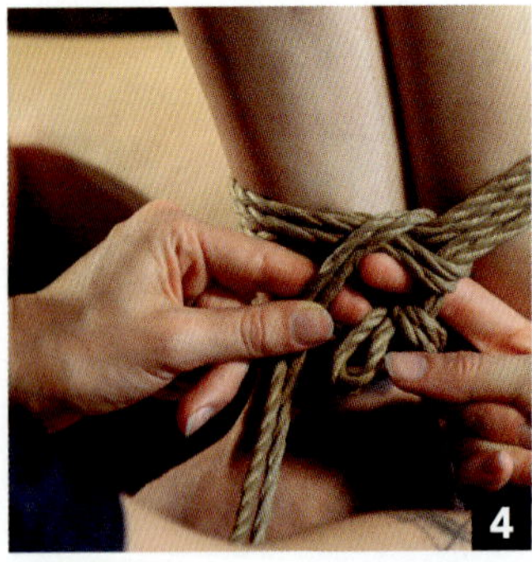

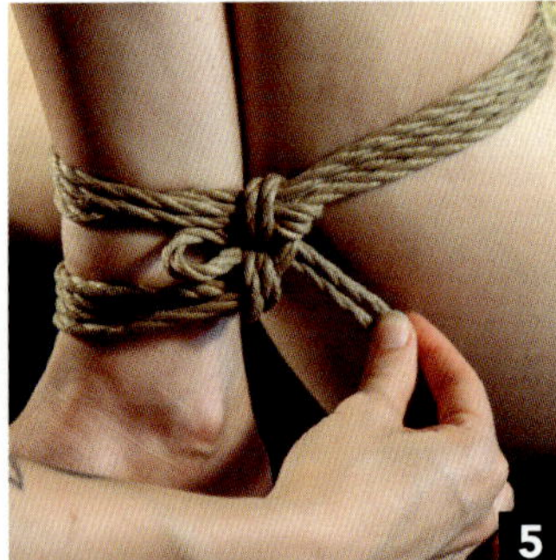

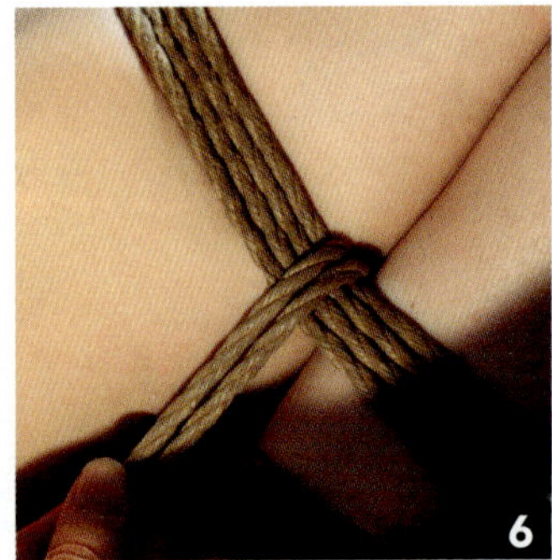

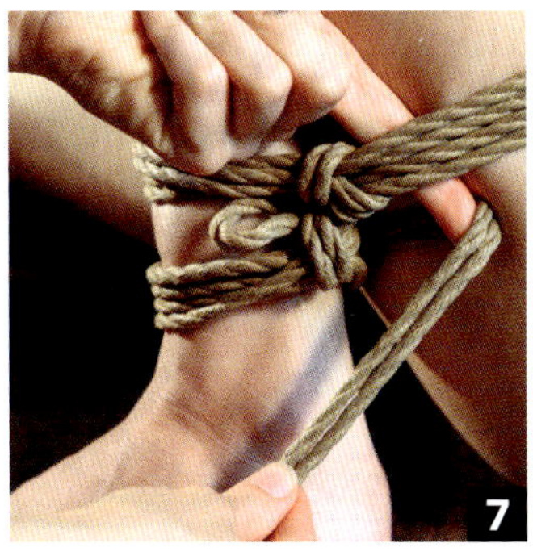
7

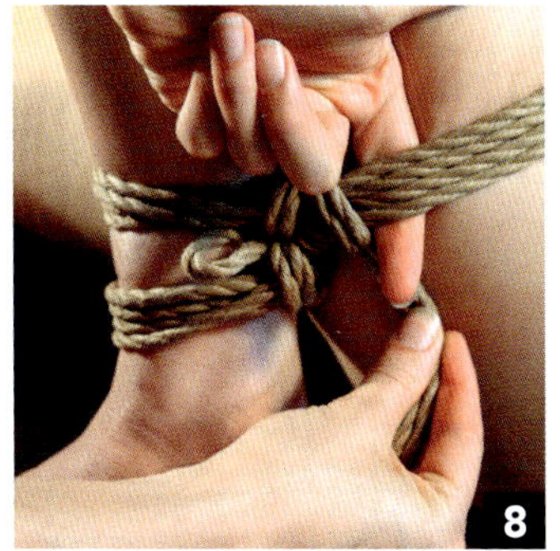
8

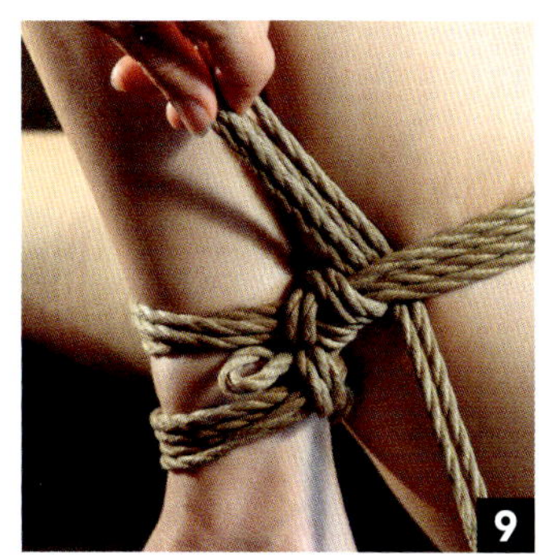
9

[7] Hook the working end up, so it comes out above the wrap.

[8, 9] Then pass it down and make a full turn around the wrap. To keep the friction balanced and secure, make this turn on the opposite side to the wrap of the no-dome.

[10] Because I have finished this friction on the right side, I will begin my next wrap tying to the left.

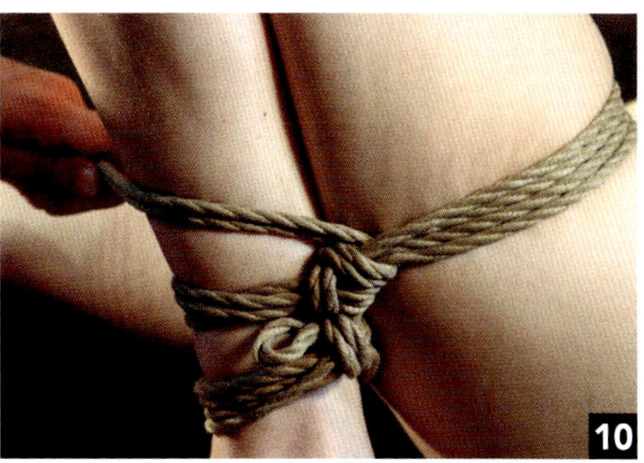
10

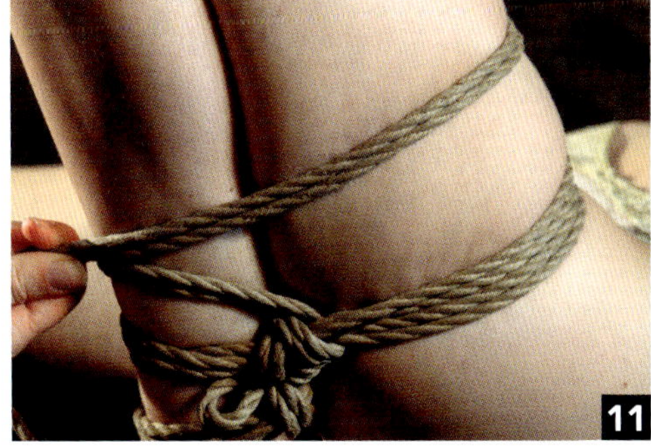
11

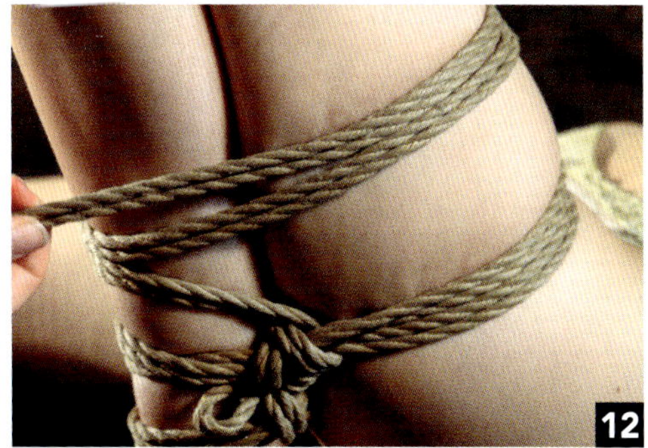
12

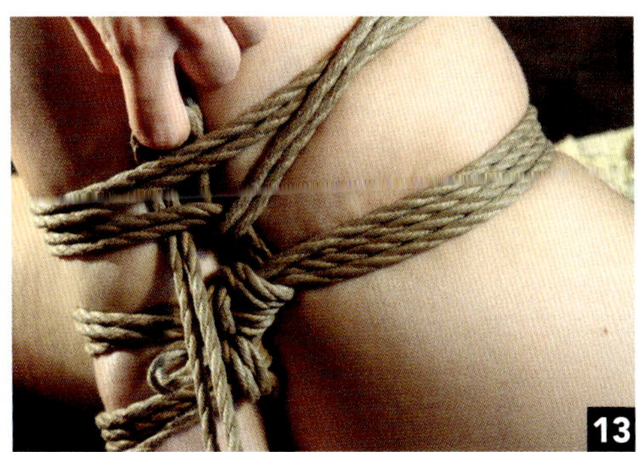
13

[11, 12] Make two wraps – I have made this quite a bit tighter than the lower wrap because I will not use a kannuki this time

[13] Hook the working end over the stem and under both wraps.

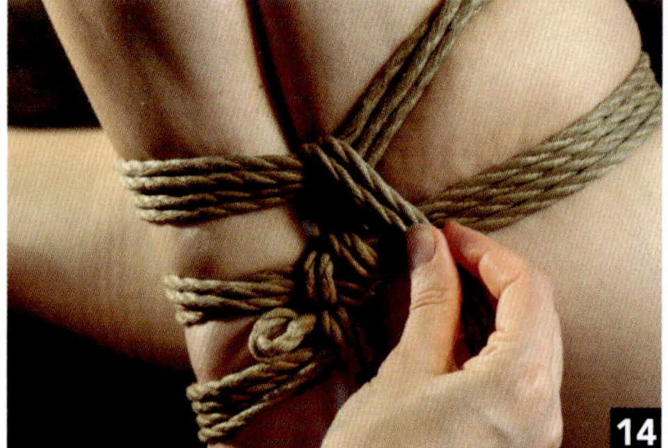

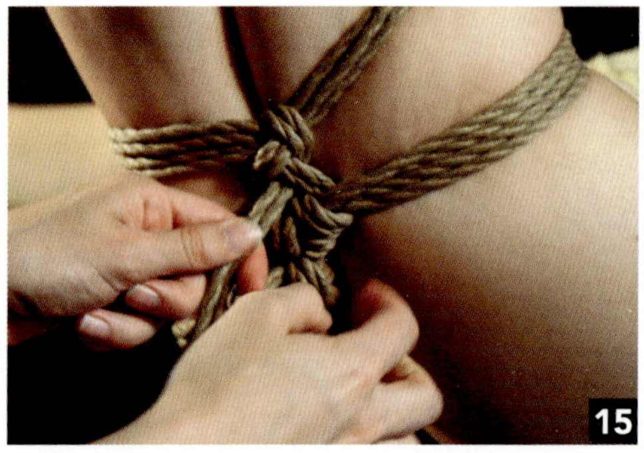

[14, 15] Close with a no-dome.

[16, 17] Make a full turn over and under the lower wrap.

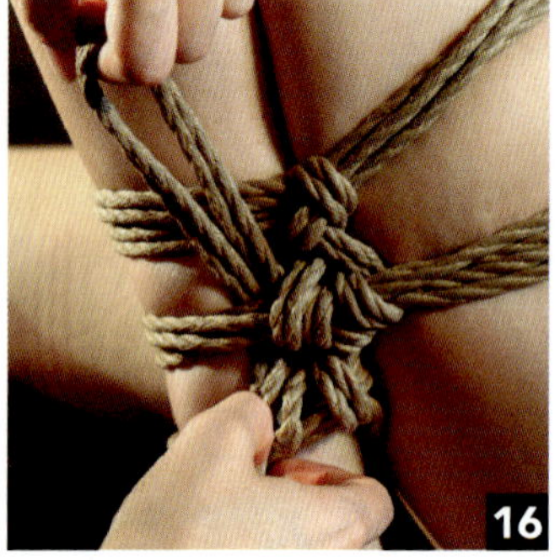

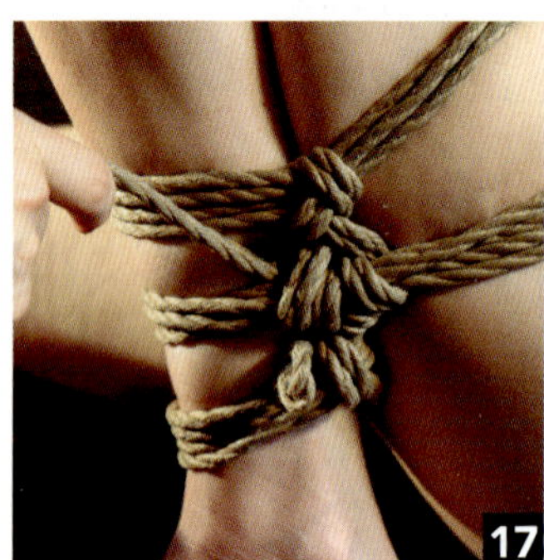

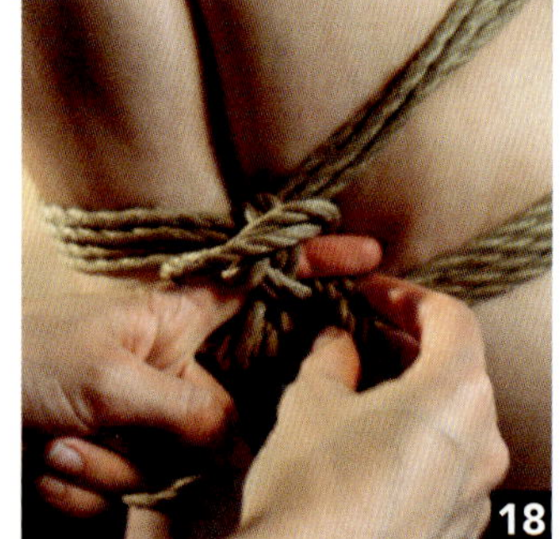

[18, 19] Lock with a half hitch around the stem between the two wraps.

[20] The tie is finished.

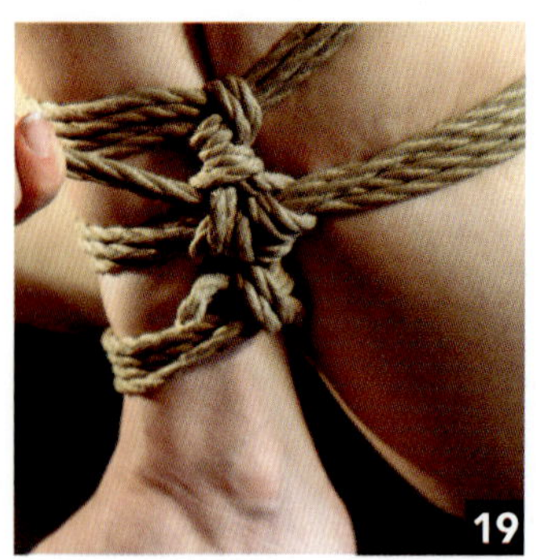

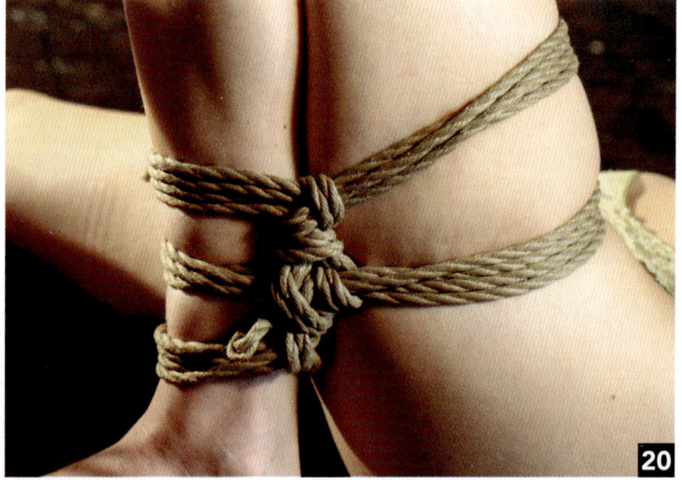

Futomomo in Suspension

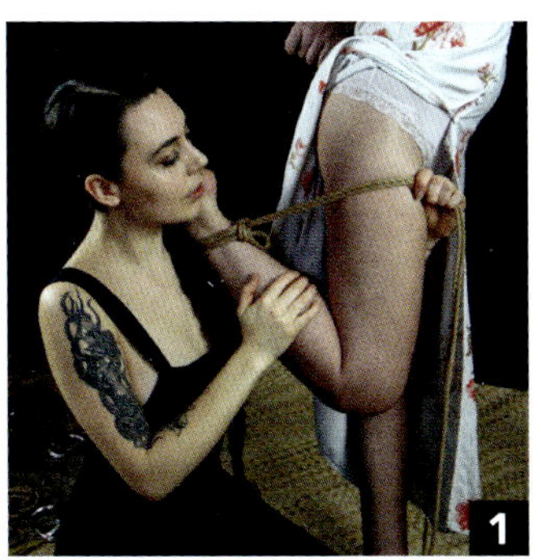
1

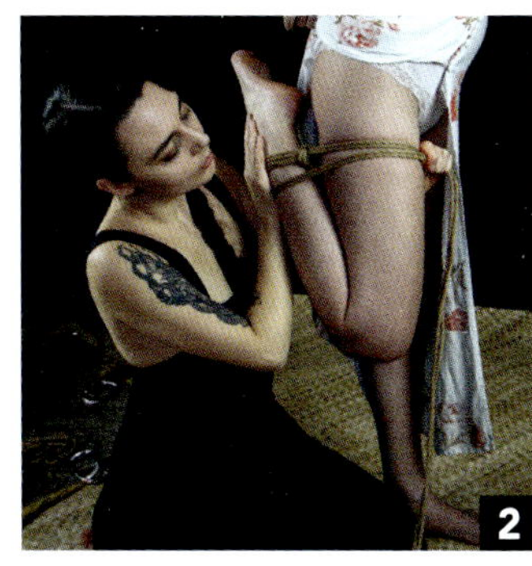
2

It can be difficult to tie a futomomo smoothly when the model is already suspended rather than sitting on the floor. Here are two ideas to help.

Option 1: [1, 2] Support the model's leg by resting their foot on your shoulder whilst you set the tension of the wraps. Once the first wrap is locked, the rest of the tie becomes much easier to complete.

Option 2: [3] Temporarily suspend the leg with a wrap around the thigh, just above the knee, to give the model support (information on suspension lines starts on pg. 106).

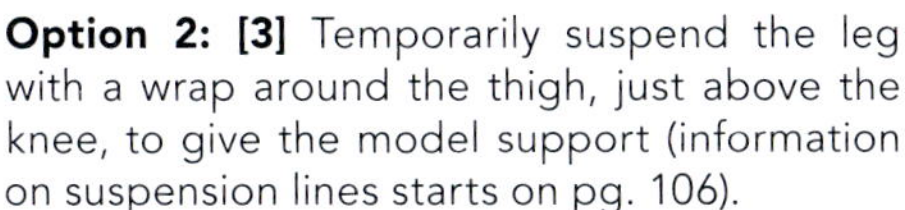

[4] Bend the leg and tie the futomomo over the top.

The temporary line can be removed once the futomomo is suspended. It can be hard to remove the single column from inside the leg, particularly if the model has bare skin, but you can leave it in place and wrap the excess rope around the leg over the finished futomomo.

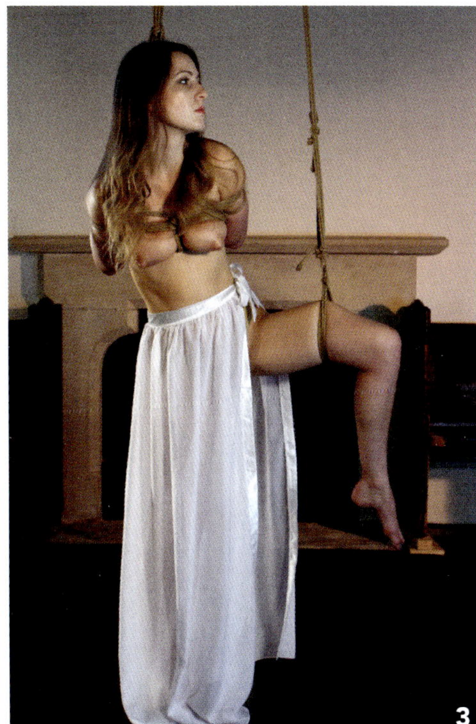
3

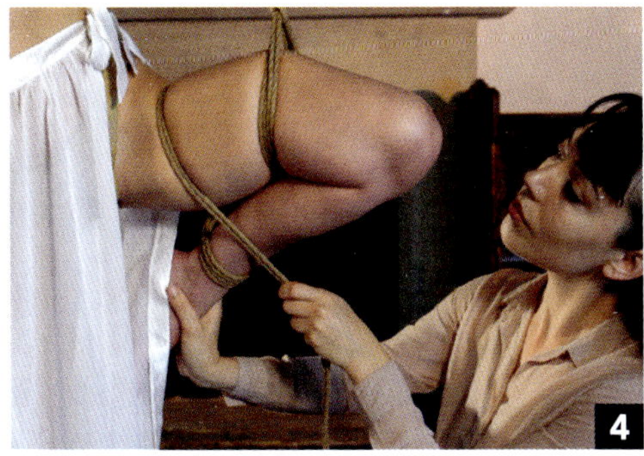
4

Attachment Points

You can attach the suspension line using either:

[B] A single column tie (pg. 107) around the stem

[C] An ypsilon (spiral pg. 100) around the top wrap, as shown

depending on which direction the suspension line is going to be pulling in.

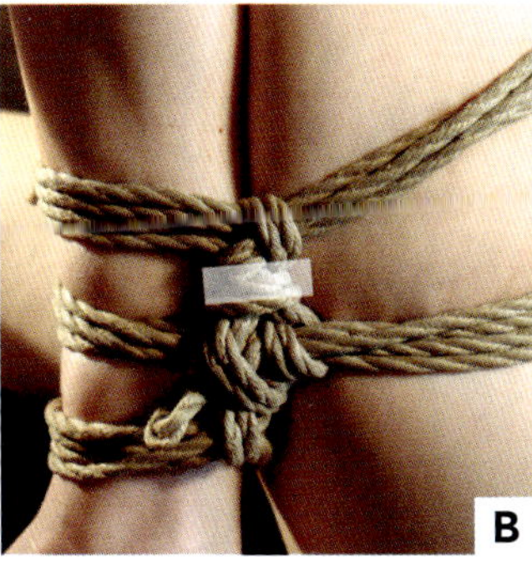
B

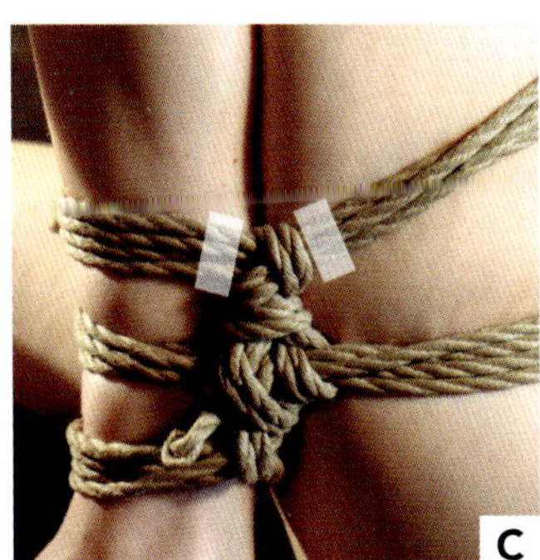
C

Chest Harness for Floor Work and Partial Suspensions

The takate kote (pg. 50) can also be used for **floorwork** and partial suspensions, however many people like to use a tie that omits the lower arm wrap to reduce the risk of nerve compression. In full suspension, rope is placed over both the chest and the arms to spread the load away from the ribs, which can be painful and restrict breathing – however, in situations where there is less pressure overall it may be more tolerable on the ribs.

In this harness, the rope that covers the chest will add some support and help prevent sliding, but it is also there just to give the feeling of pressure holding the body, which many models enjoy. In play situations, it can also be nice to take the extra time to add rope to the body as part of building your scene, even if it isn't strictly necessary. The large amount of detail at the front of this tie means you get to face your model as you tie and connect in a different way.

I have tied this with the hands in a low position (pg. 48) – which allows more freedom of movement for the model to adjust themselves, reducing the stress on the shoulders and also letting the elbows stay closer to the body so they don't dig into the floor if the model is lying on their side. As ever, feel free to use whichever hand position feels right for you.

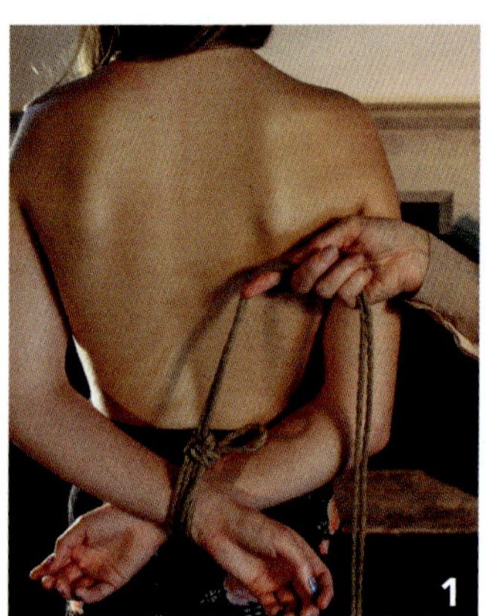
1

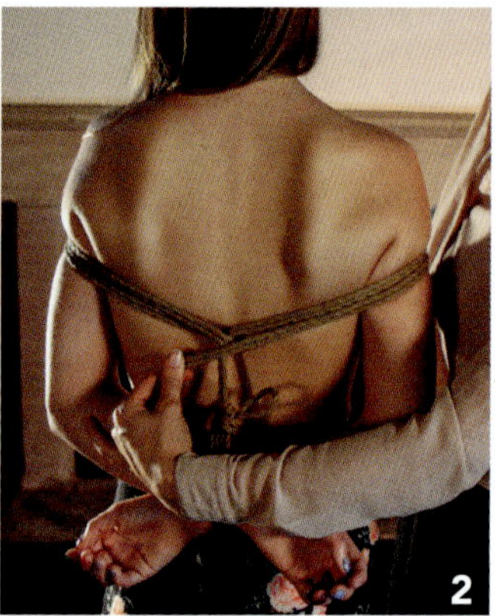
2

[1] Start with a single column tie around the wrists.

[2] Create the upper wrap – I have done this using reverse tension (pg. 38) because the low hand position makes the stem long.

[3, 4] Make one full turn around the wrap to isolate the tension.

[5] Wrap the working end down the stem, and through the wrist cuff.

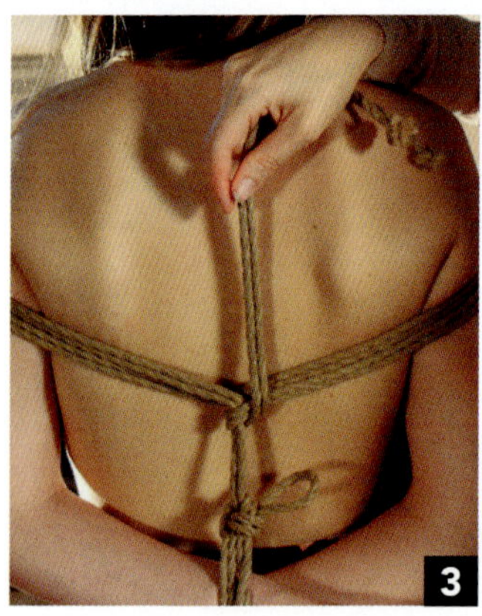
3

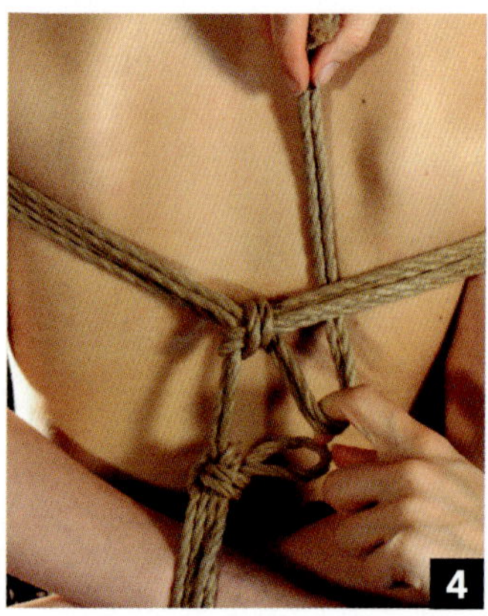
4

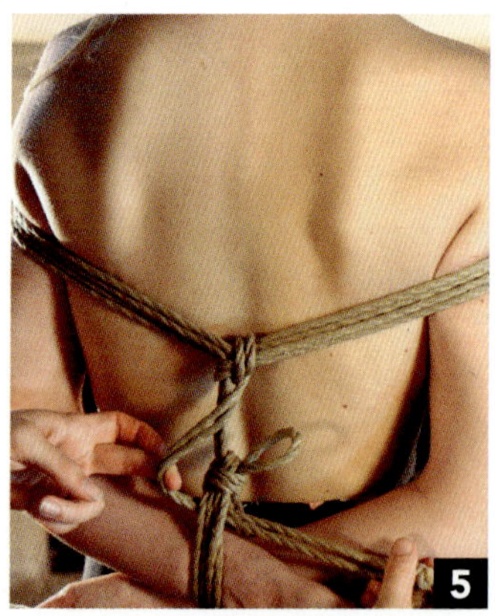
5

[6, 7] Here, I am locking off the first rope around the wrist cuff using an overhand lock (pg. 40). You may lock off in whatever way works for you, depending on the amount of rope you have left.

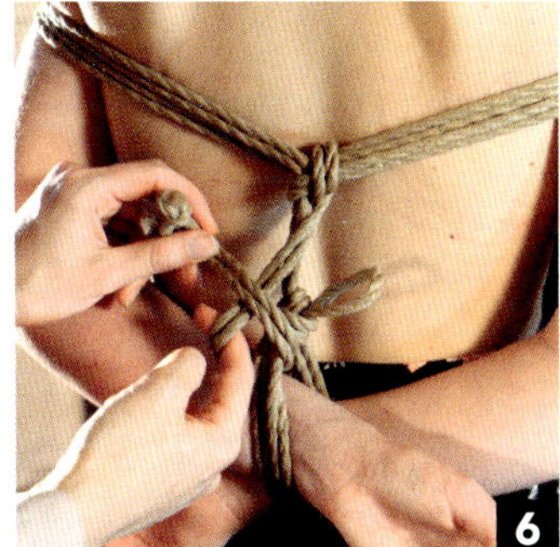

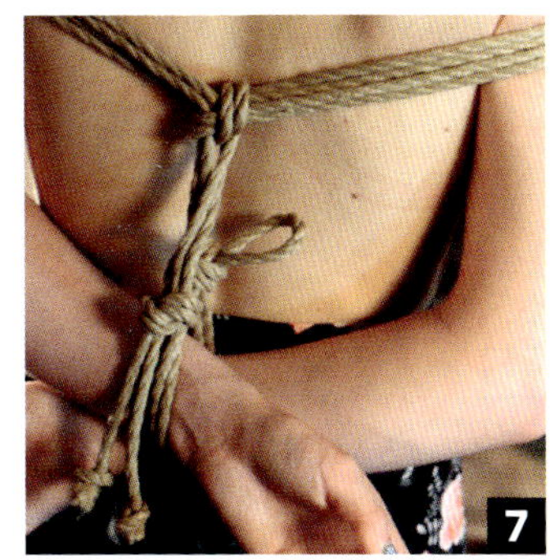

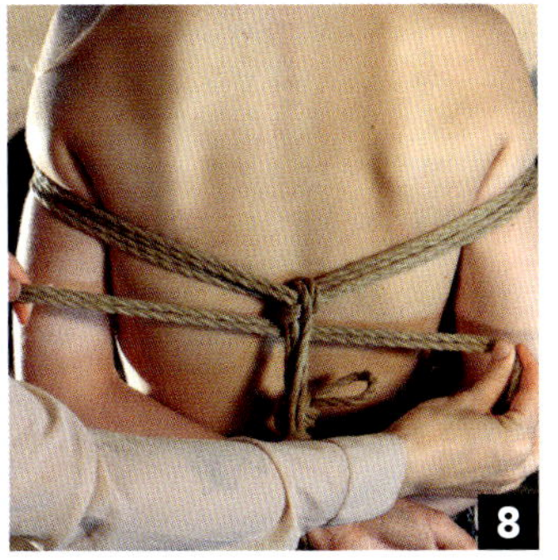

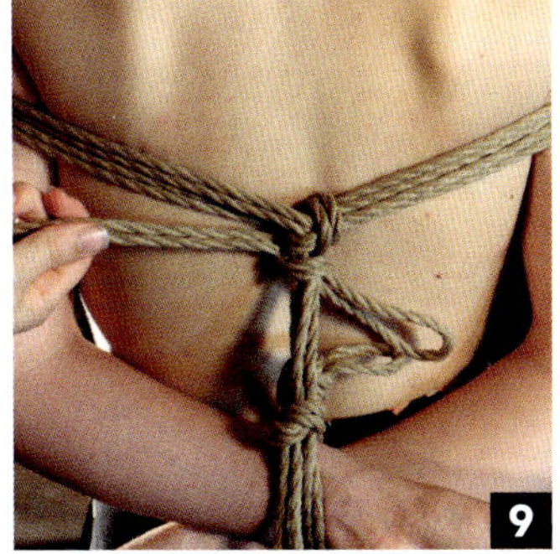

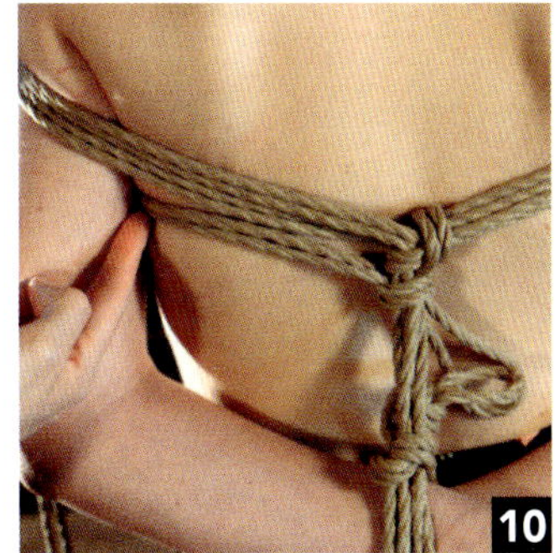

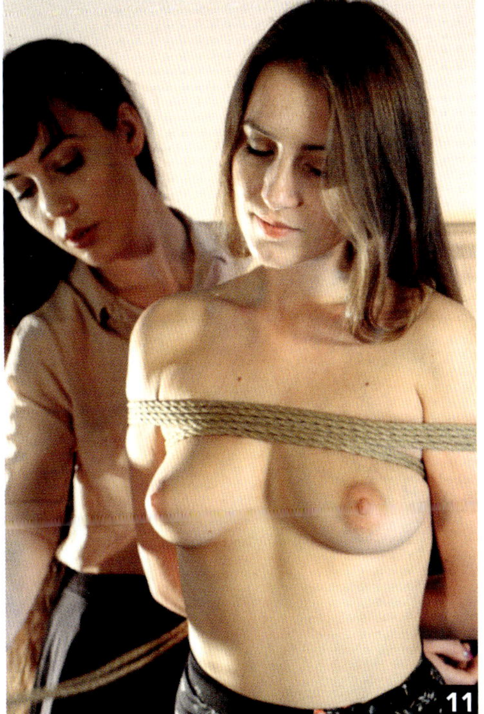

[8, 9] Attach a new rope using an overhand knot around the stem (pg. 34).

[10] Pass the working end underneath the arm.

[11, 12] Make two wraps around the chest, going under the stem as you pass it. You need to make these wraps considerably looser than the first wrap in step 2.

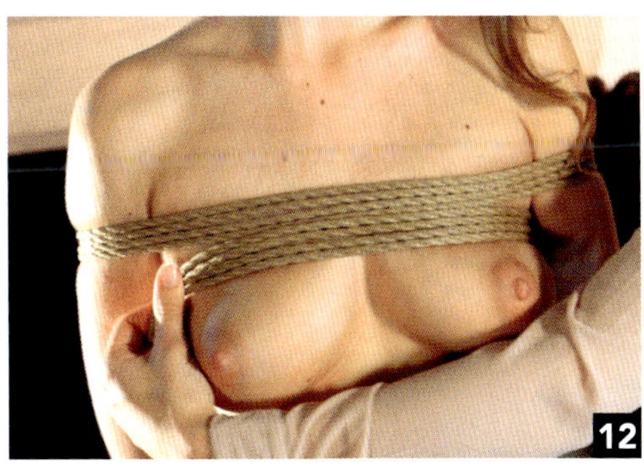

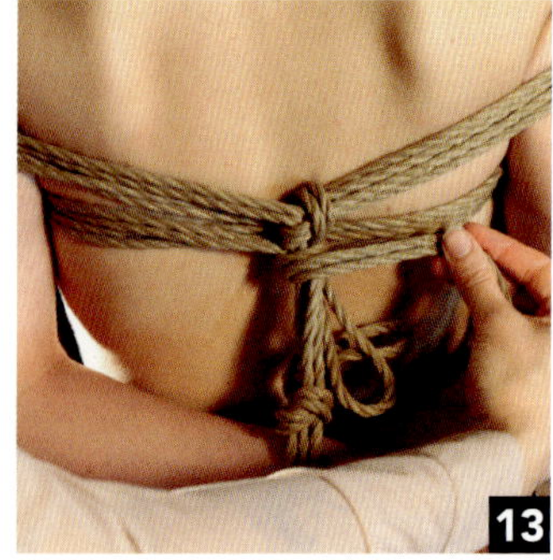
13

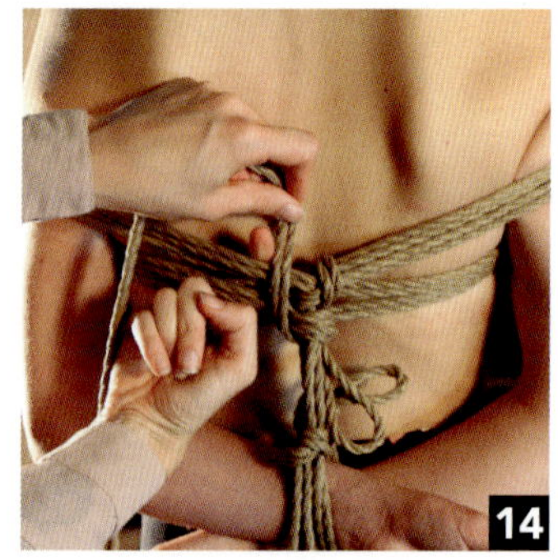
14

[13] Make a full 360° turn around the stem.

[14, 15] Pass the working end over and under both the shoulder and chest wrap and **[16]** wrap once more around the stem.

[17] Pass the working end back underneath the arm – this time below the pectoral muscle.

[18] Now we're going to begin opening up the chest wraps into a diamond shape. Make sure the lower wrap passes over the upper wrap when you do this.

[19] Pass the working end around the upper wrap and pull down a little.

[20] Make a twist by wrapping the working end around the lower chest rope and take the rope back through the opposite arm.

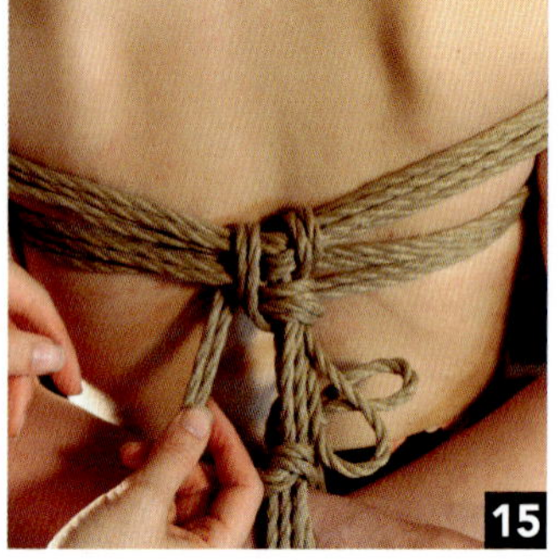
15

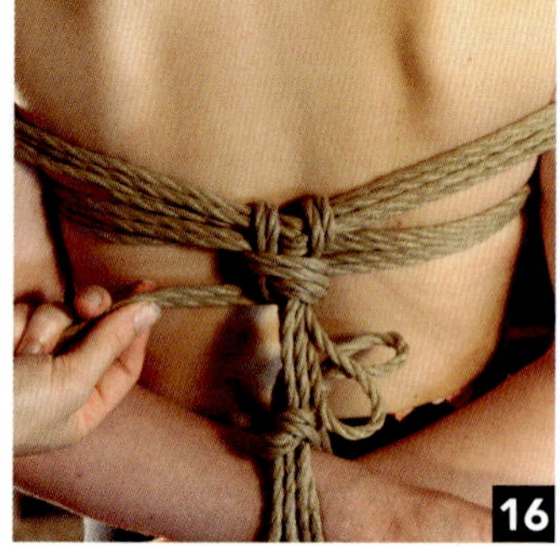
16

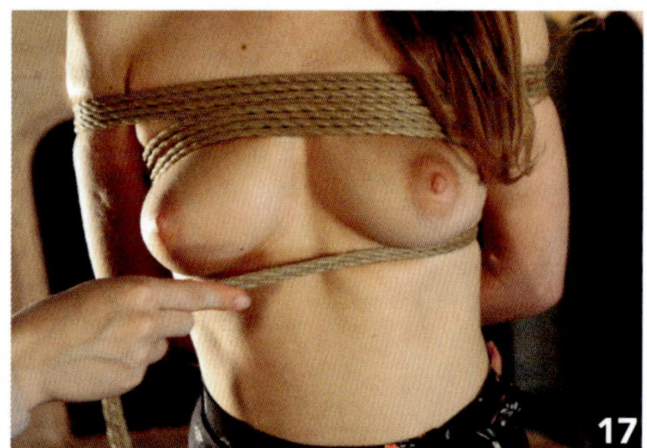
17

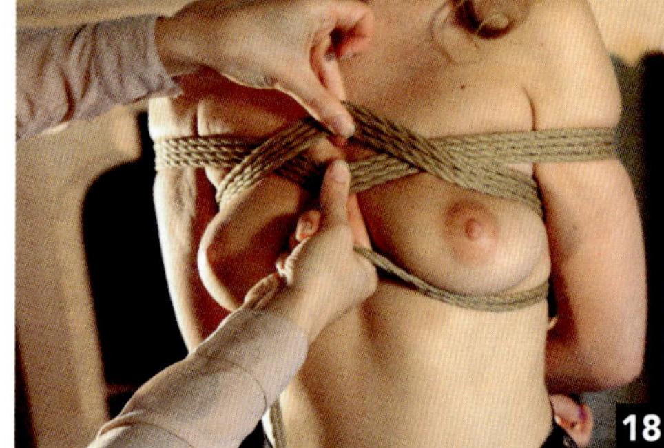
18

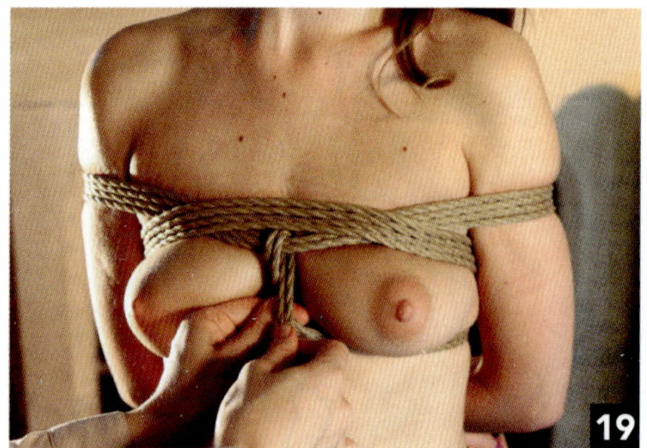
19

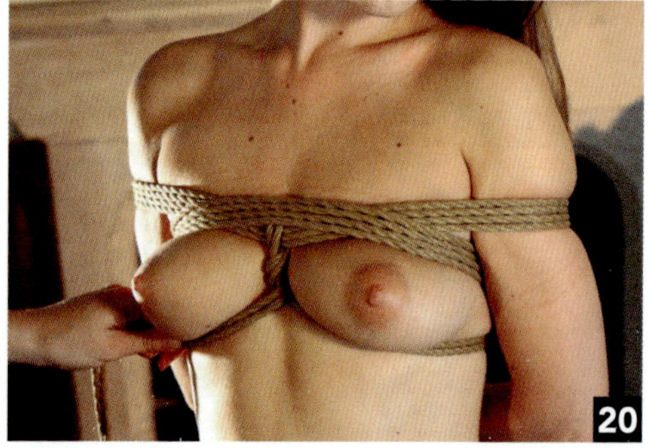
20

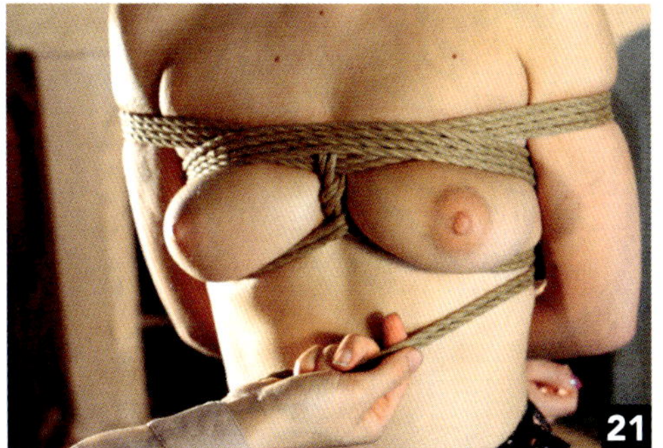

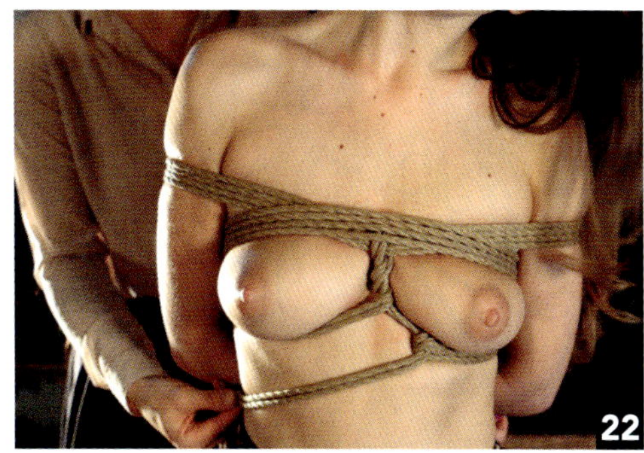

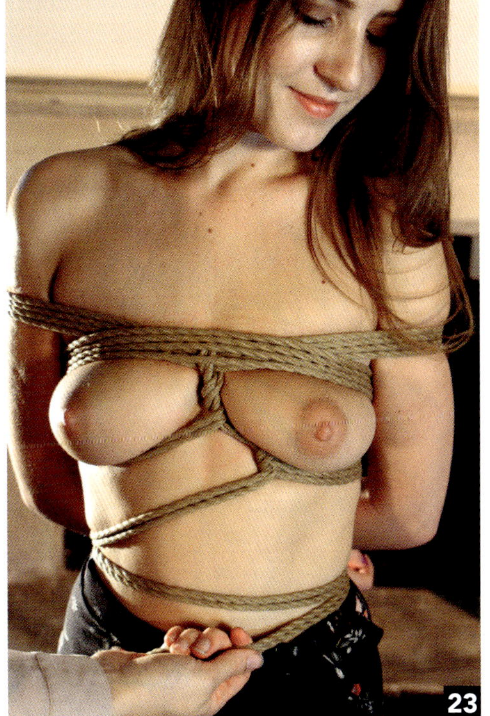

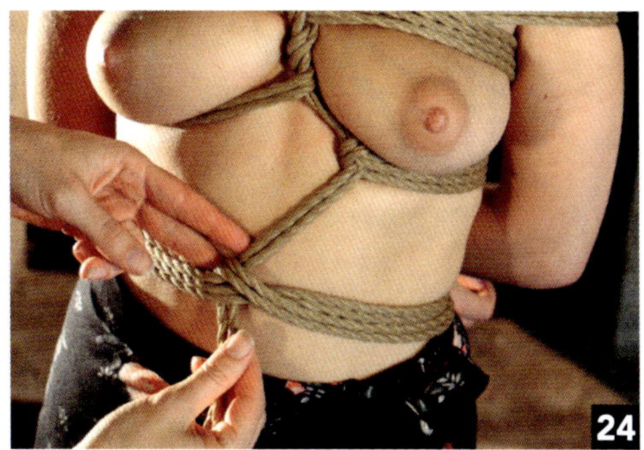

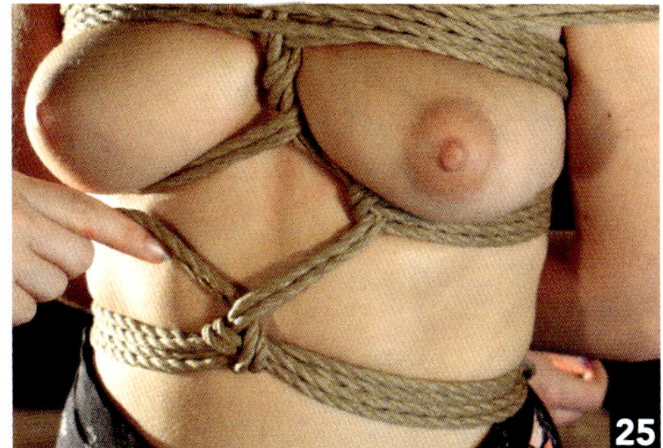

[21] Pass the working end around the back, under the stem, and back out under the opposite arm.

[22] Make a half hitch on the lower chest wrap – the exact placement will vary depending on the model (see step 18, pg. 91).

[23] Take the working end diagonally down and wrap twice around the waist.

[24, 25] Secure the waist wrap together with a no-dome (pg. 36).

[26, 27] Make another half hitch, symmetrical to the first, and take the working end to the back under the arm.

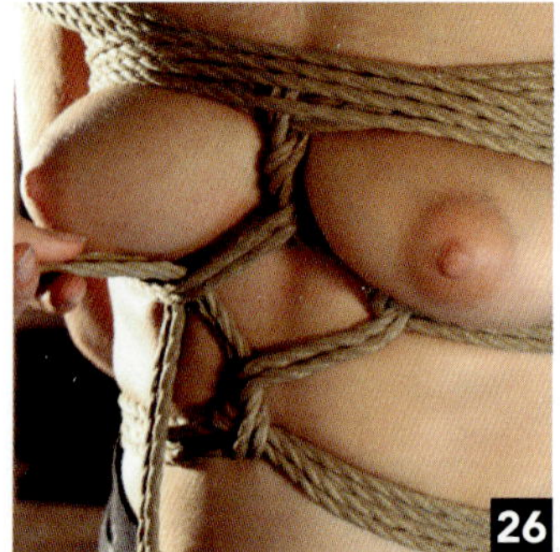
26

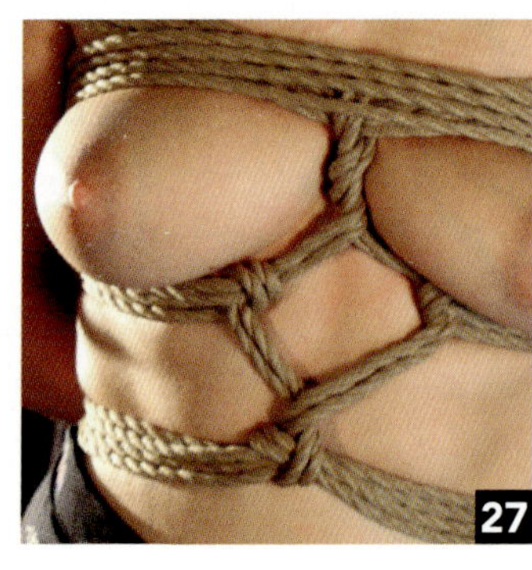
27

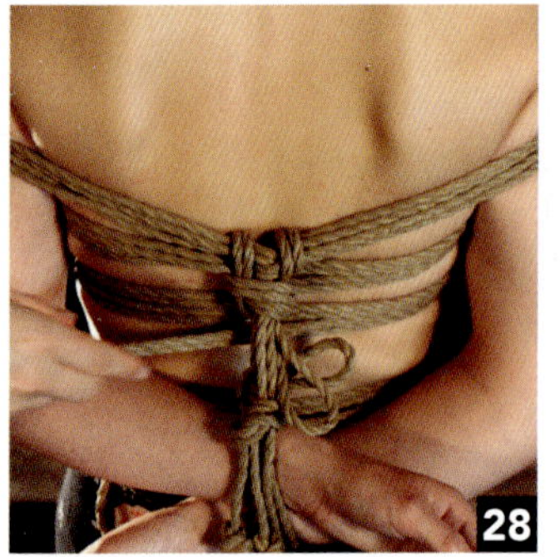
28

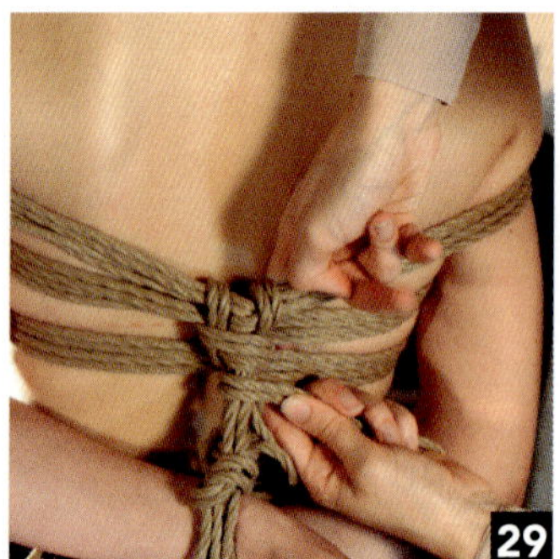
29

[28] Pass the working end under the stem.

[29, 30] Reverse around the stem, and pass up underneath everything.

[31] Make a full turn around the upper wrap and take the working end diagonally across the back and over the shoulder.

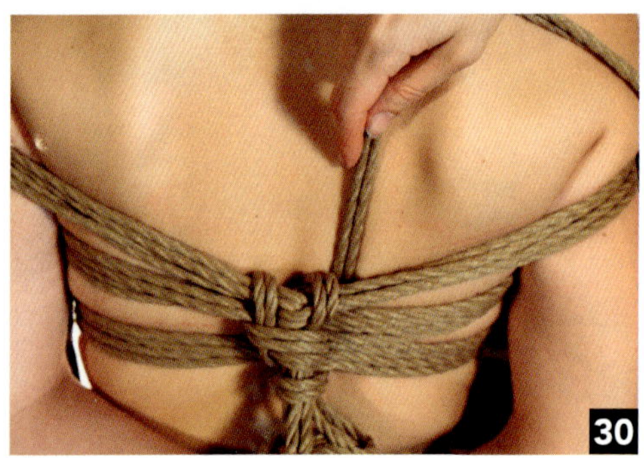
30

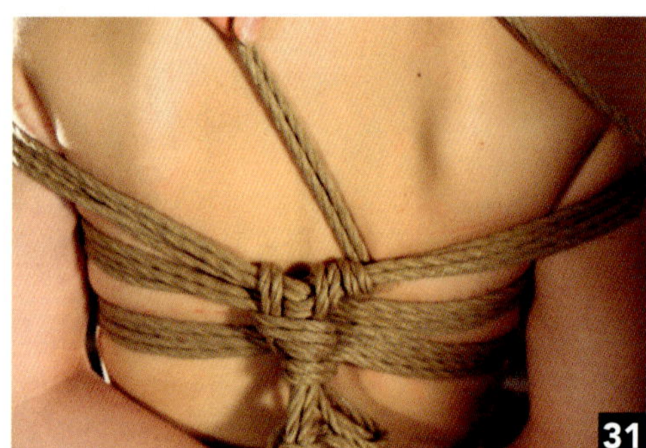
31

[32] Pick up the chest wrap, and pull it up to open the second half of the diamond. Make a simple twist and pass it back over the opposite shoulder.

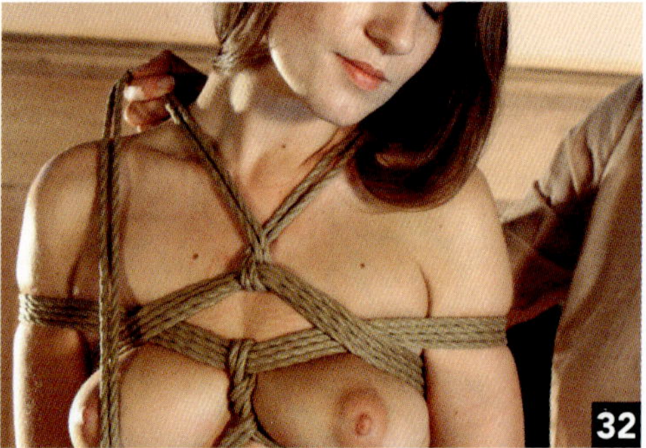
32

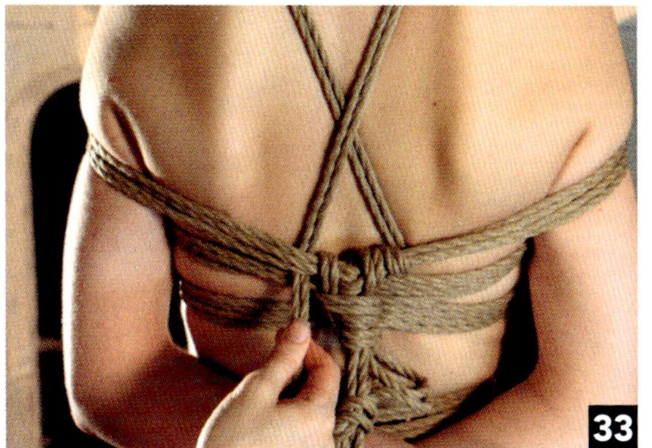
33

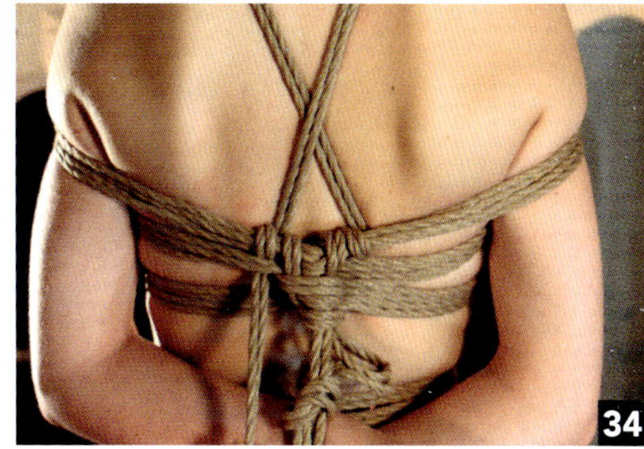
34

[33] Pass the working end diagonally across the back and under the upper wrap **[34]** then make a full turn around the upper wrap to mirror the other side and pass under the wrap from the chest.

[35, 36] Lock off to finish the tie according to the amount of rope you have left. In this case I have wrapped back into the stem to centre the rope, then built a hojo cuff (pg. 31) on one arm.

[37] The finished tie.

Tip

Sometimes the ropes over the neck can come loose if you're putting vertical pressure on the tie. If this bothers you, rather than finishing the rope off neatly at step 35, 36 just make a really simple lock that's easy to untie – then you can always tighten and re-lock the neck rope. Remember when the upward pressure is released the neck rope might suddenly get tighter again so you should be ready to undo it at this point.

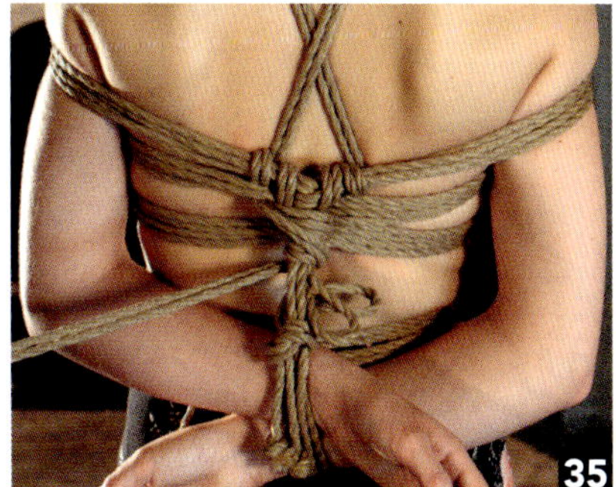
35

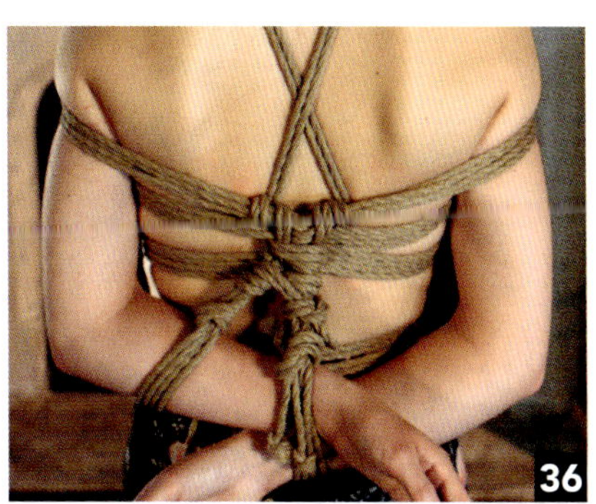
36

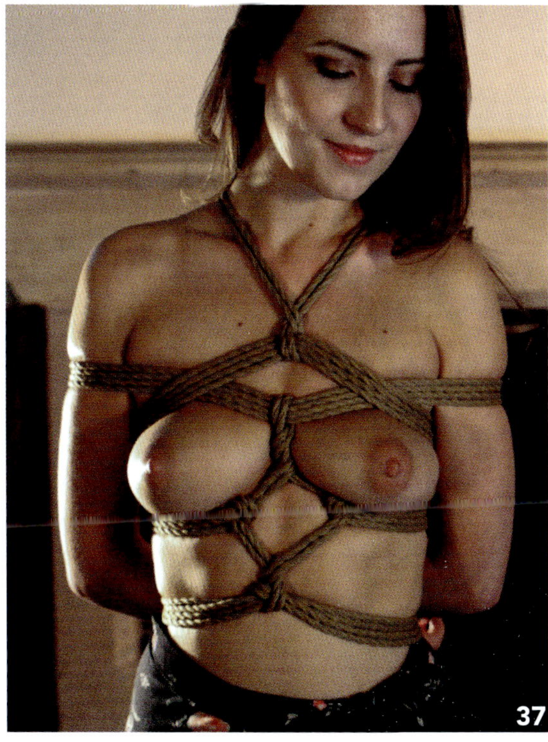
37

Attachment Points

When attaching to the back of this harness you can use an ypsilon (spiral – pg. 108) either:

[D] Around the shoulder wrap, which seems to be more comfortable for most models.

[E] Around both the shoulder and upper chest wraps.

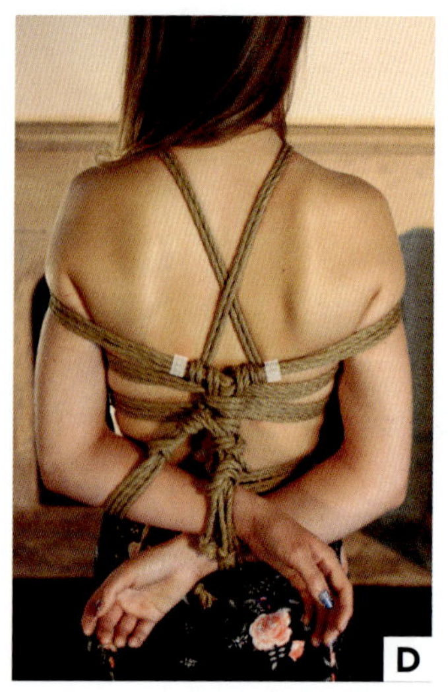

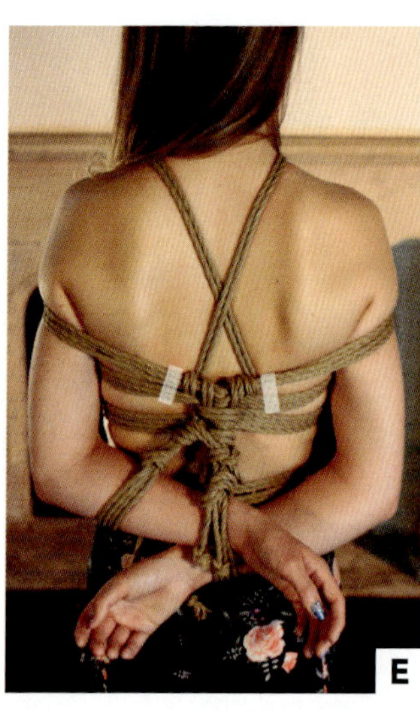

[F] A similar chest harness, tied with the waist wrap (steps 22-26) omitted.

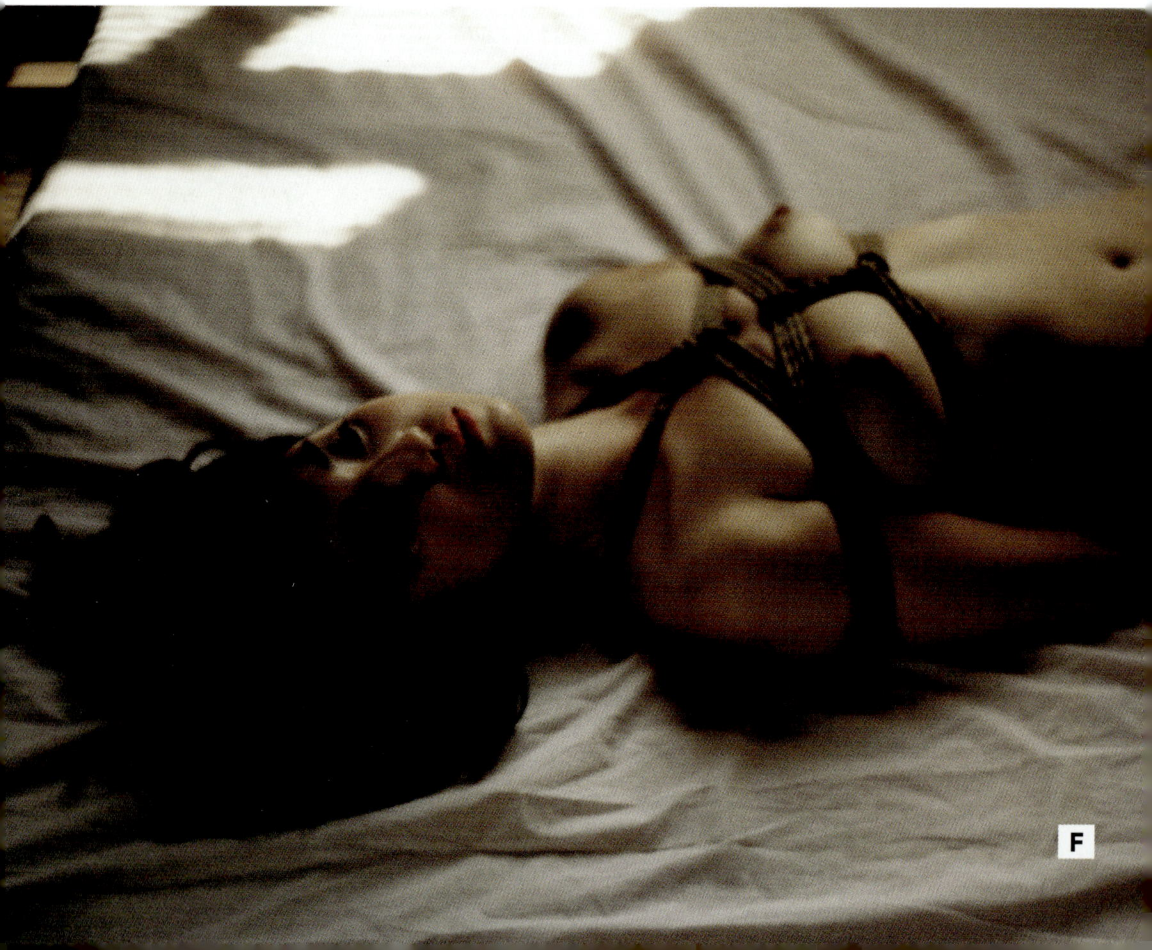

Hands Free Hishi Harness

Using a hands free chest harness is a versatile option when you wish to avoid tying the hands, or wish to have the freedom to change the hand position throughout the tie. The downsides are that some people find this harder on the breathing and more painful on the chest when there are no arms there to spread the load.

'Hishi' or 'hishigata' simply means 'diamond shaped' and refers to the diamond patterns made with the rope.

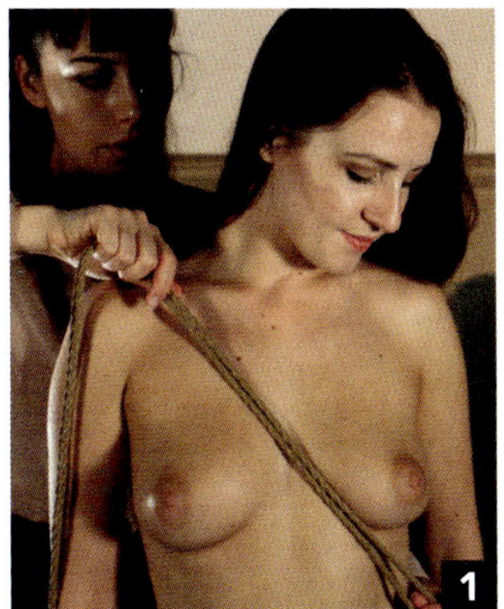

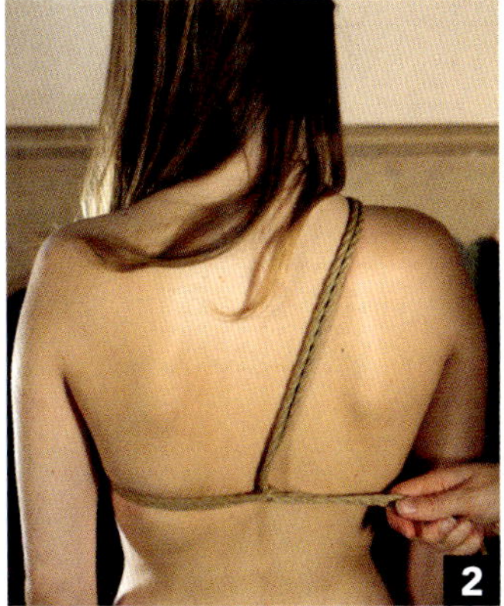

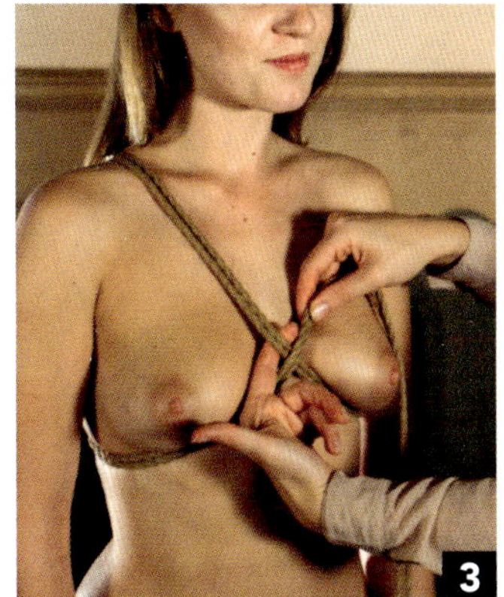

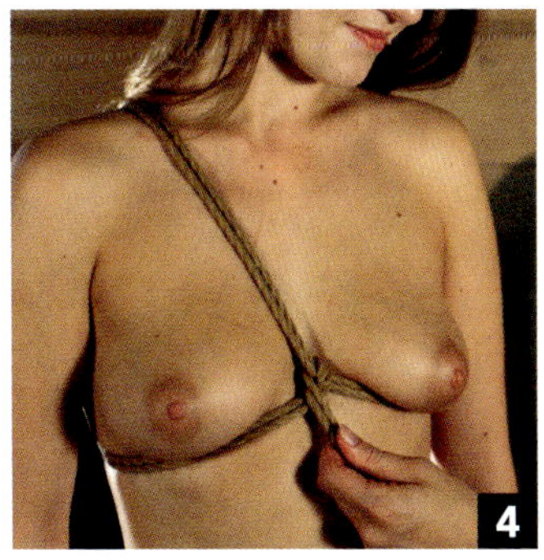

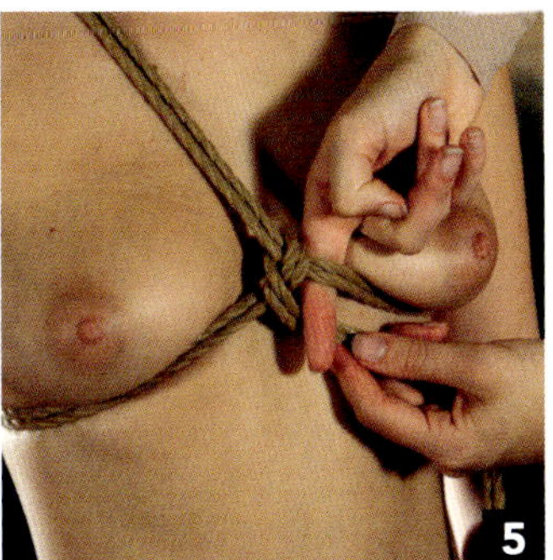

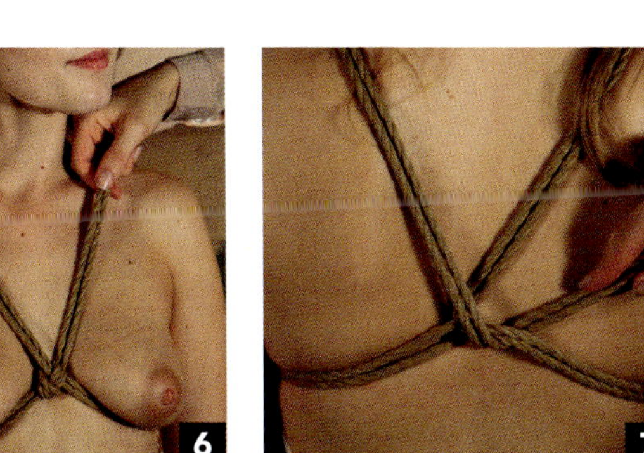

[1] Start by placing the rope diagonally across the chest, with the bight end under the pectoral muscle, and the working end over the opposite shoulder.

[2] At the centre of the back, thread the working end through the bight, pull gently against it to change direction and pass it back around to the front.

[3 - 5] Create a no-dome (pg. 36) at the point where the two ropes cross.

[6] Take the working end back over the shoulder.

[7] Hook the working end over and under the horizontal wrap at the point where all the ropes meet at the centre of the back.

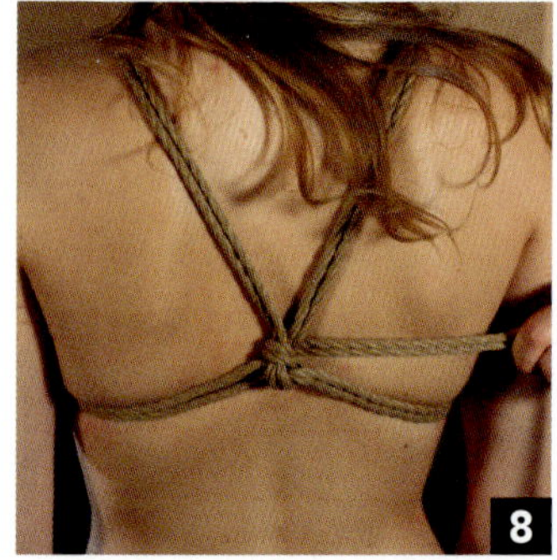
8

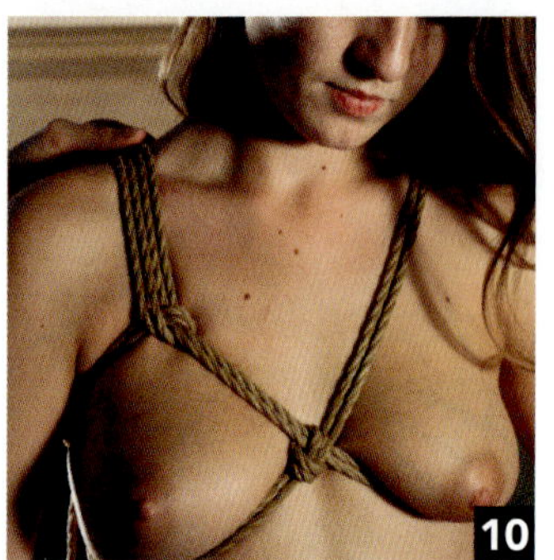
10

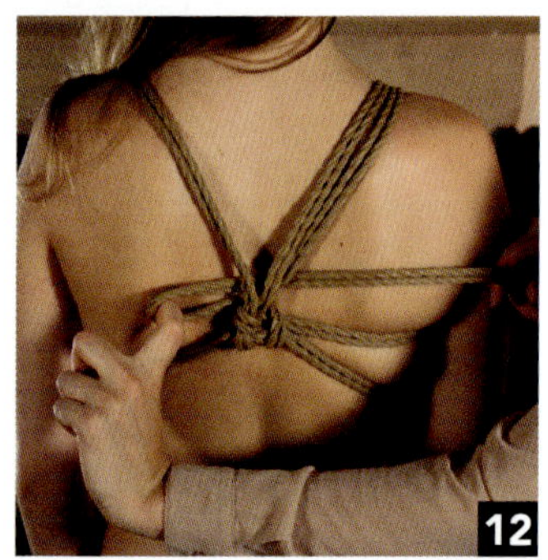
12

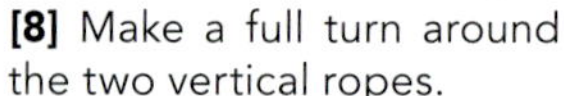
[8] Make a full turn around the two vertical ropes.

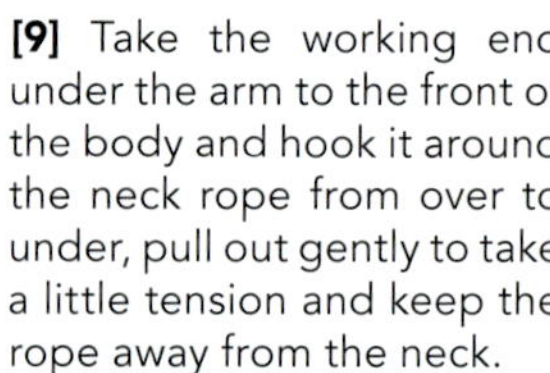
[9] Take the working end under the arm to the front of the body and hook it around the neck rope from over to under, pull out gently to take a little tension and keep the rope away from the neck.

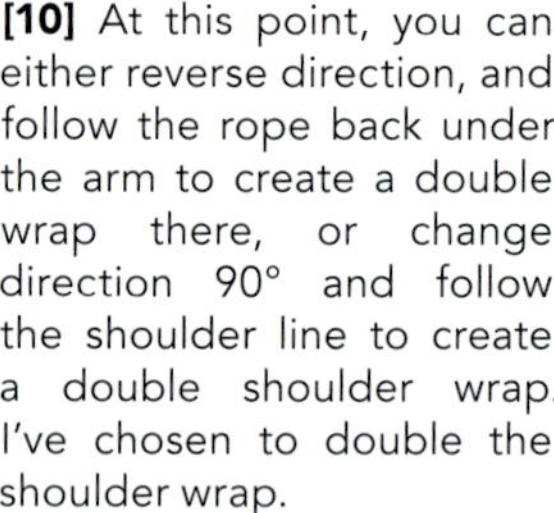
[10] At this point, you can either reverse direction, and follow the rope back under the arm to create a double wrap there, or change direction 90° and follow the shoulder line to create a double shoulder wrap. I've chosen to double the shoulder wrap.

[11] At the back of the harness go under then over the two horizontal ropes **[12]** and then behind the two vertical ropes.

[13, 14] Create a half hitch on the horizontal wrap to mirror the shape on the other side, then go back over the shoulder.

(N.B. if you have made two under arm wraps you can skip 11-14 and instead make a full turn around the vertical wraps to go back under the arm on the other side.)

[15, 16] Create a half hitch to mirror the one on the other side and pull outwards to create the same tension.

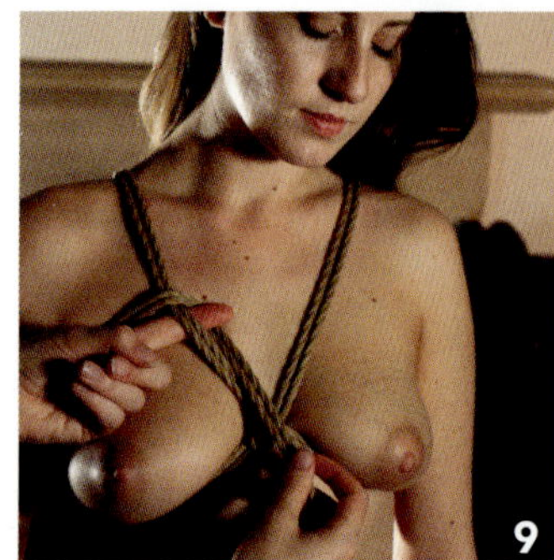
9

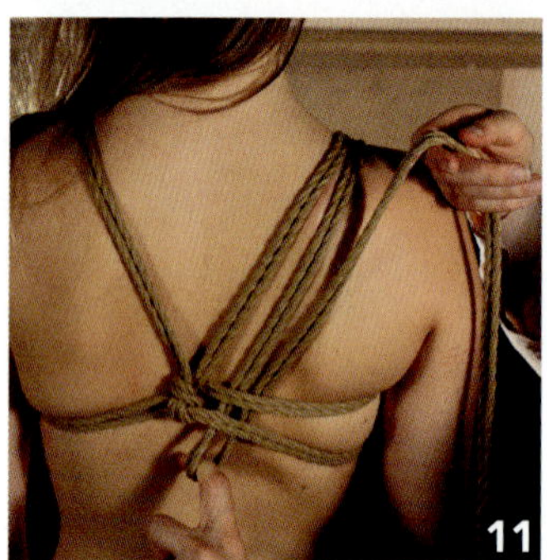
11

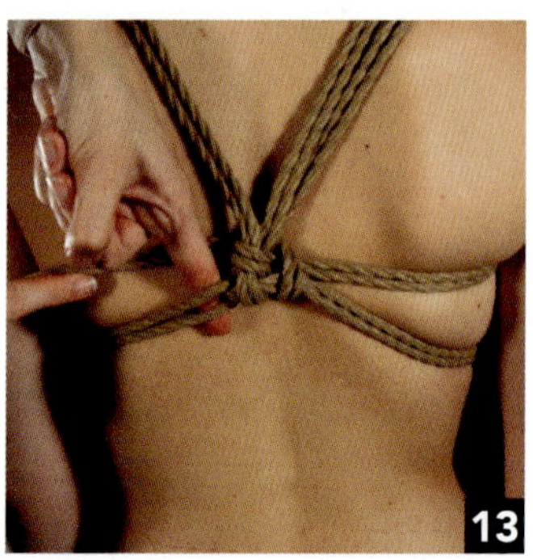
13

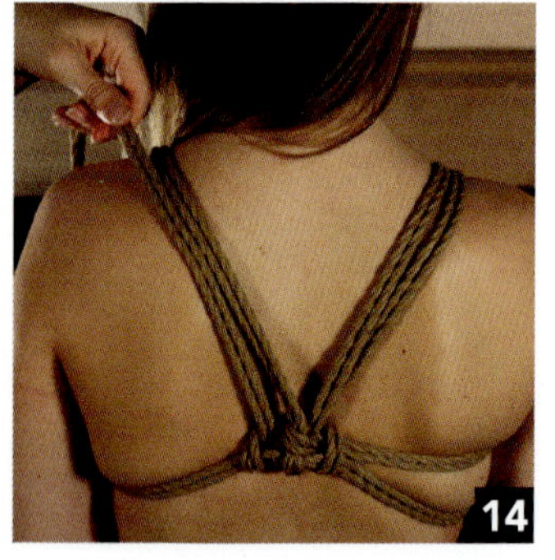
14

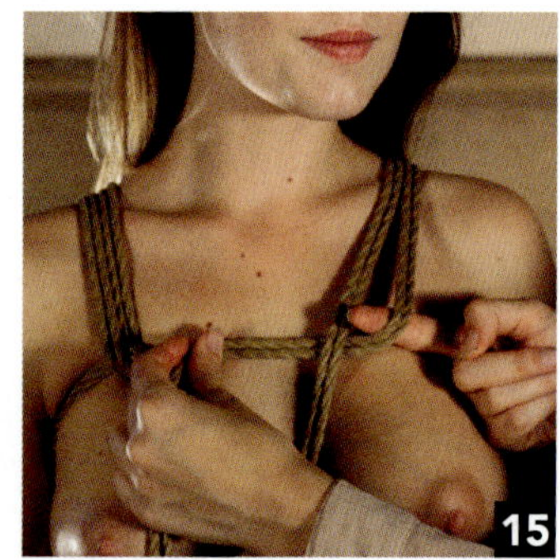
15

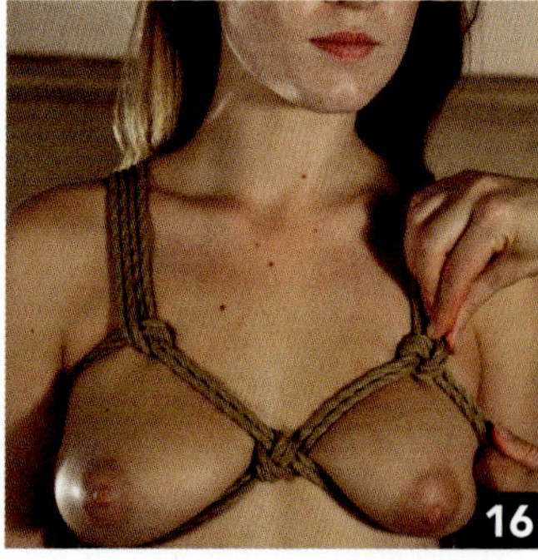
16

[17] Pass the working end to the back and wrap a full 360° around the vertical stem. Pass back to the front on the opposite side, following the rope underneath the pectoral muscle.

[18] Create a half hitch on the rope to change direction. The most comfortable placement of this is quite individual so you can test out various places pressing the half hitch down with your thumb to simulate the pressure of suspension. Then start spiralling the rope down across the stomach.

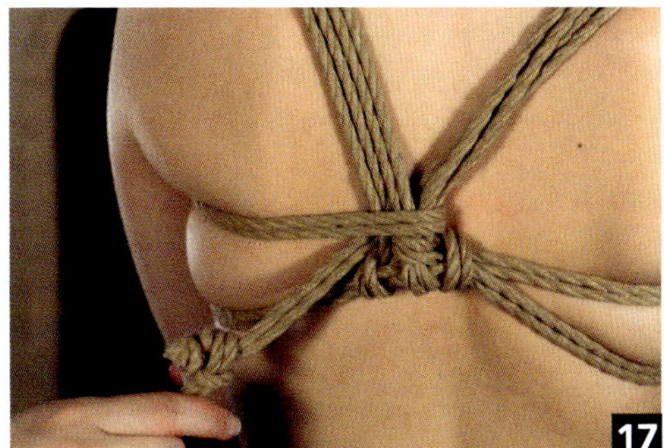

17

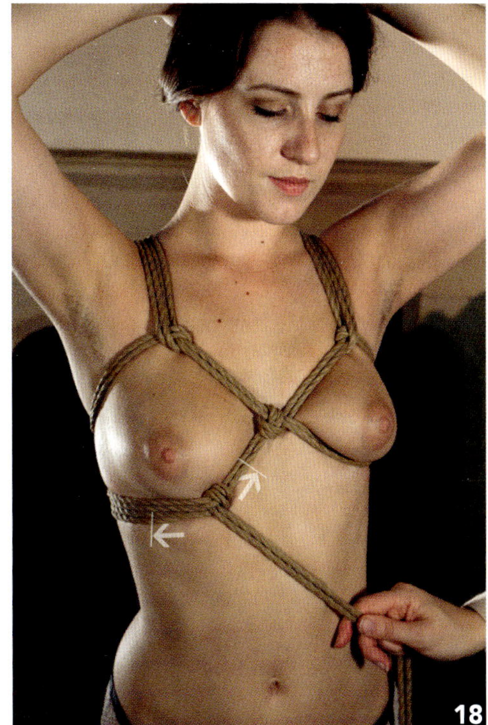

18

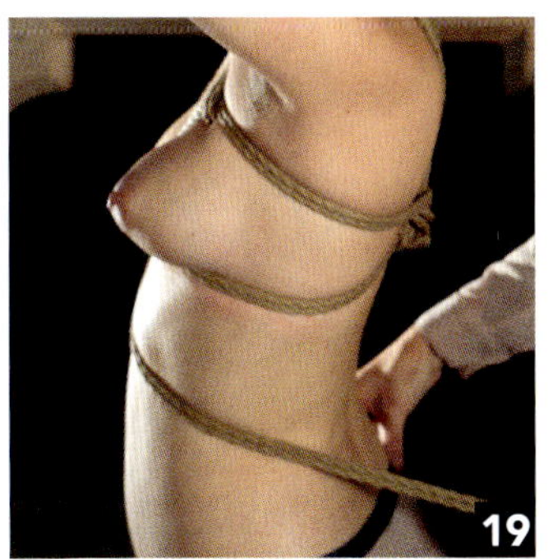

19

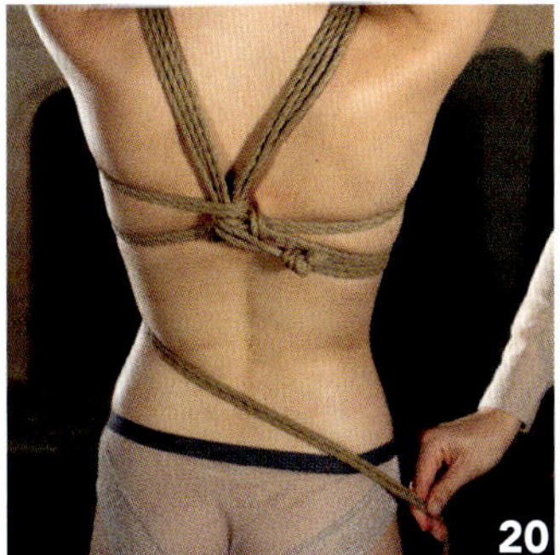

20

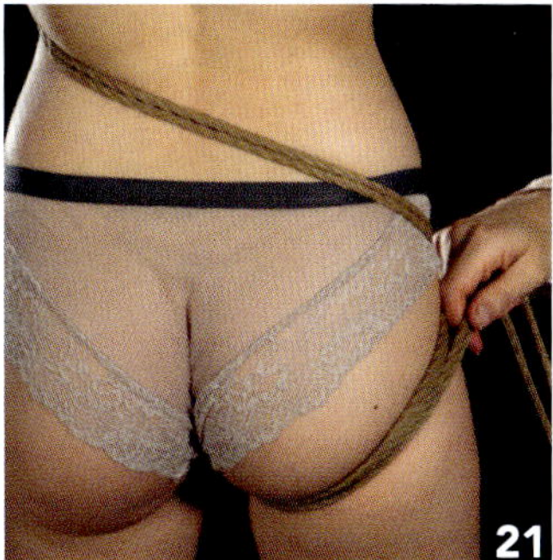

21

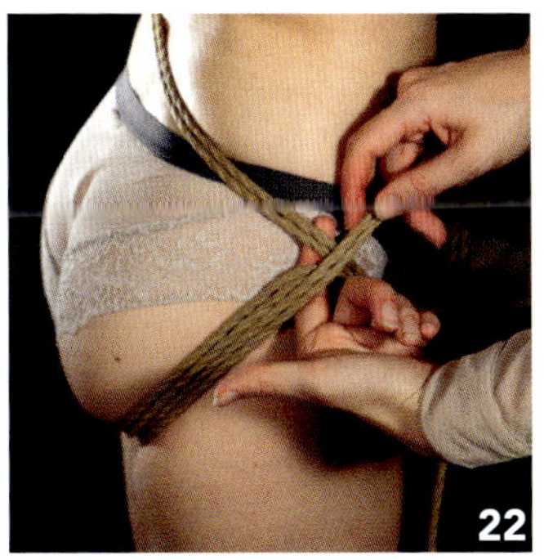

22

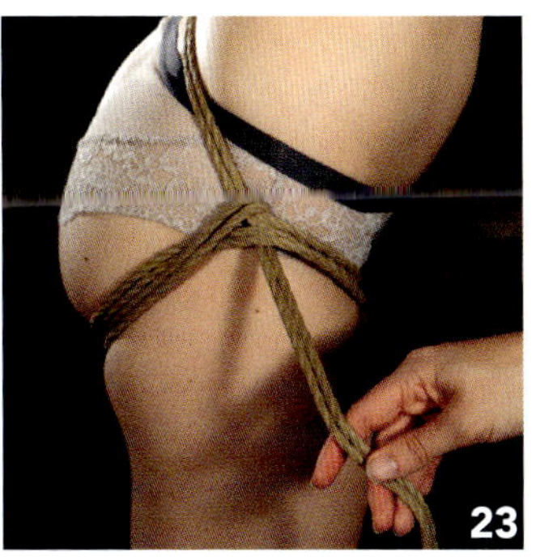

23

[19, 20] Continue the spiral across the back and **[21]** make two wraps around the top of the thigh, from front to back and from the outside of the hip to the inside of the leg.

[22, 23] Slightly loosen the wrap and pull upwards into a gentle 'V' shape. Hook the working end over and under both wraps.

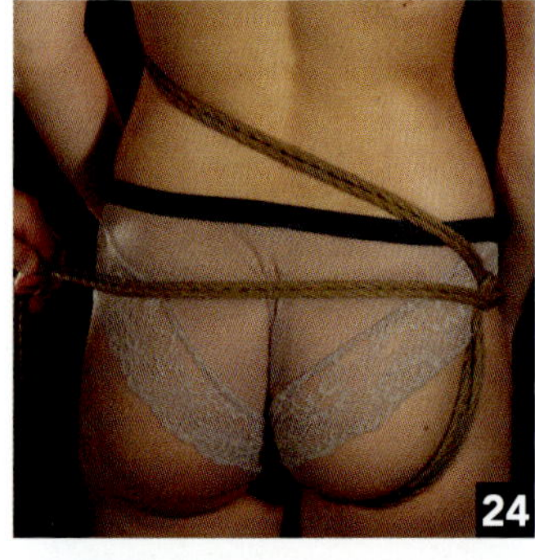

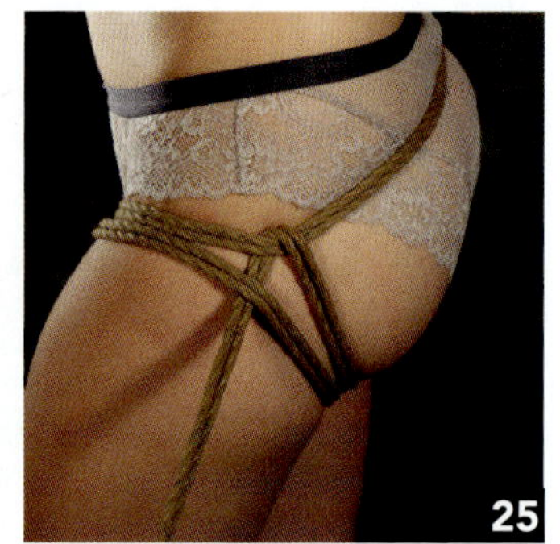

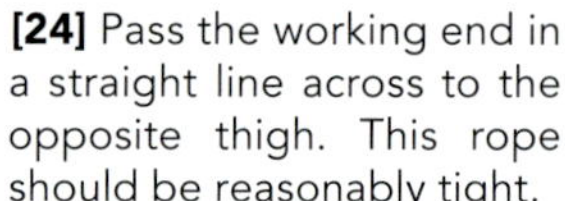

[24] Pass the working end in a straight line across to the opposite thigh. This rope should be reasonably tight.

[25] Repeat steps 21-23 to make a wrap around the other thigh.

[26] Pass the working end to the centre of the back and hook it under both the crossing lines, from top to bottom. Pull the higher line downwards to meet the lower one.

[27] Create a no-dome to fix the crossing lines together.

[28-30] Pass the working end back around to the front, symmetrical to the one on the other side and make a no-dome in the centre, where the two ropes cross.

[31, 32] Make a half hitch on the wrap underneath the pectoral muscle, symmetrical to the one on the other side.

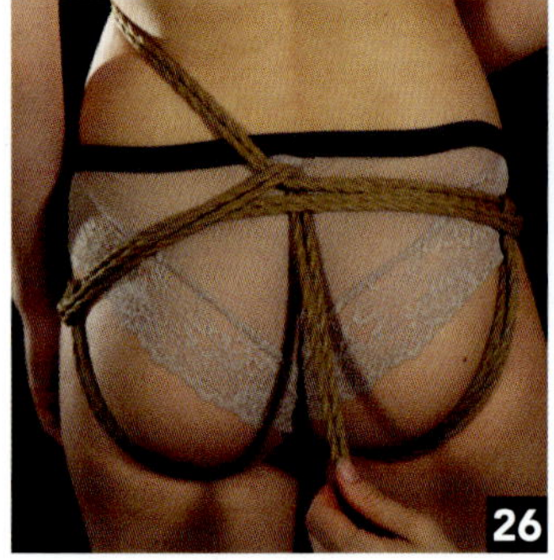

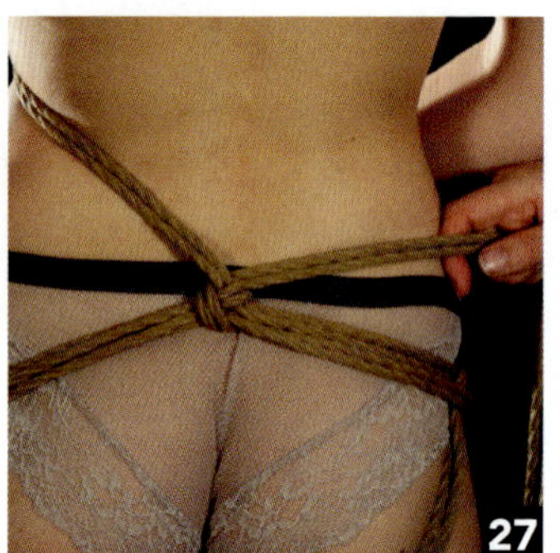

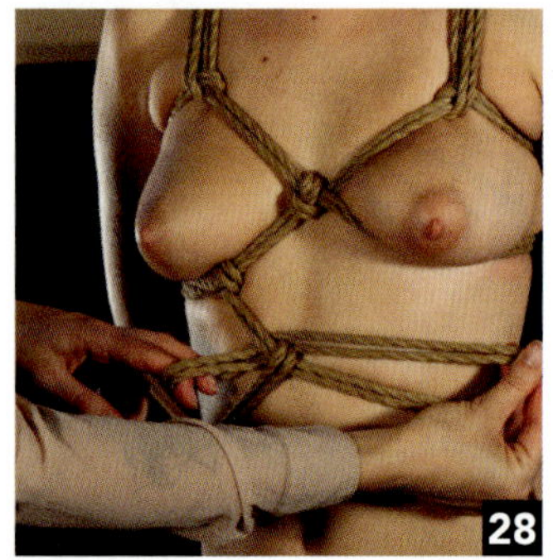

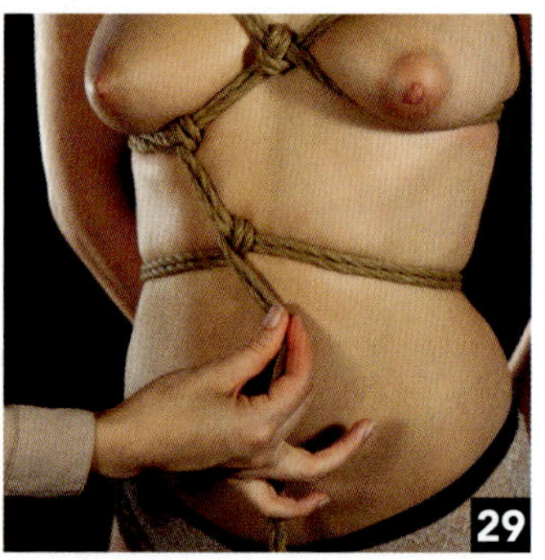

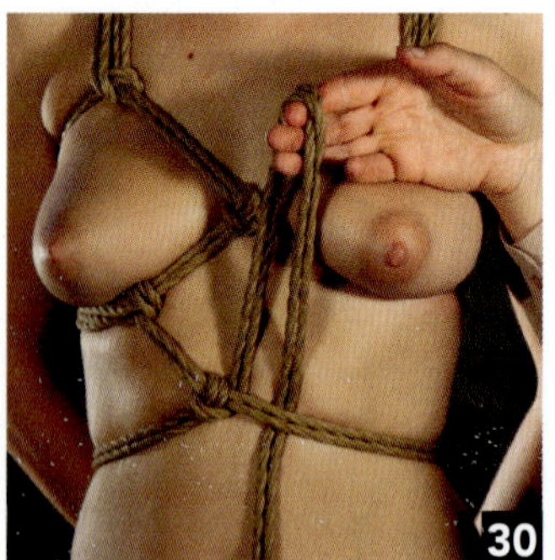

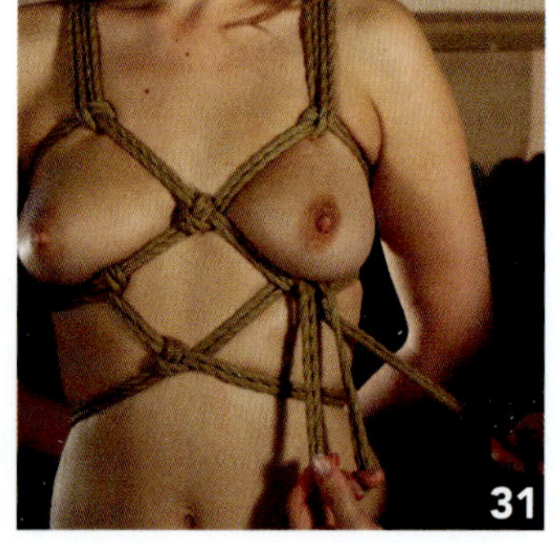

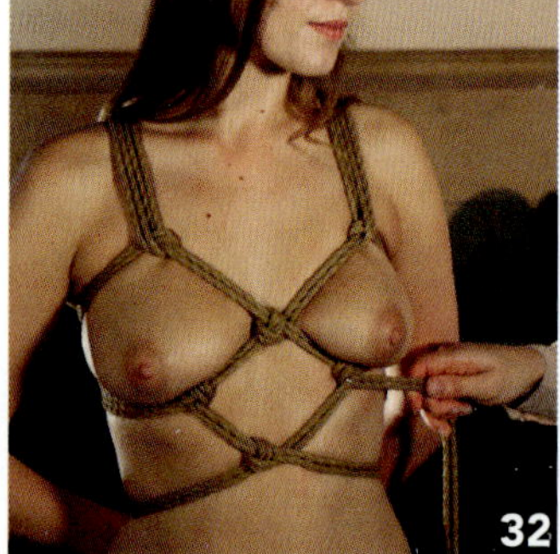

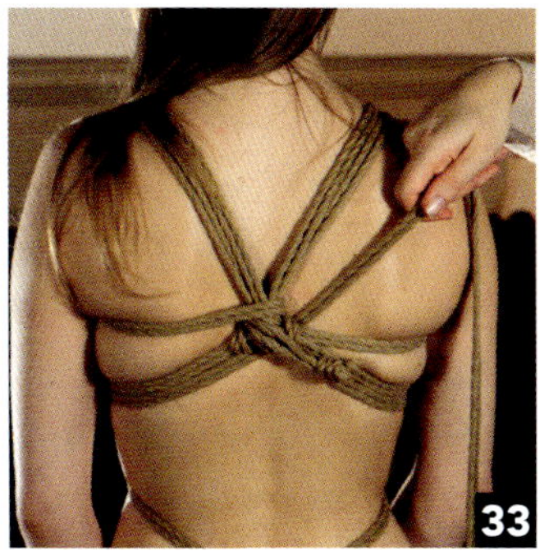

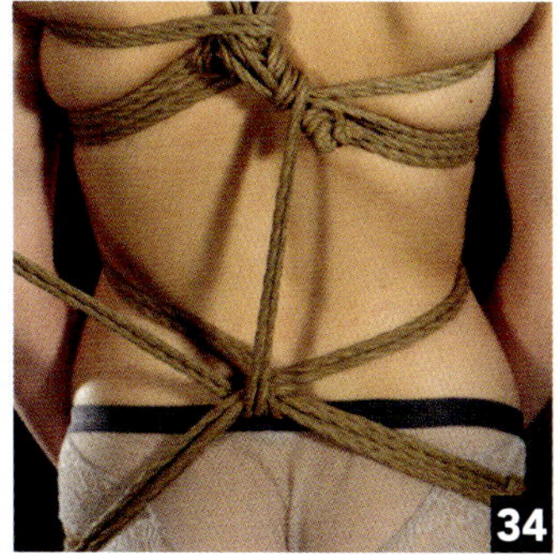

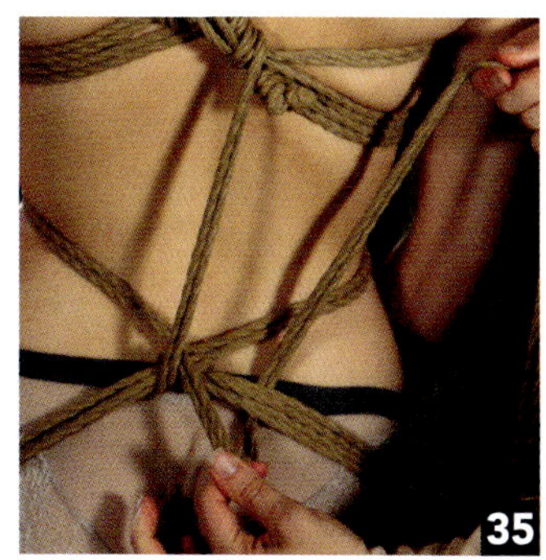

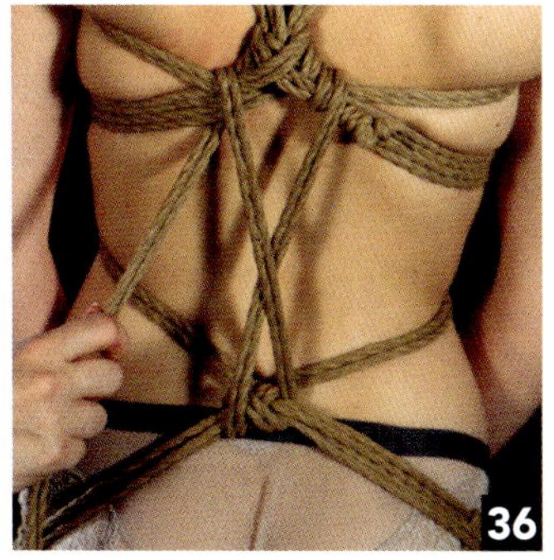

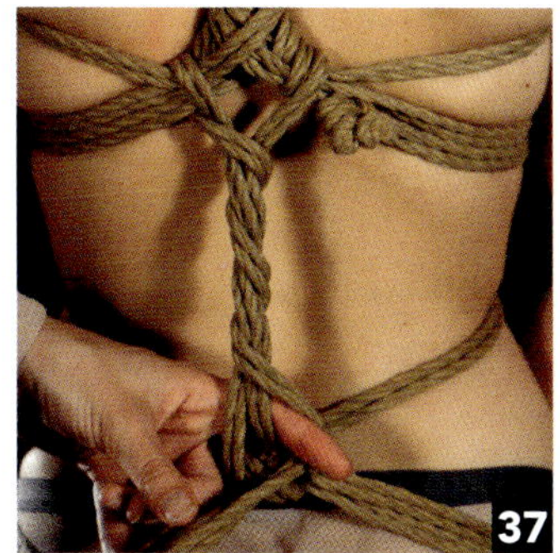

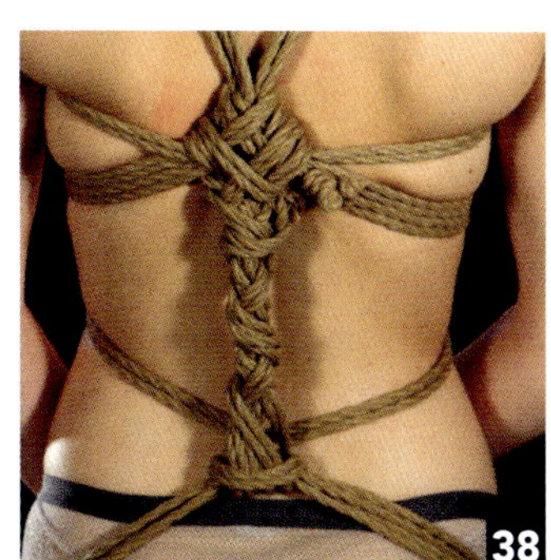

[33] Follow the wrap around to the centre of the back and pass under the central point.

[34] Take the working end down and hook it around the hip rope on the opposite side that you just came from. Pull a little bit of tension in this.

[35] Wrap around to the opposite side.

[36] Pass the working end back up and hook it around the top wraps at the opposite side. This should have created an 'X' shape. Make sure the tension is equal on both sides.

[37, 38] Use whatever rope you have left over to wrap up and down, reinforcing this new central stem that you've just created. Making it solid will help ensure that some of the tension is distributed onto the thighs when in vertical positions.

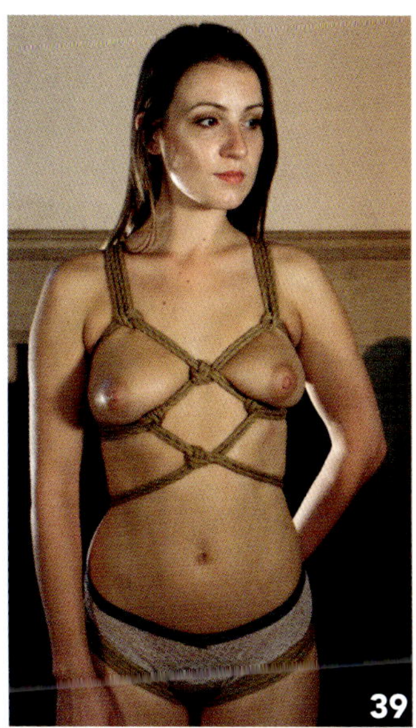

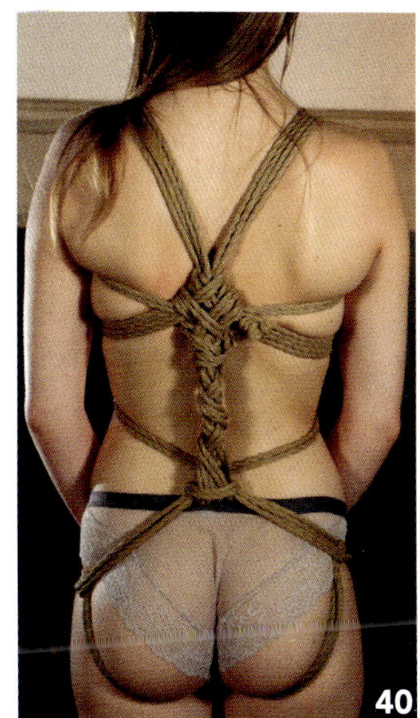

[39] Finished tie: front view.

[40] Finished tie: back view.

Attachment Points

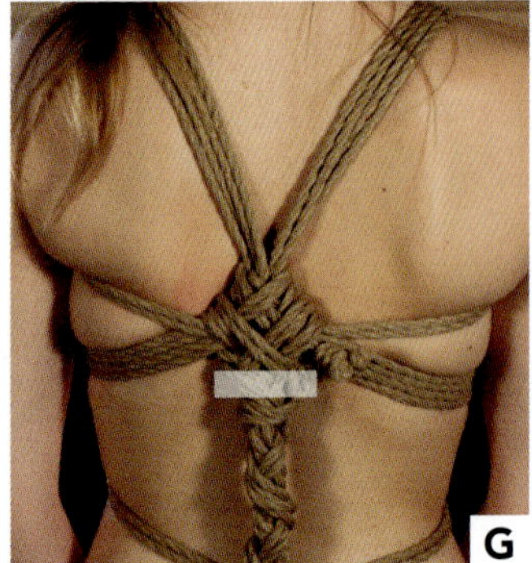
G

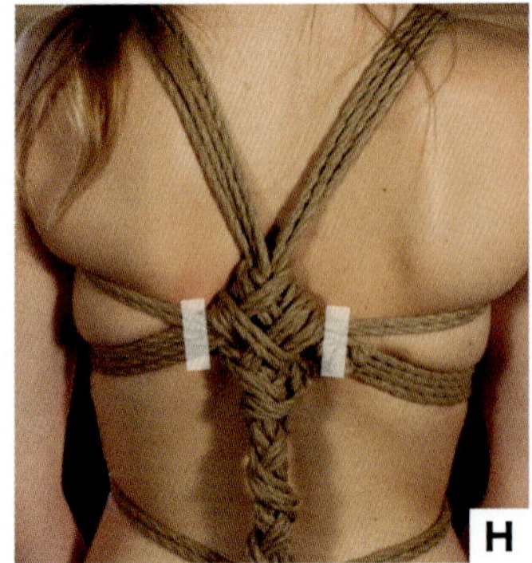
H

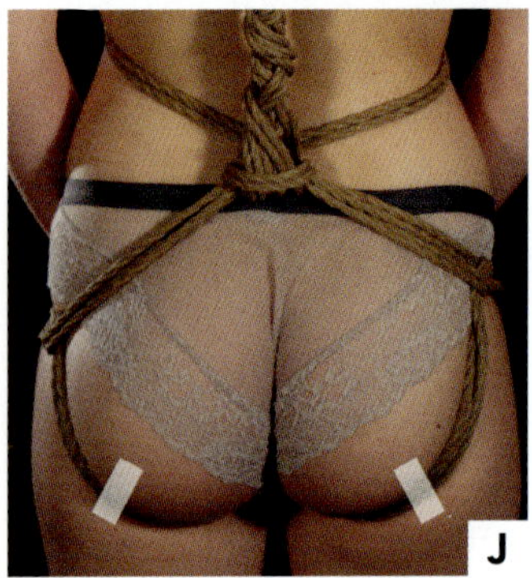
J

When attaching to the back of this harness you can use:

[G] A single column (pg. 107), compacted tightly at the top of the thick central stem. If you are doing a suspension where the body is in an upright, vertical position then the strong central stem should mean that some of the load is automatically distributed to the leg wraps.

[H] An ypsilon (spiral – pg. 108) around the horizontal chest wraps.

[J] If using this harness for face down suspension you can add hip support by threading the excess rope from the ankle lines under the leg wraps, rather than creating hojo cuffs (pg. 162).

[K] You can try tying the hands in many different positions when using this harness. One option is to tie the arms to a piece of bamboo after finishing the rest of the tie. Although changing the hand position won't alter how the harness functions, it may change the feeling in the chest.

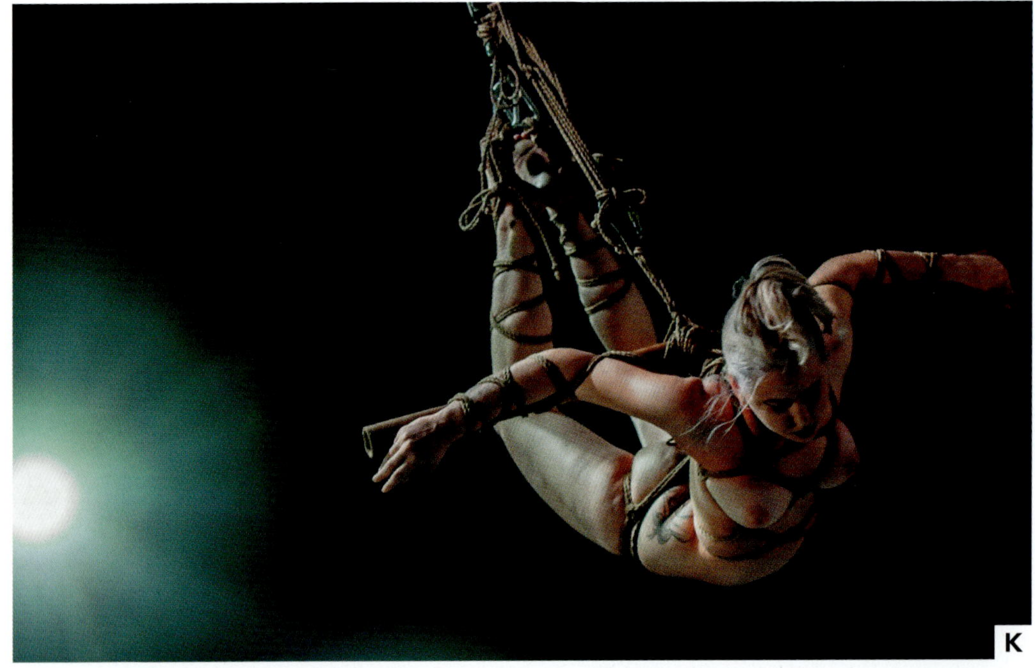
K

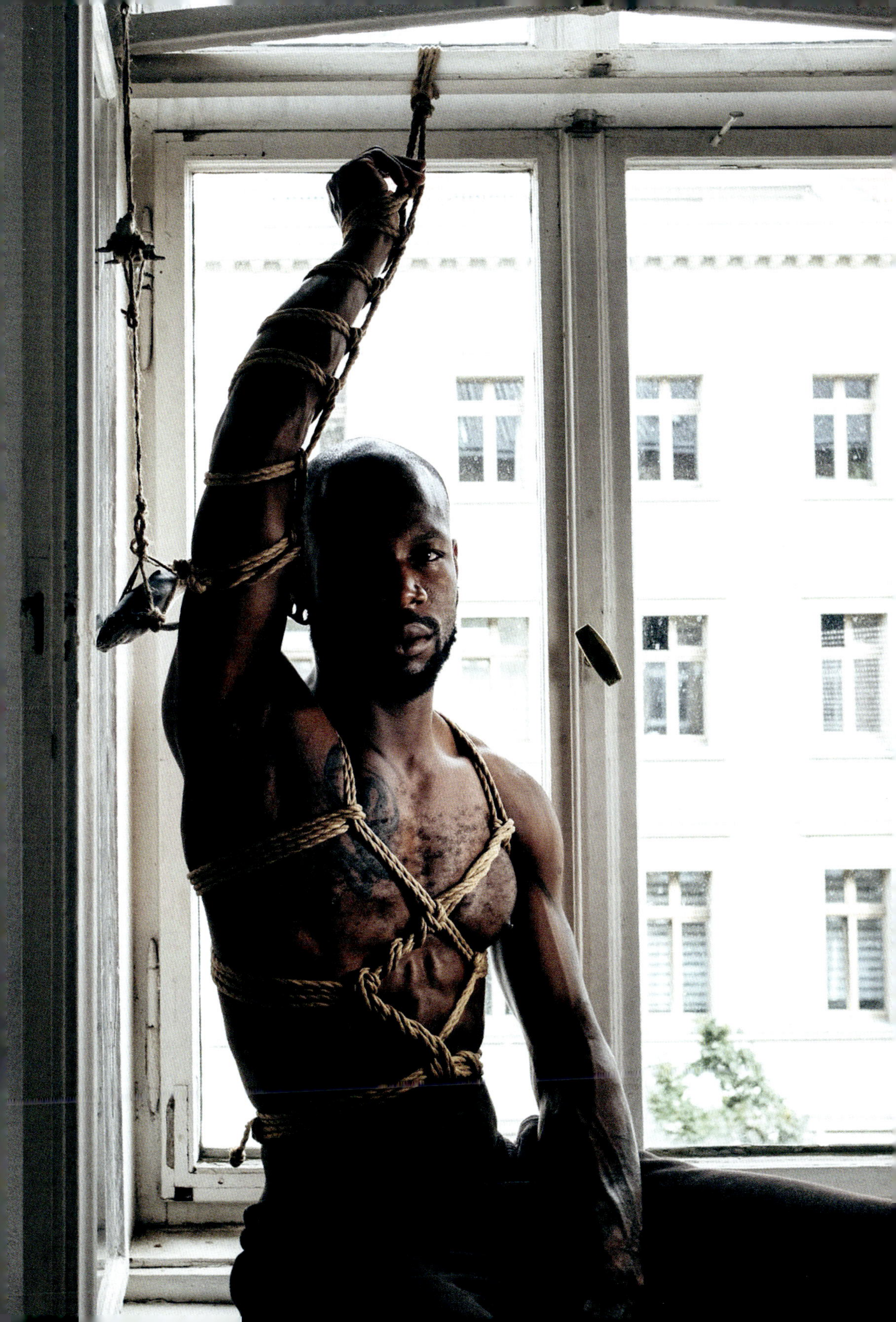

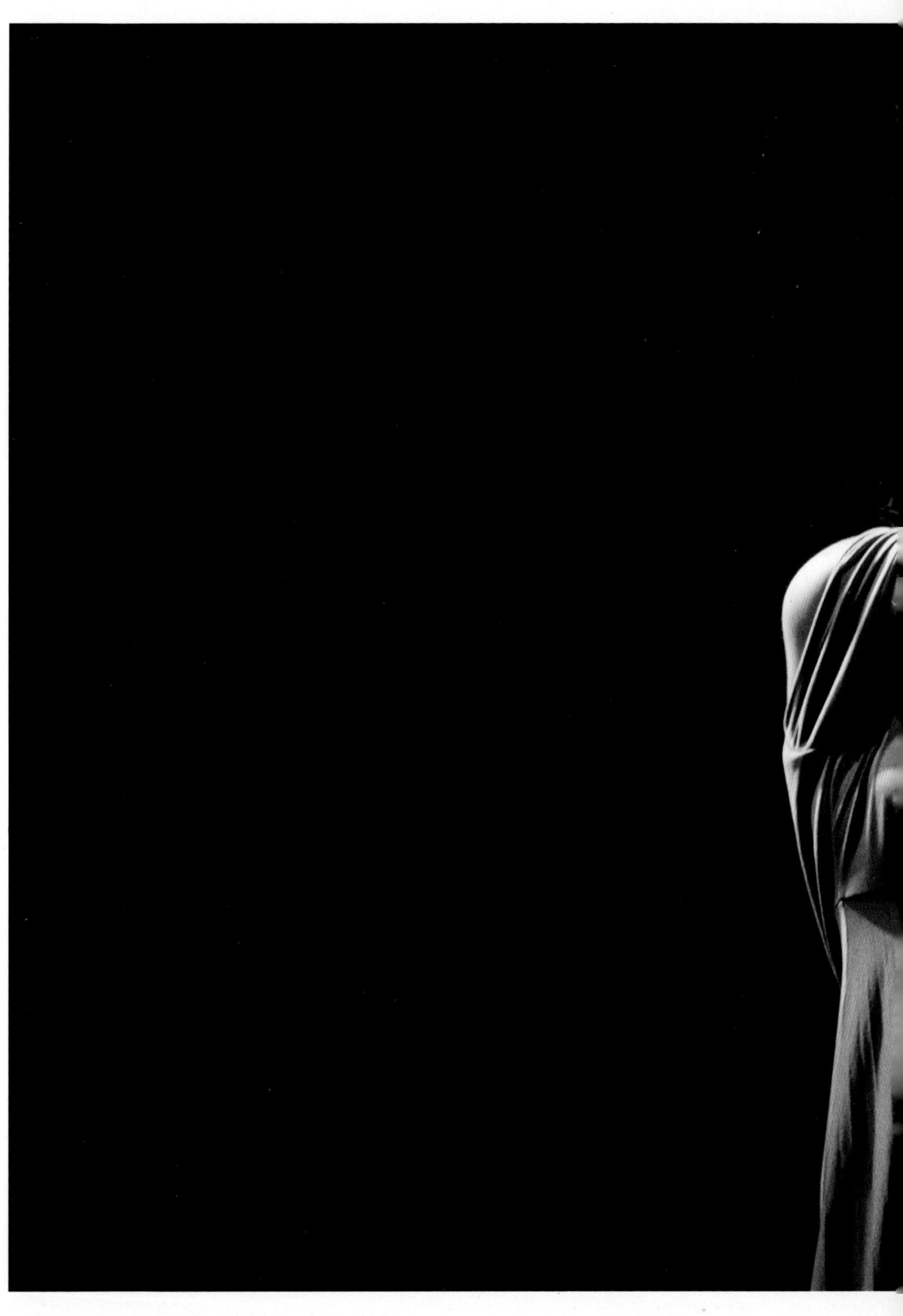

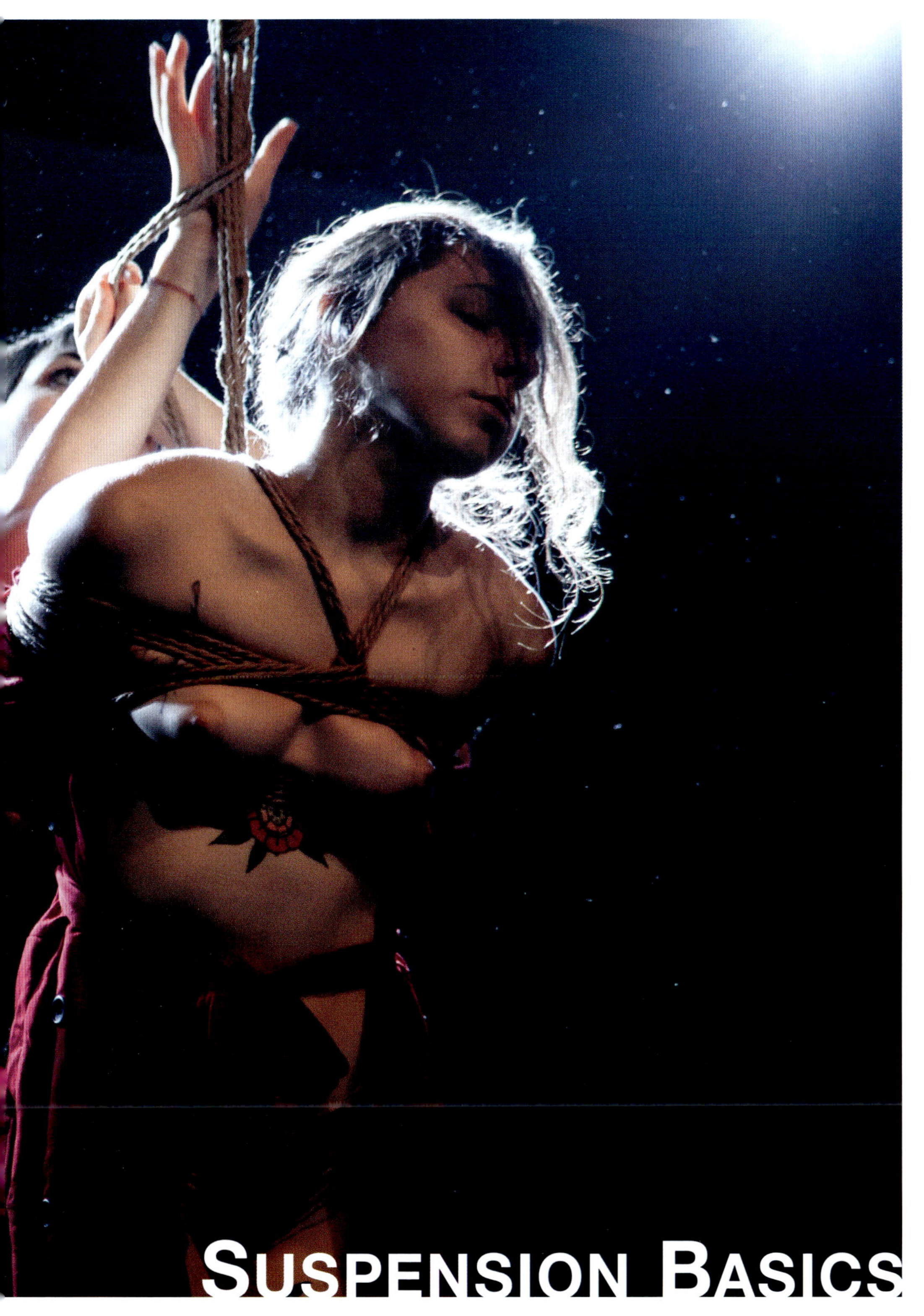

Suspension Basics

Suspension Basics

This chapter explains what I'd consider the absolute minimum knowledge of suspension hardware and line management techniques needed to perform basic static suspensions. Whilst I've gone into some detail on these things, I've not provided nearly enough information to perform more advanced suspensions or transitions safely.

I recommend reading 'Am I Ready to Suspend?' on pg. 12 if you haven't already.

This information is just as relevant for models as it is for riggers. Making informed decisions on the equipment you feel safe to be suspended from, and being able to judge a riggers knowledge and skill level is a part of defining your risk profile (pg. 18) and taking responsibility for your own safety. As with everything else, there are many possible 'right' ways to work so the information contained here can't be 100% comprehensive – but it will at least give you an idea of what to look out for and what kind of questions to ask if in doubt.

The Hardpoint

The hardpoint is whatever load bearing structure your suspension equipment (pg. 101) will be attached to. This could be hooks/bolts fixed directly into in the ceiling, a structural beam, or a suspension frame – which might either have been bought pre-made from specialist suppliers or custom built in situ, and will normally be made from wood, metal, or scaffolding.

In writing the following I have sought the advice of a range of qualified specialists. It is intended to act as a guide to assessing whether a hardpoint is suspension worthy before you use it. None of the information given here should be taken as advice on how to install a hardpoint yourself; if this is something you're thinking of doing then you need to get a professional to assess the structure of your building and install it for you.*

To assess a hardpoint you can first make a basic visual inspection – which will give you an idea of what questions you may need to ask the person responsible (such as the venue owner). In some cases you may be able to perform a basic weight test on it yourself.

How Strong Does a Hardpoint Need to Be?

A hardpoint installed or certified by a qualified engineer can be given a load rating, telling you exactly how much weight it is safe to suspend from there.

As a general rule of thumb your **minimum** working load limit (WLL) should be at approximately 4 times the weight you are actually planning to suspend from it (so, if you want to suspend a 60kg model, you should have a WLL of around 240kg). A working load limit takes into account an additional factor of 4, so a 240kg WLL will actually have a breaking point of around 960kg.

This might seem like a lot but in this case the 60kg weight of the model is what is

* If you're worried about the need to be discreet you can try asking around in your local rope community to find someone with the necessary qualifications who already understands the requirements, and won't need to ask difficult questions about what it's for.

referred to as **static load**, i.e. the weight exerted on the point when the model is hanging completely still. When performing suspensions you also need to account for **dynamic load**: which is the considerable additional force exerted by acceleration or deceleration; such as lifting, lowering, swinging, or dropping motions.

However there are further factors to consider when deciding a suitable load rating for a hardpoint, which could include:

- ◊ The amount of time it's been installed – in some venues the hardpoint could have been in use for many years.
- ◊ How frequently it's used.
- ◊ What kind of things it's used for; there will be a big difference in the forces exerted from gentle static suspension, and aerial circus.
- ◊ How frequently it is possible to inspect it within that time; if the point is difficult to access, such as in a venue with very high ceilings, you can't assume that it's examined in detail on a regular basis.
- ◊ The surrounding environment; are there changes in temperature or humidity which could affect the materials.

In order to account for general wear and tear, environmental factors, and possible misuse it's sensible have a WLL of 1000kg in any venue where the point is used over a long period of time. This figure is a standard in many commercial industries.

> People often ask why the hardpoint needs such a high load rating when the rope itself is nowhere near as strong.
>
> Whilst the same hardpoint is often left in place and used over many years, your rope should be considered a consumable item and replaced frequently if you are practicing suspensions. You should also be inspecting it often for signs of wear, and treating it to maintain a good condition (pg. 23).
>
> Slings and carabiners could also be considered consumable items.

What to Look for

1. LOOK AT THE MATERIALS USED

CONCRETE is brittle and can fail without warning or any prior deformation. You may wish to avoid a point installed in a concrete ceiling if you aren't confident knowing what to look for.

If you are using a concrete ceiling there should be a minimum of 2 or 3 fasteners (generally made of steel) of at least 12mm in diameter, spaced at about 20cm apart. A chemical fastener (eg. epoxy resin) is stronger than a mechanical fastener. A plate screwed into the concrete with multiple bolts is also a good option. Wrapping a load rated sling around a structural concrete beam can also be ok.

WOOD/STEEL (and also bamboo!) are preferable to concrete as they can bend, crack or otherwise deform before breaking, giving you some warning.

If the hardpoint is in the form of an exposed beam then once again the easiest option is probably to wrap a load rated sling around it. However, in many situations this may not be practical and so once again, you'll be looking out for a secure steel bolt, preferably passing horizontally through the beam. When this is not possible you can once again look out for a system of two steel bolts set vertically into the beam. Ideally these need to pass all the way through the beam and be secured with a plate/washer and lock nut on the other side.

2. LOOK AT THEIR CONDITION

Check that the fasteners are screwed all the way in and that they aren't going in at an angle. Look for fraying, metal chips, rusted metal, signs of wear or distortion. Also look for any breakouts near the fastener, or any cracks elsewhere in the ceiling.

3. LOOK AT THE STRUCTURE

Any beam that a hardpoint is attached to should load from the structural foundations that hold the building together.*

In the case of having two or more fasteners securing the structure they could be attached in **[A]** one of these ways. In this

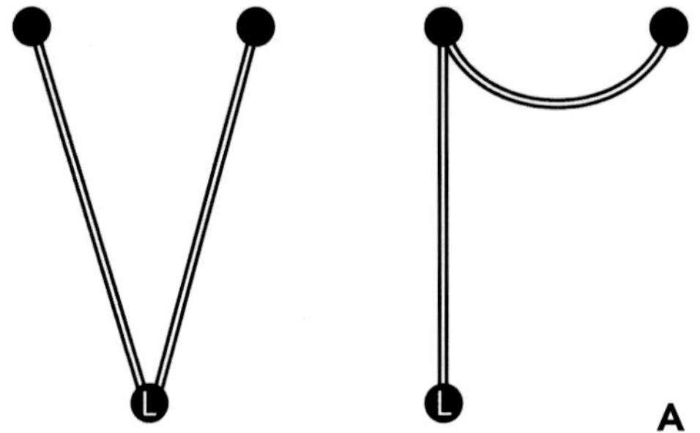

example, on the left the load (L) is equally distributed between all points, so each point individually is less likely to fail. On the right the main point takes all the load but there are unloaded safety points in place should it fail – bear in mind that, if this were to happen, the remaining point(s) could be shock loaded which could potentially cause a second failure.

In the example on the left, you should also pay attention that the points are not set so far apart that the **[B]** point at which the two connecting ropes meet has an angle

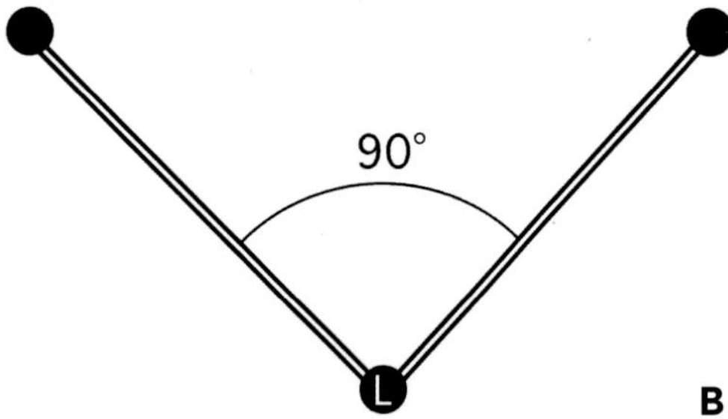

of more than 90° as this causes the load on each point to increase, rather than be spread between them. If the angle between the two points is 0° (or close to 0°) both points will be equally loaded with 50% of the models weight supported on each point – so a 60kg model will load each of the points with 30kg. At 90° each point is already taking 70% of the model's weight – so a 60kg model will load each point with 42kg and this increases exponentially. By the time you reach 120° each point will be taking 100% of the weight (60kg), and at 150° it will take 200% (120kg) per point etc.

In terms of rock climbing 90° is considered

Asking the Right Questions

The person in charge of the venue should be knowledgeable of how their equipment works and happy to answer your questions. Anyone who seems dismissive or unable to give clear, confident answers should be a cause for concern.

Questions you could consider asking:

- ◊ Can you tell me how this works?
- ◊ What materials is this made of?
- ◊ Do you know how long ago it was installed?
- ◊ What do you typically use it for (eg. partial suspensions, aerial circus classes)?
- ◊ How often do you test it?
- ◊ Do you know what temperatures

* In some cases, you won't be able to see the structure of the building itself, or the material that the hardpoint is made of (for example, if the beams are covered with plaster or otherwise obscured) - in this case the best option is to ask the person responsible for the venue for clarification.

(caused by either weather or friction) these points are exposed to? Do you know how this might affect the materials used?

- Do you know how this building was constructed?
- Who installed these points, and what were their qualifications?
- Has the point been rated or certified by an engineer?
- What's the dynamic load of the hardpoint?
- Do you have inspection records?
- Is it made from rated construction materials/climbing gear?

Testing the Point

Once you've gathered as much information as possible from asking questions and visual assessment, the last thing you can do if still unsure is to test the point by putting weight on it.

You can do this by holding onto the point yourself and loading it; first gently and then swinging from it. If possible, do this with the weight of several people simultaneously.

This test is mostly useful on a hardpoint made of metal or wood as you should be able to see if something isn't right before they actually begin to break – so look out for bend, movement or torque. You can also listen out to the sound it makes – in the case of wood, some creaking is not a bad thing – and look to see if any debris falls from the point.

> **Tip**
>
> You can also perform a slightly more gentle version of this swing test if you are using a tripod frame (that is, one with 3 legs that is usually designed to be light and portable), to make sure that it's pinned/weighted to the ground properly and can't fall over.

Suspension Equipment

Your suspension equipment hangs from the hardpoint and is what you will be attaching your suspension lines to (pg. 106). It could be in the form of carabiners, a ring, or a piece of bamboo.

The advantages of using bamboo are that you can leave a good distance between each of your suspension lines making it easier not to get them jammed or tangled together. It also gives you more flexibility in the kind of shapes it's possible to make as you can choose to pull lines in closer together (mimicking the effect of suspending from a ring) or space them further apart. This is not just an aesthetic difference: when suspension lines meet at a central point they create a triangular shape meaning that the body will be very compressed if the distance between it and the suspension point is small. Bamboo can also be easier to work with as you don't have to compensate for spinning and swinging – some models also find this stillness more comfortable. The downsides of working with bamboo are that it's not very portable and not every venue has the space available to hang them (as they effectively take up two hardpoints rather than one). Bamboo in good condition is very strong – but I would still generally look for a bamboo of around 1.5m in length to have a minimum diameter of 8cm. The strongest points are at the ridges so I tend to make the hardpoint attachments on these areas (pg. 104). Like rope, it is a natural material and can start to weaken or crack over time particularly if left in hot, dry, conditions and not properly treated.

Using a ring (made from either wood or metal) or carabiners means that your equipment will be much more portable than bamboo, and easier/quicker to set up. It also gives you the freedom to play with movement such as spinning. I personally prefer using carabiners over rings because they're easier to arrange exactly how I need them to prevent jamming when I have a complex formation of multiple suspension lines. Using a **[D]** combination of a small ring and carabiners can also help to prevent jamming. Load rated carabiners can be bought from any climbing store. Rings are often made specially for bondage so you will have to ask the manufacturer for their load rating.

Attaching Rings/Carabiners

Rings and carabiners can be **[C]** attached to your hardpoint with a piece of rope. I use the same method that I use to attach a main line (pg. 107-114). Some people prefer to use a synthetically reinforced rope such as hempex for this.

[D] Alternatively, you can use a climbing sling which, like carabiners, are widely available at climbing shops and are load rated. Although they tend to be rated far above anything you would ever need in normal usage, it's worth being aware that **[E]** the way you use them can have an effect on their strength.

[F] As a beginner – I would recommend that you don't set your ring/carabiners any higher than you can comfortably reach with your fingers when standing in a relaxed, flat footed position.

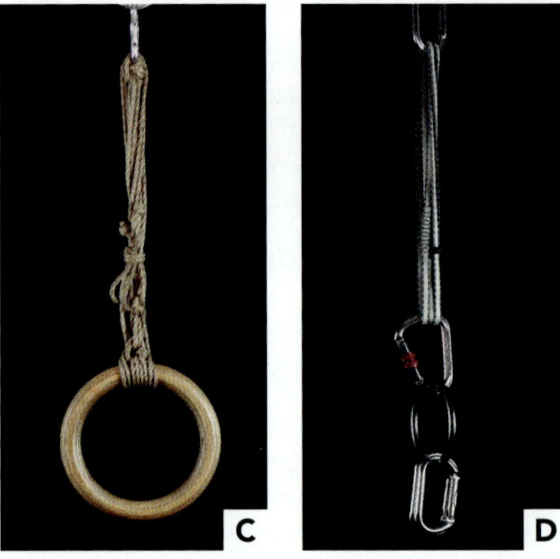

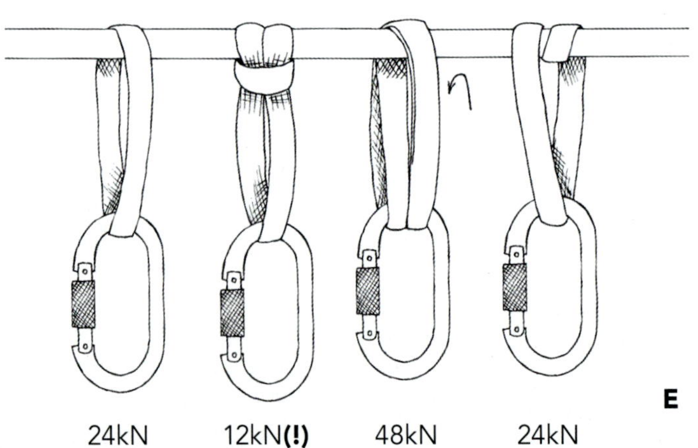

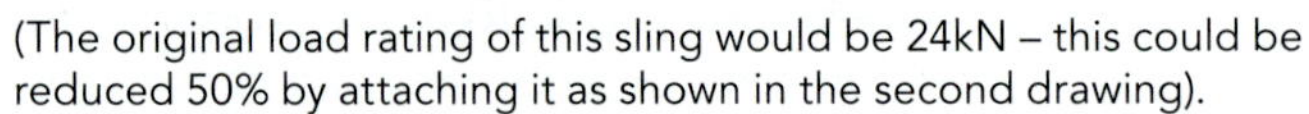

(The original load rating of this sling would be 24kN – this could be reduced 50% by attaching it as shown in the second drawing).

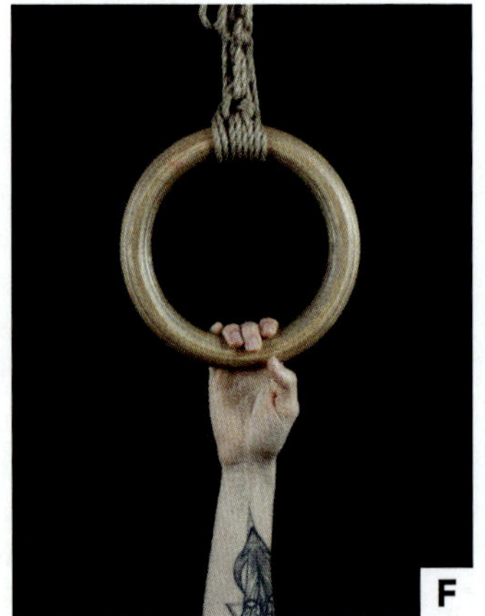

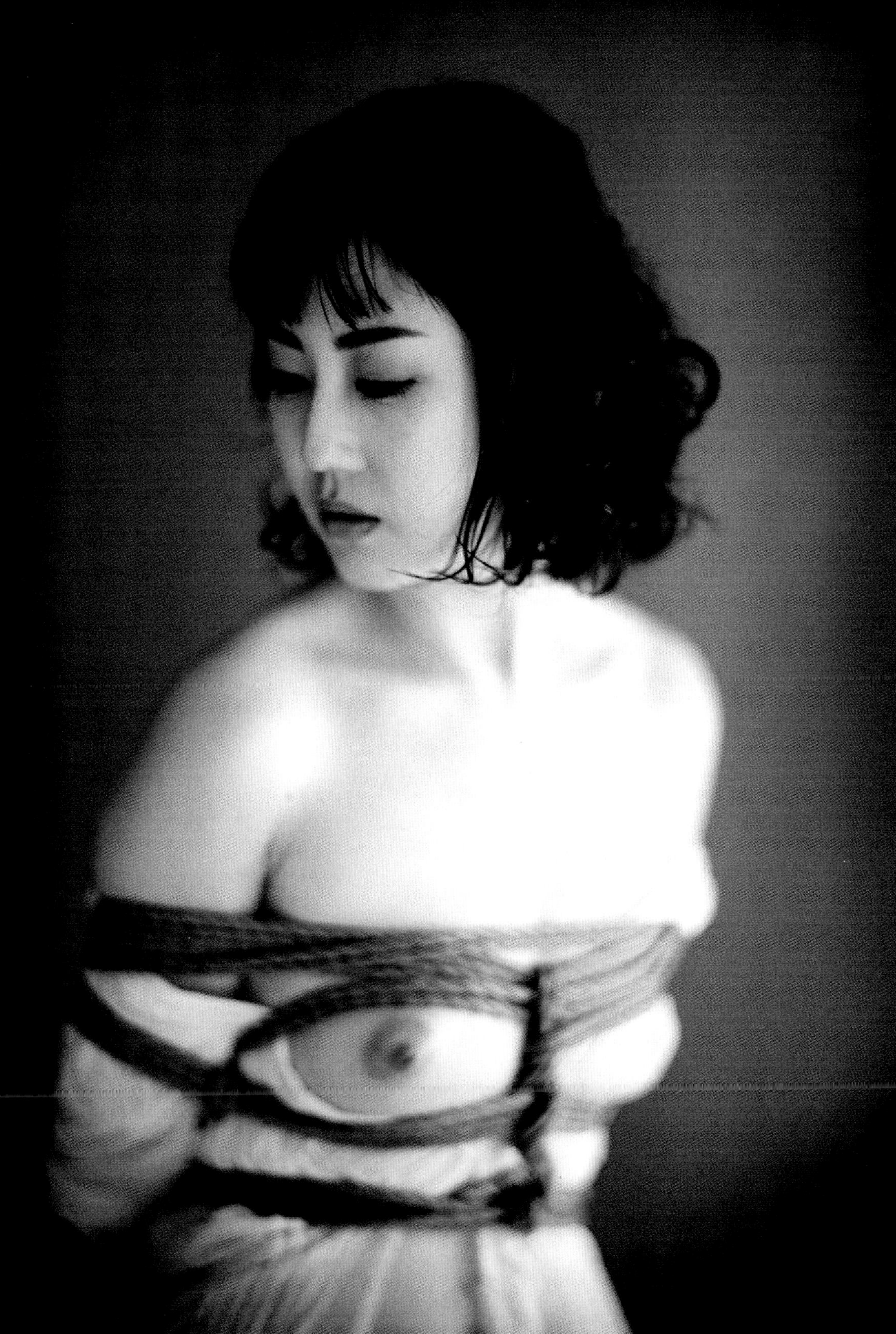

Attaching Bamboo

Tying bamboo to a hardpoint can be less straightforward than attaching a ring/carabiner, and I often see methods used that put undue strain on the ropes. This is one method that should be easily replicable.

[1 - 3] Tie a single column tie (pg. 27) tightly around the bamboo. Aim to put it on (or just to the centre of) the first ridge to help prevent sliding.

[4, 5] Add a double bight (pg. 109), and pass the working end up to your hardpoint, then back down and through the bight.

[6] Temporarily lock your line at the bottom (pg. 115) and repeat this process at the other end of the bamboo.

[7] Take a moment to check your bamboo is level and at a good height for you – adjust as necessary.

[8] Generally, it's best not to place the bamboo higher than you can comfortably reach your hand over.

[9-10] Undo the temporary lock and take the working end back up to the hardpoint to lock as you would a normal suspension line using a 360° friction and half hitch (pg. 112-114).

[11] Pass the remainder of the working end back under the bamboo.

[12, 13] Make a 360° wrap around everything and **[14, 15]** secure the ropes together with a hojo cuff (pg. 31).

[16] Use up the remainder of the working end by passing it back over the hardpoint, and secure using an overhand lock (pg. 118). If your remaining rope is considerably longer, use it up by passing it up and down between the hardpoint and bamboo.

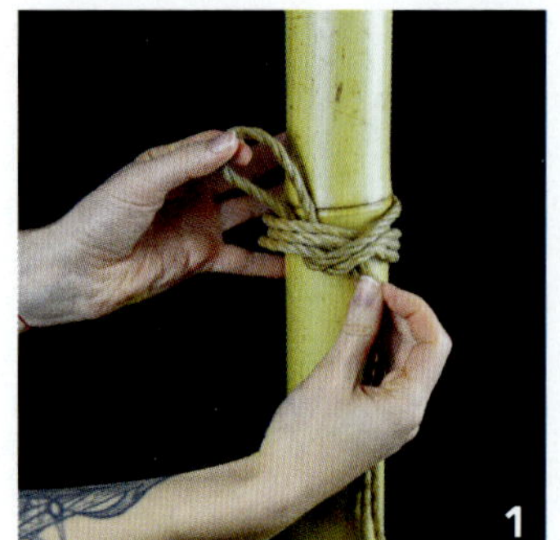

1

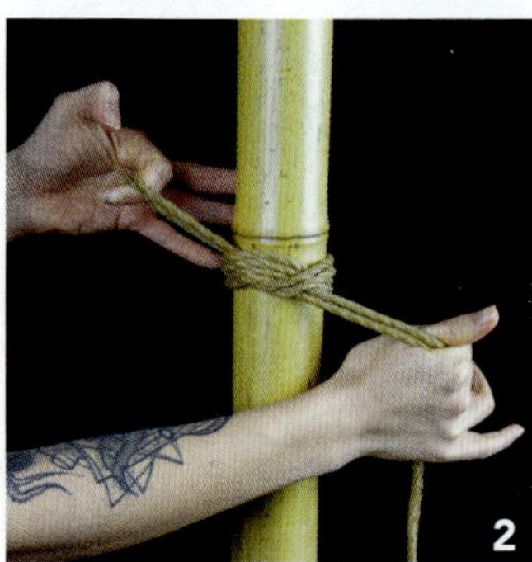

2

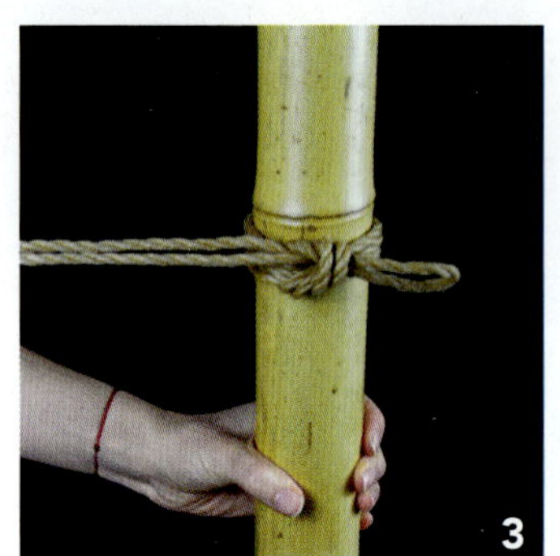

3

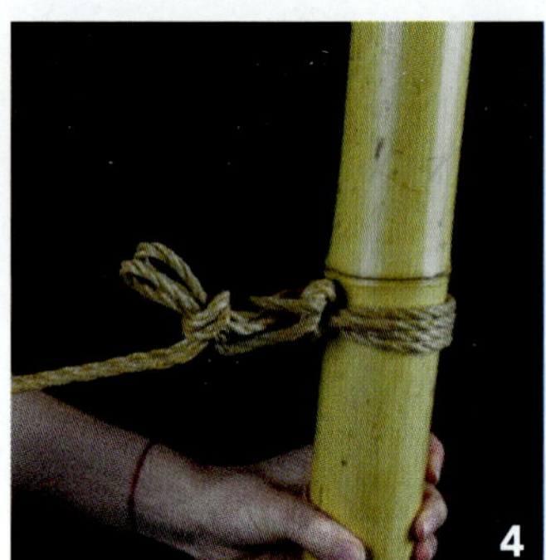

4

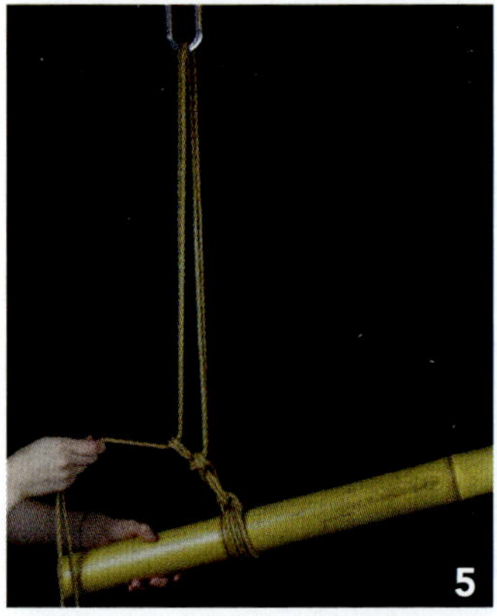

5

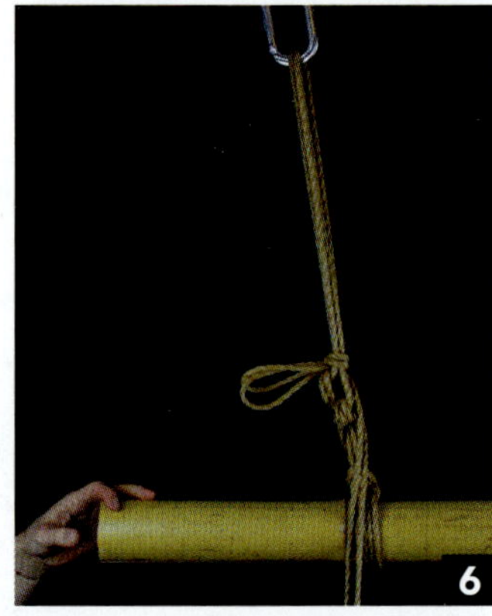

6

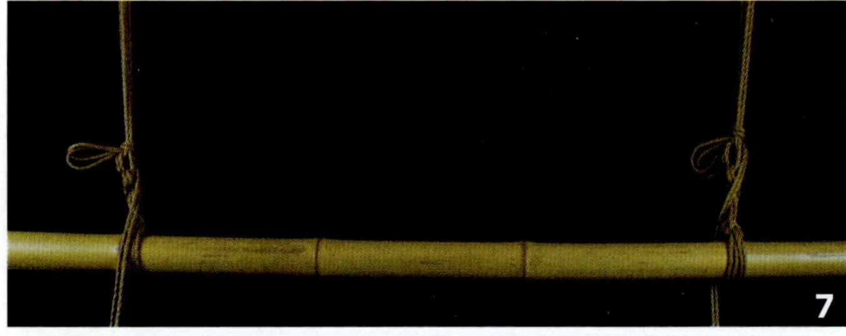

7

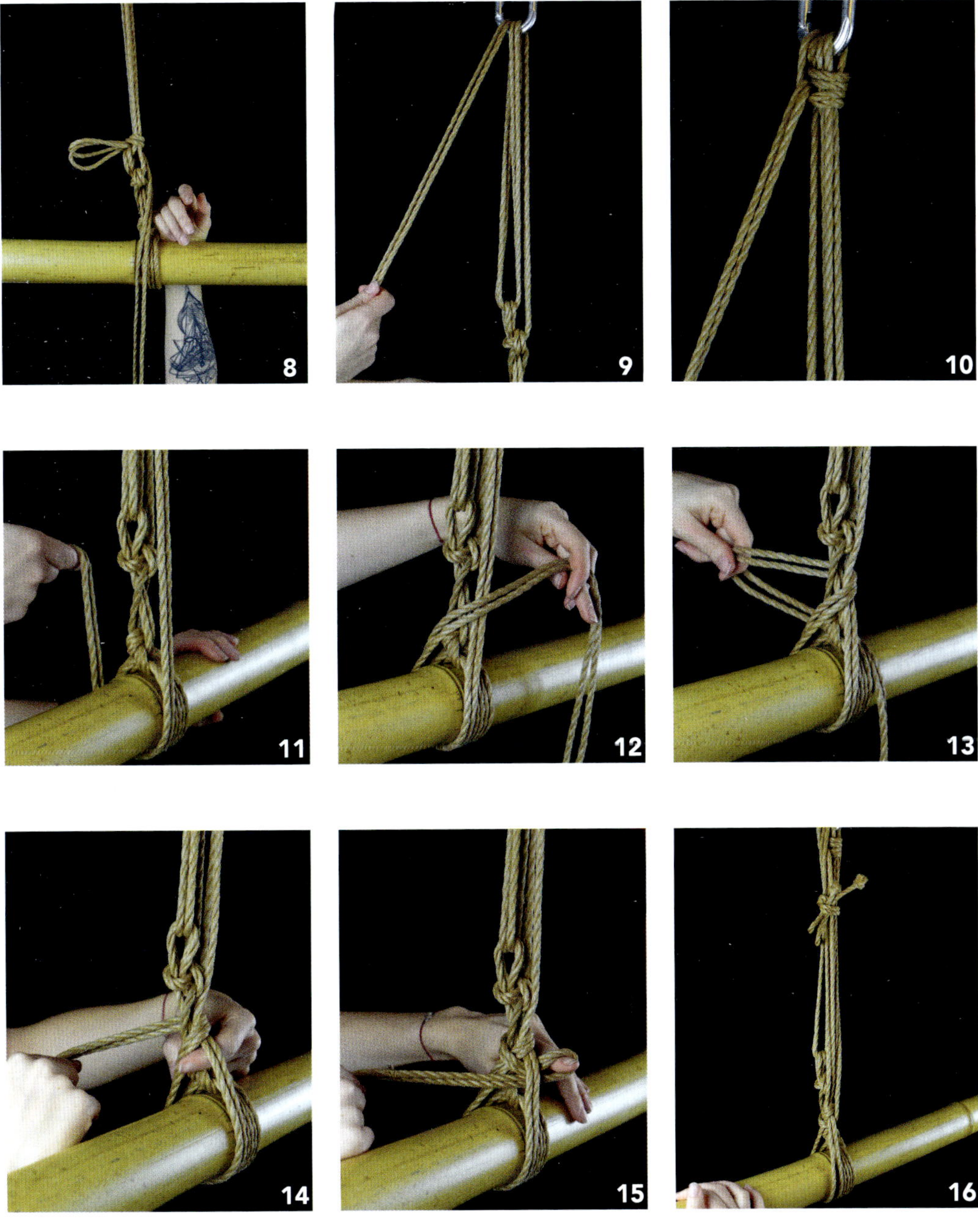
8
9
10
11
12
13
14
15
16

Suspension Lines

Suspension lines are the ropes connecting the body to the suspension point. You might also hear them called 'tsuri' lines.

You should have the whole process – attaching, raising, and locking, and more importantly unlocking, lowering, and removing – firmly lodged in your muscle memory. I recommend that you practice on a heavy object (e.g. a suitcase, bag, or box) before you practice on a real person. In addition to helping you memorise the locks themselves, this will also help with lifting and lowering smoothly so you don't jolt the model too much, ironing out the kind of common mistakes that lead to your lines becoming twisted and tangled, and understanding what it feels like to lock and unlock a line that's under tension. You can vary the weight of the objects that you practice on to see how that affects things, and I also like to practice lifting the objects to different heights in order to vary the amount of excess rope I have so that I can practice using it up efficiently (pg. 118).

Main Lines and Secondary Lines

I use the term 'main line' to refer to whichever line(s) is giving the most critical support, and 'secondary line' to refer to all other lines. Which line that is will change depending on the situation but normally it will be the one that's taking the most weight and/or the one that would, were it to slip, result in the most serious consequences. For example, in **[G]** the main line is attached to the takate kote, as it is holding the most weight (the torso), and could potentially result in an injury to the face/head were anything to go wrong with it. Whilst we obviously don't want anything to go wrong with the secondary lines (on the legs) either, this is less likely to cause a critical injury.

For the sake of safety, all of the full suspensions I have chosen to demonstrate in this book have the main line attached to the takate kote, and it will always be the **first** line you attach and the **last** line you undo, but if in the future you progress onto more advanced suspensions this won't always be the case. Getting into the habit of thinking about your main and secondary lines differently will be useful right from the very beginning.

I recommend using your strongest rope for the main line (pg. 23); some people

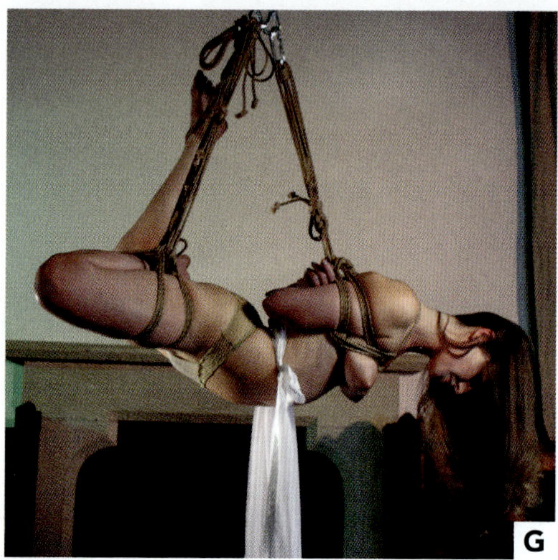

G

may even choose to use a synthetically reinforced line. You might find it useful to lock your main line slightly differently to the secondary lines – for example by putting an extra half hitch in – so that if you are untying quickly you know that you've come to the main line, and can pay extra care and attention to the situation. It is surprisingly easy to undo the wrong line if you're feeling panicked! Some types of lock are suitable for secondary lines but quite risky on main lines – the locking at the bottom technique (pg. 115) would be one example of this.

As a beginner, it's reasonably safe to experiment with simple transitions by adjusting the heights of your secondary lines to see how this might alter the tie, but I would advise against making any height adjustments to your main line until you have more training and experience than this book can offer.

Attaching Suspension Lines

There are many ways to attach suspension lines to the body dependant on the situation – these are the most common.

In the examples below I've shown them tied very loosely, leaving lots of space so you can see clearly – but in some cases you might want to collapse them down so they grip the harness more tightly.

Single Column

This is tied in exactly the same way as on pg. 27.

[1] It can be tied onto the stem/wraps of a harness or **[2]** directly onto the body and used as a suspension line. How tight it needs to be is situation dependent and will be addressed at the relevant parts in the book.

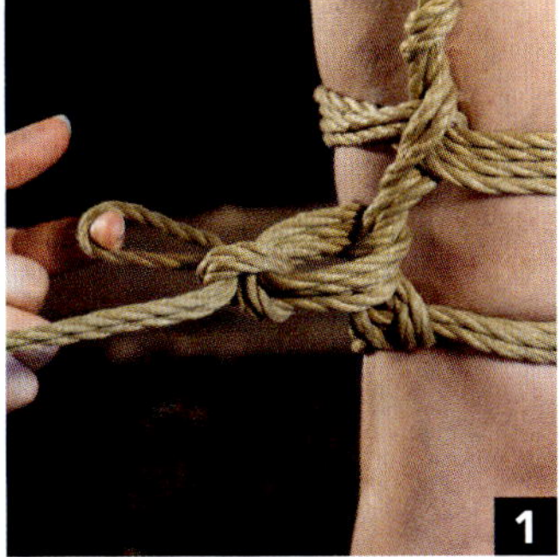
1

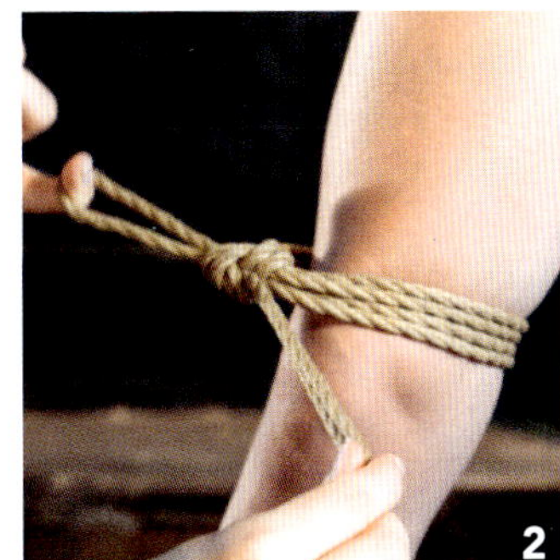
2

Ypsilon

An ypsilon (sometimes called 'Y-hanger') attachment is used when you want to load two points on a harness simultaneously. This type of ypsilon is used between two wraps, so that the load can be spread evenly whilst still maintaining the distance between them.

[1] Start by threading the bight under both wraps.

[2] Pull up the rope in-between the two wraps to create a loop.

[3, 4] Fold the bight and working end into the centre so that they line up parallel with the central loop.

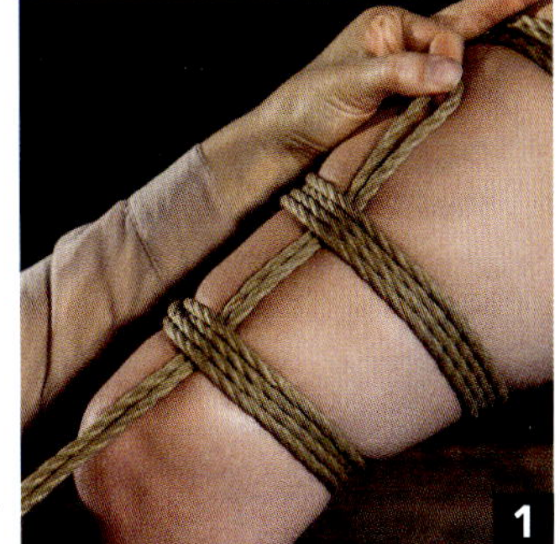
1

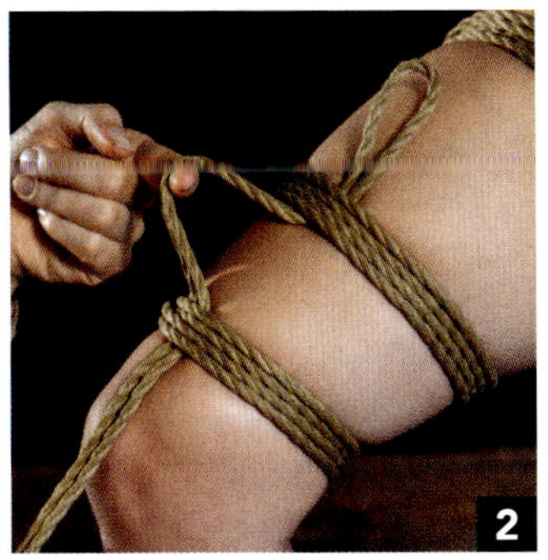
2

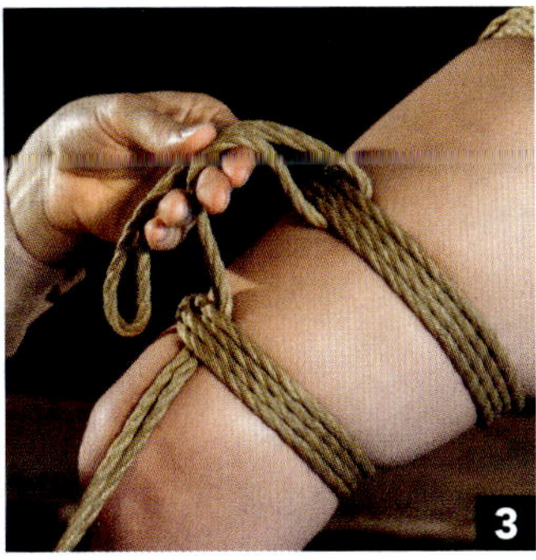
3

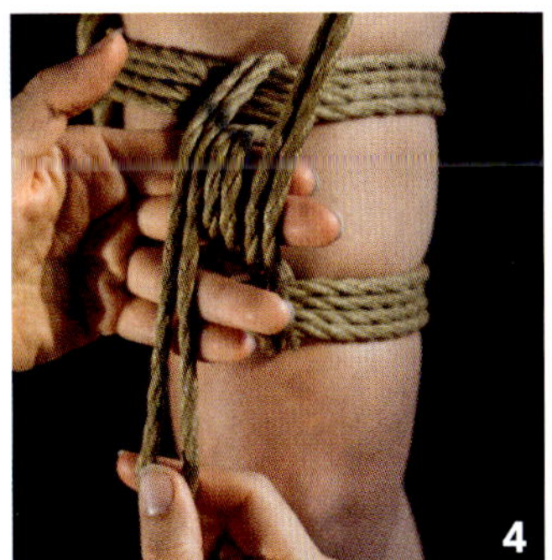
4

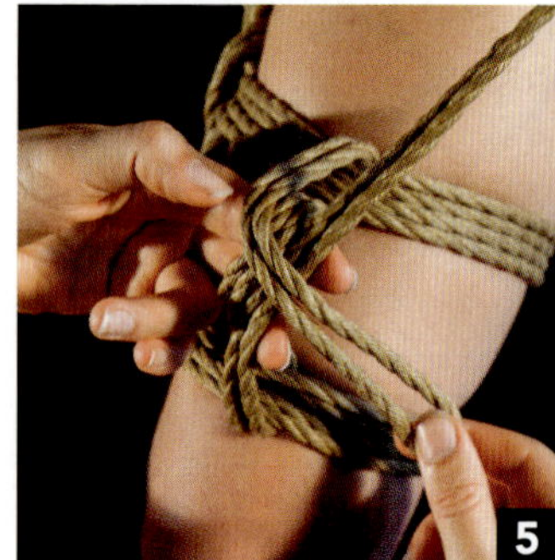
5

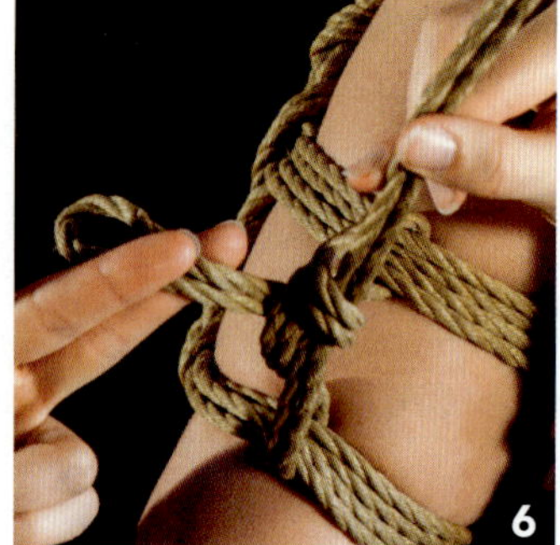
6

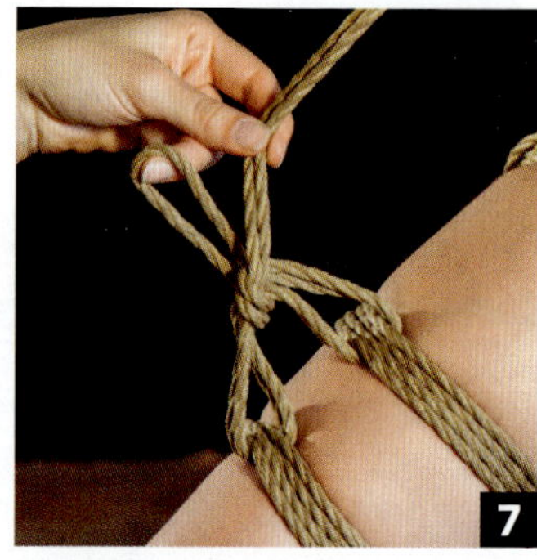
7

[5] Pass the bight over the top of both other ropes **[6]** then back underneath them, through the centre of the loop.

[7] You should now have something that looks like this. Take a moment to check that the tension is as you wish and adjust if necessary. If you're planning to collapse the ypsilon so it grips the harness you can do so now by pulling on the working end.

You can close this in the same way you would a single column tie.

[8] Create a U-turn with the working end.

[9] Pass the bight through the loop so that the working end is trapped in the centre.

[10] Pull tight to finish.

If you wish to load one wrap a little more than the other – for example, in a yokozuri (pg. 146) some people prefer to take more weight on the top wrap of the takate kote – then you can achieve this by making the two sides of the ypsilon slightly uneven. The shorter side will be taking more weight.

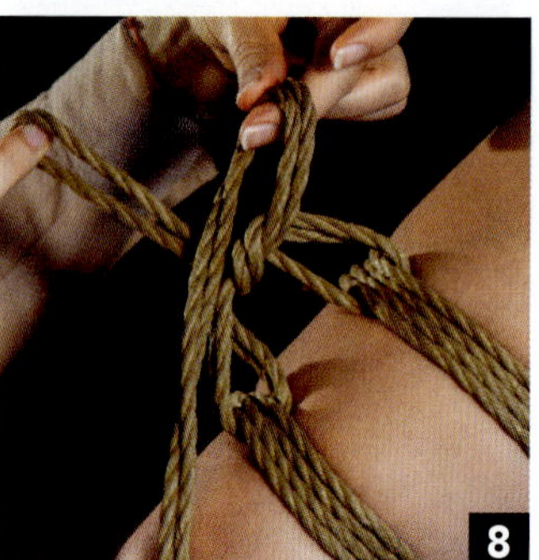
8

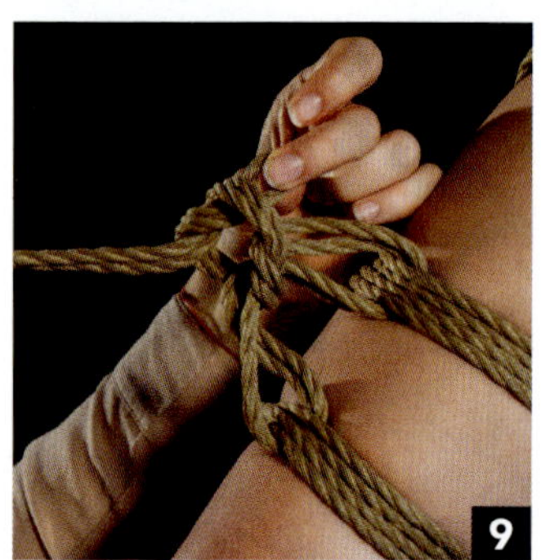
9

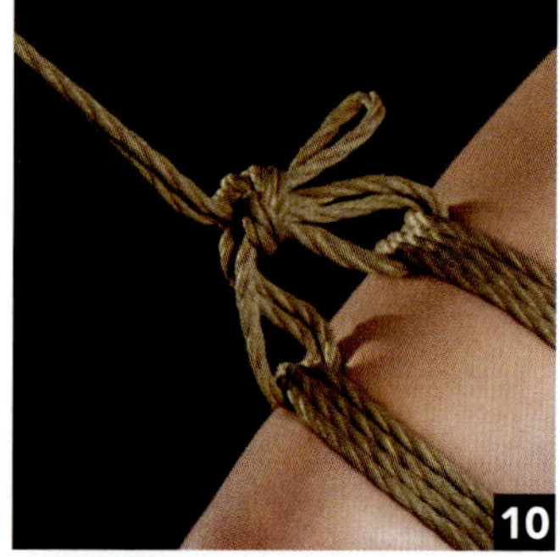
10

Ypsilon (Spiral)

Normally this is also referred to just as 'ypsilon' – I am using the term 'spiral' here to help distinguish between the two. This version is used when you want to place a suspension line on the point at which two crossing ropes intersect either at **[H]** an X-shaped junction or **[J]** a T-shaped junction.

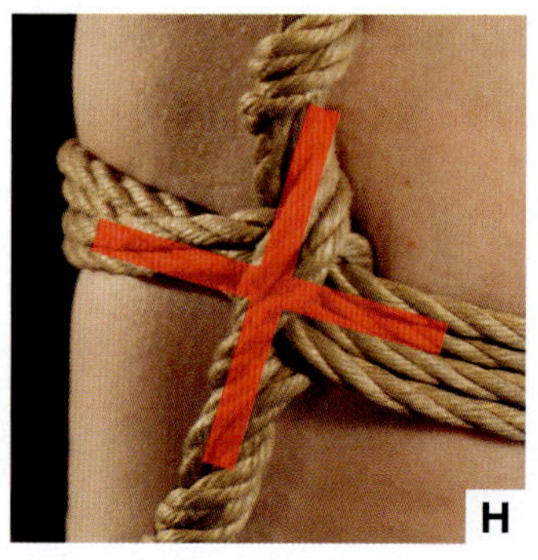
H

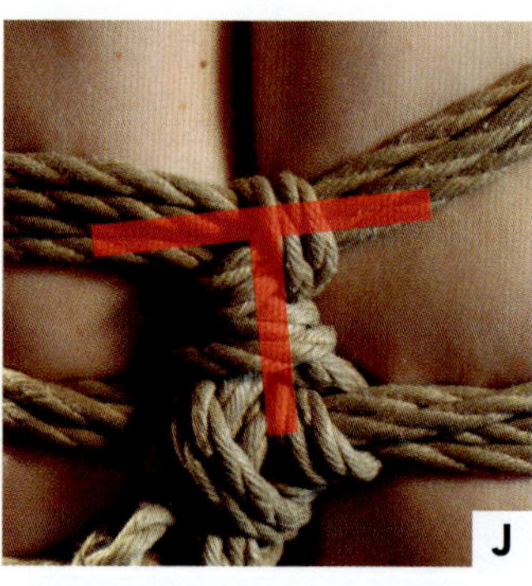
J

Here, I am attaching across an X-shaped junction.

[1] Thread the bight underneath your harness on one side of the junction.

[2] Take the bight diagonally across the point of intersection and thread it under the other side in the same direction as before. Pull up the diagonally crossing rope in the centre to form a loop.

[3, 4] Fold your bight and working end into the centre parallel with your loop.

You are now at the same point as in step 4 of the ypsilon/Y-hanger. Repeat steps 5-10 to finish.

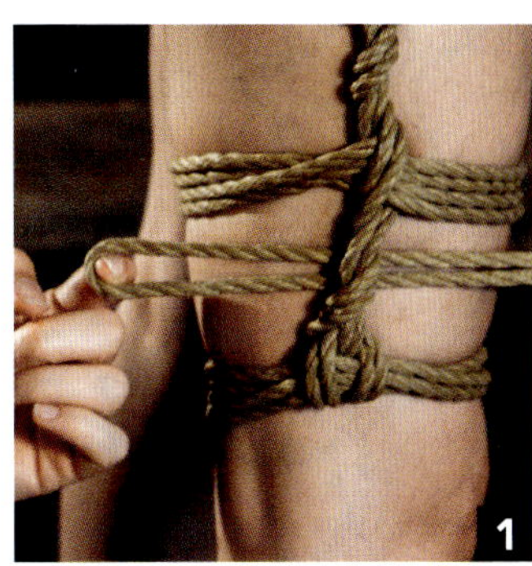
1

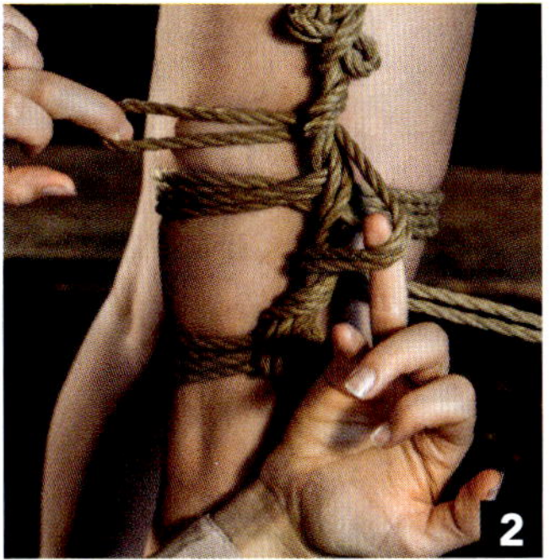
2

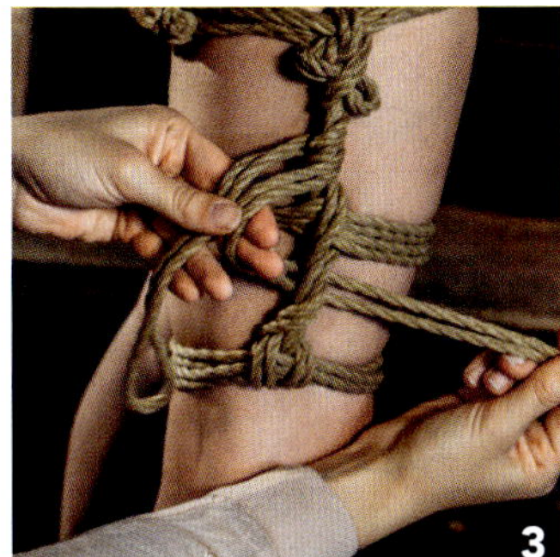
3

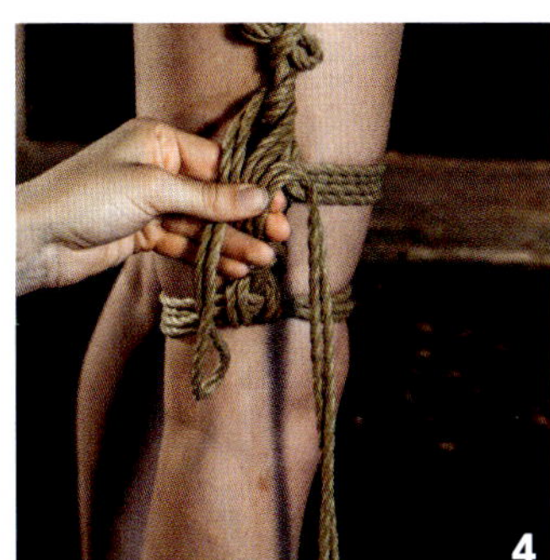
4

Double Bight

You will often see people **[K]** suspending directly through the bight of their suspension line. This is something I sometimes do on secondary lines, but not main lines. If you repeatedly use this technique the bight will get worn down much faster than the rest of the rope – and this worn part is a single point of failure, putting all of the load on one strand of rope rather than the rope folded double like the rest of the suspension line.

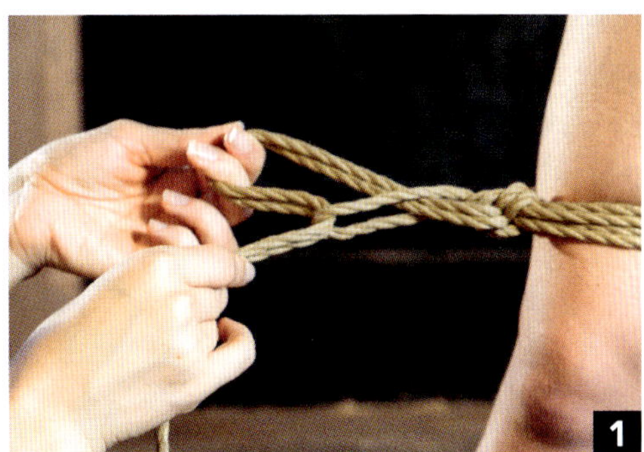
1

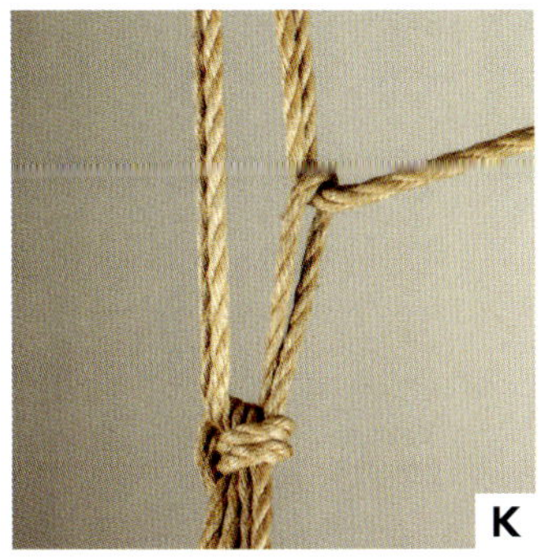
K

[1, 2] You can avoid this issue by making a yuki knot (pg. 37) in the place of your original bight. This means the rope is now doubled, and that the point of wear will change slightly every time you use that line.

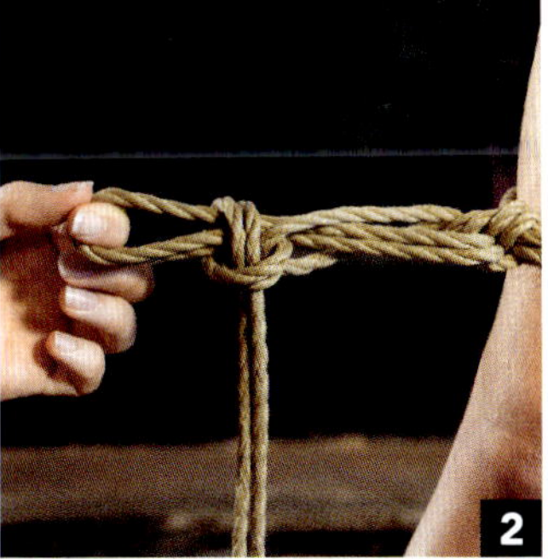
2

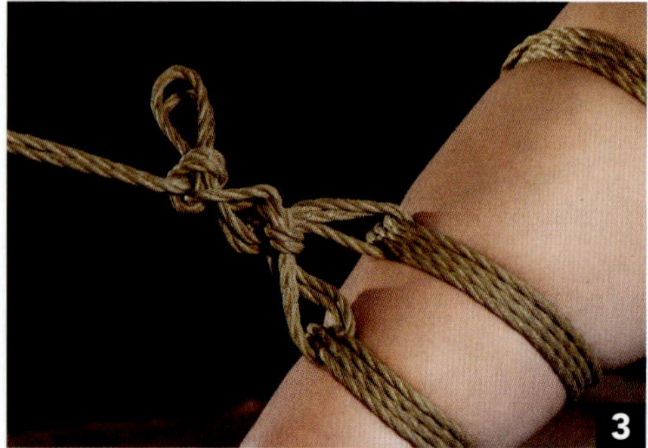
3

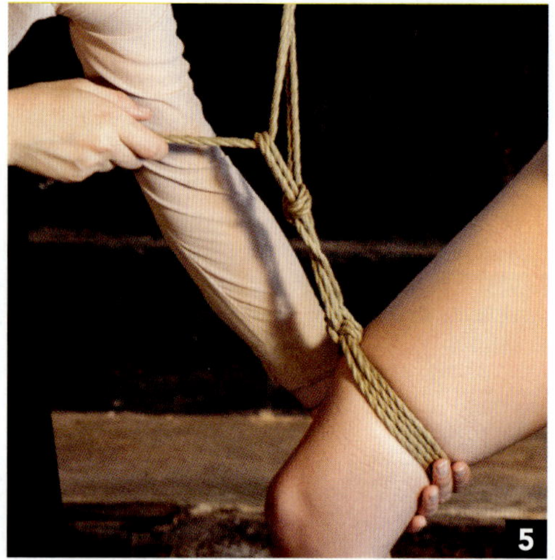
5

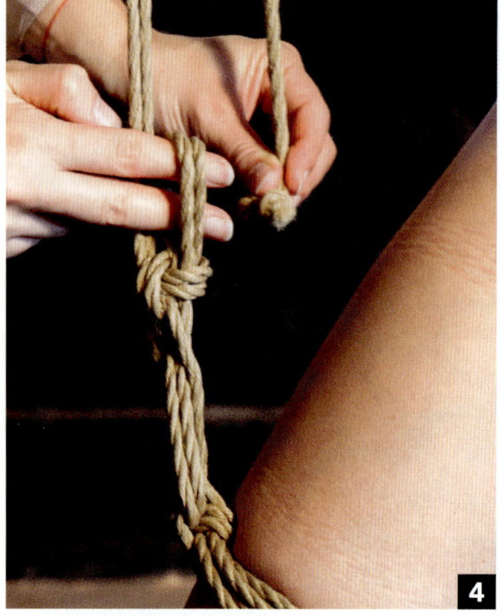
4

[3] This technique works in exactly the same way whether you are using a single column tie or an ypsilon.

[4, 5] The double bight is now used just as the regular bight would have been.

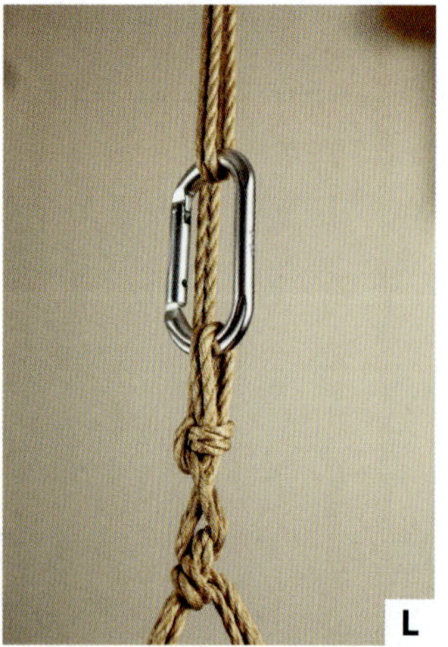
L

Tip

[L] None of the suspensions demonstrated in this book should require too much heavy lifting because they all take the weight of the heaviest part of the body (the torso) first, and then gradually take the weight of remaining body parts with other lines. However if you are someone who struggles with lifting, or you are a lot smaller than the person you're tying, then you could consider putting a carabiner in the bight to reduce the friction.

Bear in mind that this reduction in friction will also cause the lines to fall much faster should you lose your grip on them whilst tying or untying so you will need to be extra careful.

Locking Suspension Lines

I strongly recommend taking time to regularly practice this whole process – taking the line over the point, raising, locking, unlocking, lowering – on a heavy object before practicing on a person. Although it seems straightforward there are many small things that can twist/jam very quickly leading to much bigger problems – you will hopefully come across some of these while practicing so you know what to look out for in the future.

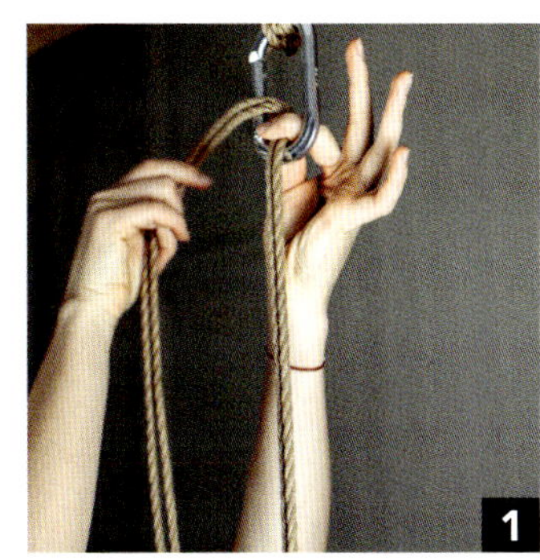

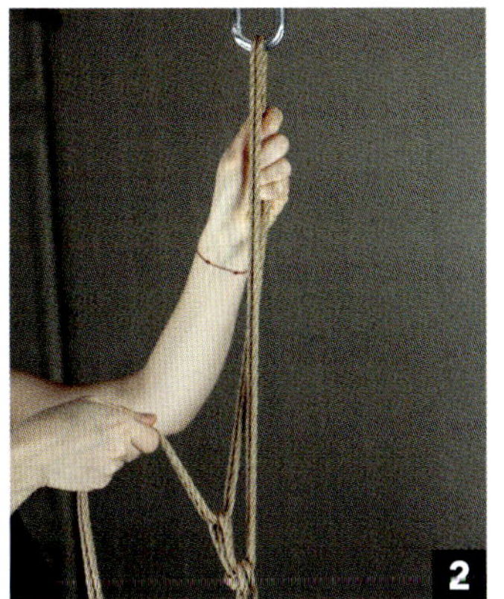

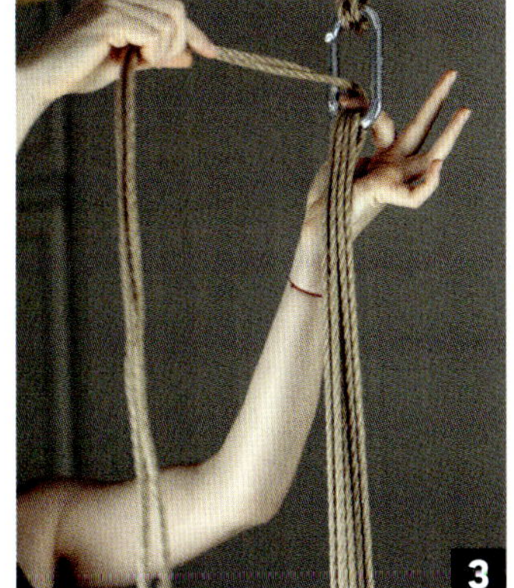

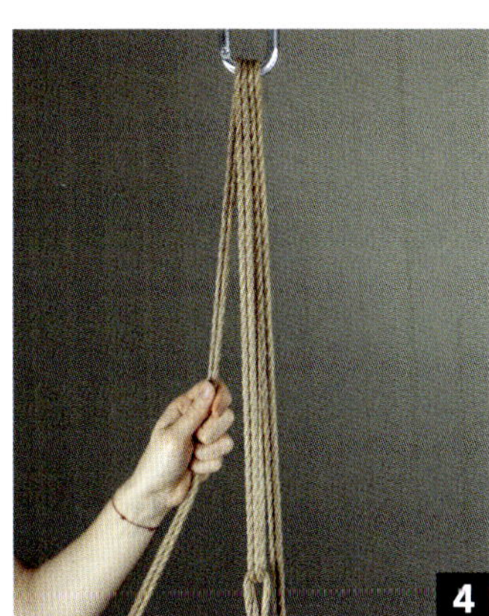

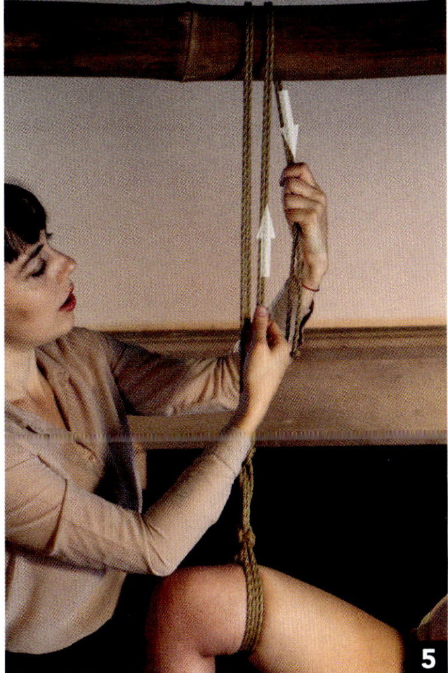

[1] Starting from whatever suspension line attachment you are using, run your working end up and over the point – taking care to follow the line all the way along with your fingers as you do so to ensure that there are no twists in the rope.

[2] Take the working end back down and through the double bight.

[3] And back up and over your suspension point again. Here you need to take care that the working end has passed over the suspension point in the same direction (in this case from front to back) both times – if the two lines are running in opposite directions, it will cause additional friction when you need to raise the line.

[4] Take a moment to ensure that all your ropes are flat; with no twists, or places where they are crossing over each other.

[5] Raise the line to the required height. You can reduce friction as you do this by holding the rope ends with one hand and pulling down, whilst simultaneously holding the rope going up to the point with the other hand and lifting up.

360° Friction on Carabiners and Rings

A 360° friction is used to 'block' the suspension line, which removes the load so you can hold the working end easily. This makes it far easier to lock and unlock and prevents half hitches (pg. 114) from jamming.

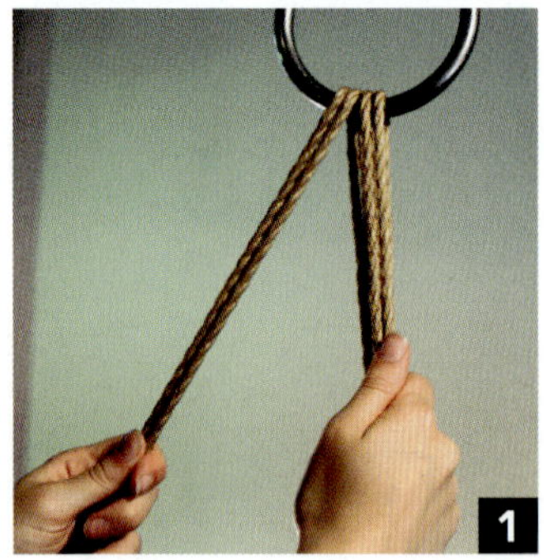

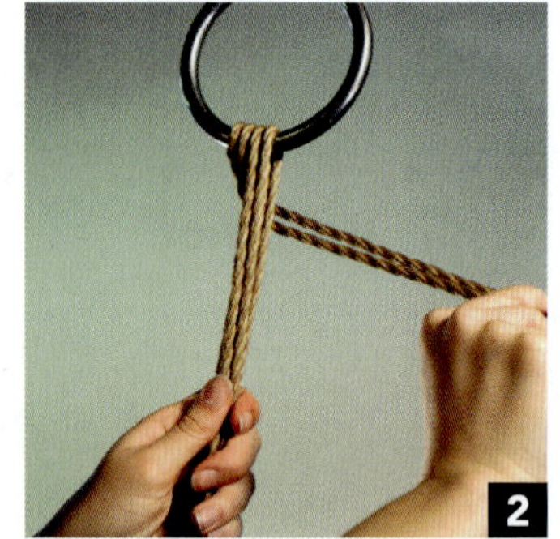

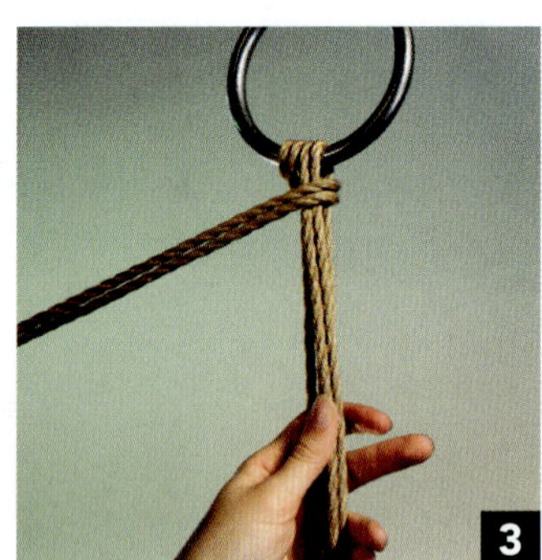

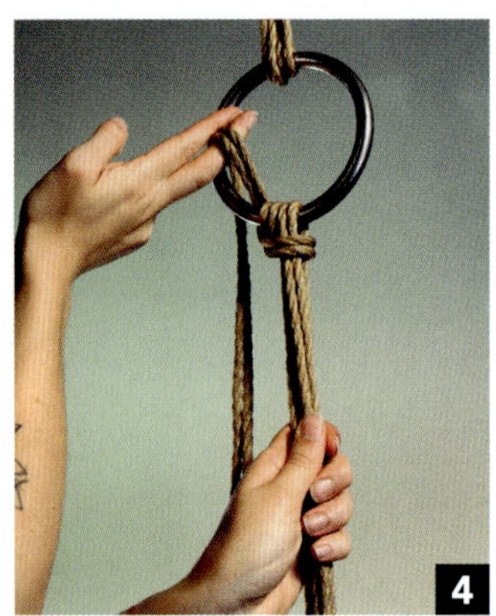

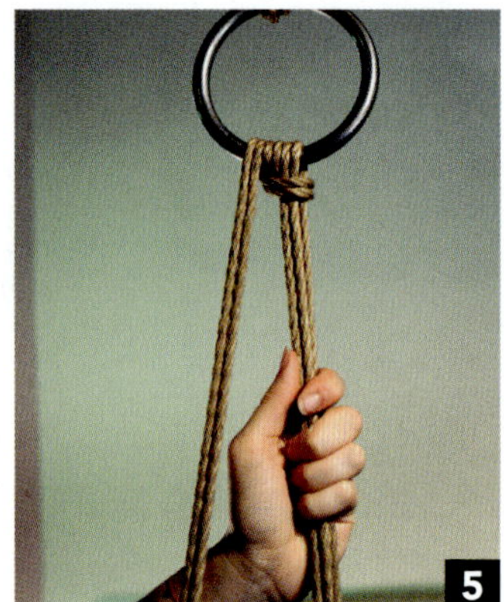

[1] Start with the working end at the front.

[2] Take it straight back under the ring/carabiner, then cross behind the suspension line.

[3] Wrap back in front of the suspension line so that you have now passed 360° around the line.

[4] Cross back under the ring from front to back, and over through the middle of the ring from back to front.

[5] The 360° friction is finished, but the line is not locked yet so you must keep hold of your working end. You should find that holding the rope now takes relatively minimal effort.

360° Friction on Bamboo

As bamboo is considerably wider than a carabiner or ring the ropes have a tendency to want to pull apart, which can make it more difficult to secure. This method leaves a little gap between the bamboo and the friction, reducing the strain by allowing the ropes to come together at a gentle angle.

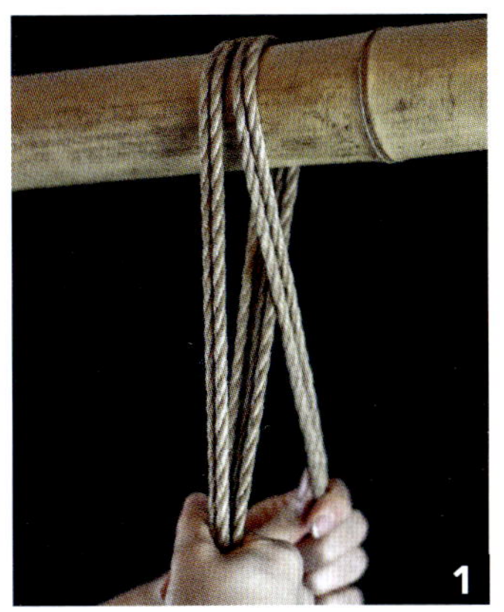

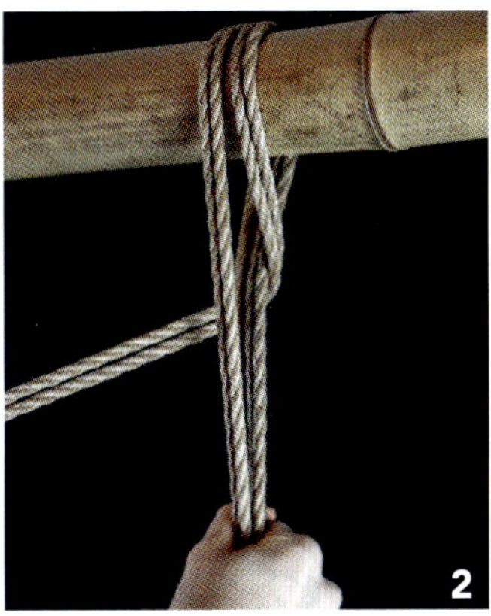

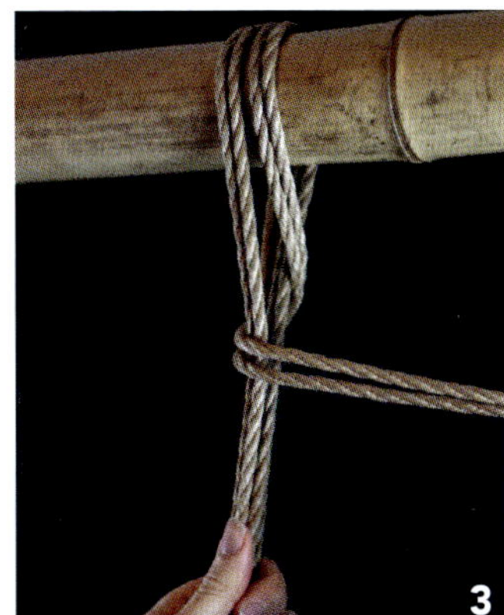

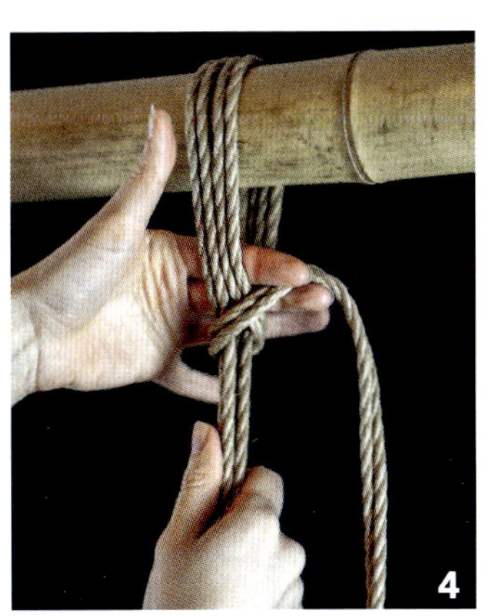

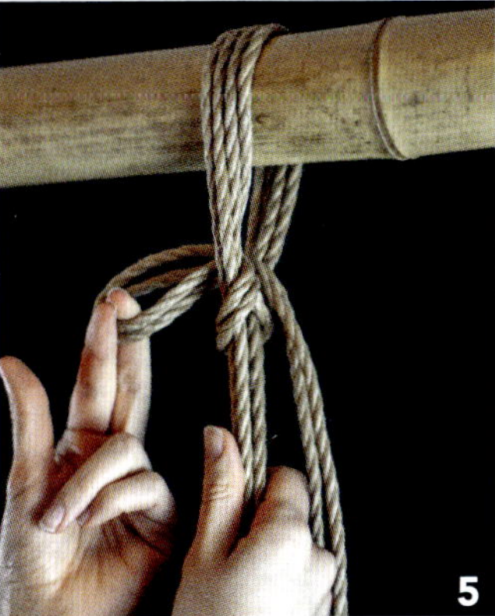

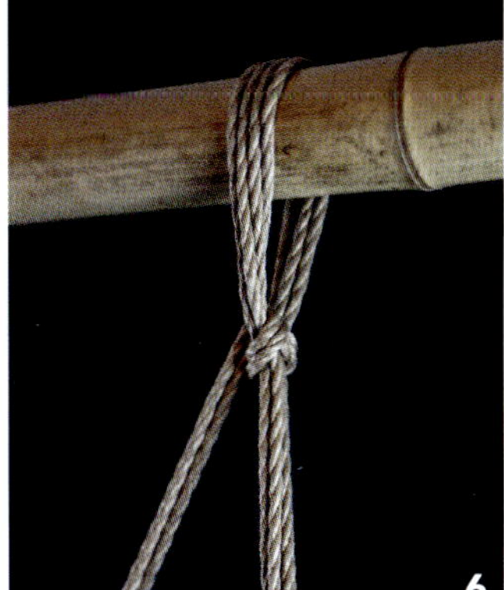

[1] Start with the working end at the front.

[2] Wrap the working end straight back under the bamboo, then cross behind the suspension line.

[3] Wrap back in front of the suspension line so that you have now passed 360° around the line.

[4, 5] Put two fingers through the gap in between the front and back of the suspension line and pull the working end through, holding the line firmly with your other hand as you do so.

[6] Pull down to tighten. For extra security, you can repeat this process if you wish.

The friction is finished, but is not locked yet so keep hold of the working end until you have locked with a half hitch *(pg. 114)**.*

Half Hitch

Once you have made the 360° friction you need to secure it somehow. Here I am using a half hitch for this. This works in exactly the same way on bamboo, carabiner, and ring.

Placing a single half hitch right the way up at the top of the ring as demonstrated here should **only** be done if the 360° friction is there, otherwise it's likely to jam and become very difficult to undo.

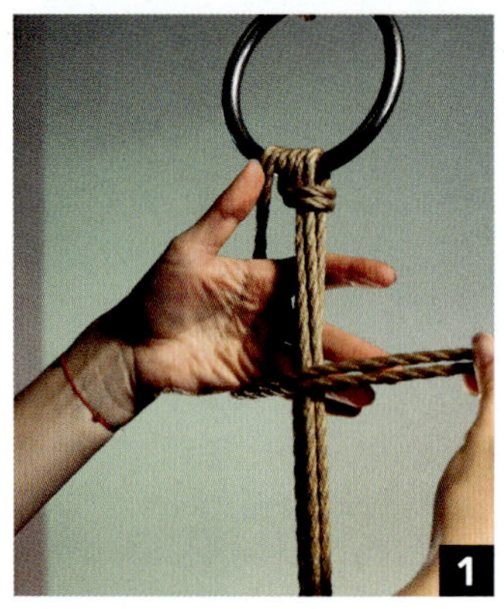

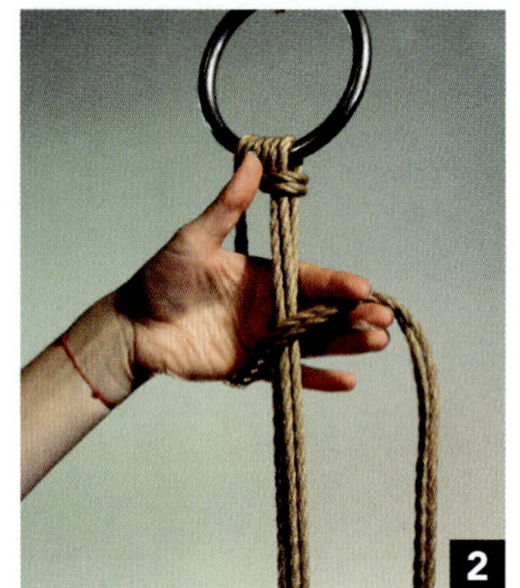

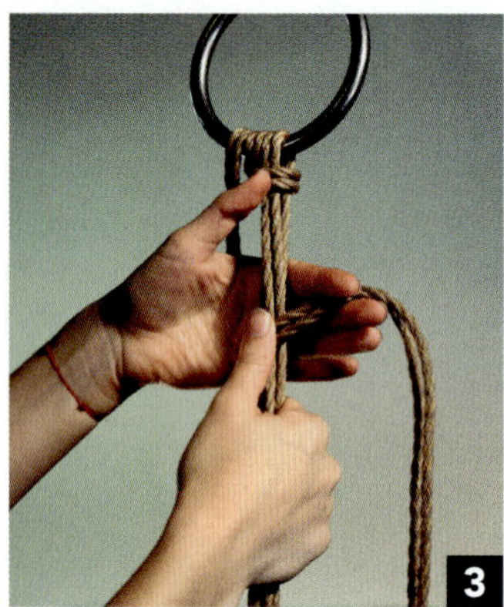

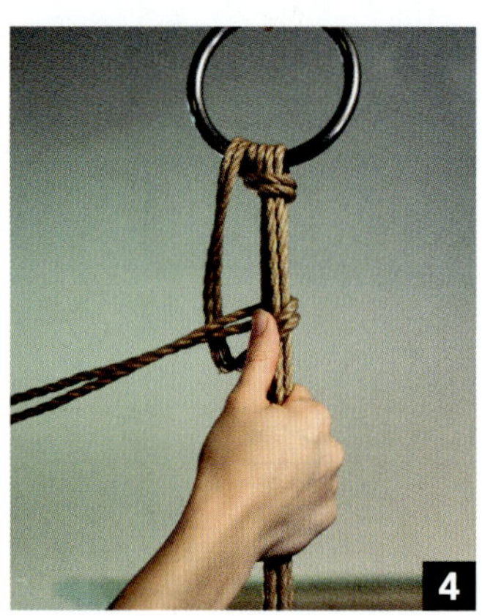

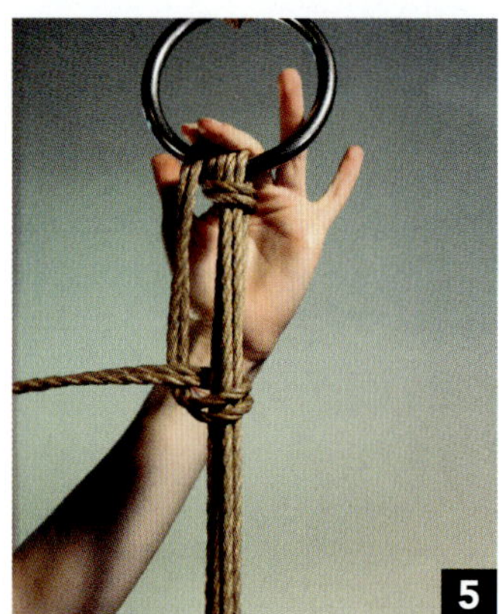

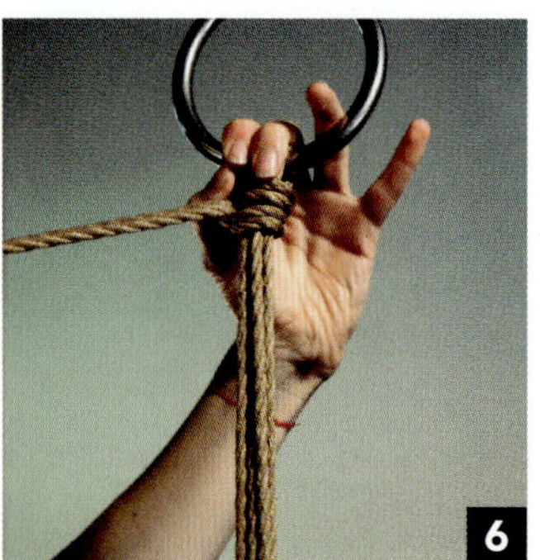

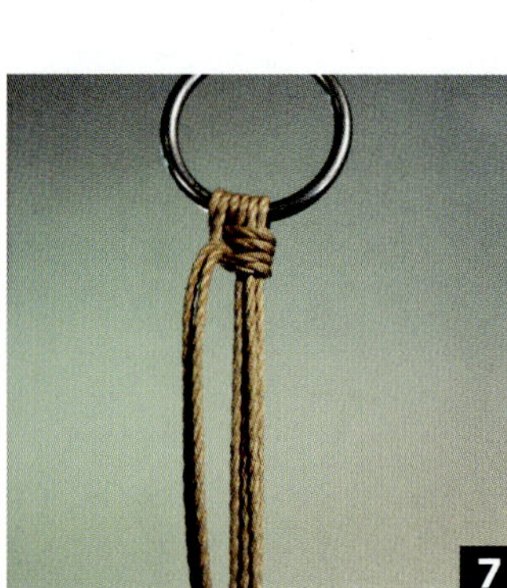

[1] Place your left hand behind the suspension line with the working end running behind the knuckles and across to the front of the line, forming an 'L' shape.

[2] Grab the working end between the index and middle finger.

[3] Hold the suspension line with the fist of your right hand, and firmly block the working end into the line with your thumb as shown. This will keep the loop you have made with your hand open.

[4] Pull the working end backwards through the loop.

[5] At this point, you might find it useful to block the 360° friction with your right hand.

[6] Pull the working end upwards and outwards so that your half hitch sits snug against your 360° friction.

[7] Now the line should be secure, so you can let go.

[M, N] Using a single half hitch only works when it has something to lock against (such as the 360° friction). If you wish to make a lock further down the line then you should use a double half hitch so that they can lock against each other.

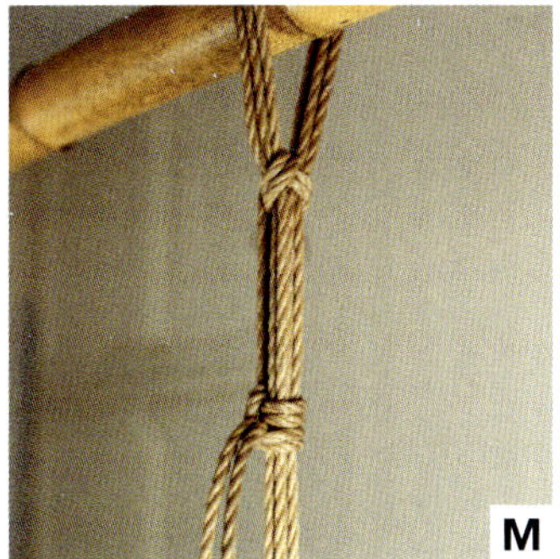
M

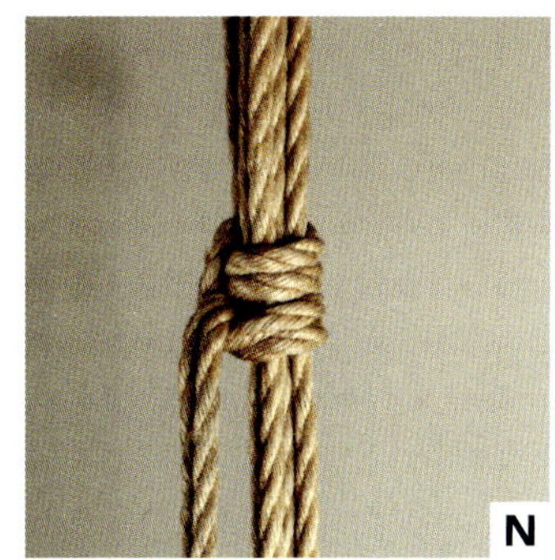
N

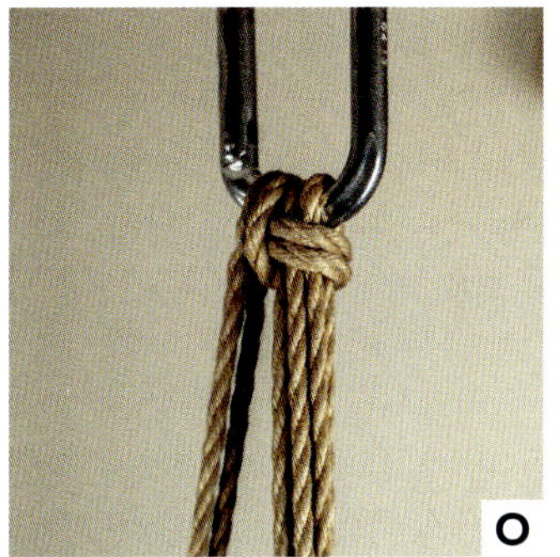
O

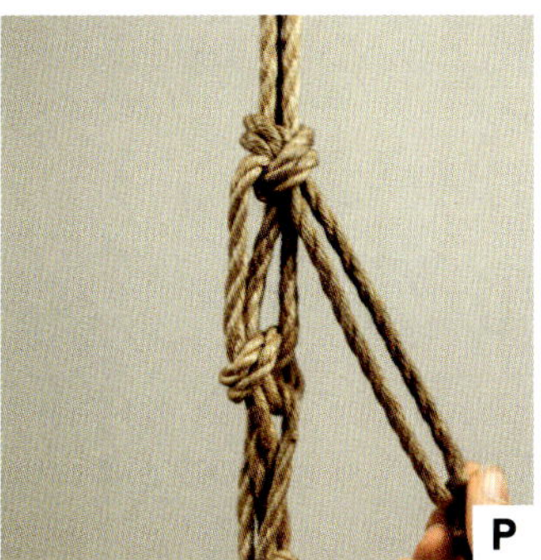
P

[O, P] You should never use a half hitch at the top of your line without a 360° friction. You should also avoid pushing the half hitch down to the bight/carabiner at the bottom of the line.

Both of these locks are almost impossible to undo under tension.

Locking Lines at the Bottom

The yuki knot (pg. 37) can also be used for creating a lock at the bottom of a suspension line, before you've made a second pass over the point. I only use this technique on secondary lines, as the suspension line will only be made up of 4 strands of rope rather than 6, and will be more difficult to save if it falls. Having the lock close to the body also makes it more likely to be knocked around and loosened.

This is useful if you wish to lock a line low to the floor and don't have enough rope to make the second pass over the point – or if you wish to have some rope left over to use elsewhere in the suspension.

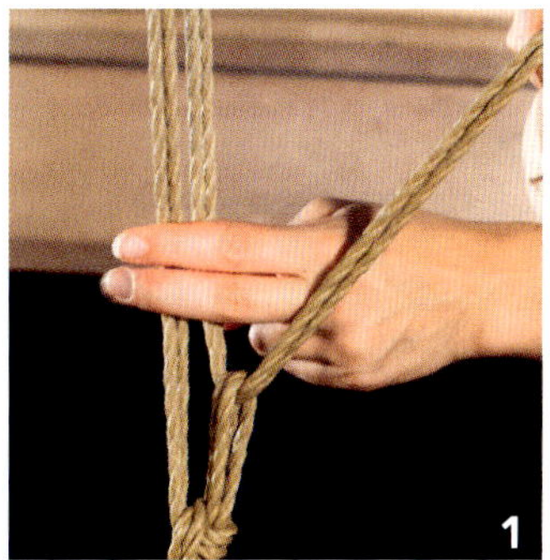
1

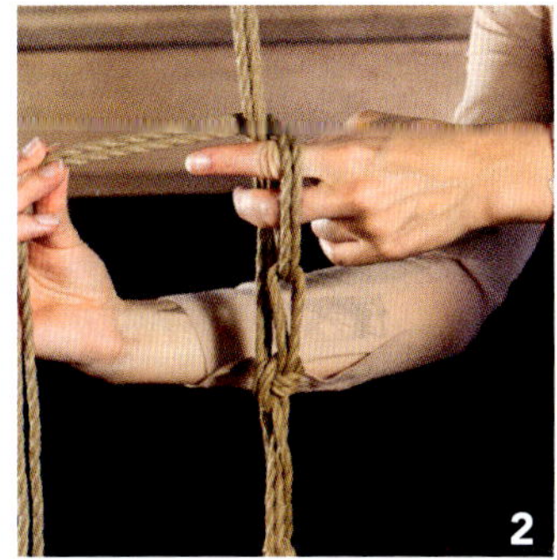
2

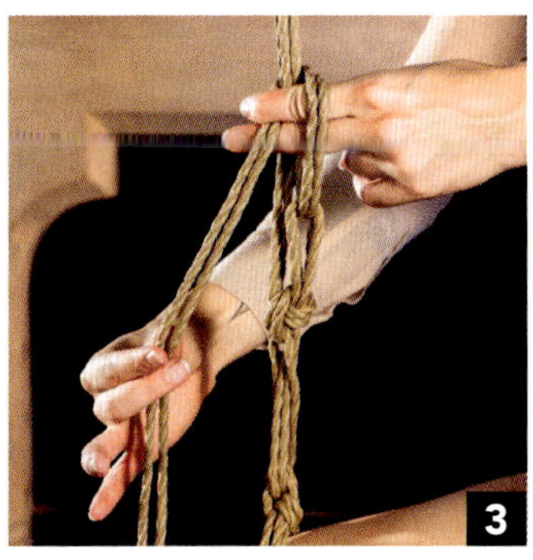
3

[1, 2] Place your left hand in front of the suspension line with the working end running over the knuckles and across to the back of the line, forming an upside down 'L' shape.

[3] Grab the working end between the index and middle finger.

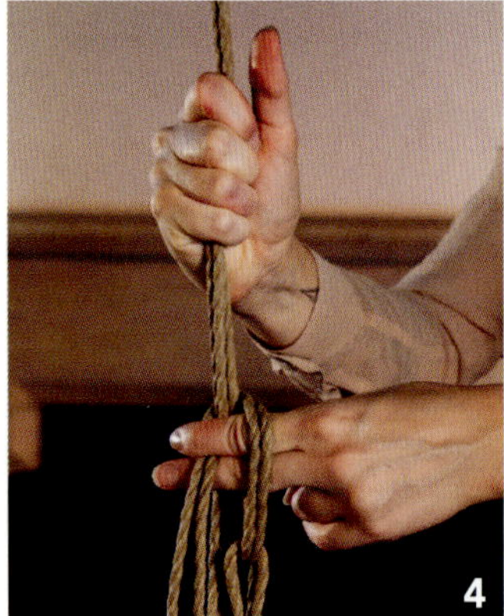
4

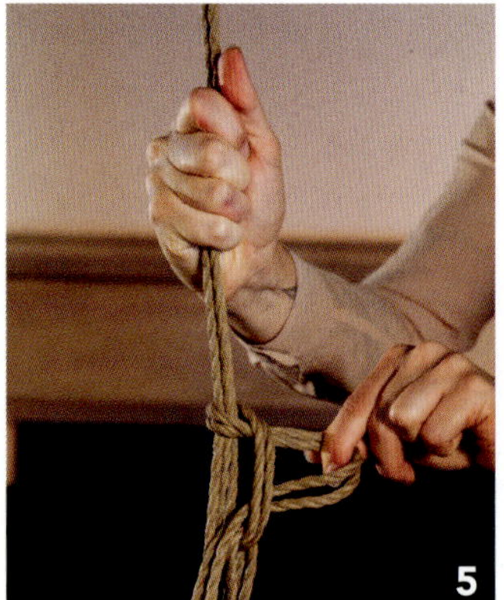
5

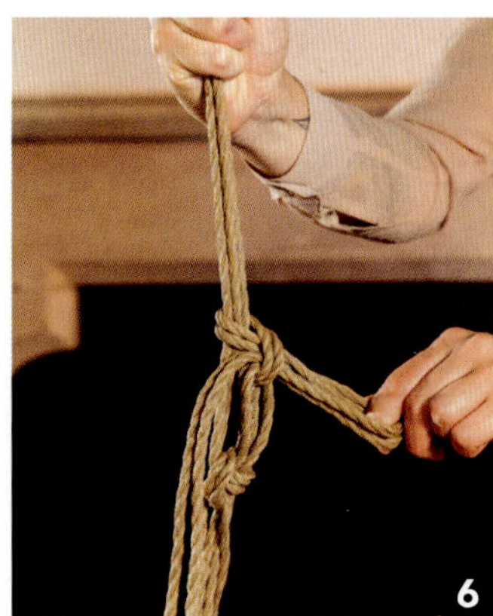
6

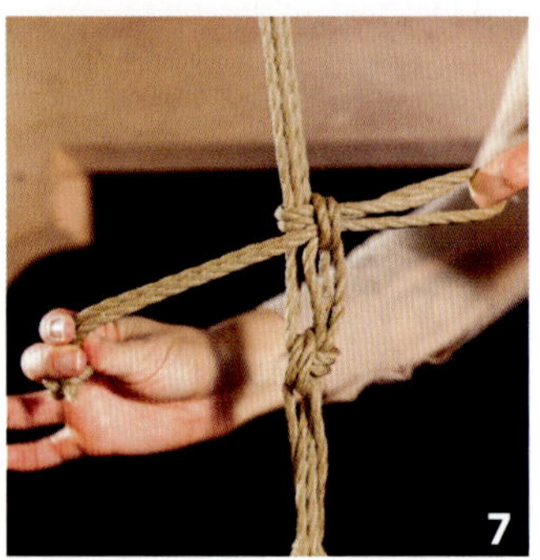
7

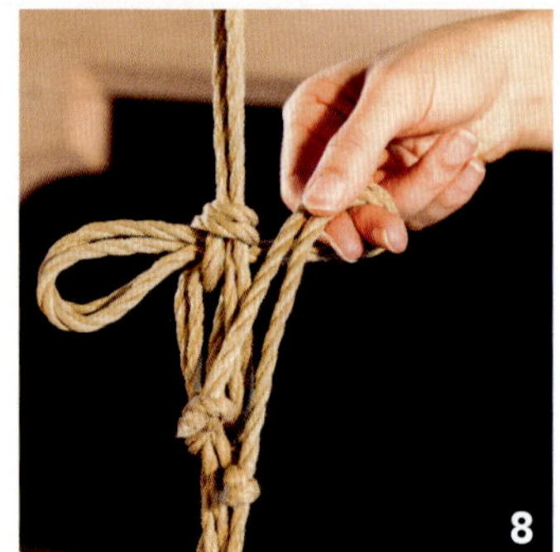
8

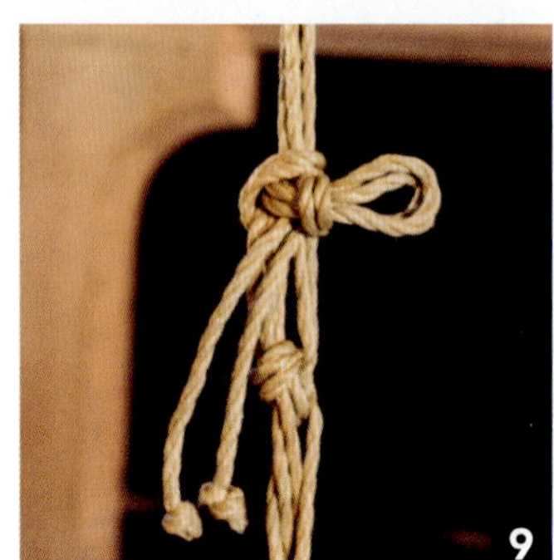
9

[4] Hold the suspension line with the fist of your right hand.

N.B. I have shown this in distinct steps for emphasis, in reality you might have to get from step 2 to 4 with a fairly swift movement due to the amount of load the line is under, and perhaps even temporarily block the line by closing your left hand into a fist around it as you move your right hand to block the line further up.

[5, 6, 7] Pull the working end half way through the space made with your fingers and secure it downwards onto the bight.

[8, 9] Finish the yuki knot (steps 3-5, pg. 37). I prefer to wrap the working end to the other side of the suspension line before I make the loop so that it is trapped in the middle.

Notes for Models

Once the first suspension line is securely locked off you can 'test' the tie by moving and shifting your body slightly, expanding into it, and loading it slightly to see how it feels before the rest of the body comes off the ground.

This can help you to identify anything that might already be causing a problem so that you can ask the rigger to change it for you before continuing the suspension.

This might also make you aware of things which are fine for now but might cause problems futher on in the session. You can store these at the back of your mind for reference so that if something does become difficult you might find it easier to identify the source of the problem.

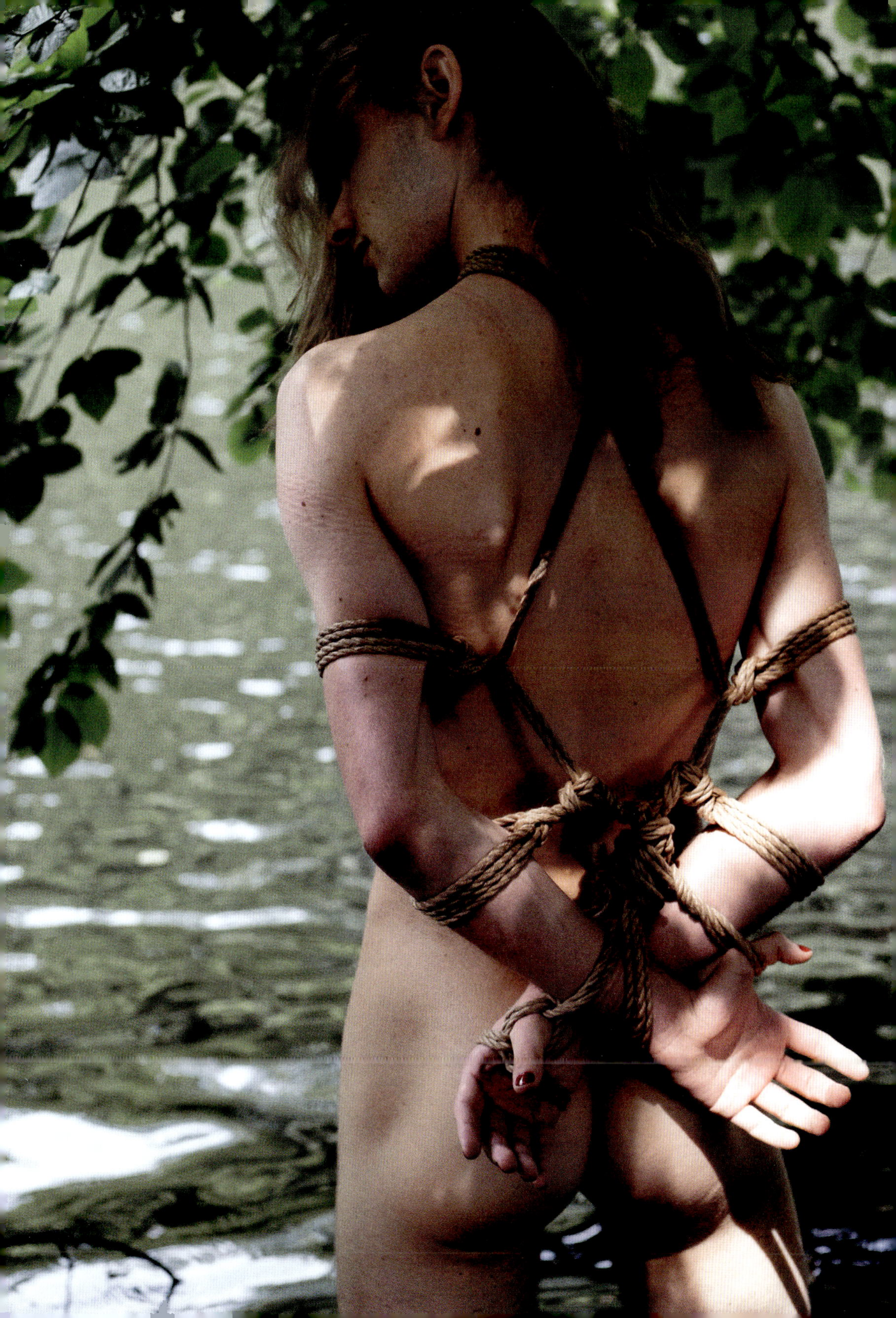

Using Up Leftover Rope

You will often be left with some surplus rope after you have locked your suspension line. It's important to find a way to use this up because trailing rope ends could pose a risk by becoming caught in the rest of your tie which could slow you down considerably if you are in a hurry to untie.

Overhand Lock

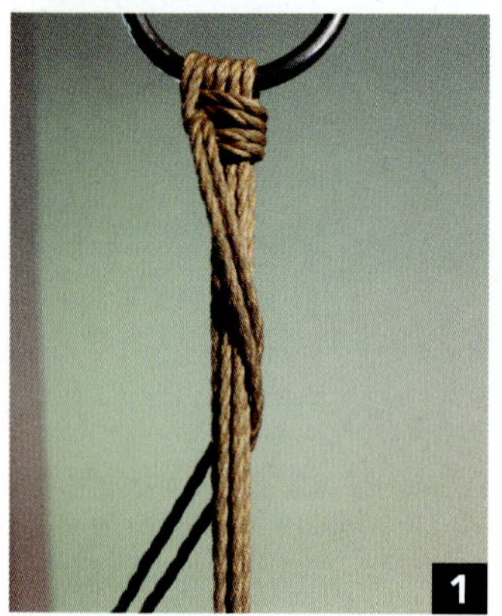

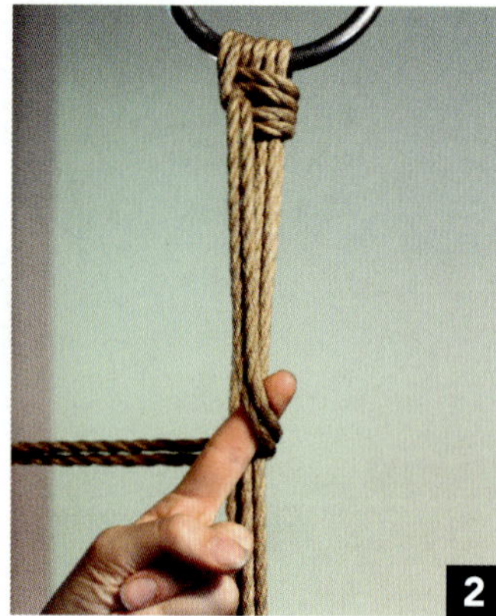

[1] Wrap your working end loosely around the suspension line.

[2] Hook the twist you have just made with your index finger and pull down.

[3] Pass the working end over the top of the twist and behind your index finger.

[4] Turn your index finger around and hook the working end.

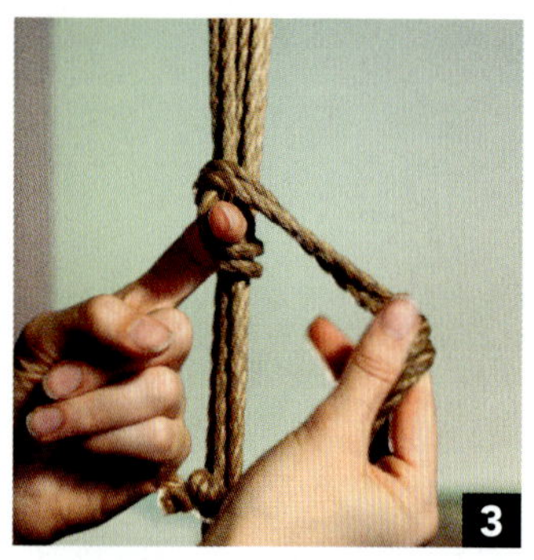

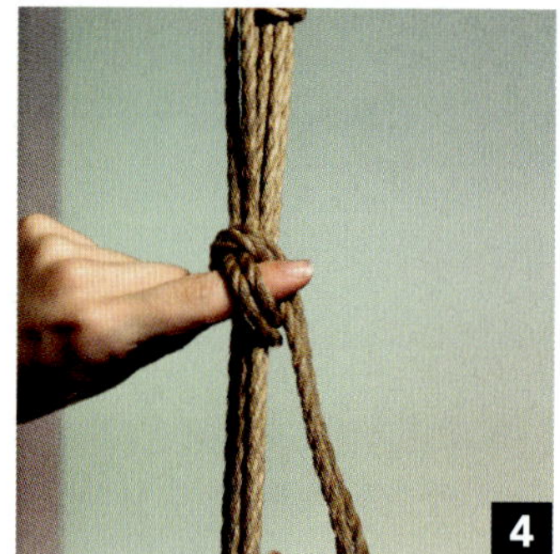

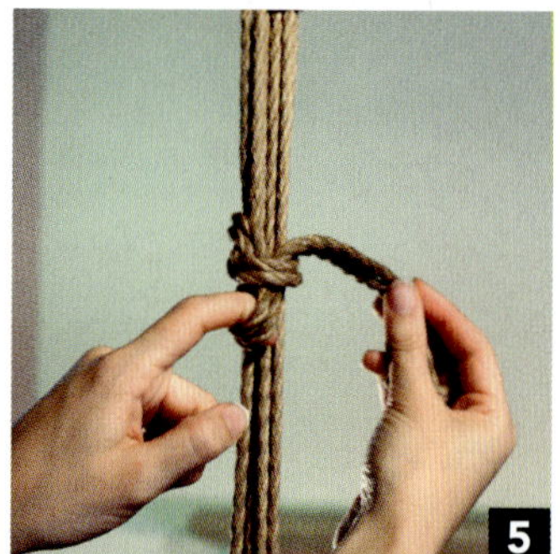

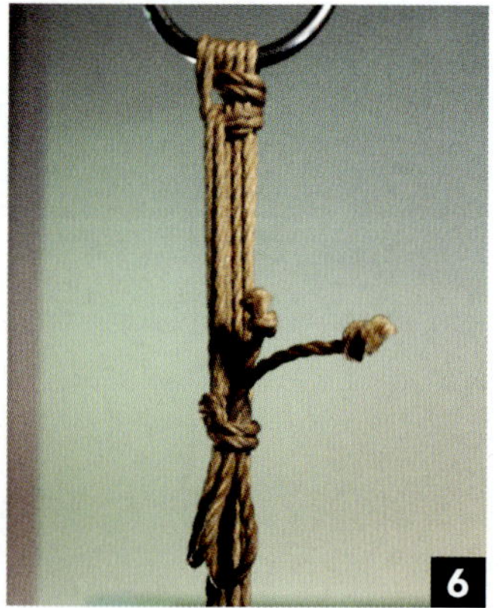

[5] Pull halfway through to form a loop.

[6] To get this friction really tight and secure you can hold the whole friction in your fist and pull down firmly. The friction is now finished. To undo, simply pull on the knots (nawajiri) of your rope.

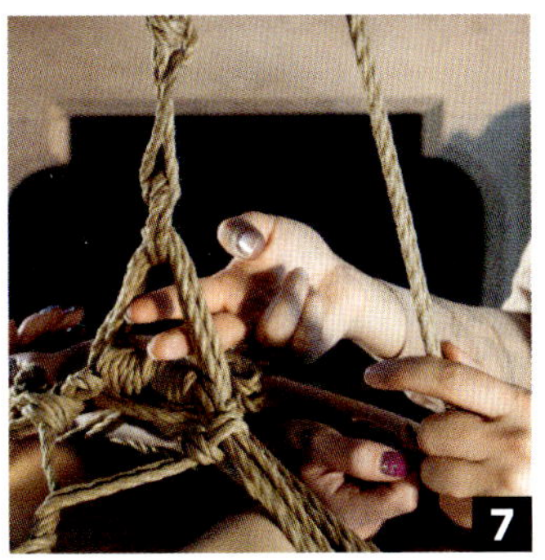

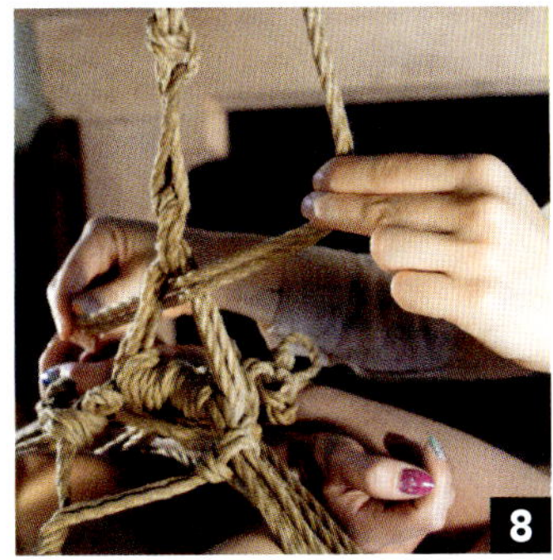

If you have a lot of rope left over at the end of the tie, you can still use this method.

[7, 8] Just take the working end and pass it through the gap in the line attachment.

Then pass it back through the carabiner, or through the gap in the 360° bamboo friction (pg 113) and complete steps 1-6.

Making a Bundle

Sometimes, you will find yourself in a situation where you have a lot of rope left over, but feeding the rope back through the attachment point isn't an option; usually because the space is too small, or is too close to the skin. In this case, you can use your rope up at the top of the line by making a bundle out of it.

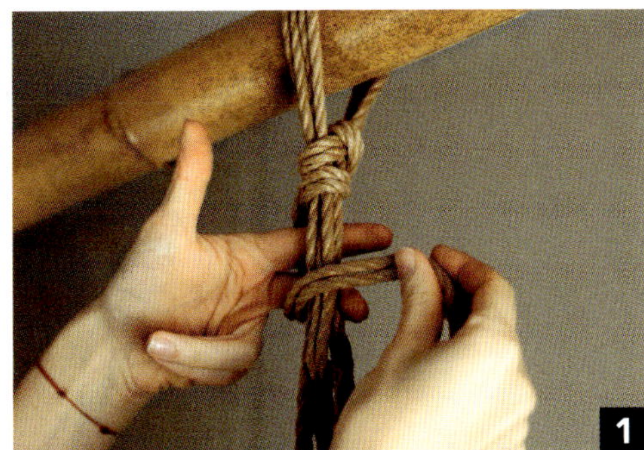

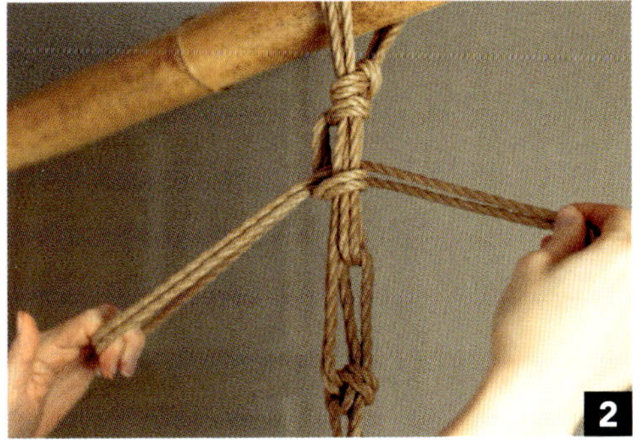

[1] Begin to make another half hitch an inch or two underneath your original lock, **[2]** but this time just pull the rope half way through.

[3] Now you should have your rope ends at roughly the same length as the loop you have just pulled through.

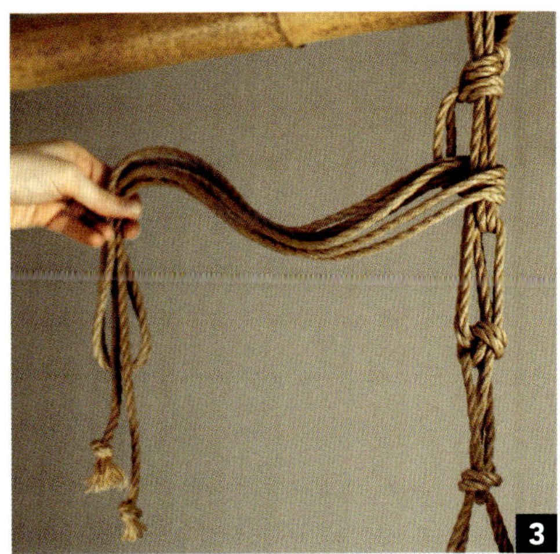

[4, 5, 6] Take all the ropes together and make another half hitch *above* the first one. Pull this one just half way through as well.

[7] As you pull this through, tighten by making a fist over the bundle and pulling downwards to jam the two 'half hitches' together firmly.

[8] Finished. To undo, simply pull on the knots (nawajiri).

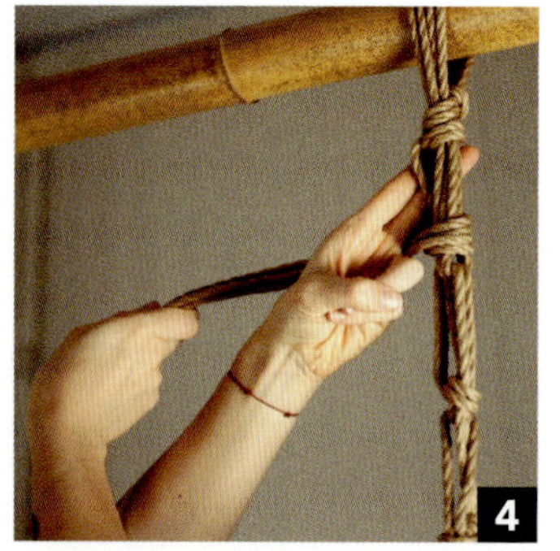
4

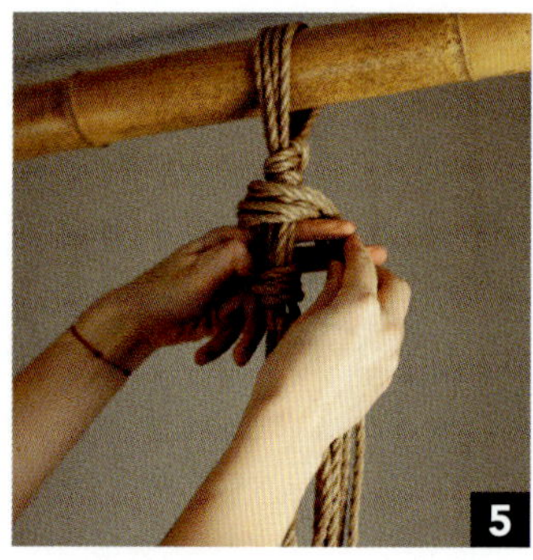
5

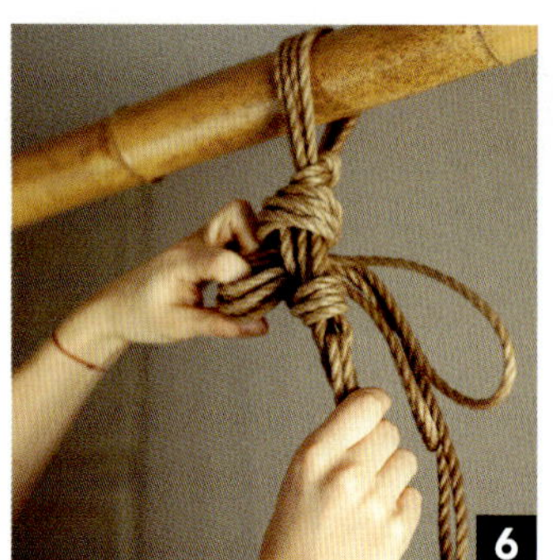
6

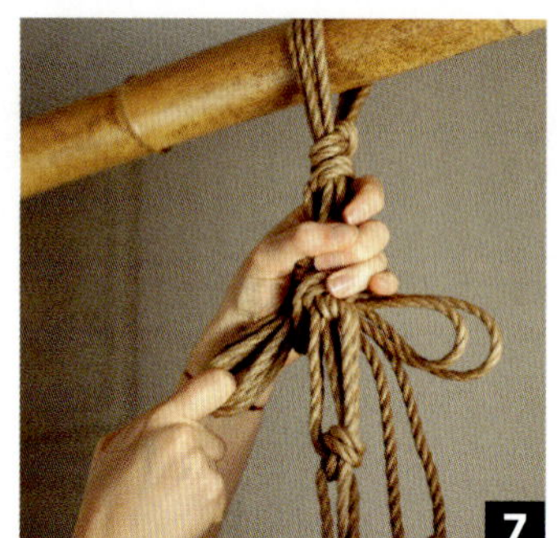
7

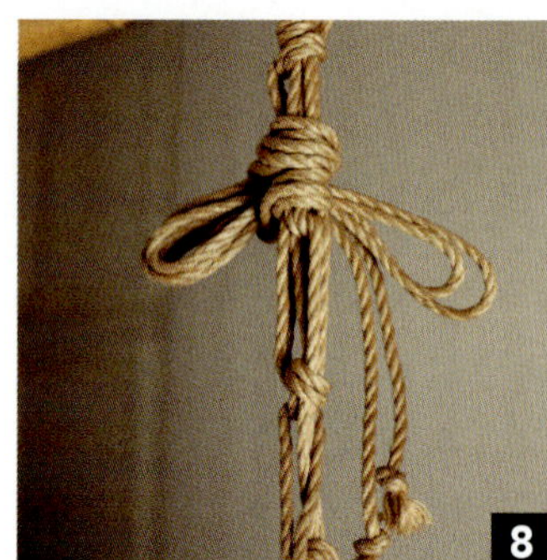
8

Both of the methods above are very quick to both tie and untie.

[Q, R] I also see techniques such as these used from time to time that are less efficient. Using one of the methods shown here (or even leaving your rope ends trailing!) can be an aesthetic choice later on, but as a beginner it's really just one more potential complication that you don't need to worry about.

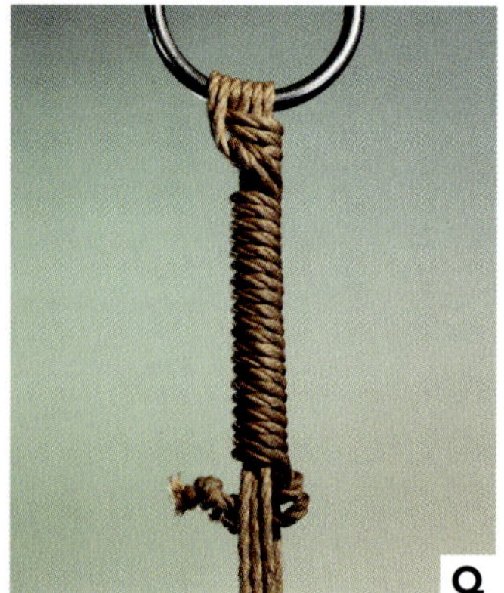
Q

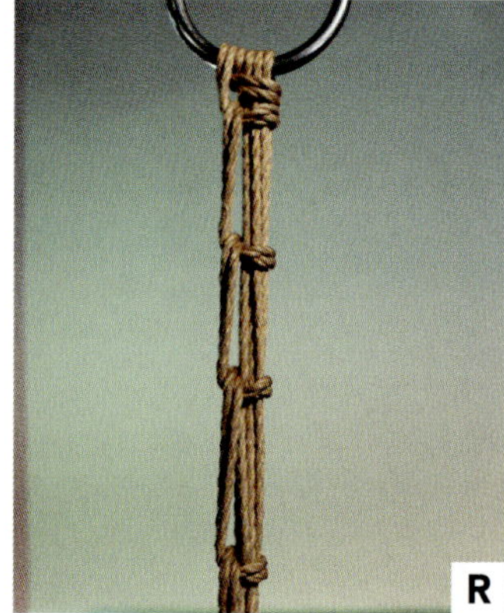
R

Carabiner Formations

If you're working on a bamboo you are unlikely to struggle too much with finding enough space to place your suspension lines, but on carabiners this can be a little harder. In the following pictures, the main line is the only line locked with a 360° friction and half hitch for clarity – but in reality, all of your lines could be locked like this making it much more difficult to find enough space to work in.

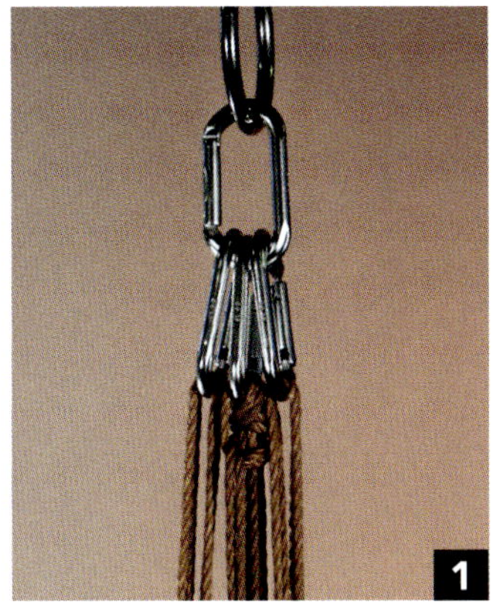

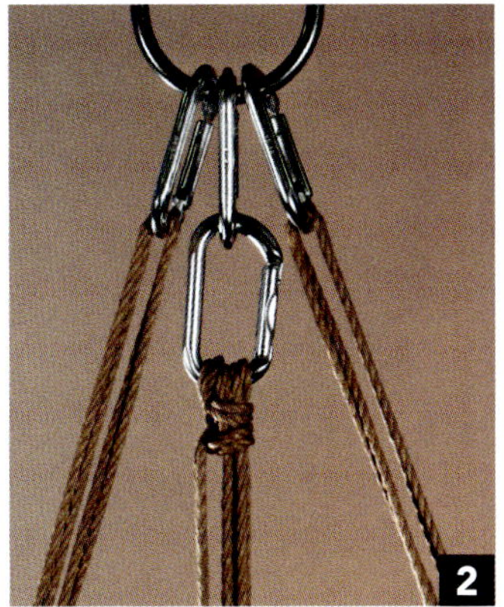

If the carabiners are **[1]** all arranged at the same level then the lines are likely to become jammed together and it can be difficult to find enough space for your fingers when you come to undo them.

[2] Placing an additional carabiner in the centre so that it is dropped lower than the others means you will have more space to be able to work with the lines.

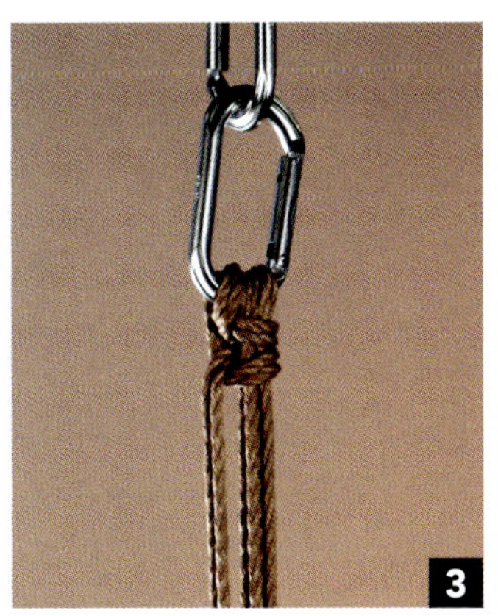

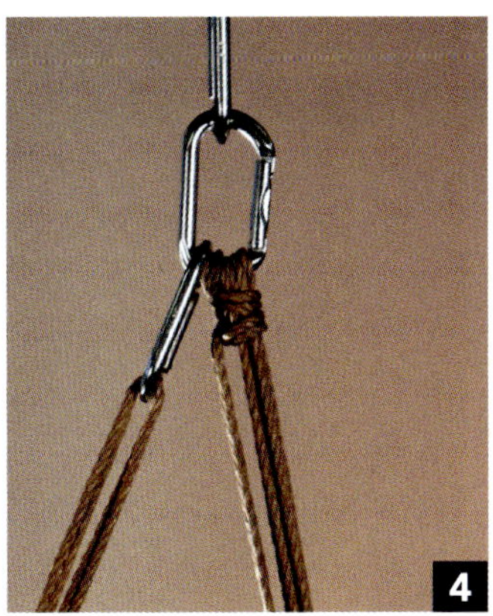

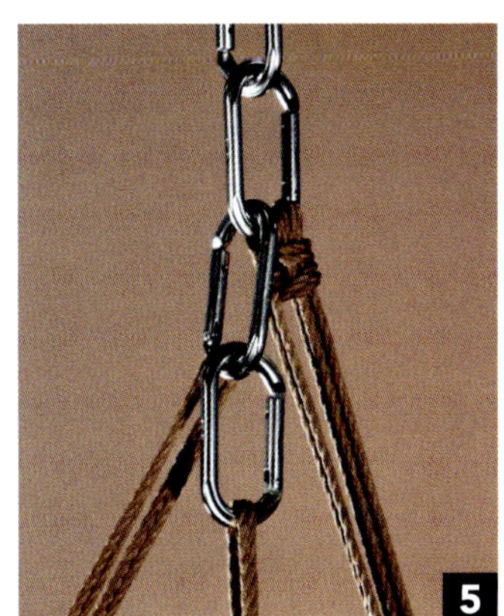

[3] Alternatively you can start with the main line on a carabiner at the top.

[4, 5] And then attach each subsequent carabiner to the one before it, creating a chain as you go down. This creates an easy working space for static suspensions (such as the ones in this book) but can make transitions difficult.

Getting Down

All the suspensions demonstrated in this book can be untied in the exact reverse of the order they were tied, so the main line (attached to the takate kote) will always be the last thing you remove.

The technique shown here – using your hand to 'block' the line as you undo it and supporting the part of the body you are lowering – is equally relevant for all lines, but I have shown it here on a main line attached to the upper body. Even though here, the model already has both feet on the ground, it is still important to support their weight as you release the line in case the model suddenly becomes light-headed or unstable after coming down from suspension.

Remember to practice lowering slowly and smoothly as sudden movements can cause injury.

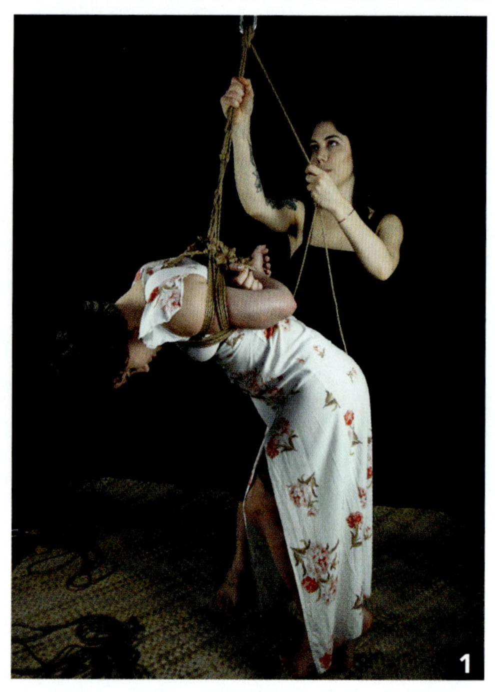

1

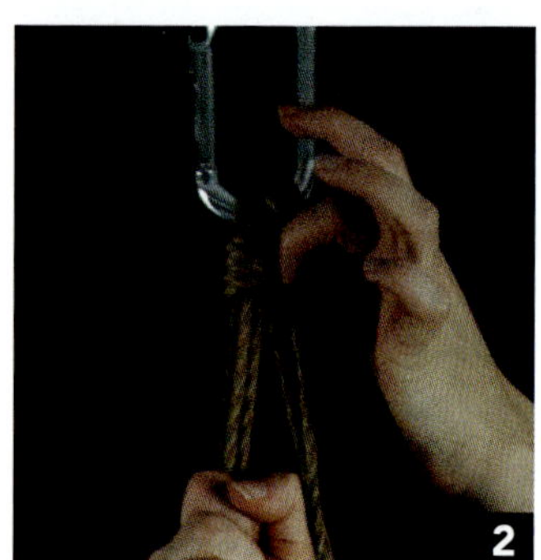

2

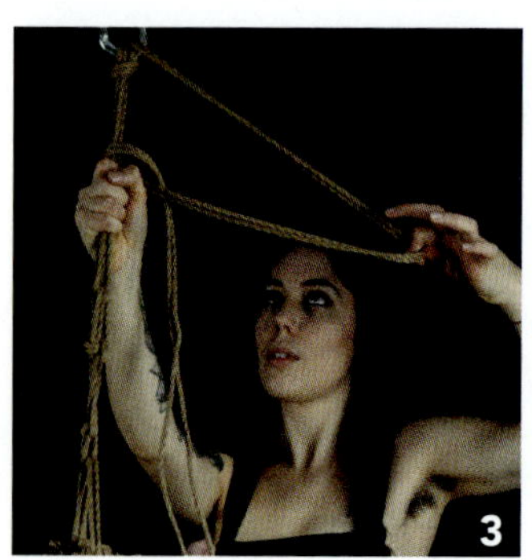

3

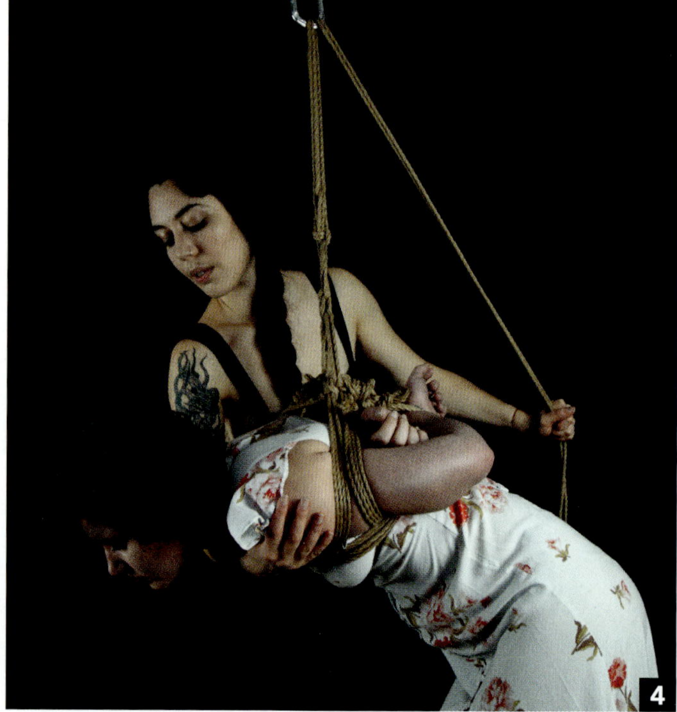

4

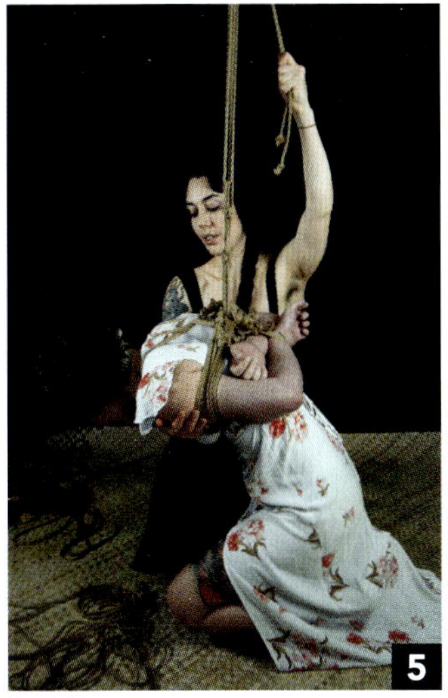
5

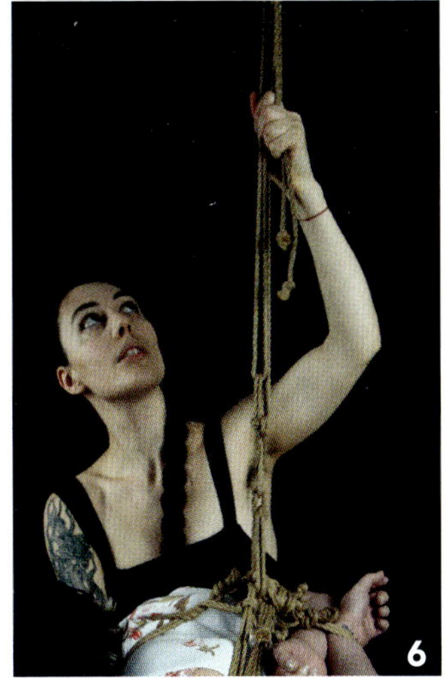
6

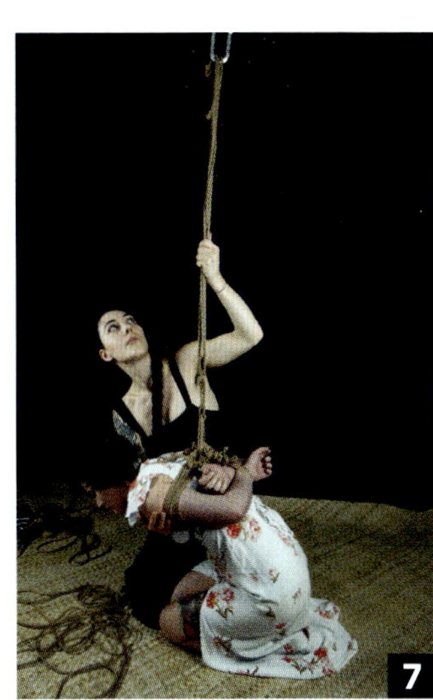
7

[1] Undo whatever method you've used to finish the rope (pg. 118) and grip the line firmly with your fist before undoing the half hitch to ensure it doesn't slip.

[2, 3] To undo the half hitch with one hand pull on the vertical rope at the side with your thumb and index finger. Then undo the 360° friction in the same way (keeping a firm grip on the suspension line with your fist at all times).

[4] Make sure that you have a firm grip of the working end before you let go of the hand around the main line. If you are lowering a very heavy load you might wish to keep your fist loosely around the main line to help you break the load a little as you lower – but in most other cases, you can use your other hand to gently support the model by placing your hand underneath their body as shown.

[5] Support your model all the way to the ground.

[6, 7] If you get to the point where you can no longer reach the rope ends, and there is still a little load on the line, you can switch back to gripping it with your fist and let go of the working end – then gradually release the tension in your fist until you are safely on the floor.

Getting Down In an Emergency

The above is fine under normal circumstances, but at some point you might find yourself in an emergency situation that you need to get out of fast. Sometimes this can be down to rigger error – but even when you reach a competent level it's best not to get complacent about the possibility of this happening to you. Everyone makes mistakes, either model or rigger could suddenly become ill, the fire alarm could go off, or any number of other external factors beyond your control.

It is outside the scope of a book to be able to give instruction on this in any great detail, so I strongly recommend that if you have the opportunity to take a lesson with a more experienced rigger you ask them to cover this topic with you.

Ideally you should always ask a spotter to help you get down in an emergency. They can:

- ◊ Take the model's weight to relieve any stress that they might be feeling in a particular area whilst the rigger concentrates on unlocking the suspension lines. For example, in the gyaku-ebi-zuri/face down suspension (pg. 161) it is common for models to feel stress in the lower back. A spotter can lift up the hips to relieve this stress.

- If one of your suspension lines has become caught or jammed, they can lift up the body part it's attached to to take that weight whilst you unjam it. In some cases there may be so much weight on a jammed line that it is impossible to undo without taking the load off.
- Take on the role of your spare arm (pg. 122, step 4) so the model has more support as they are being lowered to the ground, and the rigger has the use of both arms to untie faster.
- Occasionally, it might even be necessary for the spotter to take the whole of the model's body weight whilst you unclip the carabiners from the suspension point, so the whole body can be taken to the ground in one go. This should only really be attempted if the spotter is confident that they can lift the model's whole weight easily and, of course, will only be possible if you are using carabiners or some other form of suspension equipment that can be easily unclipped.

In the unlikely case that you find yourself in a situation where cutting the suspension lines is the **only** option available to you then, once again, ask a spotter to support each body part as you cut the line it's attached to, and then lower it gently to the ground. Sudden movements as a body is coming out of a stressful position – particularly a backbend or a torsion – can cause serious injury.

Just as when undoing the lines normally, cut everything in the exact reverse order that you attached it, making sure that the main line (attached to the takate kote) is the **last** thing you remove.

IF THERE ISN'T A SPOTTER PRESENT

I strongly advise against practicing suspensions if you don't have anyone on hand to help you should you get into difficulties – but if you should find yourself in this situation then there are a couple of pieces of advice that may help you:

- If you have a jammed line and there is no one to take the weight for you then you can attach a new suspension line to take the load so that the jammed line goes slack and can be removed more easily.
- If the model is struggling then rather than trying to support their weight yourself – only to have to lower them back down into the difficult position in order to get them down – it may be preferable just to untie directly as efficiently as possible.
- If you should find yourself needing to cut a line when you are alone (and this is not recommended unless there really is no other option), you can do so by gripping the single column tie, ypsilon, or harness firmly in one hand and lifting it up whilst you cut the suspension line with the other hand, then lowering to the floor. Once again, please make sure that the line attached to the takate kote or chest harness is the last thing to be removed.

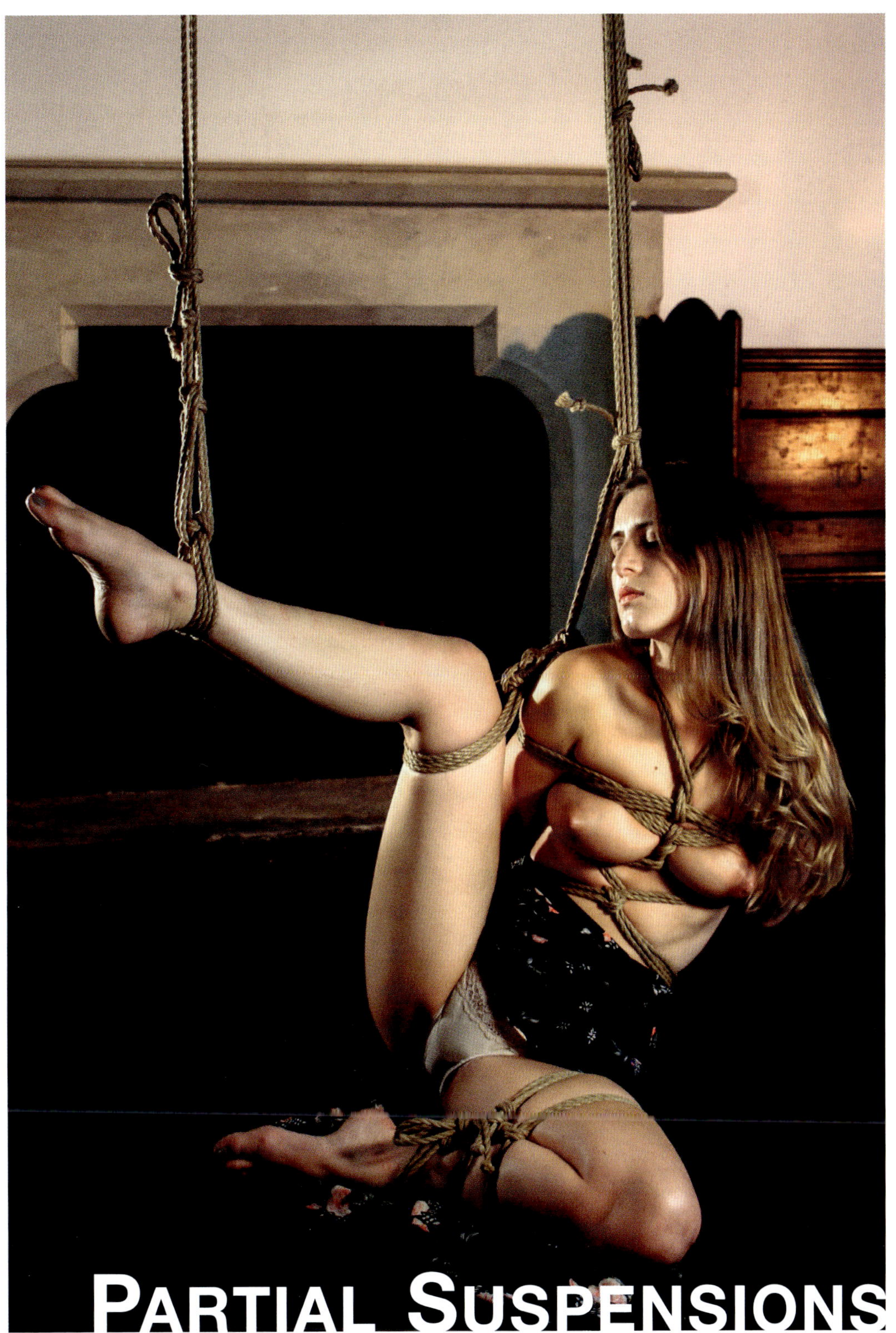

Partial Suspensions

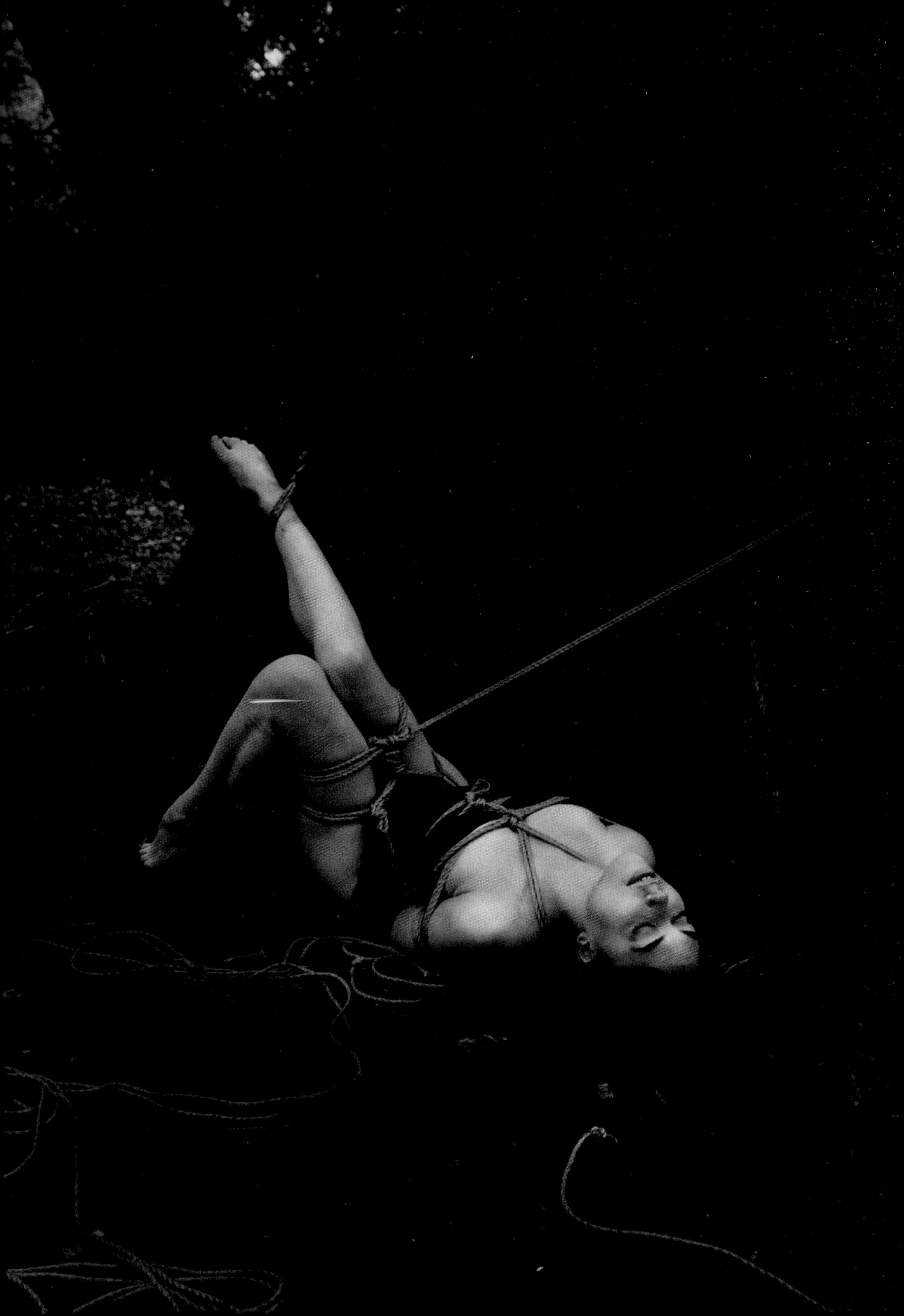

Partial Suspensions

Partial suspensions – suspensions where a part of the body remains touching the floor at all times – are sometimes thought of as an intermediate stage between floor work and the 'end goal' of full suspension, however I've tried here to present them as something very worthwhile in their own right. Practicing partial suspensions will give you an opportunity to familiarise yourself with many of the techniques used in full suspensions – but additionally the fact that they are comparatively low risk can give you the necessary mental space to begin experimenting with the possibilities adding gravity can bring to rope play sessions.

I've deliberately chosen not to talk about play in relation to full suspensions because I feel this can create a very stressful situation when you are first learning – in fact there are many people who are very experienced with full suspension but still prefer to stick to partials when they are playing more intimately. Keeping low to the floor can also allow partners to stay physically closer to each other. Some people choose never to move onto learning full suspensions, and happily explore floor work and partials for many years. I think it's important that this isn't seen as somehow a 'lesser' choice.

If it's within the limits of what you and your partner are comfortable to negotiate, you could consider adding other elements of play to the ties shown here, e.g. skin sensation play (candle wax, ice, and objects with different textures), impact play, or other toys.

Although it doesn't seem to be used so often, I have sometimes heard partial suspensions referred to as 'han'yuka-zuri' in Japan (translation: 'half floor suspension').

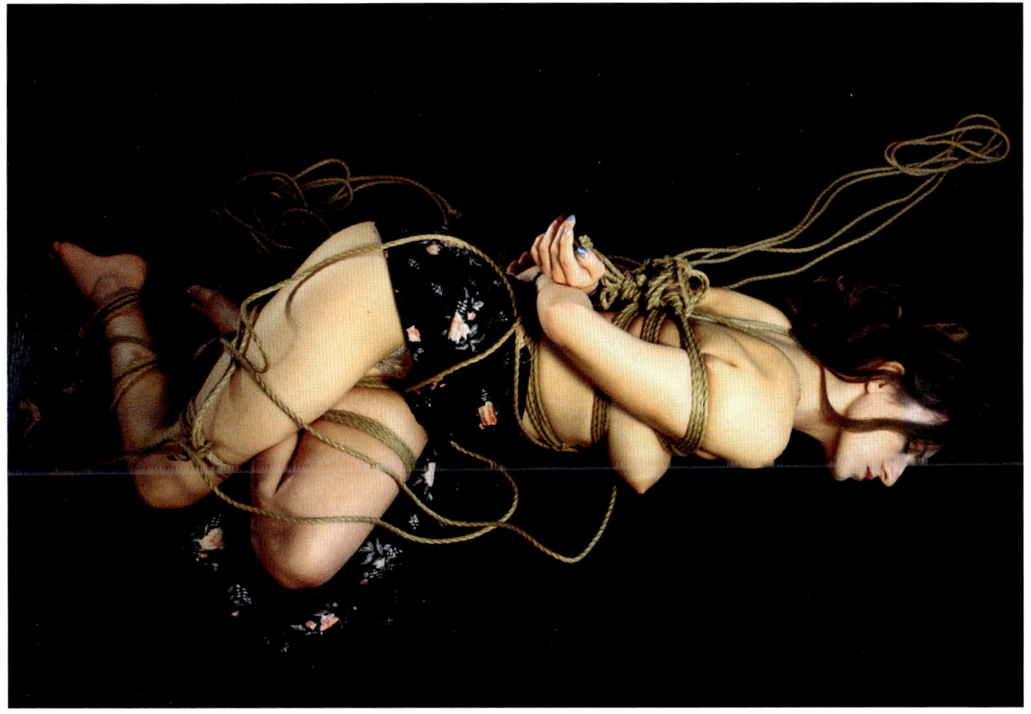

Lowering the Point

When practicing partial suspensions you'll sometimes find it easier to lower you suspension point so that you don't run out of rope so quickly on your suspension lines, and so that you can stay physically closer to your model whilst tying.

If you're mid scene and you don't wish to spend a lot of time reattaching your suspension equipment a quick alternative is to use one of your ropes.

[1] Fold your rope in half twice so you are holding the bight and rope ends together.

[2] Pass the folded rope over the original suspension point.

[3, 4] Decide on the right height for your lowered point and make a minimum of 3 alternating overhand knots at this level: 'left over right and under, right over left and under' etc. Compact the knots tightly together as you do so.

[5] Slide this knot up the top so that it doesn't get in the way and use this circle you've created as your new point.

If you're working on a single point, you can put carabiners into the bottom of this loop in order to keep the lines separated.

If you're working on bamboo, you can choose just to use an attachment like this for one of your lines (eg, the main line) and attach all other lines directly to the bamboo separately using the locking at the bottom method (pg. 115).

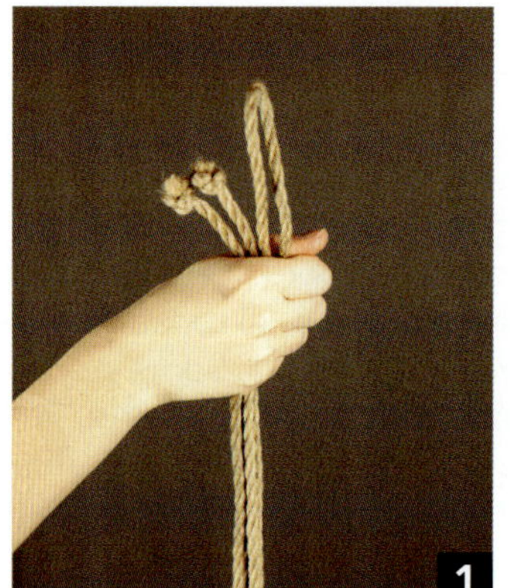
1

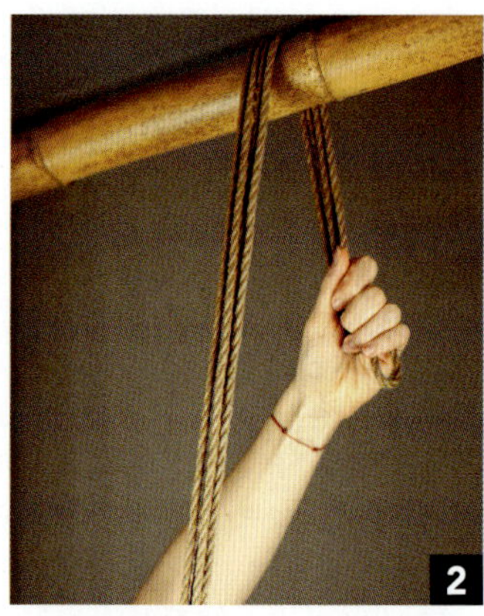
2

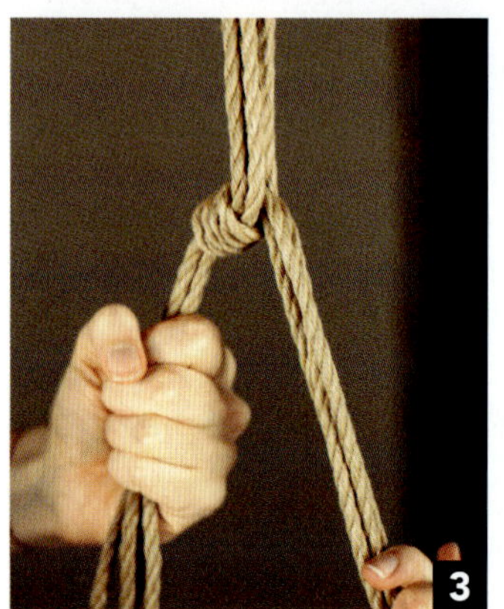
3

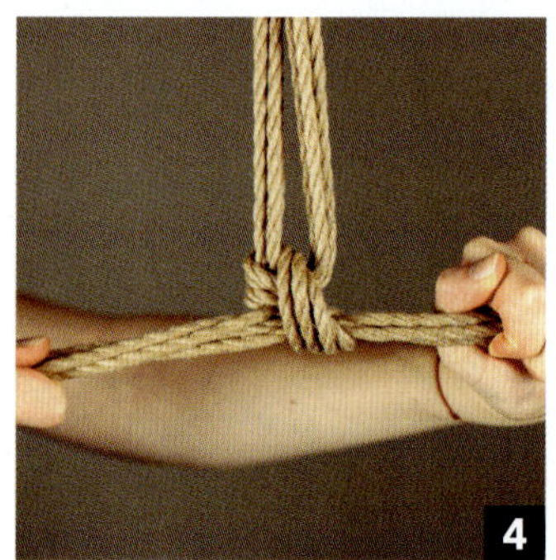
4

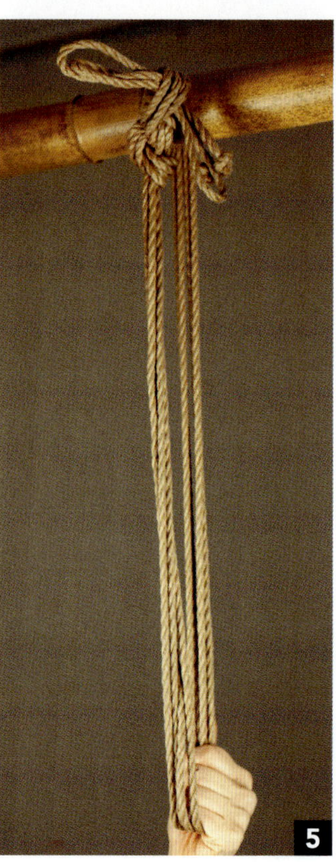
5

Opposite page: when tying on the floor you can also experiment with free tying. This harness is made using only hojo cuffs (pg. 31) and fairly random wrapping. Although it's not suitable for attaching a suspension line, it keeps the hands held loosely behind the back and gives you an alternative option if you're tying someone who prefers not to have the chest or shoulders too restricted.

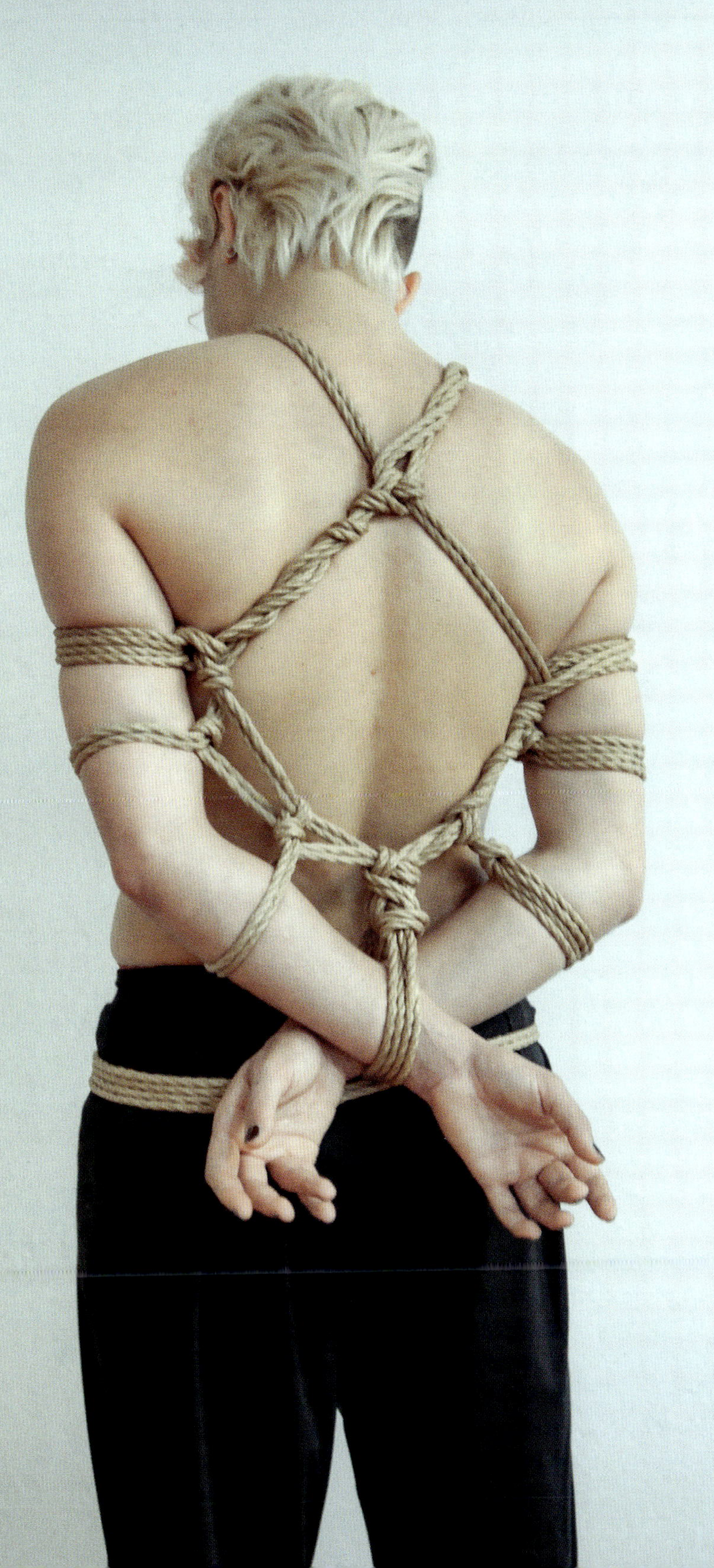

Kata-Ashikubi Partial Suspension

This is a very simple starting point for partial suspensions, but there's still a lot you can do with it as a tie. It creates exposure of the inner thighs which is great for sensation play. It also creates a small arch in the back which, in addition to the upward pull from the ankle line, adds a layer of tension in the body which many people enjoy, and often find that it makes them more sensitive to other forms of play. Here I have used the chest harness for floorwork and partial suspensions (pg. 82) but you can use another form of chest tie if you prefer.

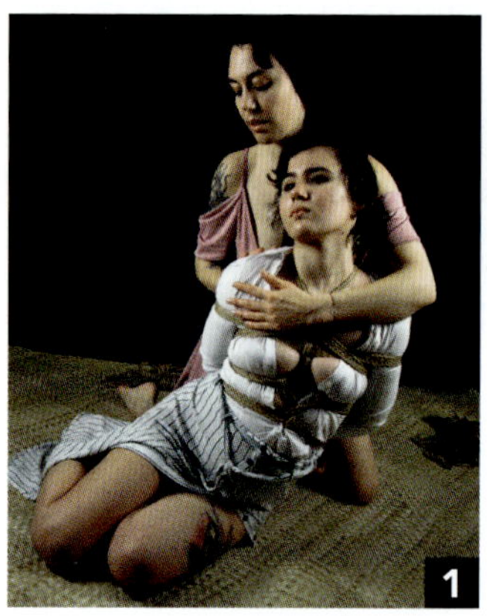

1

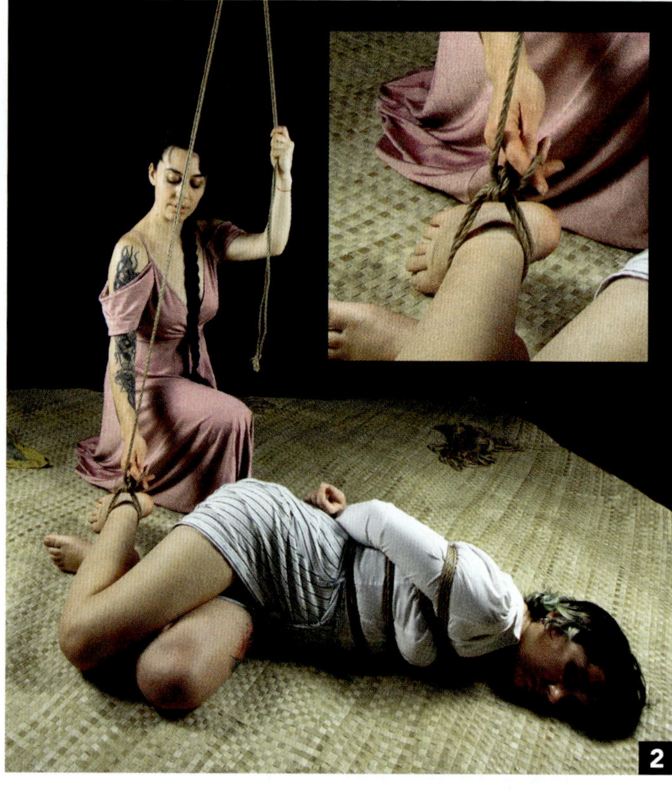

2

[1] Once you have finished tying an upper body harness, help the model to lie down on their side.

[2] Tie a single column tie in a 'V' shape (pg. 29) around the ankle closest to the ceiling and take the working end up to the suspension point. In order to leave enough room to stretch the leg out as far as desired I haven't lowered the point (pg. 128) which means I don't have enough rope to get back down to the ankle and through the bight before I start lifting. To make this movement more steady I'm putting my fingers through the bight and lifting with one hand as I pull down on the working end with the other hand. This also means that my fingers are ready to thread the working end through the bight when I get to that point.

[3] Once the leg is raised just enough that the shin is vertical, pause to dress the wrap and make sure it is in the model's preferred position (see 'notes for models' on pg. 164). If you lift this line too high before dressing the wrap there will be too much weight on the line and it will become very difficult.

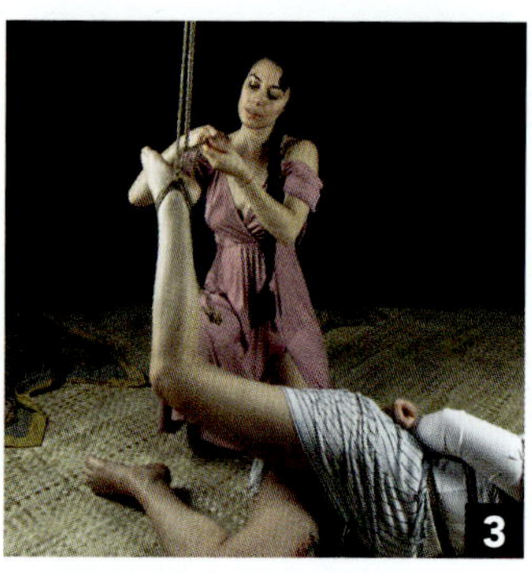

3

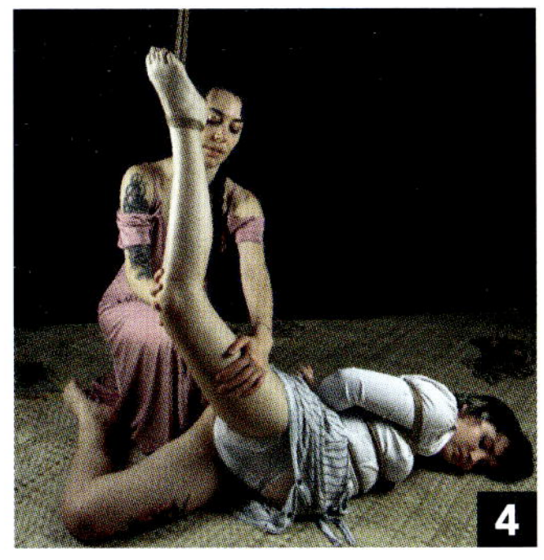
4

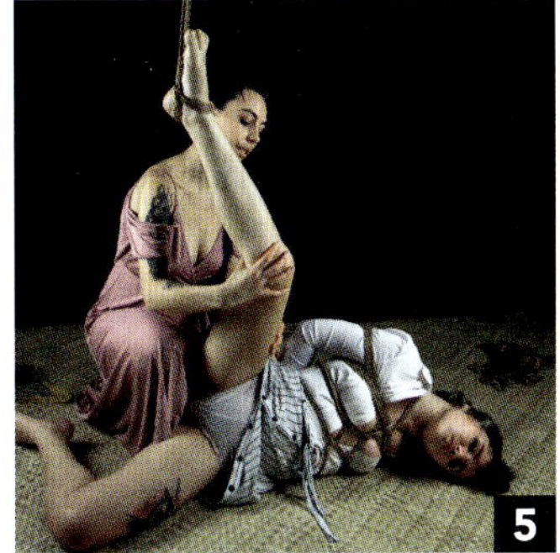
5

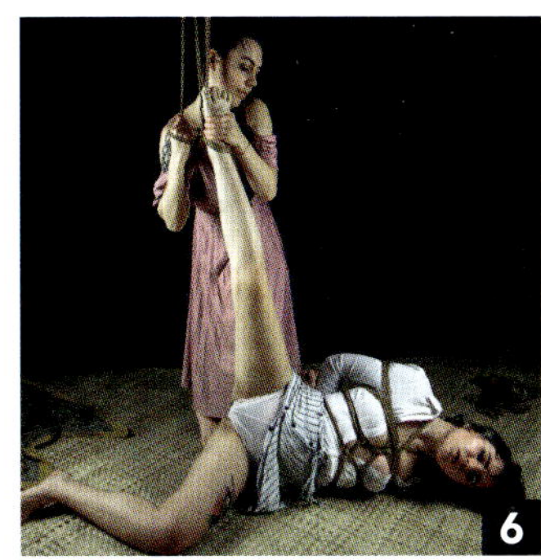
6

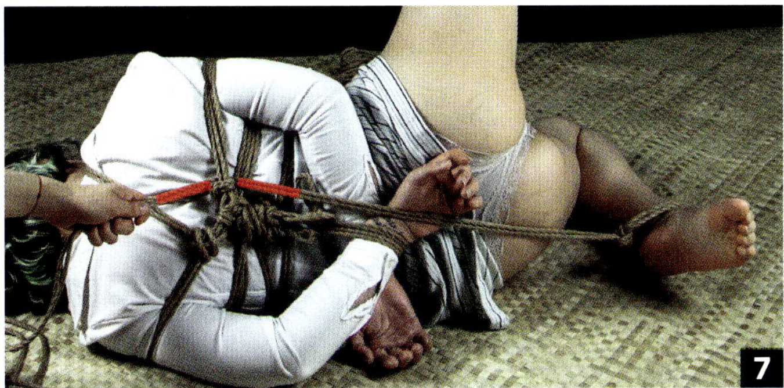
7

[4, 5] Models might find it feels smoother and more comfortable to roll the hip into the position shown in **[5]** whilst you lift, even though it's likely to change back naturally later on.

[6] Raise the leg as far as feels right for the model. I normally find that lifting just to the point that it's straight is enough; many people can find pressure on the ankle quite intense even at this level so there's no need to lift the hips off of the floor. Lock the line using whatever locking method is appropriate for your suspension point.

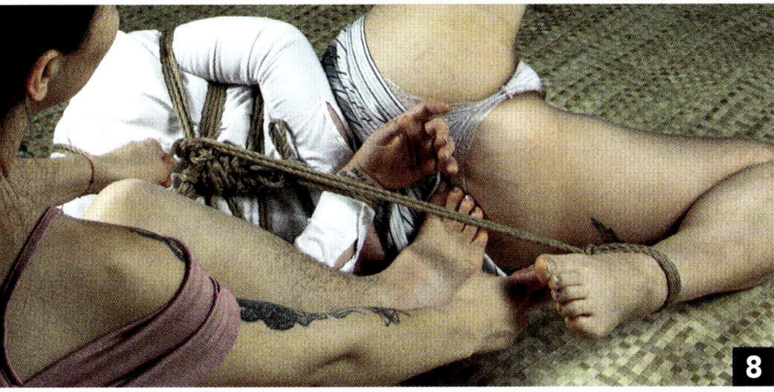
8

[7] Attach a new rope around the other ankle and thread it under the top wrap of the takate kote on the side of the stem closest to the ceiling. The parts highlighted in red show you the path of the rope clearly.

[8] Pull the ankle backwards. I find it easiest to do this by putting my foot on the model's hip to keep it forced forwards. Pull slowly enough that the model has time to adjust their body, and has enough time to let you know when it's in a good place for their particular level of flexibility. Once there, thread your working end back through the bight and lock with a yuki knot (pg. 37).

Notes for Models

After a while, lying the floor at this angle can become just as stressful on the shoulder as being in a full suspension – so be aware of your body and ask the rigger to make adjustments to your position if necessary.

Using Up the Rope

There will likely be a lot of rope left over from this second ankle tie, and using up rope doesn't always have to be strictly practical – here are some suggestions for ways of using up your rope in a more playful way.

[9, 10] Use it to wrap tightly around the thigh to create a sensation of pressure. **[11]** I secured this in place by going back through the loop of the yuki knot I made in step 8 and locking it with another yuki knot.

[12, 13] You can also take the leftover rope between the legs and hook it through the waist wrap on the chest harness, then back through the legs, creating a crotch rope.

[14] I still had a little rope left over after this so I used it to wrap around the foot – some people enjoy pressure in this area.

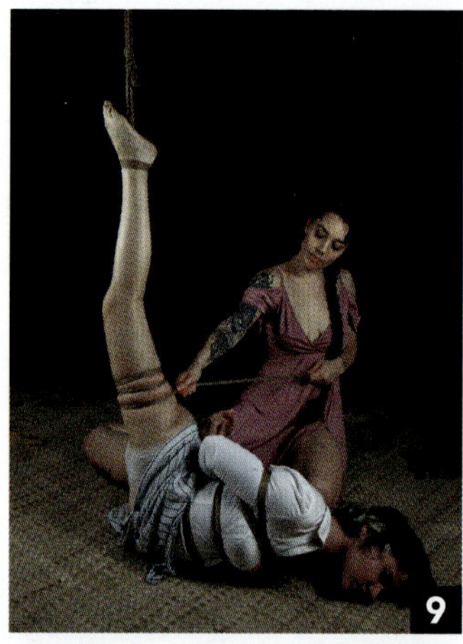

9

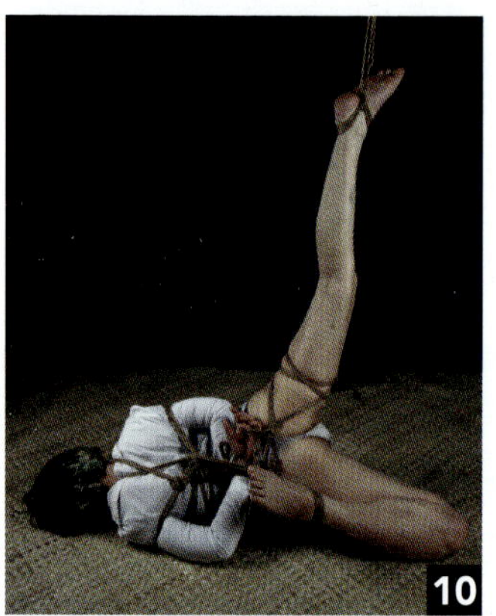

10

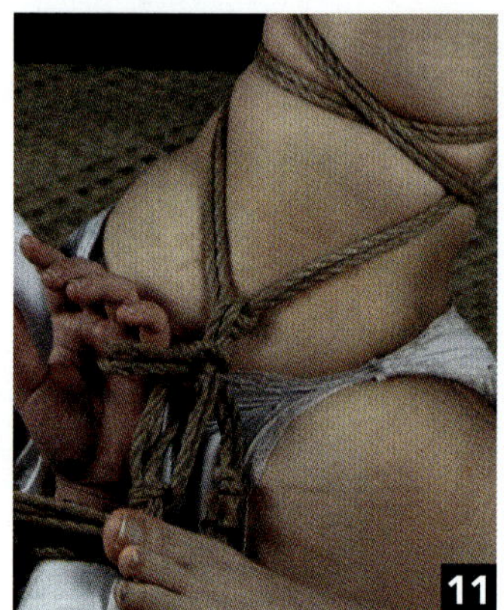

11

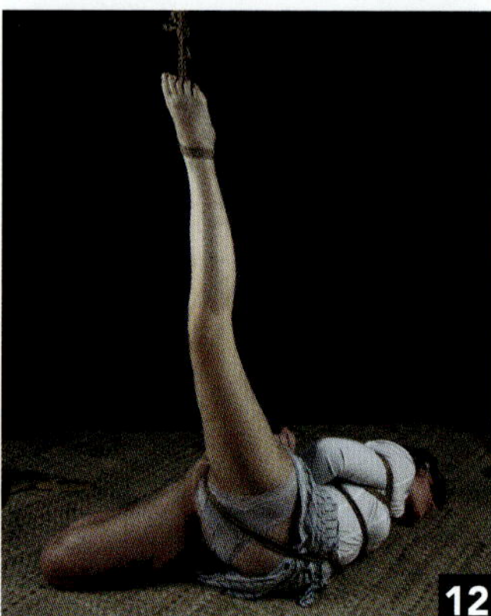

12

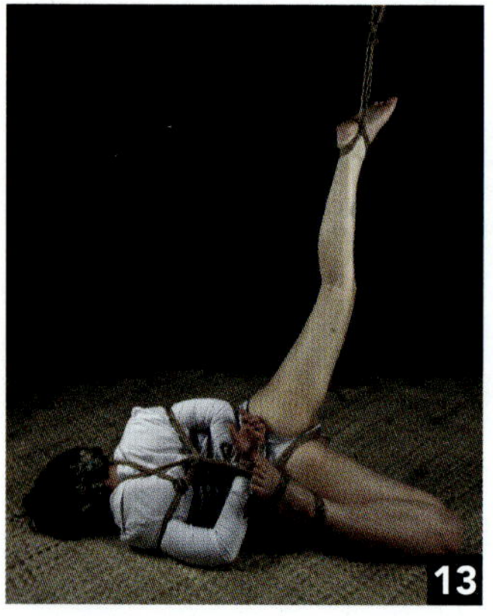

13

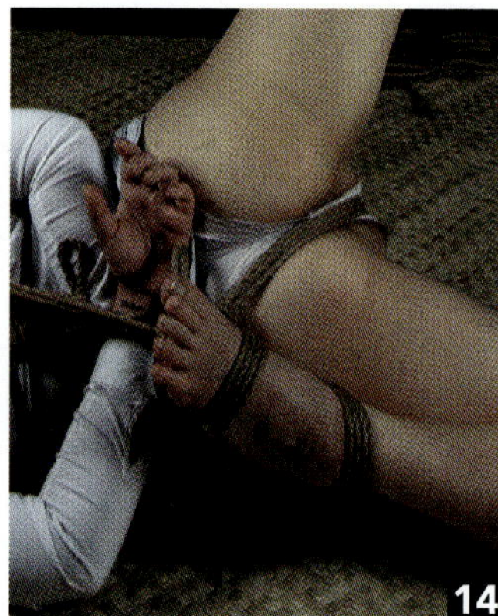

14

Futomomo Partial Suspension

The process of creating this tie is similar to the last one but it creates a very different result. Pulling the knee forwards like this creates, to my mind, a more explicitly erotic shape. Here I have attached the futomomo with the stem (and therefore suspension line) on the inside as it forces open the legs more, again helping to create exposure. You can also experiment with what happens when attaching from the outside – which also creates a lot more sensation on the inner thigh, in addition to changing the position of the body.

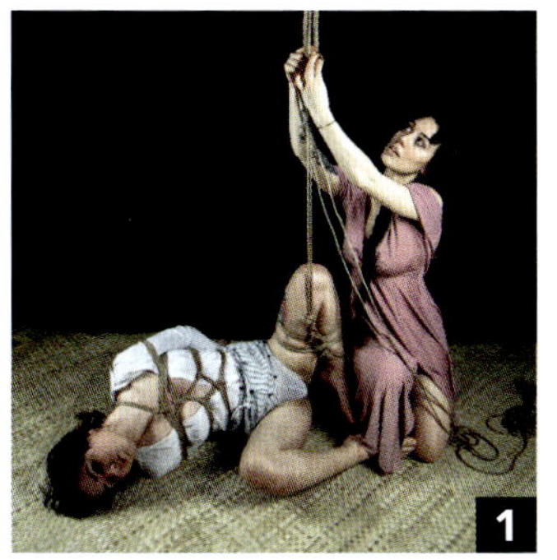

1

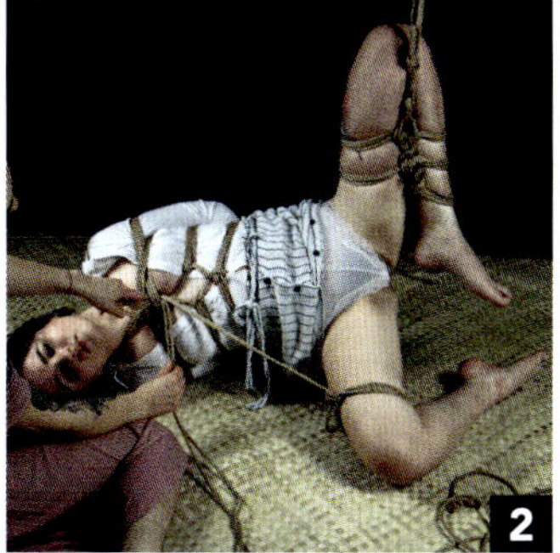

2

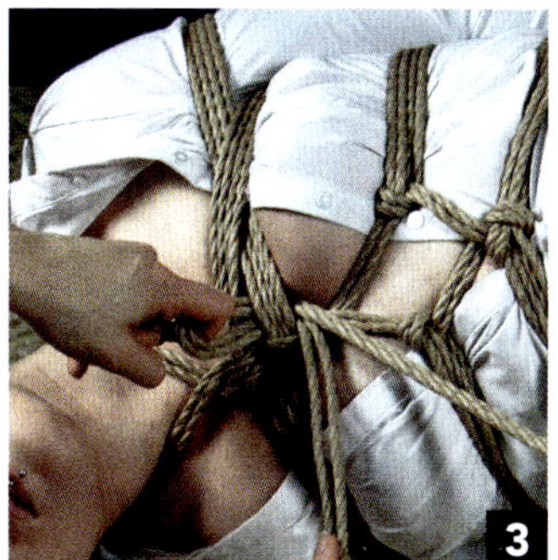

3

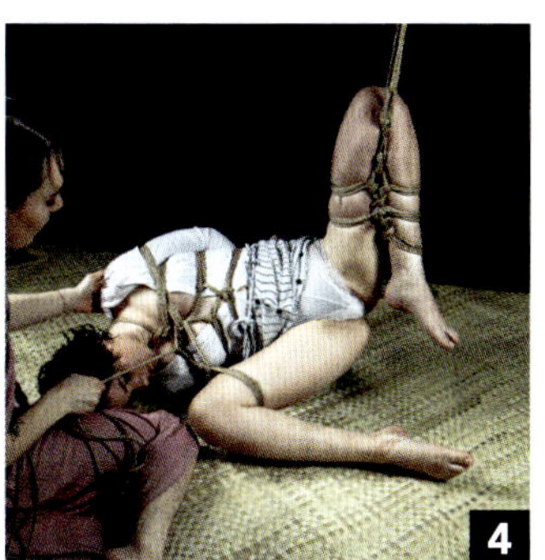

4

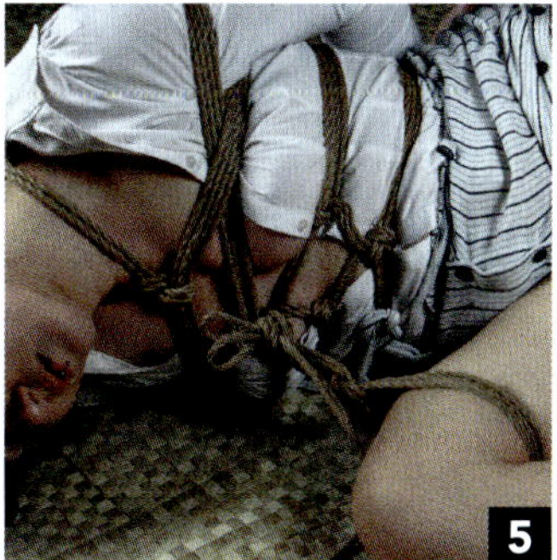

5

[1] Attach a suspension line to the futomomo. Here I've used an ypsilon (spiral – pg. 108) on the top wrap. Lift it to the suspension point. Once again, the higher it is pulled it the more intense it will become for the model but there is no real need to pull it that high. Lock the line in whichever way is most suitable for the suspension equipment you are using.

[2, 3] Tie a fairly tight single column just above the knee. Hook the working end through the front of your chest harness (in this case I have used the wrap going over the shoulders).

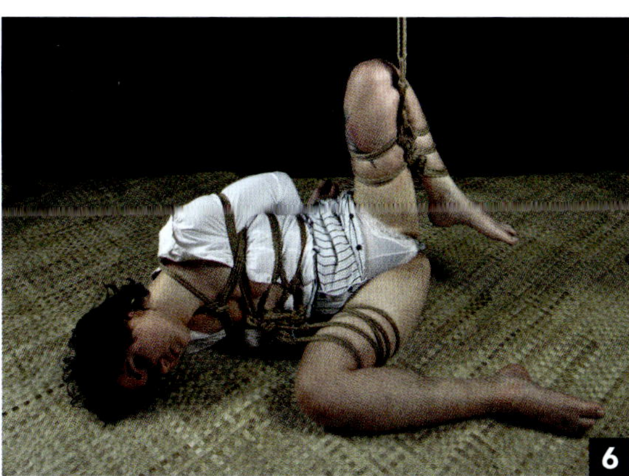

6

[4] Pull the line in as far as is suitable for the model's flexibility.

[5] Take the working end back through the bight of the single column and secure with a yuki knot (pg. 37, pg. 115).

[5] The tie is finished. I have used up my excess rope by wrapping tightly around the thigh to create pressure.

Hashigata Partial Suspension

Hashigata translates as 'bridge shaped'.

I find this simple tie one of the most effective for play; the forced backbend can create a tension in the thighs and pelvic floor area which some people find erotic.

Start with any harness that keeps the model's hands behind their back, and two futomomos. Add a koshinawa (waist rope) by tying a single column tie with a double bight (pg. 109) around the waist.

[1, 2, 3] Help the model to lie on their back and lift the line from the waist up to whatever height feels right for the model.

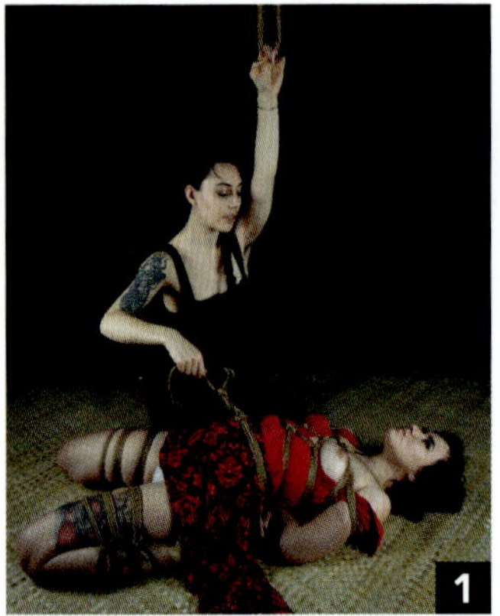

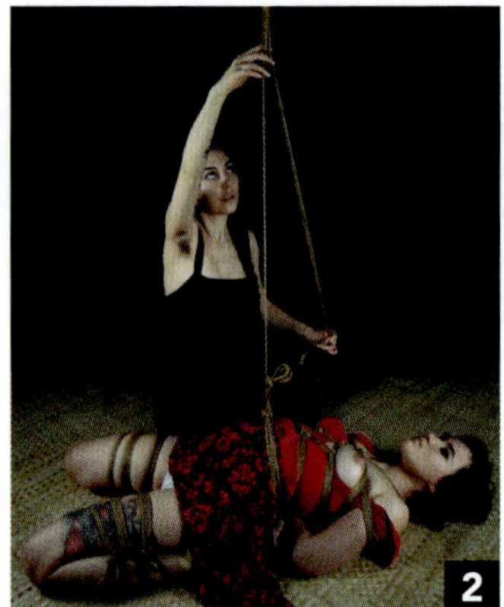

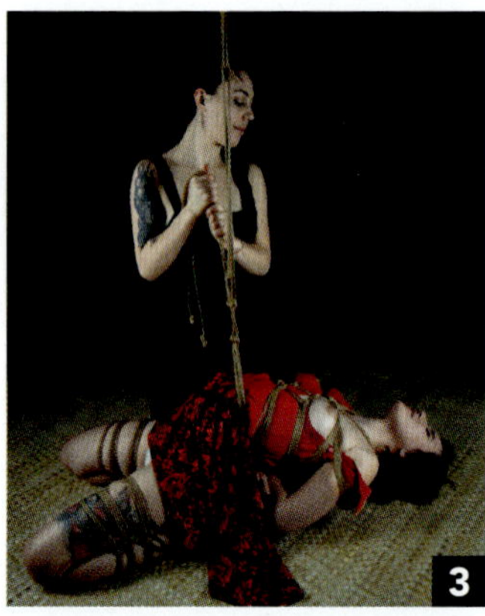

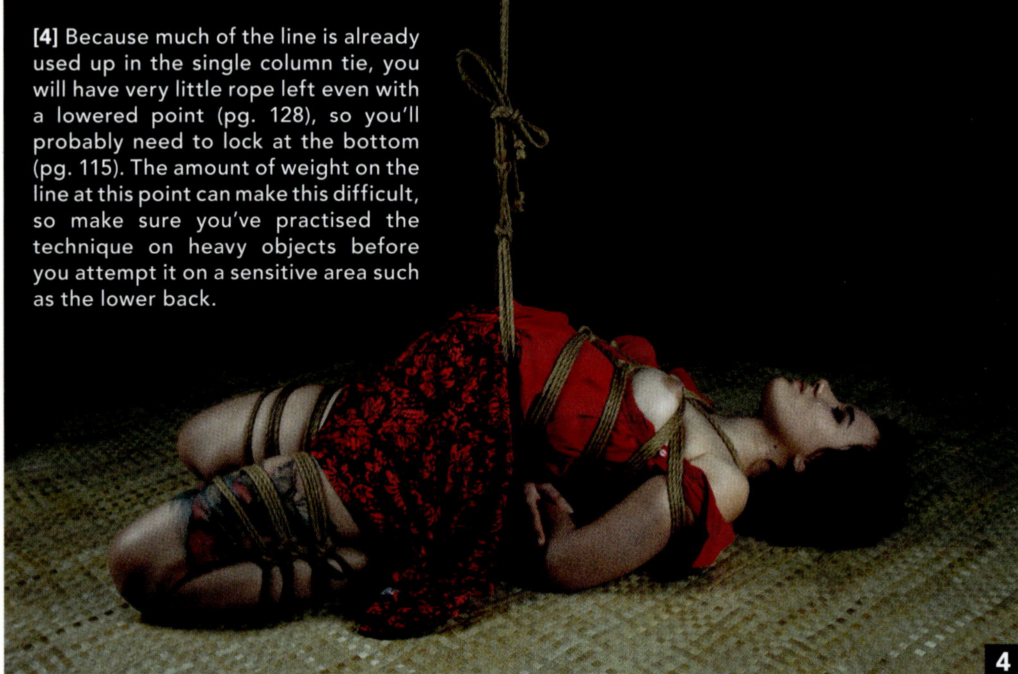

[4] Because much of the line is already used up in the single column tie, you will have very little rope left even with a lowered point (pg. 128), so you'll probably need to lock at the bottom (pg. 115). The amount of weight on the line at this point can make this difficult, so make sure you've practised the technique on heavy objects before you attempt it on a sensitive area such as the lower back.

Variation

[5, 6] You can continue to play with this shape by lifting one of the futomomos to create a little twist in the body and see how it changes the sensation. Because there's already tension in the body the pressure on inside of leg from the futomomo could be quite stimulating.

I've used the excess rope from the futomomo suspension line to tie the two lines together, compacting the shape.

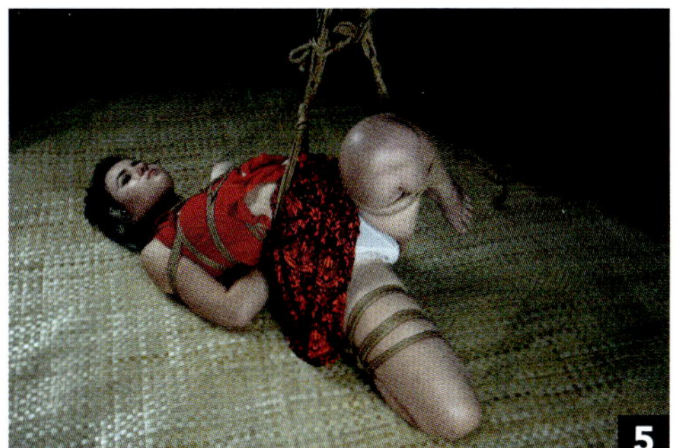
5

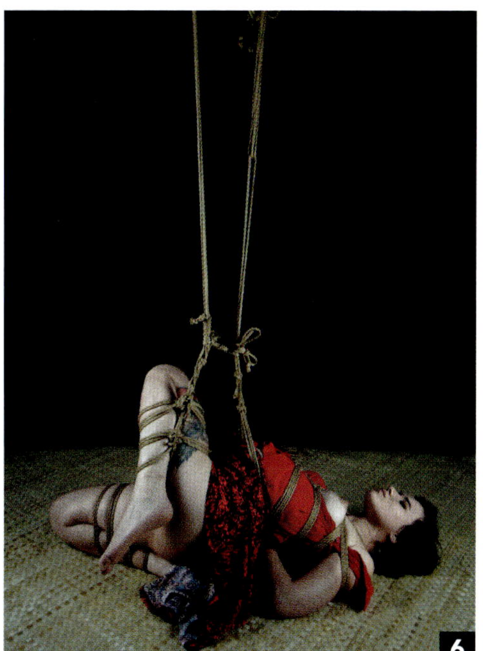
6

Gyaku-ebi (Hogtie) Partial Suspension

As in the 'hashigata partial suspension' this tie begins with a chest harness and two futomomos. This time, help the model roll onto their front. Begin by attaching suspension lines to the outside of each futomomo.

This is a more stressful position than the previous ties, and can cause restriction to the breathing – I suggest you read 'positional asphyxia' on pg. 21 before trying this tie.

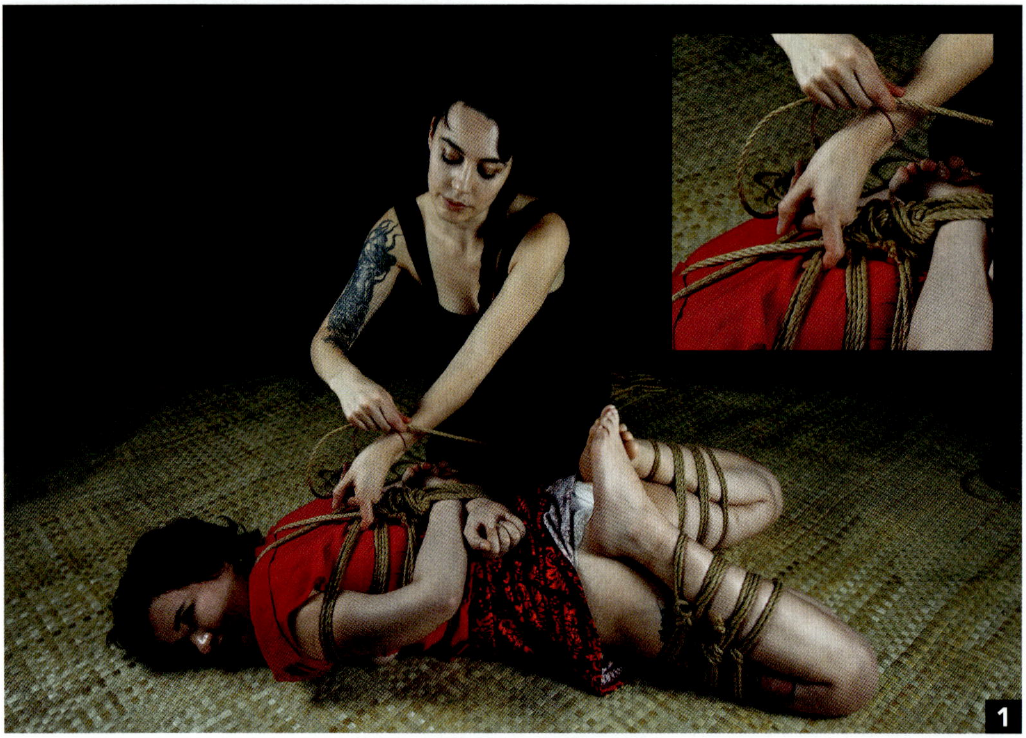

[1] Take the first futomomo line across to the opposite side of the body and hook the working end around the top wrap of the chest harness.

[2] Take it back through the bight and pull in a little tension.

[3] Lock the line using a yuki knot (pg. 37) and repeat the process on the other side. You should now have two lines crossing at the back of the body.

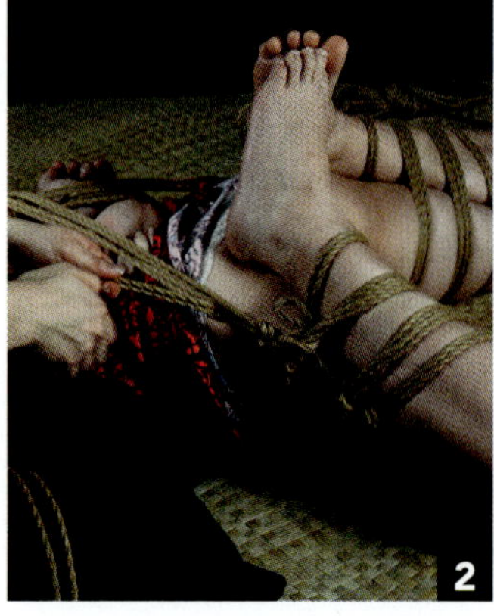

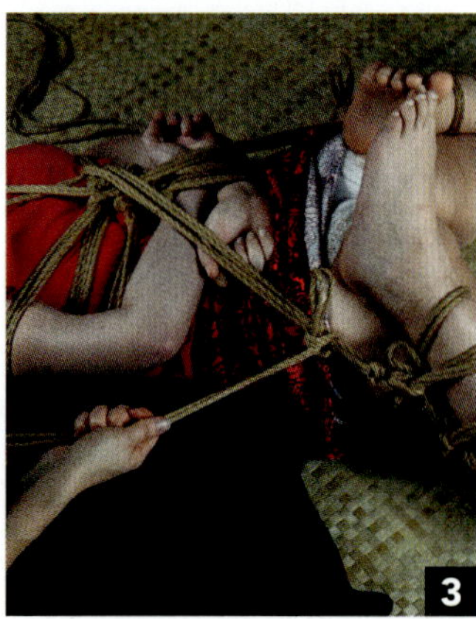

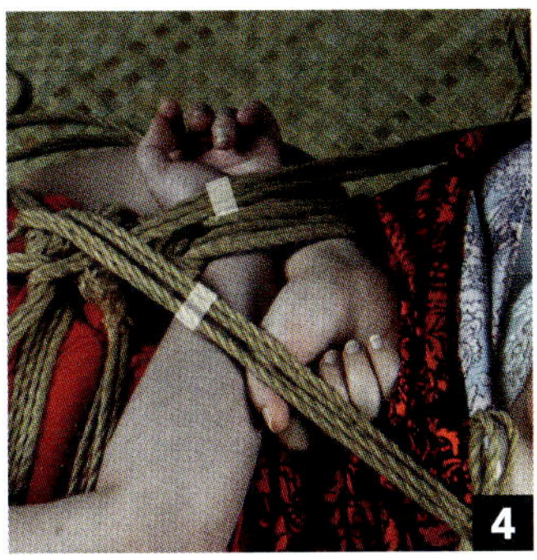

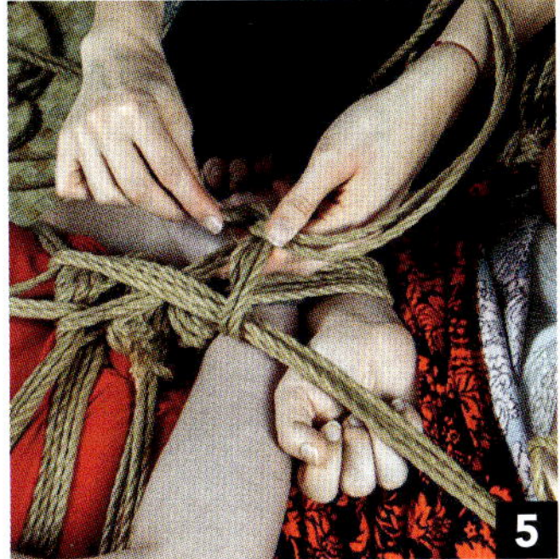

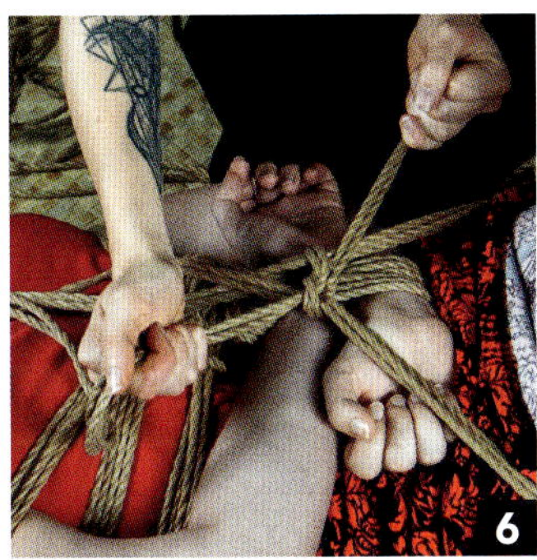

[4, 5] Take a new rope and attach it to the two crossing lines at the points shown in white using an ypsilon (pg. 107). Be **very** careful not to accidentally pick up the wrist wraps as you do this.

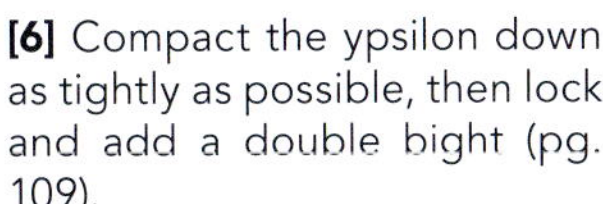

[6] Compact the ypsilon down as tightly as possible, then lock and add a double bight (pg. 109).

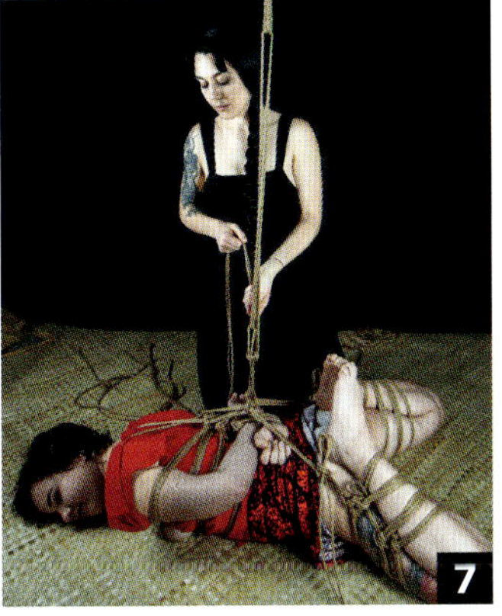

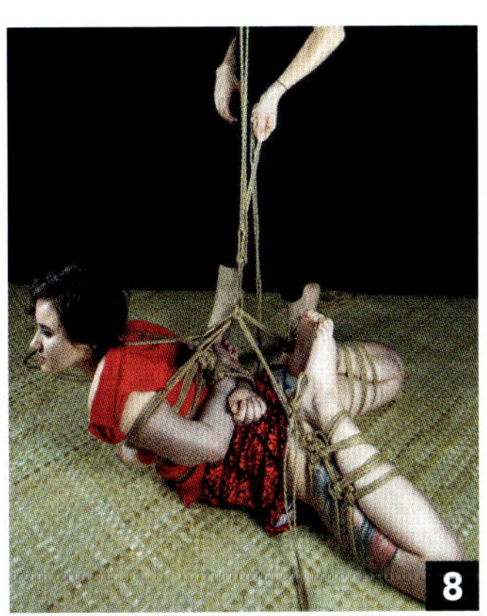

[7] Take the working end up to the suspension point – here I have a lowered point (pg. 128) – and down to the double bight.

[8] Pull up slowly on the suspension line as far as is comfortable for the model. Some people enjoy being in quite a strict position, whilst others will prefer just enough tension to create pressure. Lock in whatever way works for the type of suspension point you are using.

[9, 10] The tie is finished. I have used up the excess rope from my futomomo lines by wrapping it tightly around the legs over the top of the futomomo because I like the aesthetic, and because I can pull in a fraction more tension as I do so – but this is not essential and you can use up the rope in any way you wish.

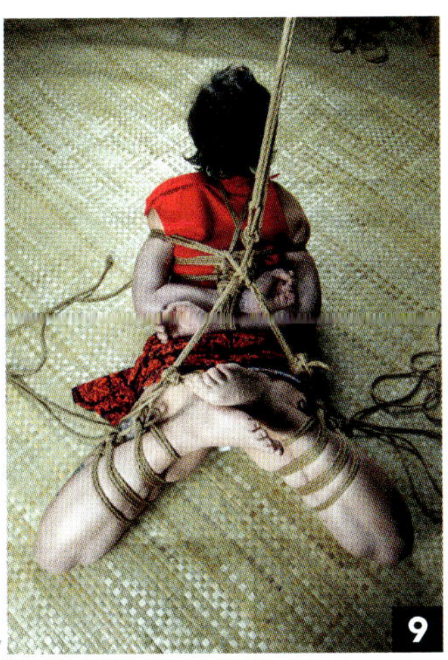

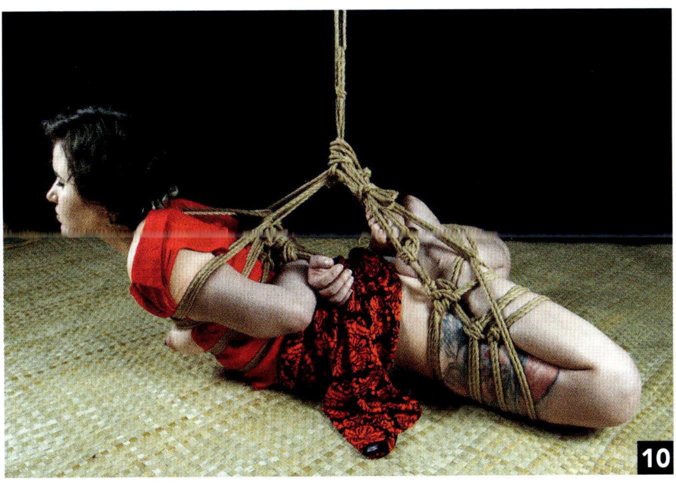

Kata-Ashi Kaikyaku Partial Suspension and Transition

This tie is a little more involved than the previous ones. It's the only tie in this book which uses a transition – a movement between two positions – which although relatively safe when this close to the floor, can still go wrong if you're not confident moving a suspension line smoothly whilst supporting the model's body.

Transitions are useful in building a scene because they can offer a change of feeling or pace and help you prolong play. In this case, the ropes around the chest are likely to become tiring for the model after a while – so lowering the chest to the ground can help to relieve this, whilst enabling you to continue the scene. The moment of release when moving from a stressful position to a more relaxed one can also be quite powerful.

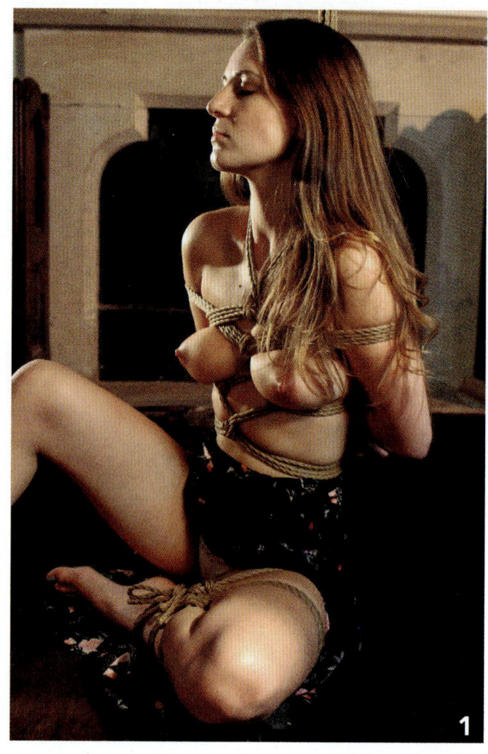

Once you've done this transition, you can probably work out how to move into one of the previous partial suspensions quite easily if you wish to play for longer. For example, removing all of the lines, rolling the model over, and creating the futomomo partial (pg. 133) will give them a chance to lie on the other side of their body if one arm is getting tired, whilst again providing a new sensation.

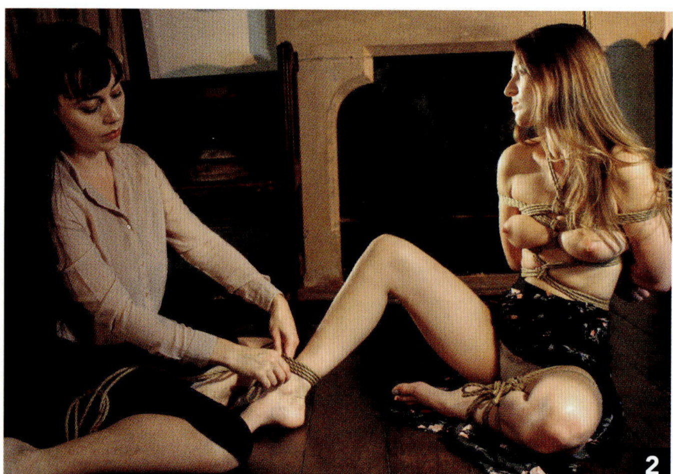

[1] Attach a suspension line to the back of the harness (pg. 88). With the model sitting comfortably on the floor, take the line up to the suspension point and create just enough tension to support them. Lock the line, and tie a futomomo (pg. 78) on one leg.

[2] Tie a single column around the other ankle. You can make this reasonably tight-fitting. Even though this is an ankle tie, we don't need to use the 'V' shaped single column in this case because the foot will never reach a fully vertical position.

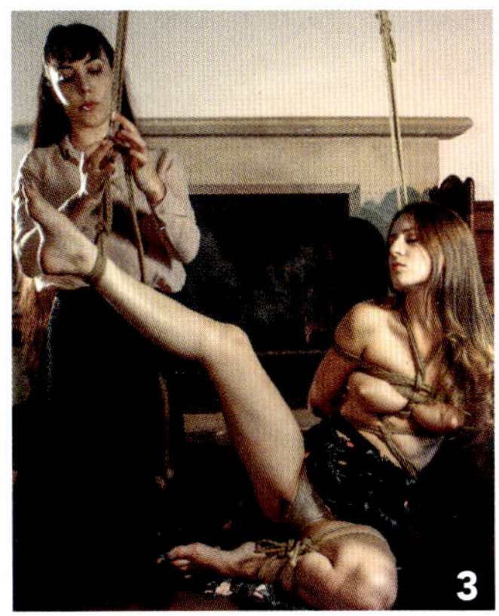

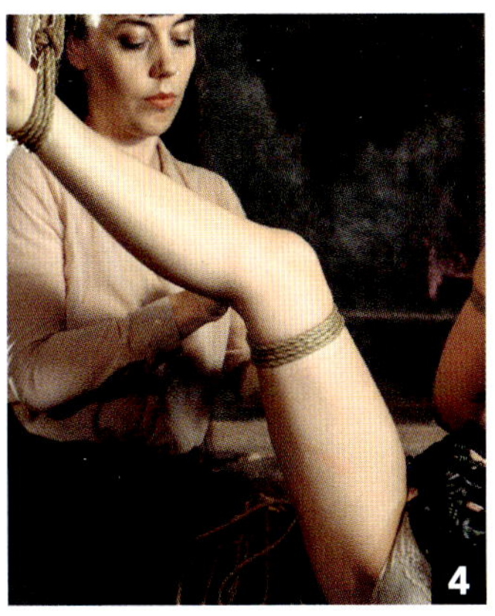

[3] Raise the ankle to a position that is comfortable for the model's level of flexibility. It's easy for the body to overbalance if the leg is pulled too far, which you want to avoid.

[4] Tie a fairly tight fitting single column tie around the thigh just above the knee.

[5] Take it through the centre of the ypsilon at the base of the main line. I have left quite a large gap in the ypsilon for this reason, but you could also go directly around the line if you wish to compact the ypsilon more.

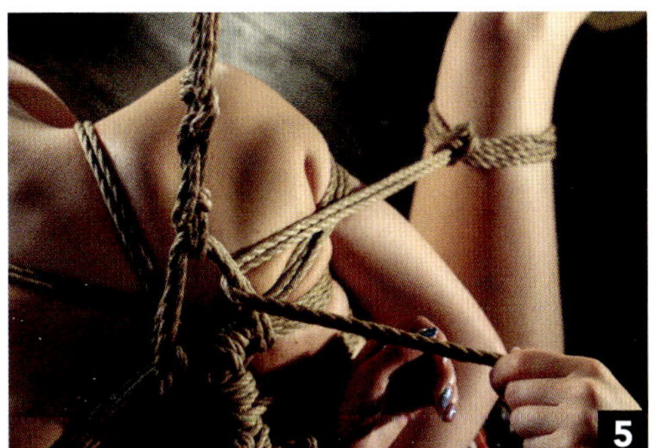

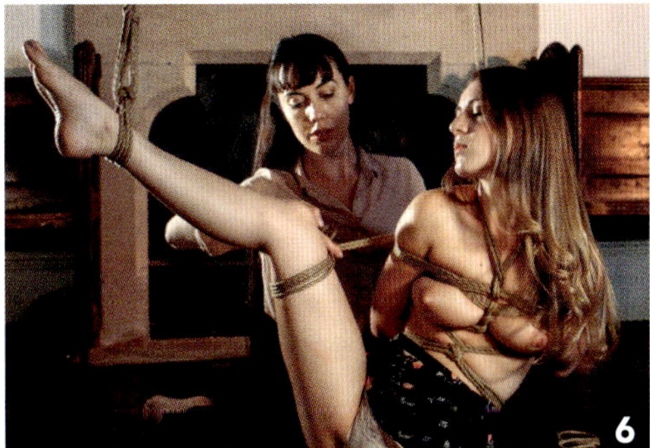

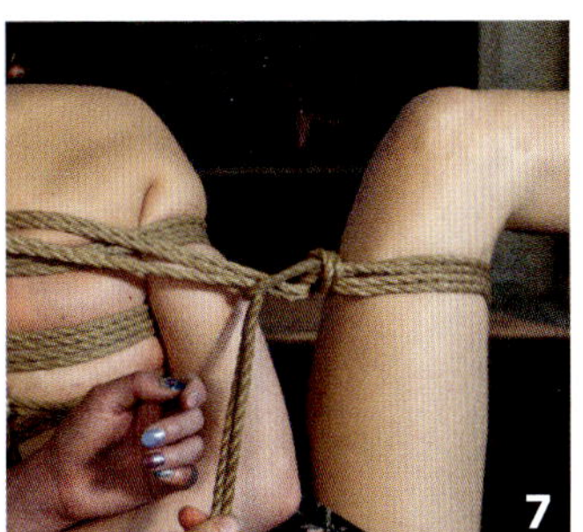

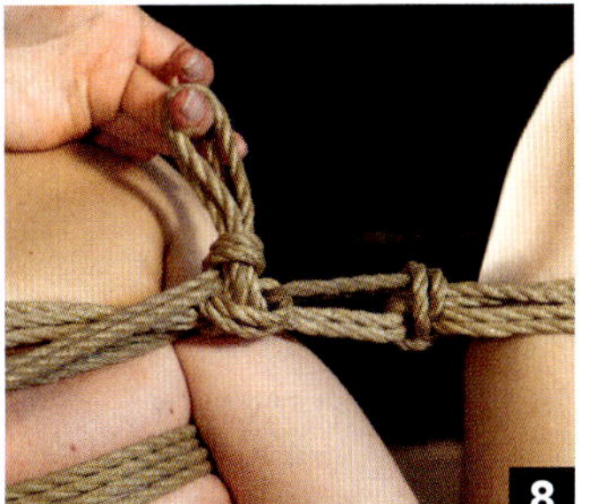

[6] Pull the knee into the body as close as is comfortable for the model.

[7] Pass the working end back through the bight.

[8] Lock with a yuki knot (pg. 37).

[9] Take the working end up to the point then back down and through the newly created double bight from the previous yuki knot.

[10] Pull the rope up to take a little weight (note the slight upward 'V' shape) and lock off using the same yuki knot technique as before.

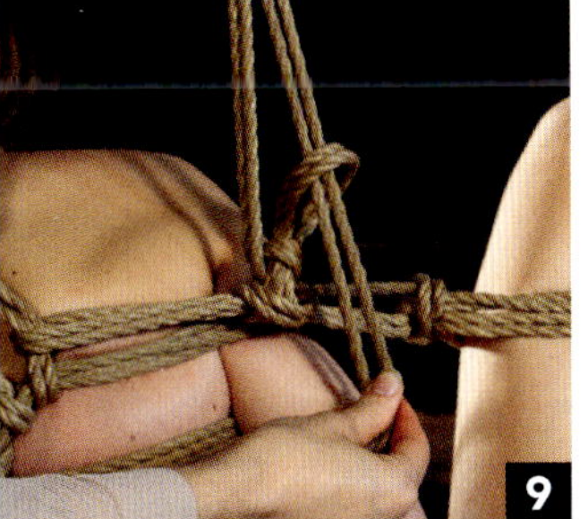

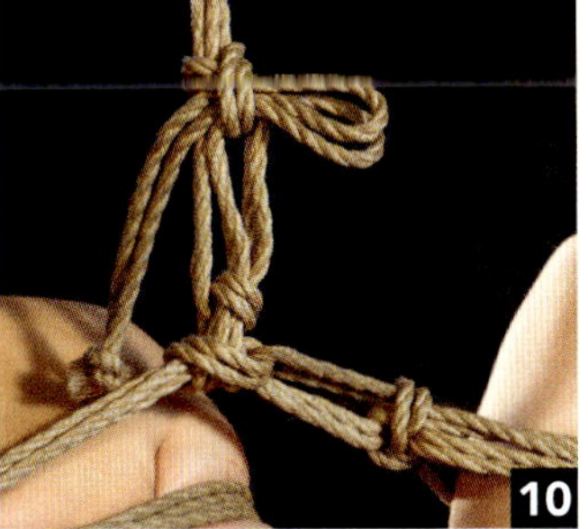

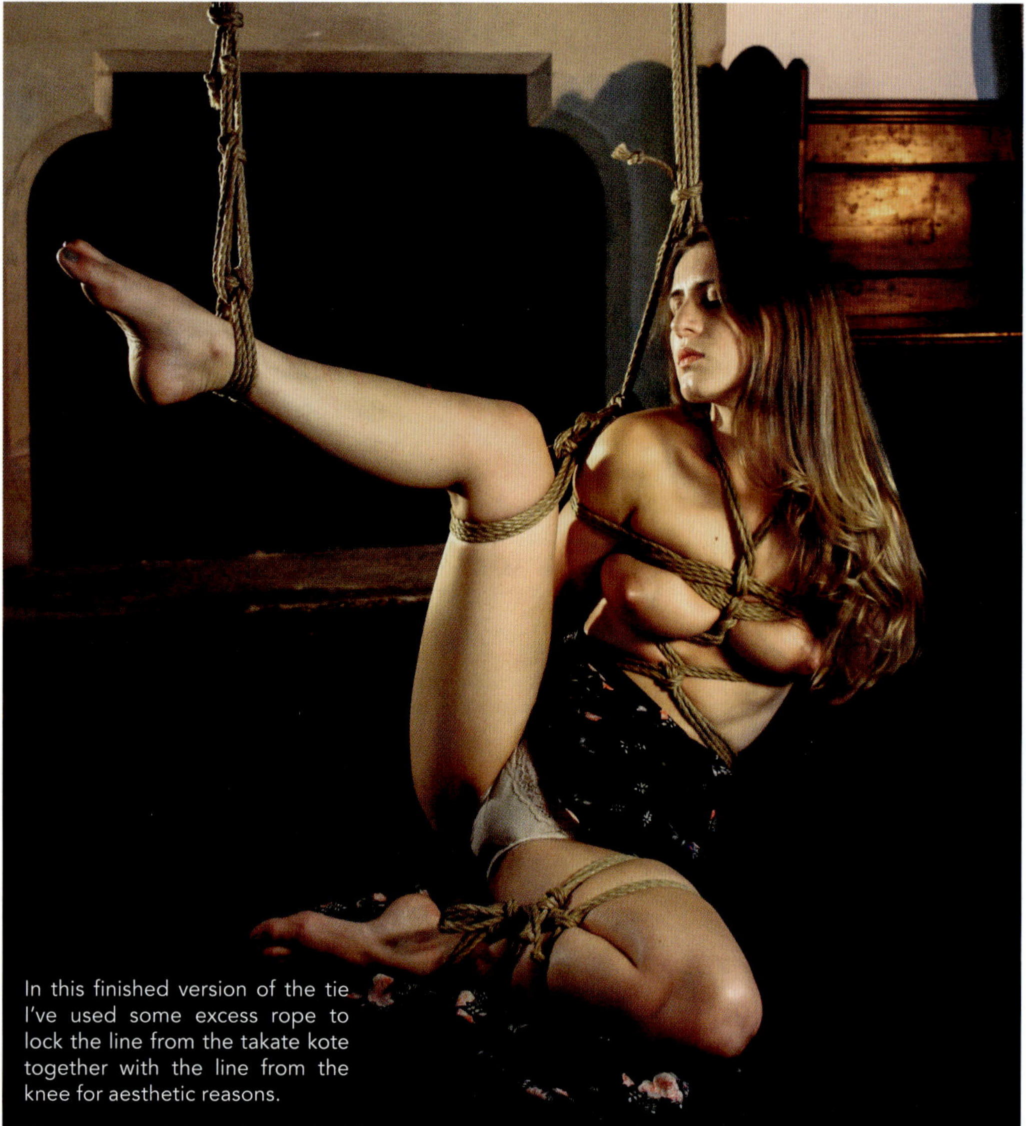

In this finished version of the tie I've used some excess rope to lock the line from the takate kote together with the line from the knee for aesthetic reasons.

Notes for Models

Depending on a combination of how your body naturally bends, and the relative heights of the suspension lines this tie has the potential to either compress the body inwards (by pulling the knee into the chest), or create a slight torsion (by pulling the knee into the back so that the chest begins to twist towards to floor). Either result is fine. Torsions are not covered properly in this book, but you can still begin to explore the feeling to a small extent in this tie.

You should be cautious not to over twist the outside shoulder joint. Be aware of your body, and ask the rigger to untie or transition if you feel too much discomfort or tiredness from holding the position.

Transitioning the Tie

When making this transition, you need to be very careful not to drop the model's torso as you move the main line.

Before you start, undo the line going up from the knee rope to the suspension point but leave the knee attached to the back of the takate kote. You could wrap excess rope tight around the thigh to create pressure and sensation, whilst keeping the trailing ends out of the way.

[13] Undo the main line, and support the model by putting your hand on the side of their neck/shoulder.

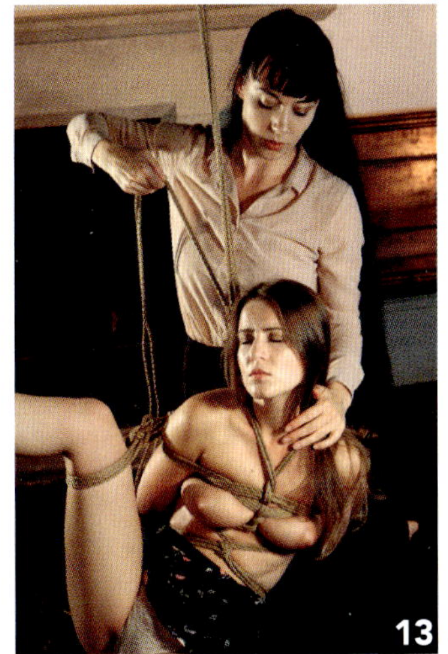

13

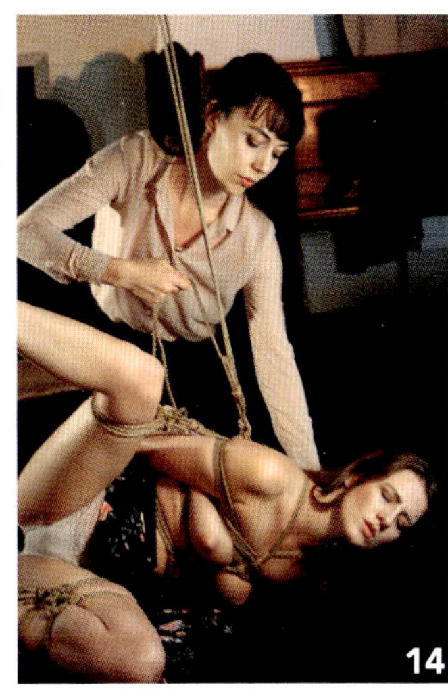

14

[14] Keeping a firm hand on the suspension line, gently lower the model to the floor.

[15] Relock the suspension line, with just a tiny bit of tension on it – use the technique for locking at the bottom of lines on pg. 115 if you don't have enough rope left to reach back up to the point.

[16] Undo the ankle line and raise it higher to stretch out the leg. The knee will be kept bent due to the attachment at the back of the takate kote, and this will create a little pressure and tension between the leg and the chest.

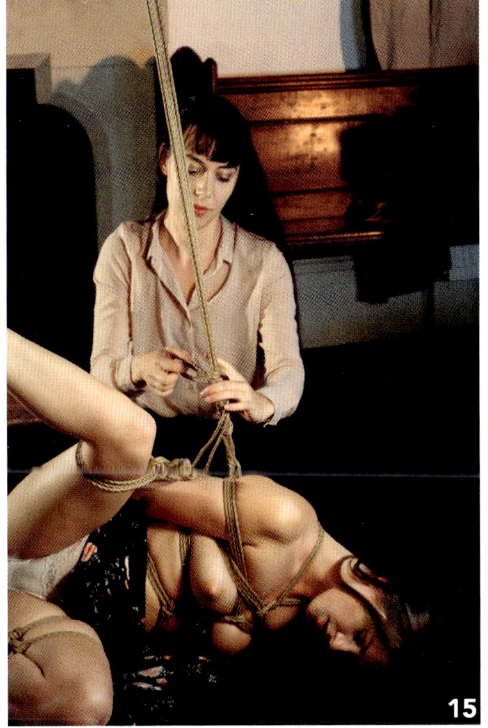

15

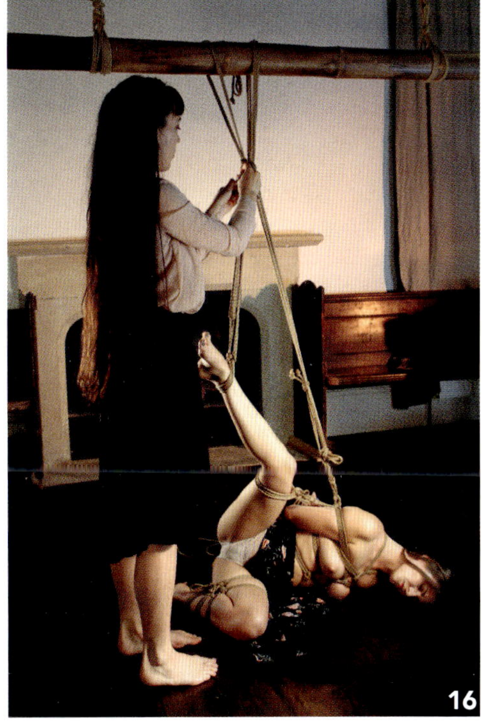

16

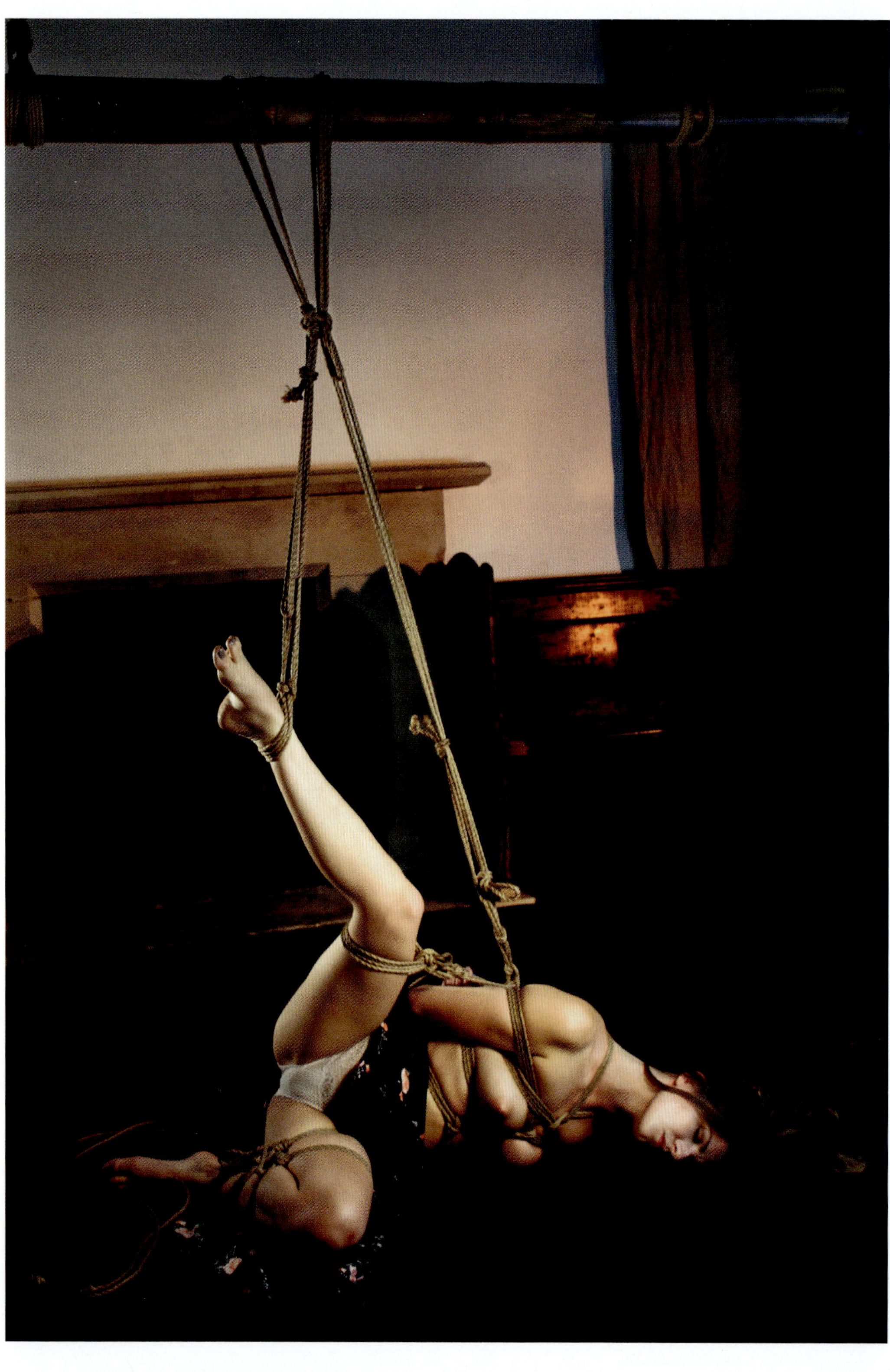

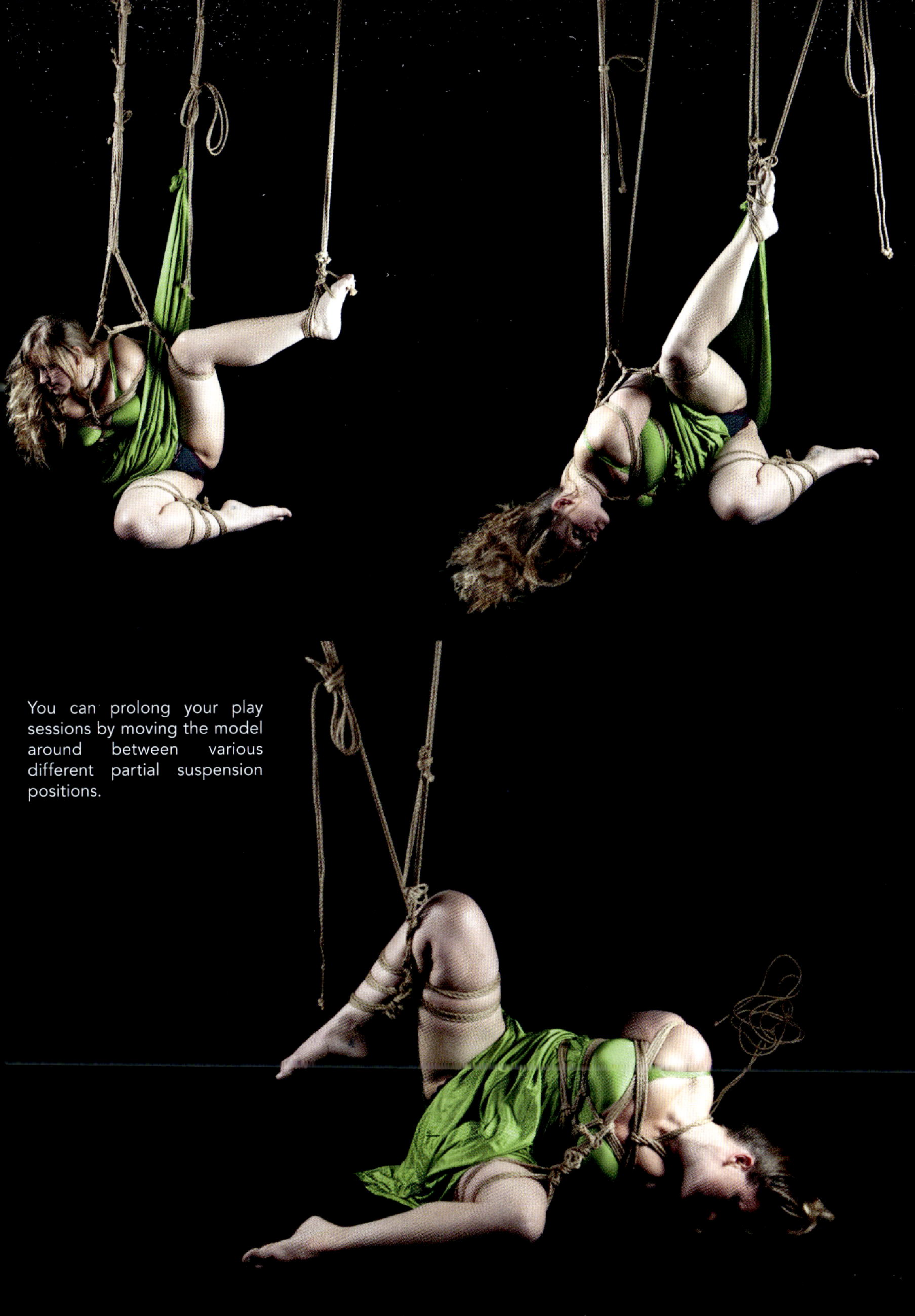

You can prolong your play sessions by moving the model around between various different partial suspension positions.

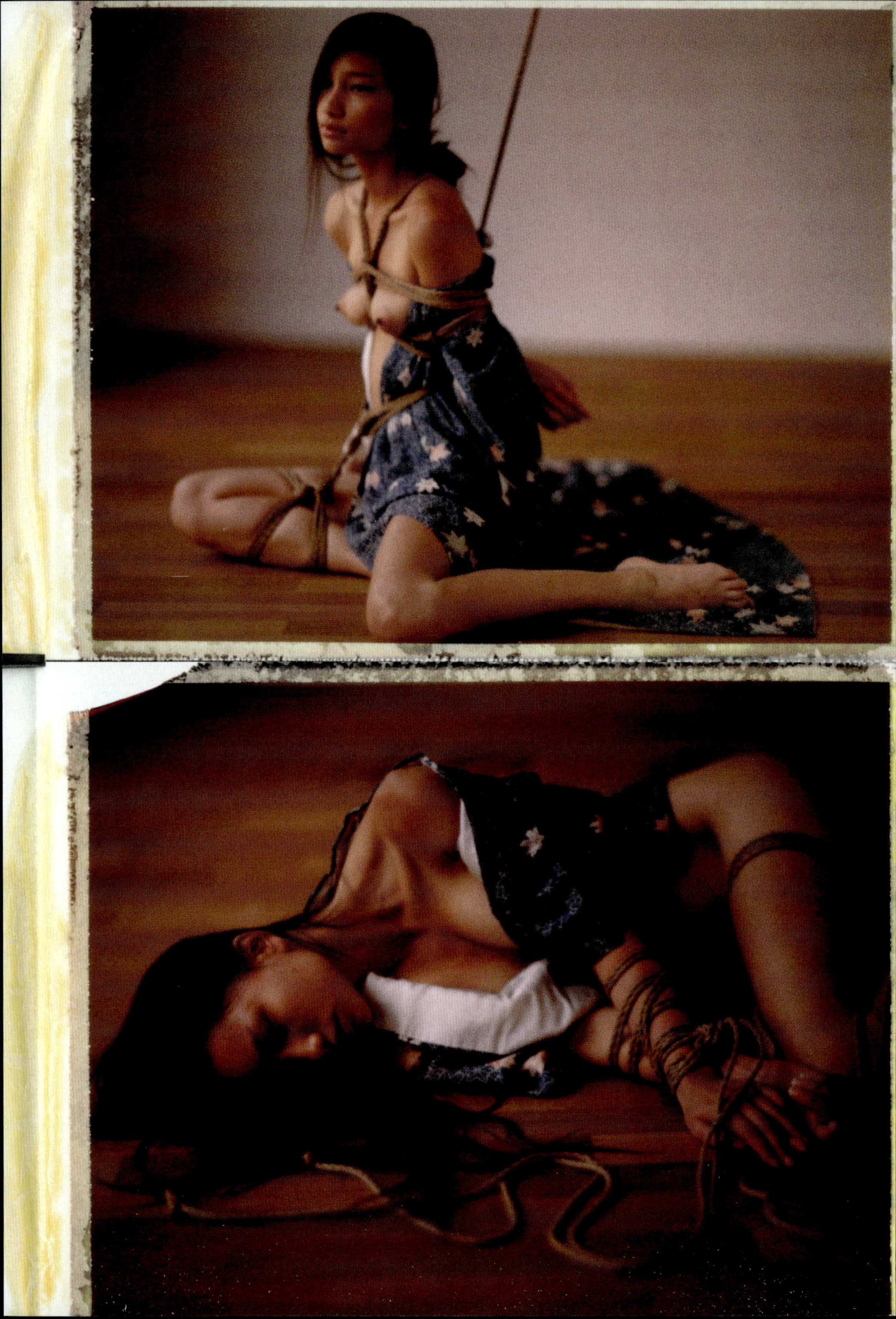

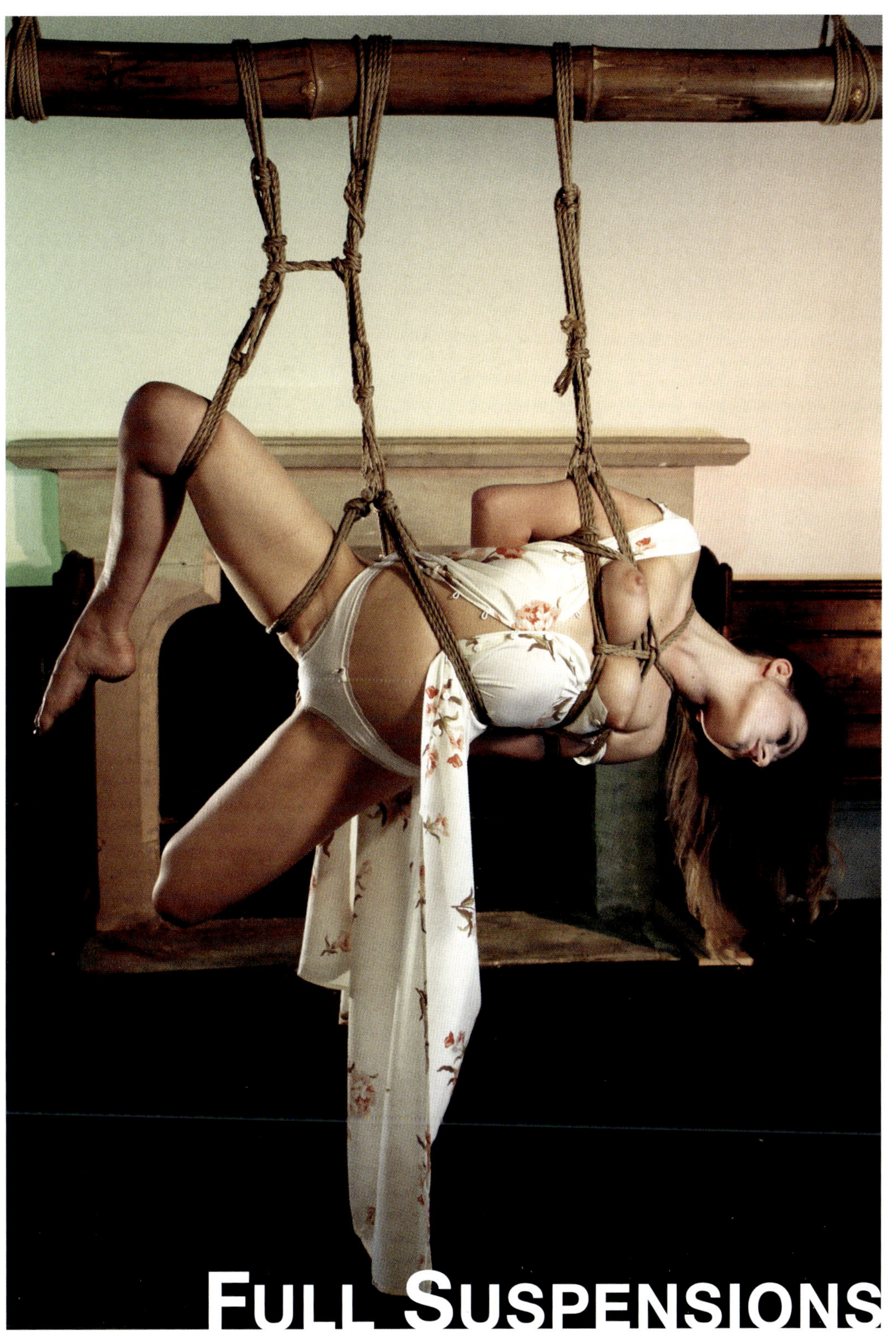

Full Suspensions

Yoko-zuri

Many models find the yokozuri (side suspension) one of the most sustainable ties as support is well distributed throughout the body and it's easy to adjust for different body types and levels of flexibility. This makes it a good starting point for both riggers and models who are new to suspension.

[A, B] It uses the takatekote (pg. 50) with basic third rope (pg. 59) and yuki knot finishing (pg. 65), and gunslinger (pg. 75).

I've demonstrated the tie on bamboo here, but would use the exact same steps on a single point – read 'carabiner formations' on pg. 121 to help you manage the suspension lines.

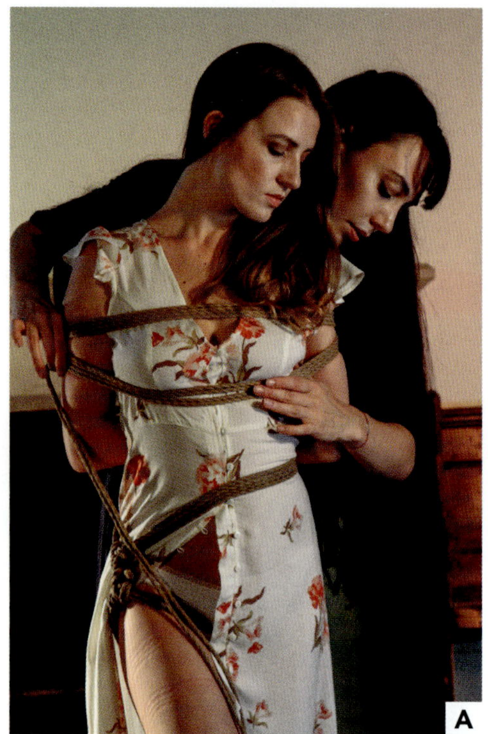

A

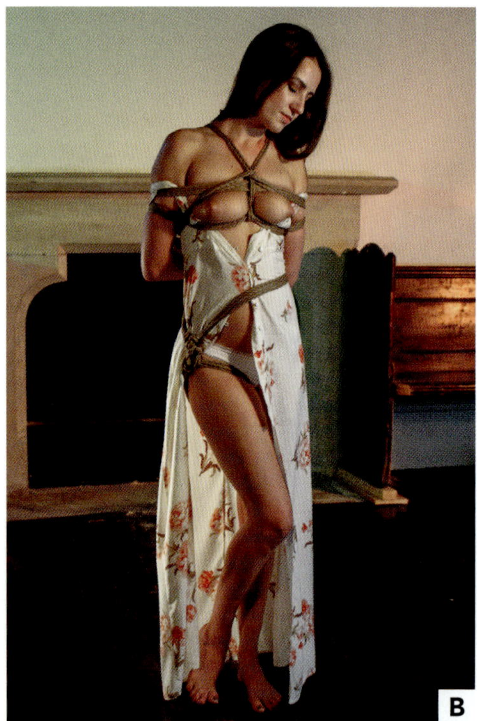

B

[1] Attach a main line to the side of the takatekote (pg. 67), pass it over the suspension point and lock (pg. 111-114). It's useful to have some tension on this line, but not so much that the model is pulled onto their toes.

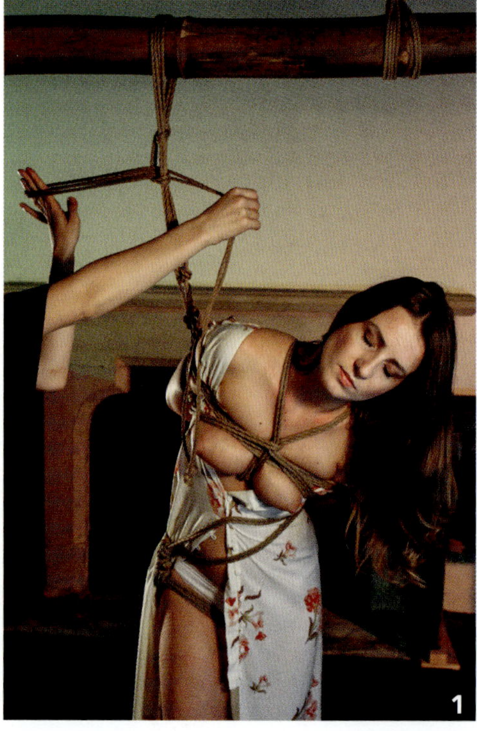

1

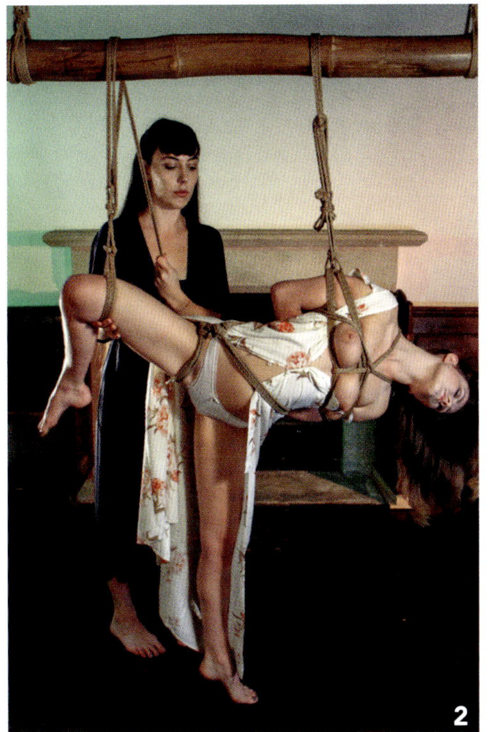

2

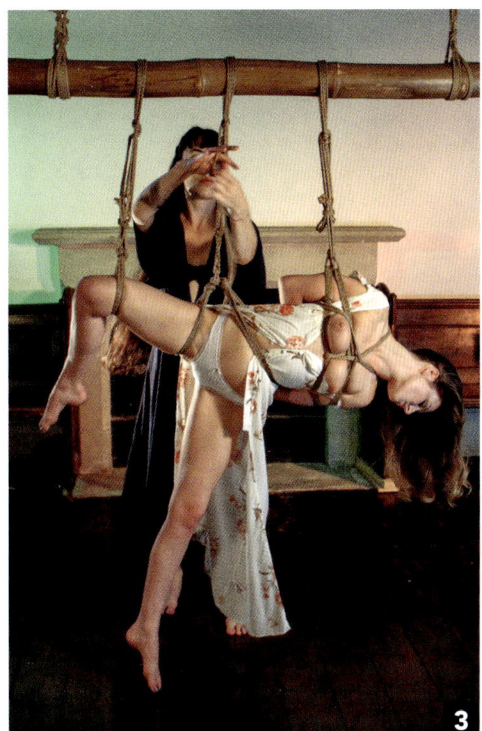

3

[2] Tie a single column tie just above the knee for the next suspension line, and raise the leg. The model can make this easier for themselves by leaning their weight sideways into the main line. The placement of the knee wrap varies person to person and the model will be best able to assess this once there is a bit of weight on the leg.

[3] Attach the next line using a tight single column tie (pg. 107) on the stem of the gunslinger and lift just enough to give support. In this case, I have made the hips roughly level with the chest but you can vary this depending on the preferences of the model.

[4, 5] On the other leg, tie a 'V' shaped single column around the ankle (pg. 29) and run the line up to the point (between the lines from the takatekote and the gunslinger if you are using bamboo). Lift just enough that the knee bends naturally; not so much that the overall body position starts to tilt. Lock at the bottom of the line using a yuki knot (pg. 115).

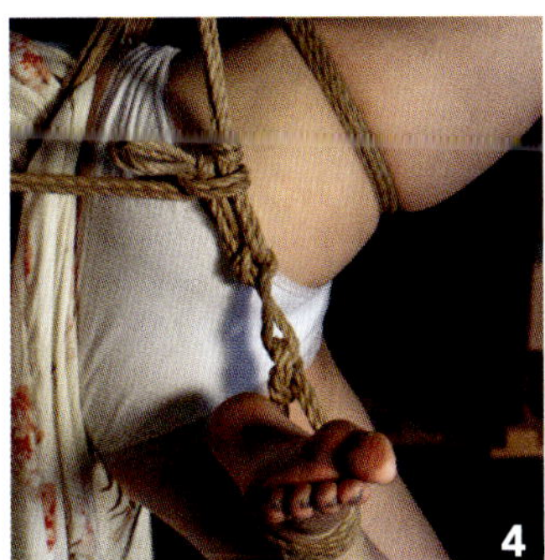

4

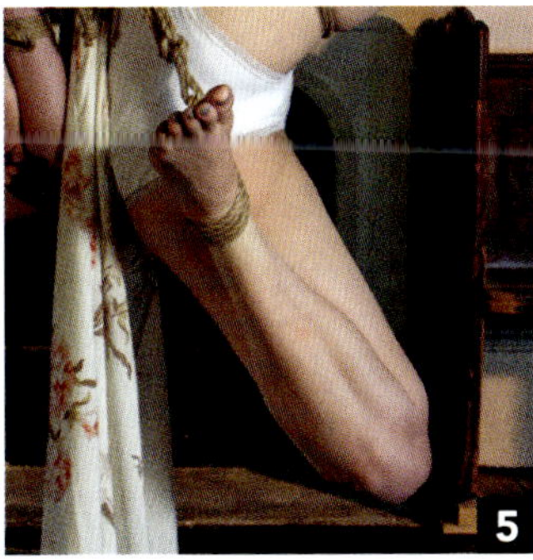

5

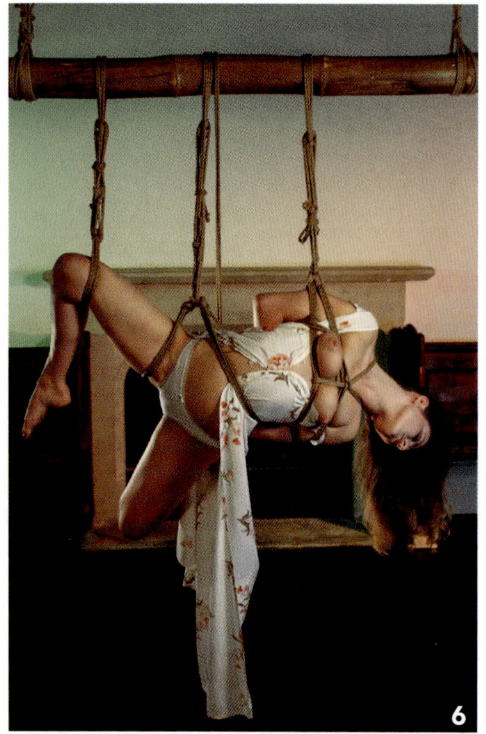
6

[6] Take a moment to check the relative heights of all the lines. You'll notice that in photo 3, the knee and torso are in alignment whereas in photo 6 the knee is higher. This is because some models find it uncomfortable to lift the leg this high in step 2, but may find it a more comfortable position in the end, so you can raise it a little more once everything else is in place if you wish.

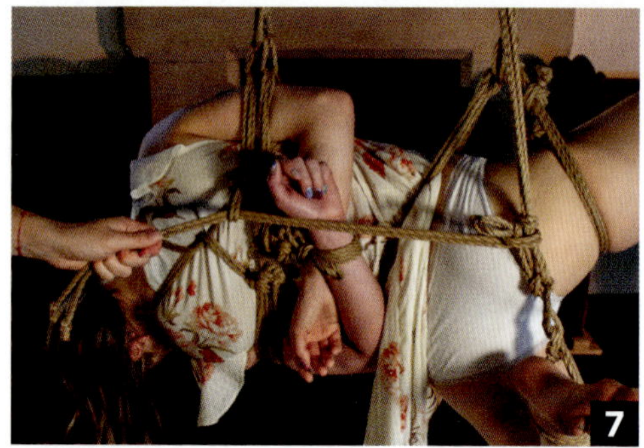
7

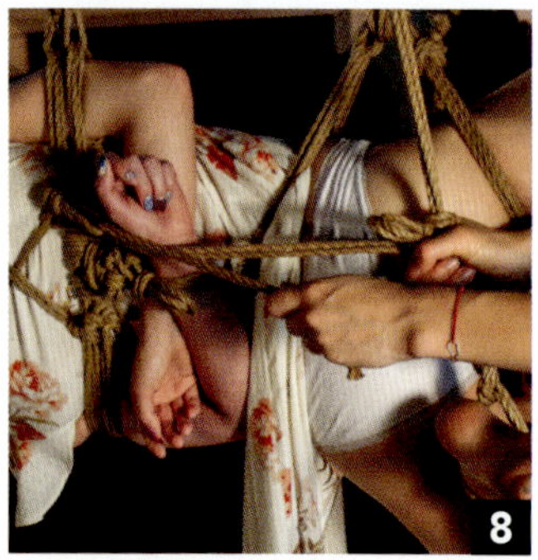
8

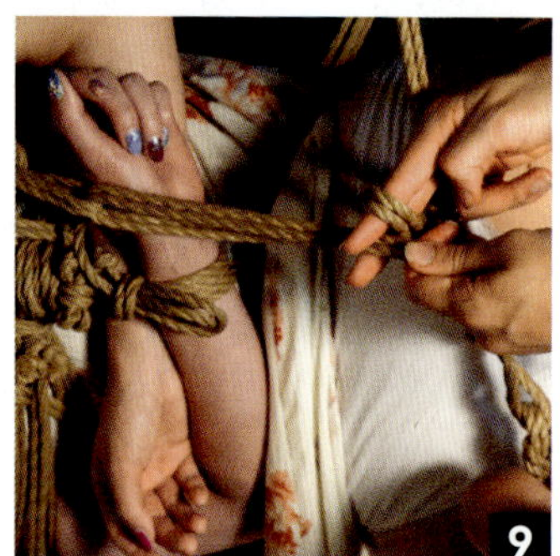
9

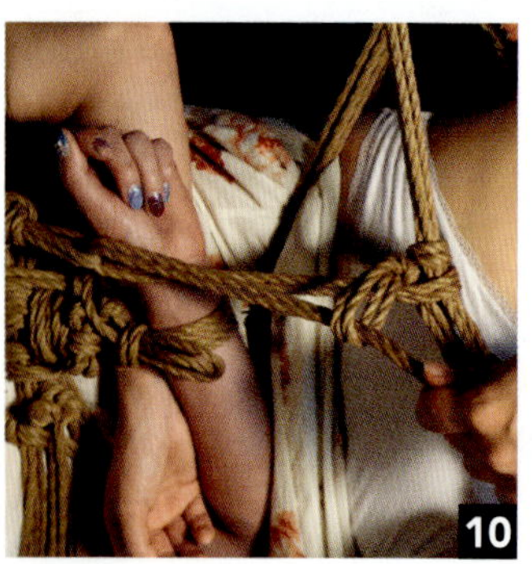
10

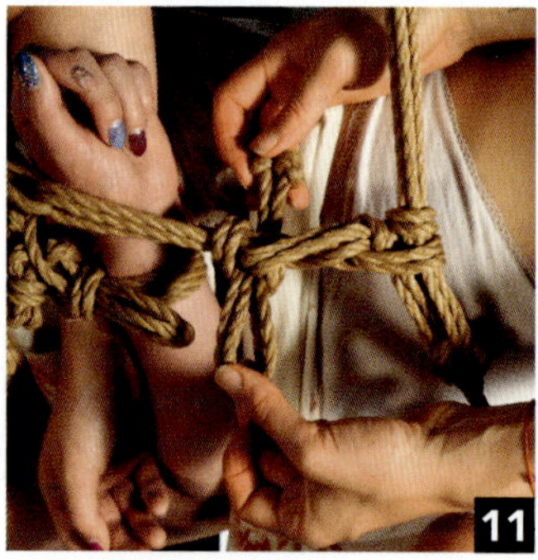
11

[7] Some people have a natural tendency to slump forward in this tie, which can restrict breathing. To help keep the body open take the excess rope from the ankle tie through the yuki knot finishing (pg. 65) at the back of the takatekote.

[8] Pull the ankle line to the back as far as is comfortable for the model.

[9, 10] Pass the working end back through the loop of the yuki knot on the ankle line.

[11] Secure in place with another yuki knot.

The main part of the tie is finished.

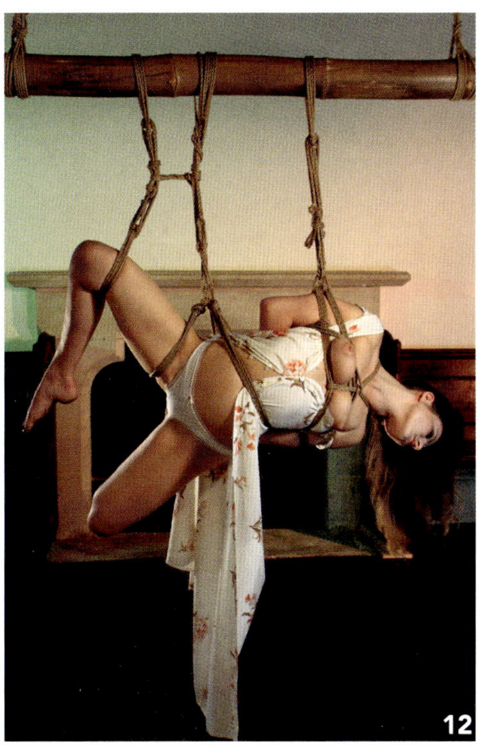
12

[12] I had a lot of spare rope on the gunslinger suspension line so have used it to tie that line together with those from the knee and ankle. This is mostly for aesthetic reasons: breaking up the blocky look of the three verticals from the chest, hip and thigh lines, whilst simultaneously hiding the stray single ankle line, which to my mind can look careless, or unfinished.

Notes for Models

When balanced well this can be one of the more sustainable suspension positions, however holding your neck to the side for long periods can be strenuous as the head is heavy. The final photo shown here is only one possible way of balancing the tie; you can try asking the rigger to experiment with raising or lowering the hips and knee relative to the takatekote as this can adjust the tilt of the spine and straighten out the neck into a more natural position.

You should pay extra attention to the feeling in the arm closest to the ground, as much of the weight will be centred here.

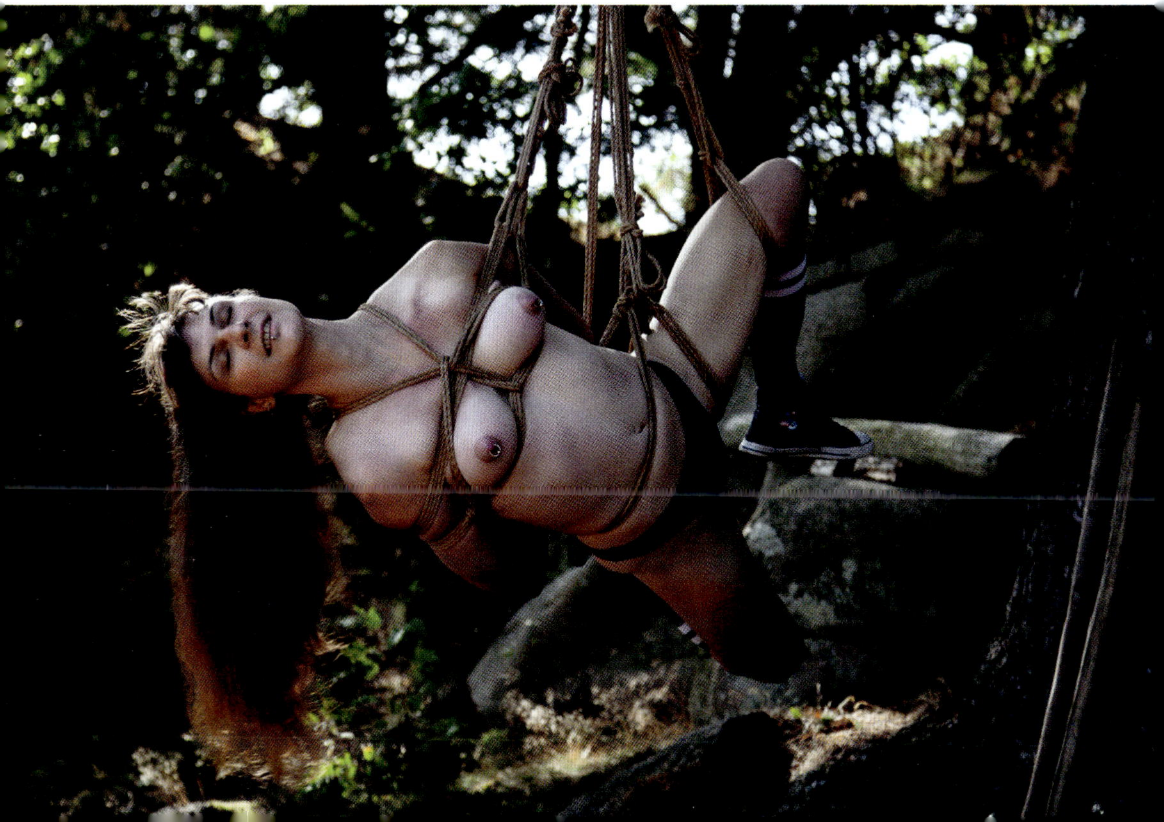

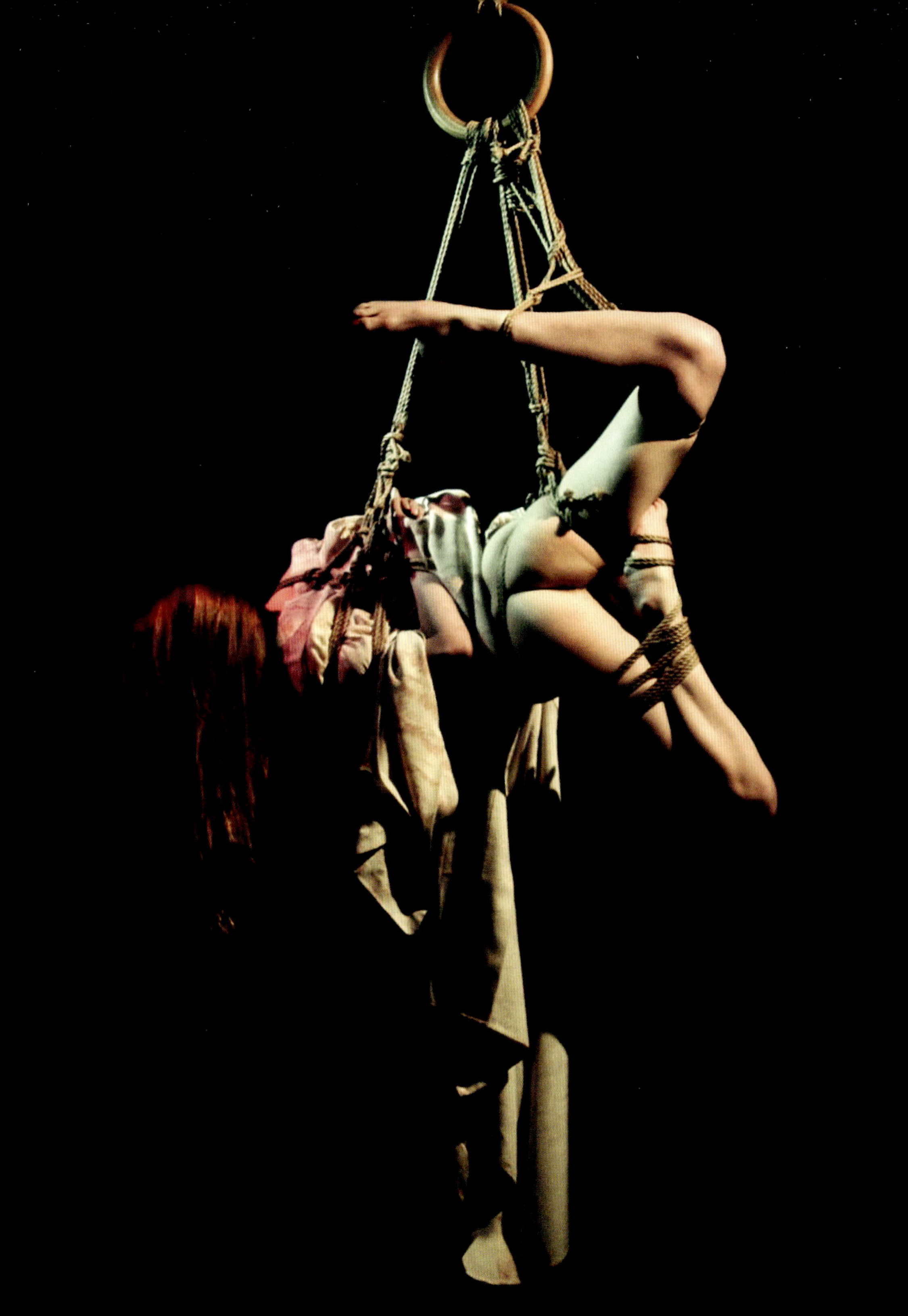

Hikyaku-zuri

Hikyaku-zuri ('running postman suspension') is more usually attached from the back of the takatekote, but in this variation it's attached it from the front as it gives a nice look and I find it a more a straightforward tie to balance for both rigger and model. Although the model might feel more stress at the back of the neck than in a 'standard' hikyaku-zuri (you might be able to alleviate this by adjusting the height of the front leg) the pressure on the ribs and wrists is avoided.

This suspension uses the takatekote (pg. 50) with the top wrap tied extra tight, and the face up third rope variation (pg. 64) with a yuki knot finishing (pg. 65).

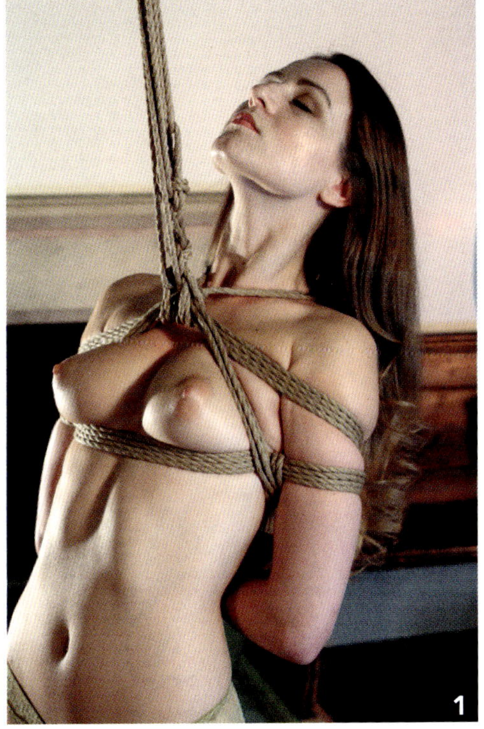

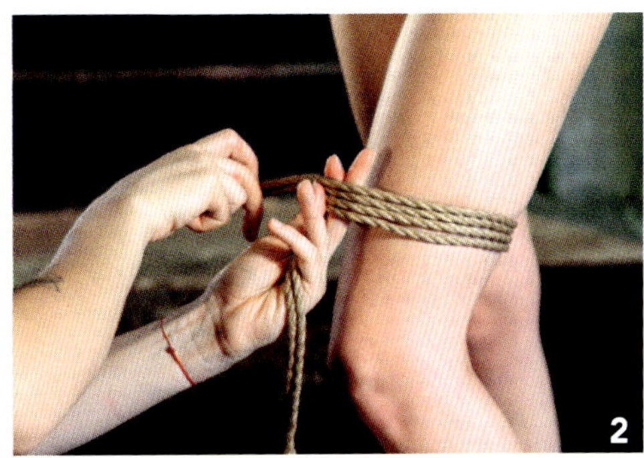

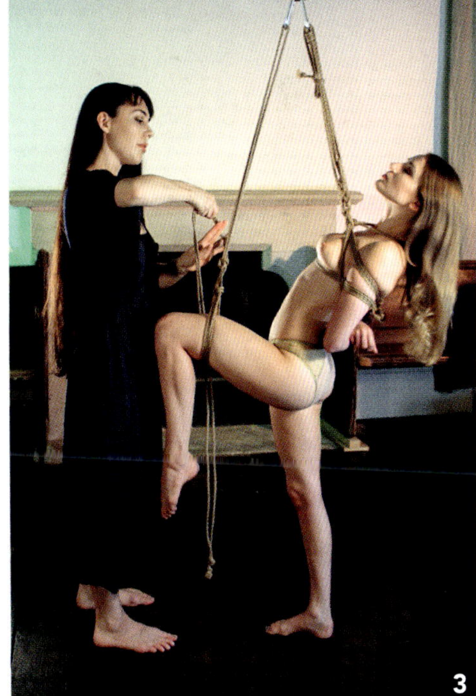

[1] Begin by attaching a main line to the front of the takatekote (pg. 66) and lock it to the point.

[2] Tie a single column around one thigh, above the knee. This doesn't need to be too tight.

[3] Raise the knee to a comfortable height – it's best not to force it up too high. The model can lean backwards into the rope to help with balance. As this tie has only two suspension lines, I have been able to use two single carabiners, without worrying about them jamming (pg. 121).

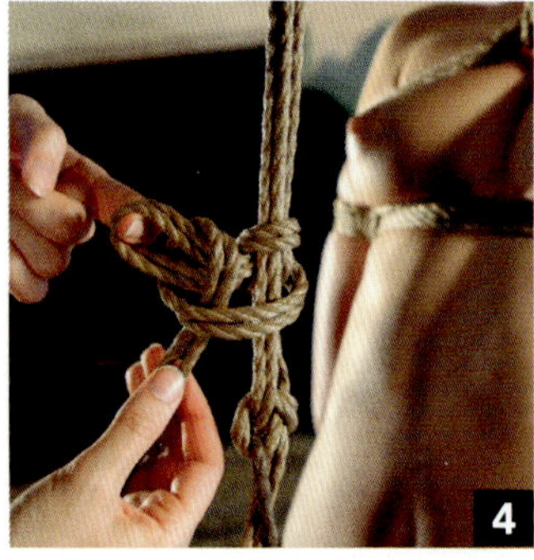
4

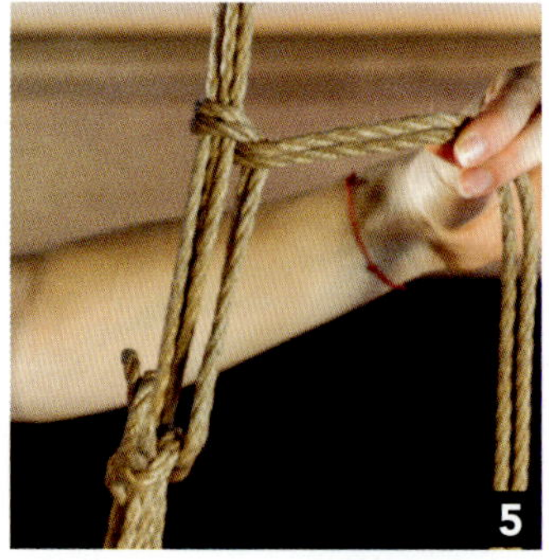
5

[4] Lock the line at the bottom (pg. 115) **[5]** and, with the excess rope, make a half hitch part way up the leg line, about level with the model's nose.

[6, 7] Pass the working end around the main line and pull the two lines together. This makes it more sustainable by helping to keep the body upright.

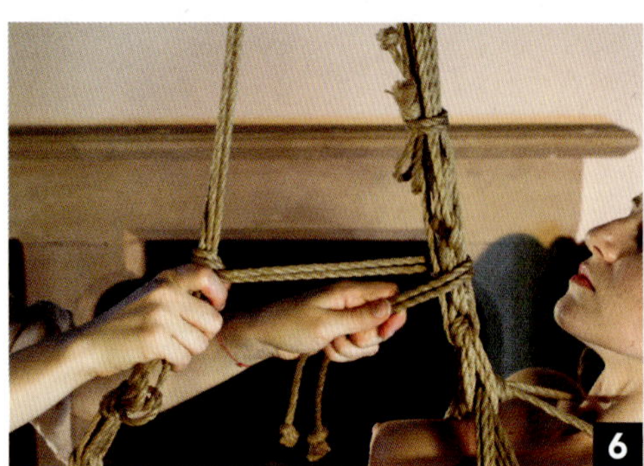
6

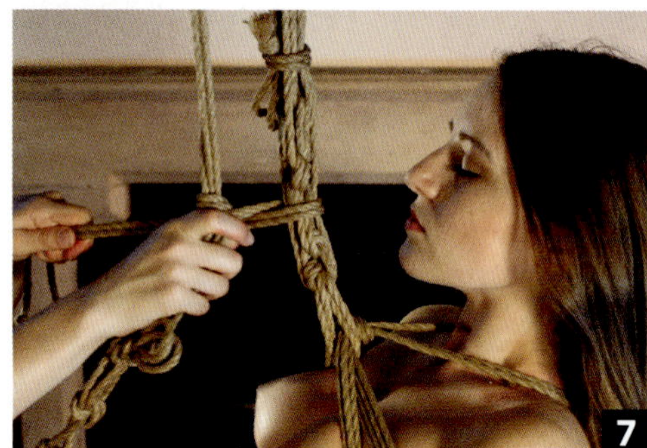
7

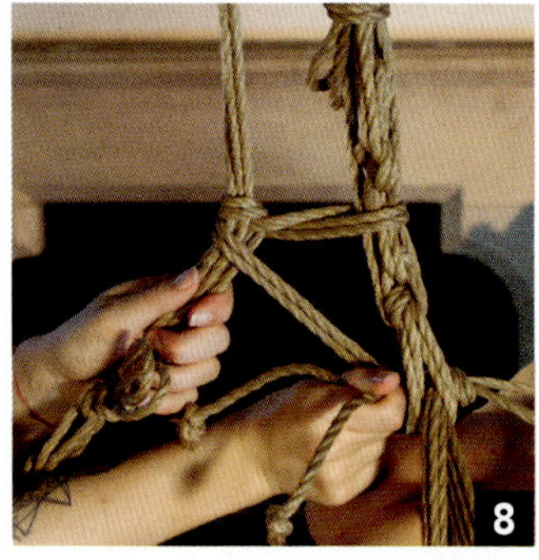
8

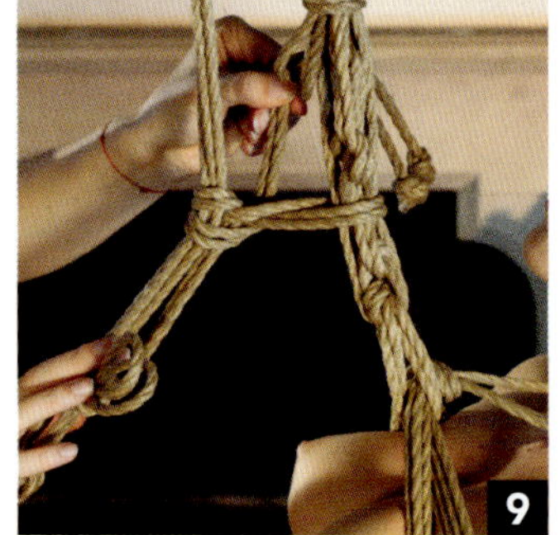
9

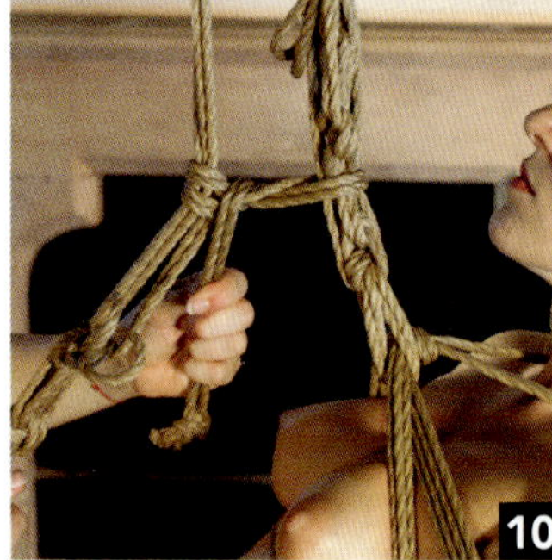
10

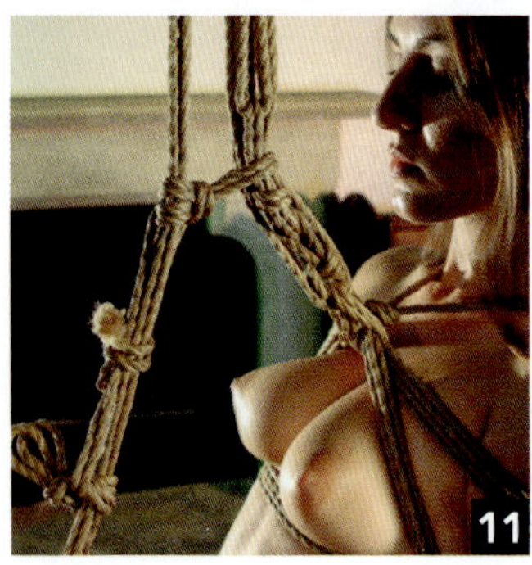
11

Hold it in place by **[8]** wrapping back around the secondary line **[9, 10]** making a full turn around the connecting rope **[11]** and locking with a half hitch (pg. 39) or overhand lock (pg. 40).

Tie your next line around the ankle of the foot still on the floor.

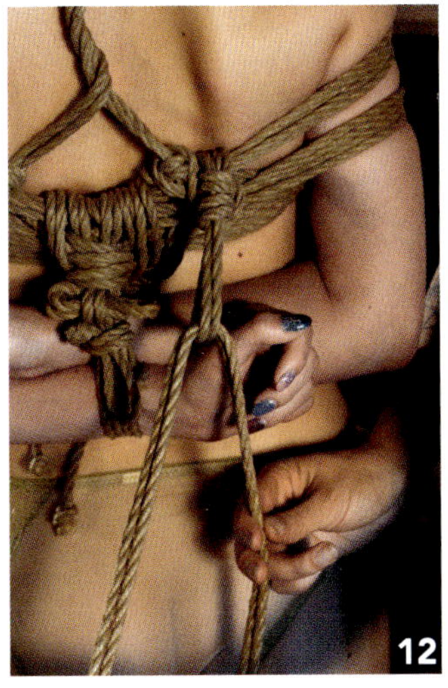
12

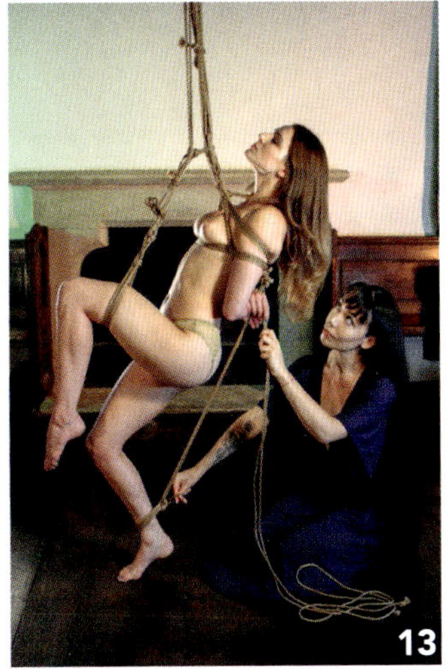
13

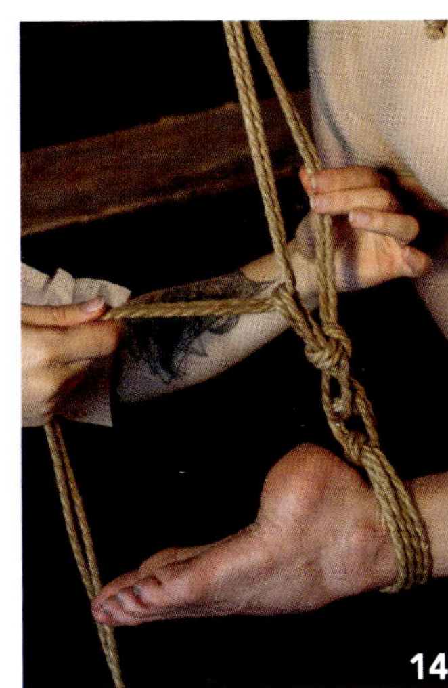
14

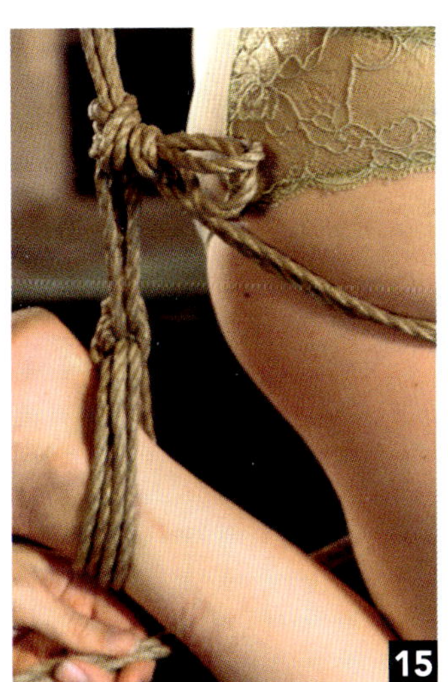
15

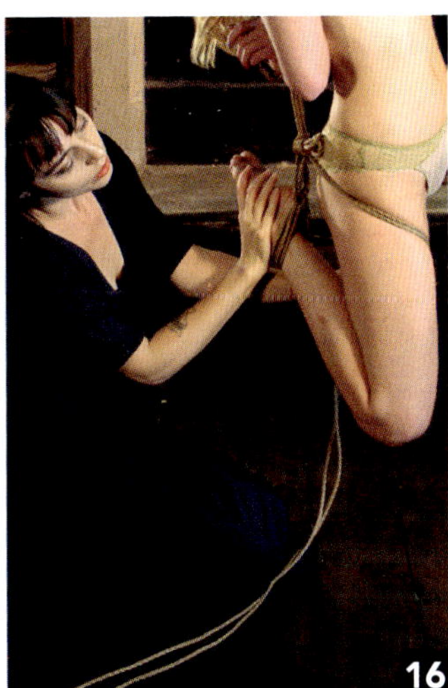
16

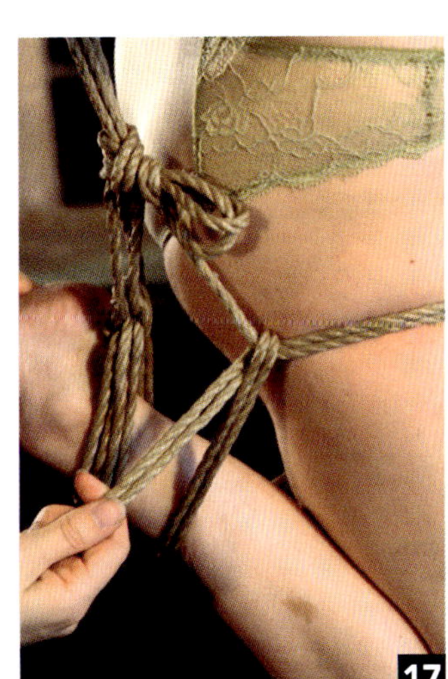
17

[12] Thread the ankle line through the loop on the back of the takatekote.

[13] Lift the ankle gently with one hand as you tighten the line with the other hand to avoid creating friction in the rope on the back of the takatekote.

[14] When the knee is bent in a natural position, thread your working end back through the bight.

[15] Lock the line at the bottom (pg. 115).

[16] You will have a lot of left over rope so you can use it up efficiently by wrapping the leg.

[17] I find it easiest to keep the wraps even by using a reverse tension after the first wrap.

[18] When you're almost to the end of the rope, pass the working end over all wraps.

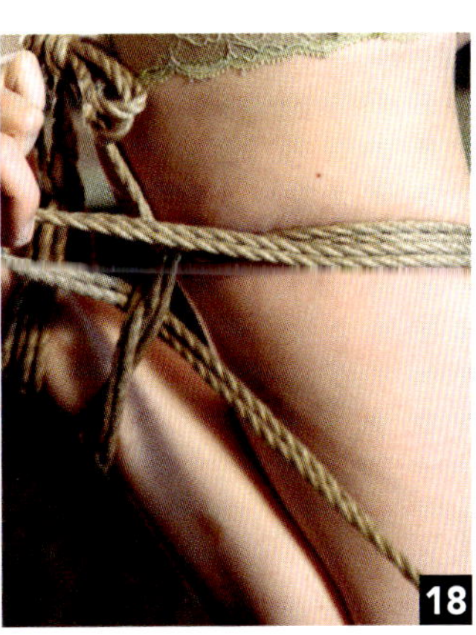
18

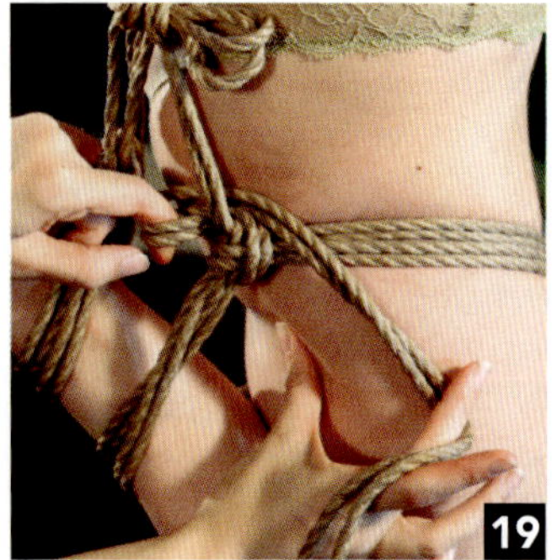

19

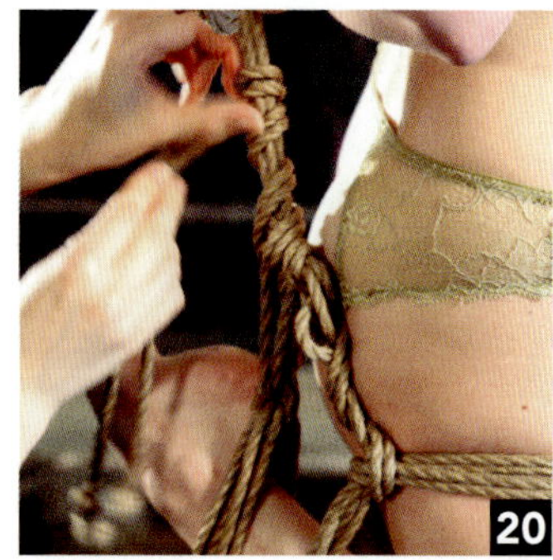

20

[19] Pass the working end back behind the 'stem' you've just made between the line and wrap to make a no-dome (pg. 36).

[20] Finish any remaining rope by wrapping back around the suspension line and locking with an overhand lock (pg. 118).

The tie is finished.

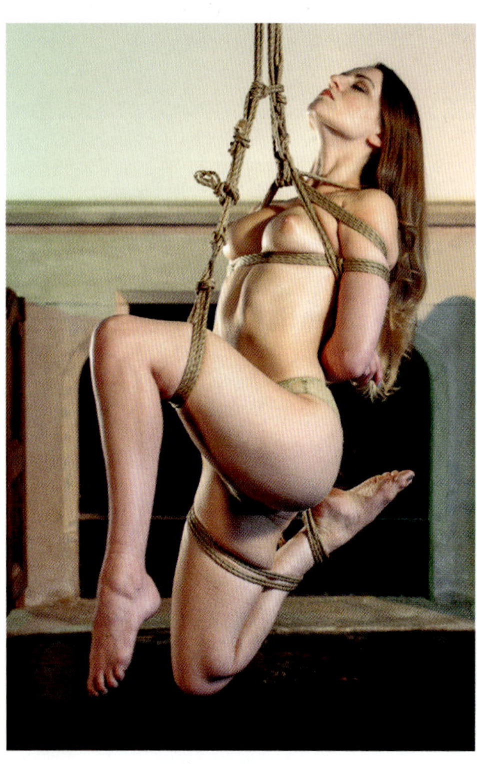

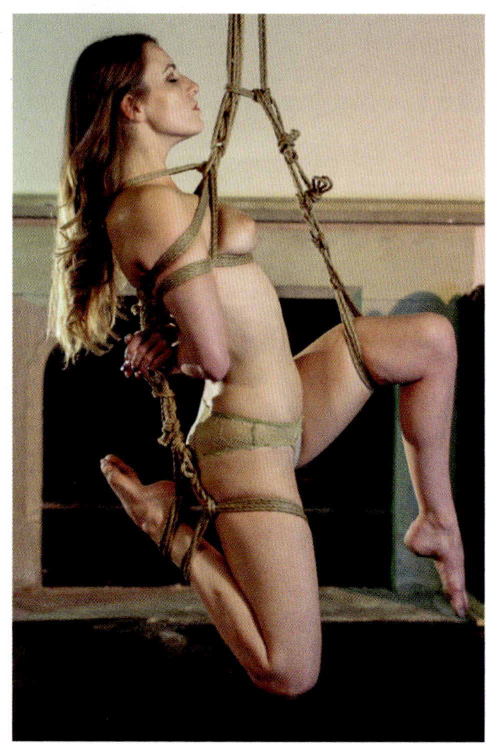

Notes for Models

The most common issue for models in a suspension where the main line is attached to the front of the takatekote is discomfort in the back of the neck as your muscles struggle to support the weight of your head. In this particular suspension, it should be possible to adjust the relative heights of the two suspension lines to find a balance that is better for you, so experiment with your rigger to see if you can find something that works. Additionally, keeping the neck a little elongated, rather than allowing the head to tip directly backwards should help to straighten out your neck and be more comfortable.

Be vigilant of how pressure on the back of the arm affects your nerves (pg. 43-47), as it will be different to side or face down suspensions. The third rope design should offer some support and help reduce this pressure, and you might wish to experiment with the placement of the third rope wrap going under your arms and across your back.

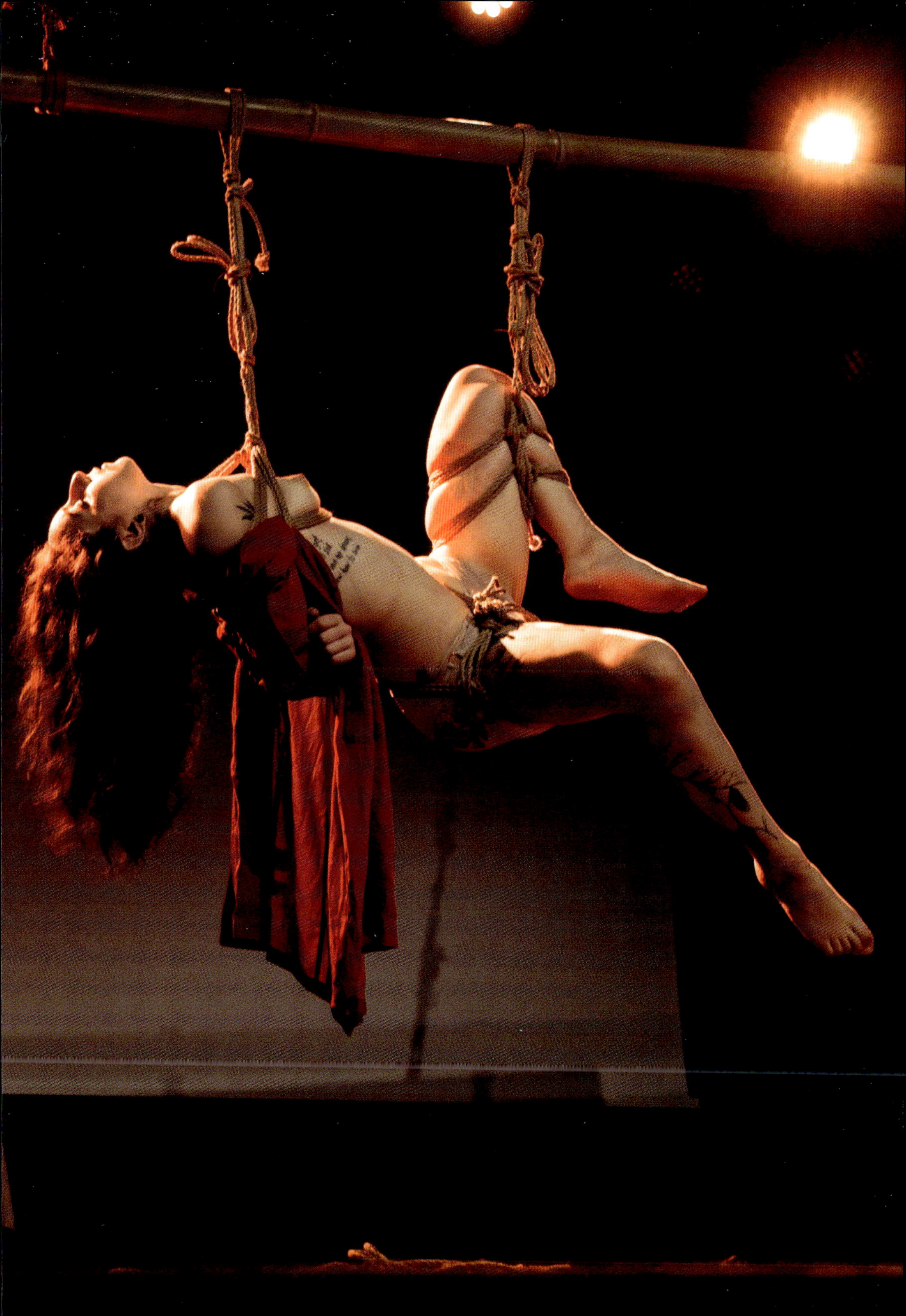

Aomuke-zuri

Aomuke-zuri (face up suspension) uses the takatekote (pg. 50) with the top wrap tied extra tight, and the face up third rope variation (pg. 64) with a yuki knot finishing (pg. 65).

This can be a difficult suspension to get into, and you will likely find the process the least smooth of all the ties in this book – even if the end result can feel quite well balanced. As the knee needs to be so much higher than the upper body, it's best to tie the main line with enough slack that the model is able to keep one leg on the ground whilst the other leg is lifted. Later on, as you become more advanced, you can explore better ways of getting in and out of positions like this, but for the time being it can still offer a lot to learn about how the body works in ropes, and the importance of working efficiently with suspension lines when the model is in a physically stressful intermediate position.

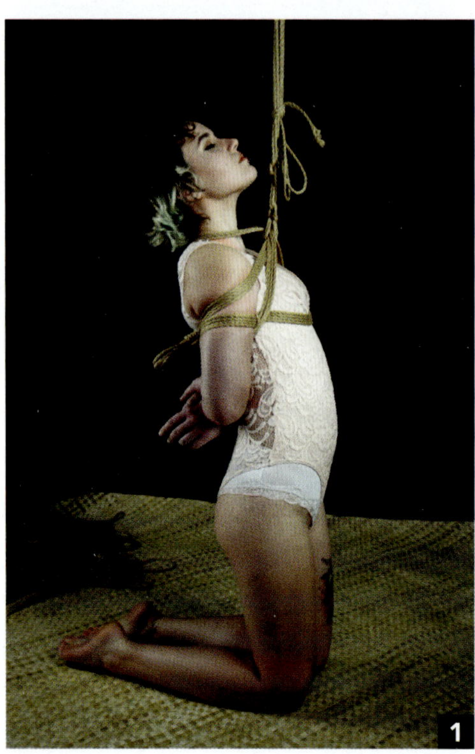

1

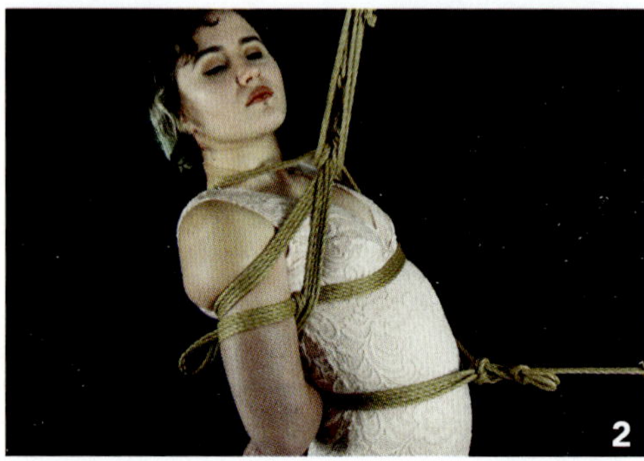

2

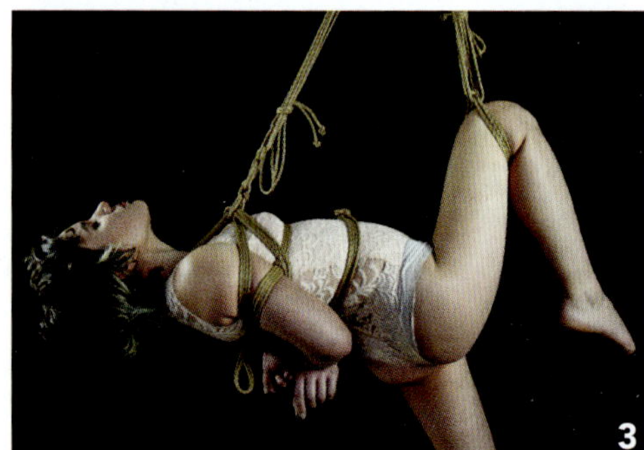

3

[1] Begin by attaching the main line to the front of the takatekote (pg. 66). Locking it with the model at kneeling height or just a little lower tends to offer enough slack for lifting the leg (step 3), depending on the model's flexibility.

[2] I suggest attaching a single column tie with a double bight around the waist now to save time in step 4 when the model is in a more uncomfortable position.

[3] Attach a suspension line above one knee and lift it upwards to the point. Some models will feel comfortable having the knee pulled up quite high at this point whereas others might prefer it left a little lower, and then adjusted to a better height after completing step 6.

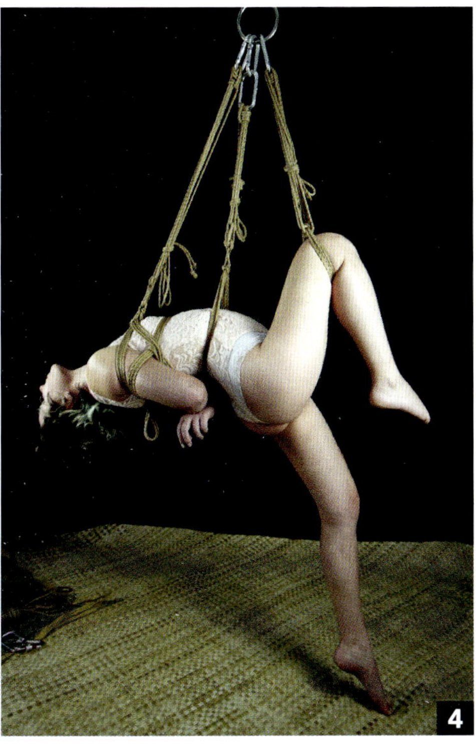
4

[4] Check the placement of the single column tie on the waist to make sure it is low enough to avoid the ribs. Pull up slowly and smoothly, checking in with your model for the correct height for the neck to be comfortable.

[5, 6] (see notes for models).

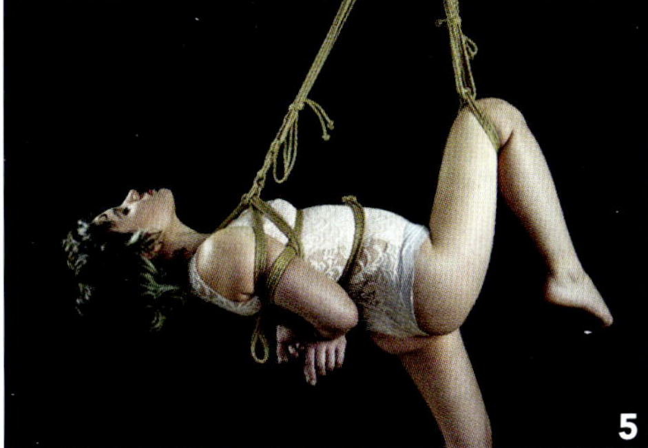
5

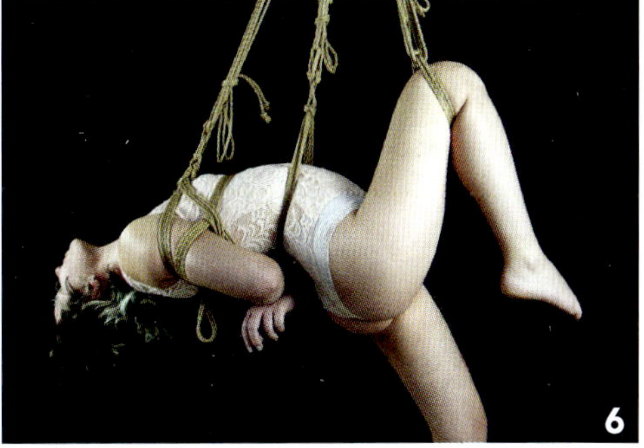
6

Notes for Models

The head is heavy so having it tilted this far back is a tough position for many people but you might well find that there is a 'sweet spot' as the waist line is pulled upwards, so ask the rigger to pull slowly, until you feel the shape of your spine elongate into a position that's natural for you. **[5]** Here you can clearly see that with the back straight and unsupported, the model is having to hold their head up to avoid their neck falling backwards at a sharp angle. **[6]** Once the back is supported into an arch the neck falls backwards into a more relaxed alignment.

You will notice how the pressure on the third rope is shifted in this tie from your back (as in the hikyaku-zuri) to the back of your neck, so pay attention to the placement of these ropes to make sure they are comfortable for you. You might find it useful to ask the rigger to dress the neck wraps before suspending to pull them a little further away from the neck and make sure no skin is being pulled underneath the ropes.

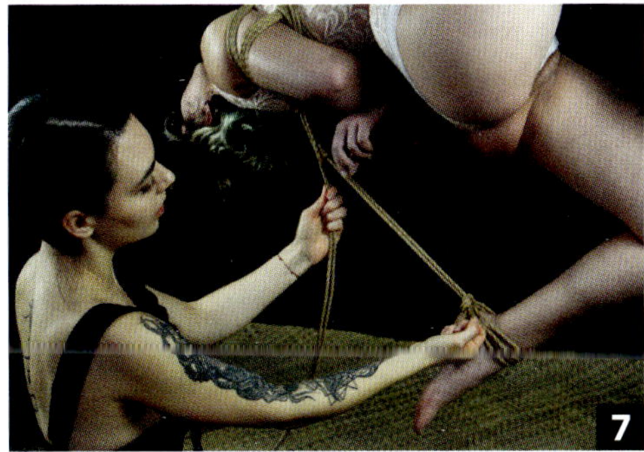
7

[7] Attach the final rope to the ankle and thread the working end through the loop on the back of the takatekote. Pull the ankle inwards as far as is comfortable for the model.

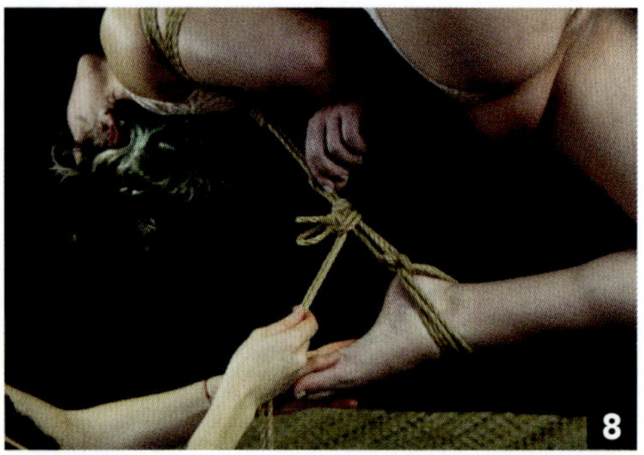

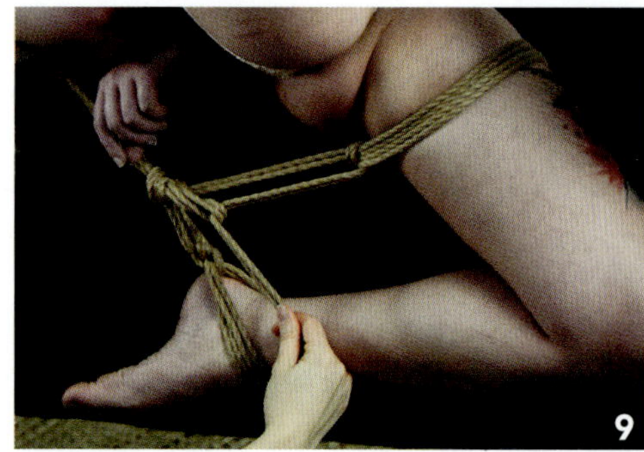

[8] Go back through the bight and secure with a yuki knot (pg. 37).

[9] I have used up the excess rope by making a hojo cuff (pg. 31) around the thigh then going back through the loop of the yuki knot. You can lock off however you wish (eg. using a half hitch or overhand lock).

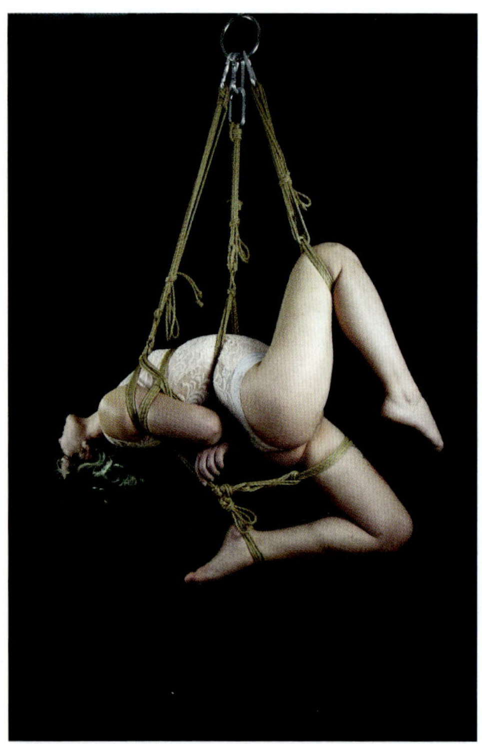

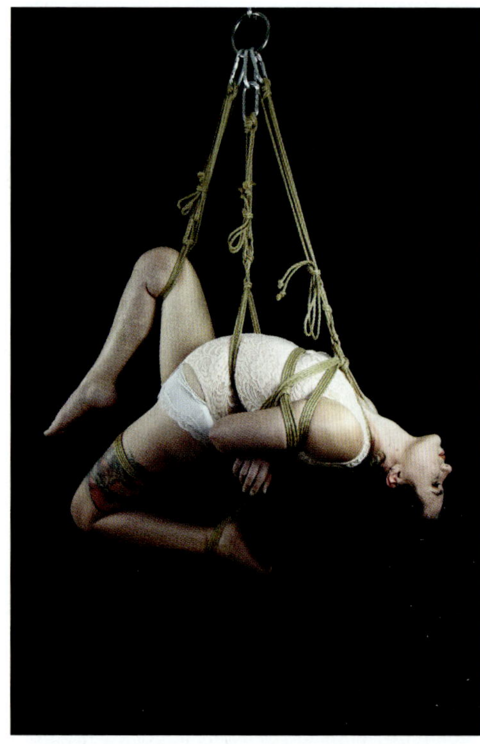

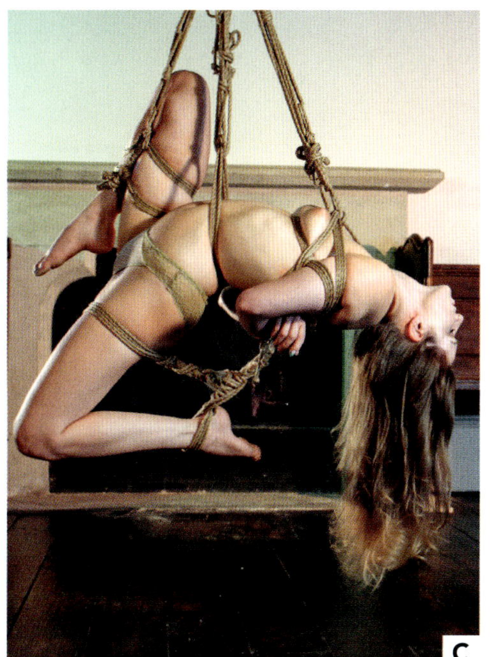
C

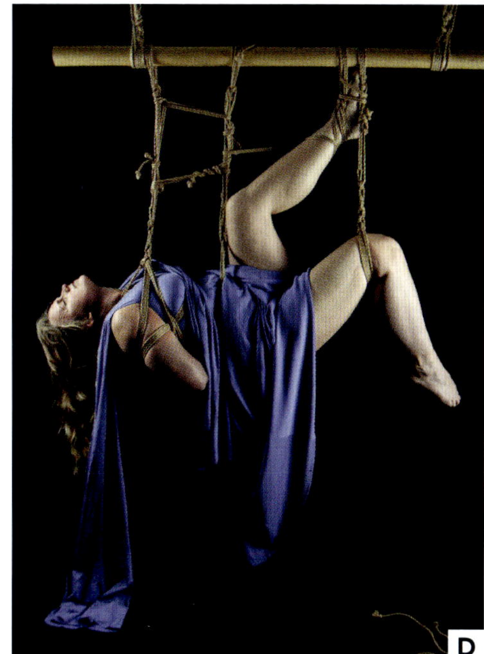
D

Notes for Models

[C] This suspension can put a lot of weight on the knee wrap, which many people find painful. An alternative could be to replace the knee line with a futomomo. Here I have attached it with a suspension line on the inside of the leg.

[D] If having your ankle pulled back to the chest puts too much pressure on the waist rope or too much bend in your back, you could try experimenting with lifting both legs up to the point instead.

If you are familiar with using some kind of hip harness, you could also try using one here instead of the waist wrap so that you have the support spread around your hip bones, waist, and upper leg.

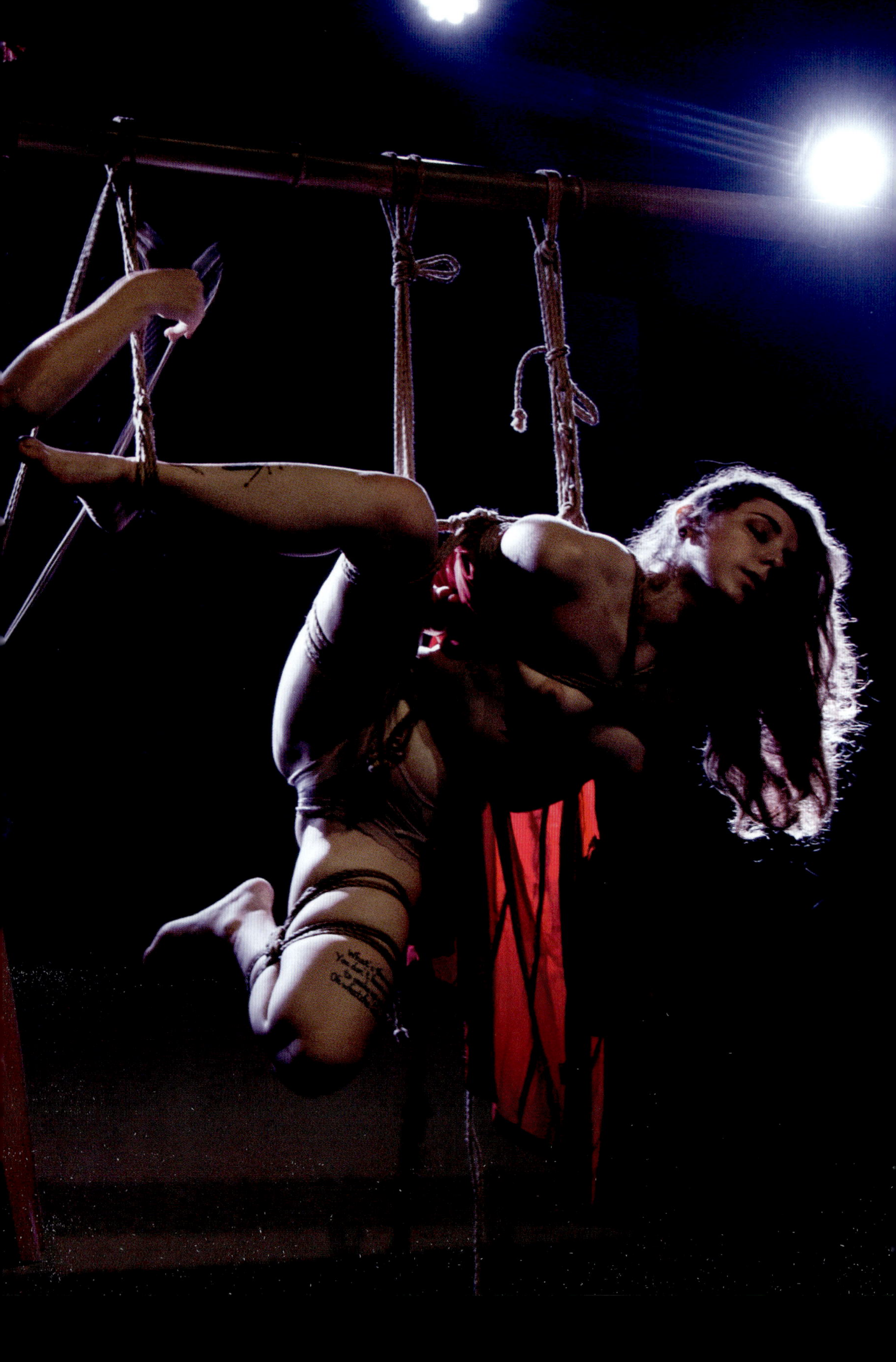

Gyaku-ebi-zuri

Gyaku-ebi-zuri (reverse prawn suspension) gets it's name because it is the reverse of the ebi tie (see **[D]** on pg. 21) where the legs are pulled forwards to the chest mimicking the shape of a prawn. In common usage, it refers to any face down suspension with the legs pulled backwards – there doesn't necessarily need to be much bend in the back.

This is often a very challenging tie for models so I would definitely recommend paying extra attention to the notes for models section.

It uses the takatekote (pg. 50) with the face down third rope variation (pg. 63).

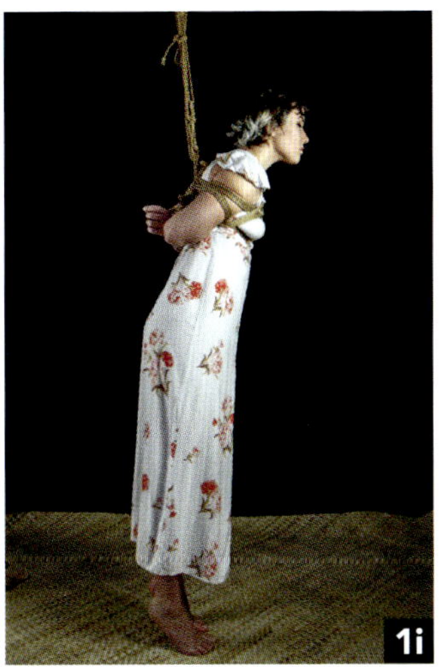

1i

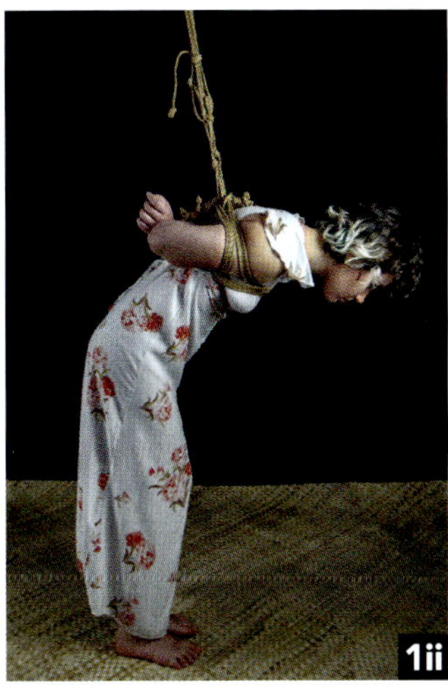

1ii

Start by attaching a main line to the back of the takatekote (pg. 66).

[1i] Pulling the line up so that the model is high on their toes will create a more extreme final position, which can be enjoyable for some, but might also be more stressful on the lower back. It will also be harder for the model to keep balance going into the tie.

[1ii] Letting the model lean forward at a natural angle so there is more slack in the rope can help alleviate these problems.

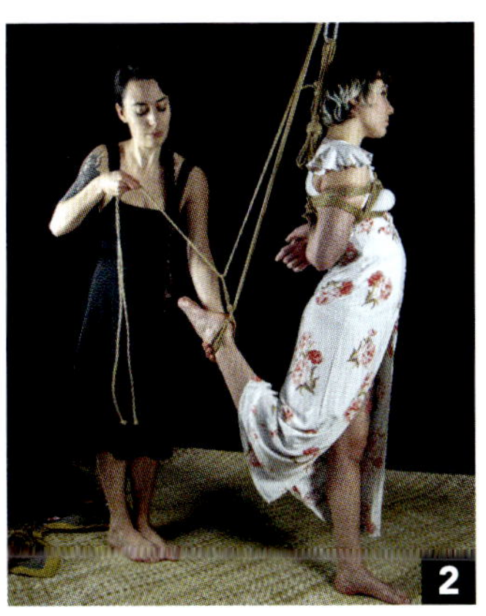

2

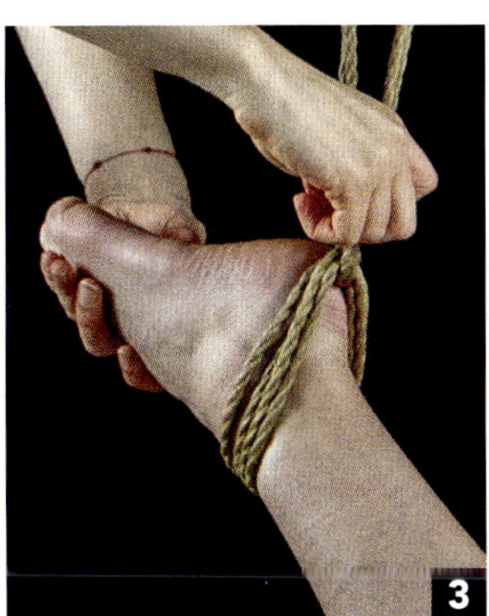

3

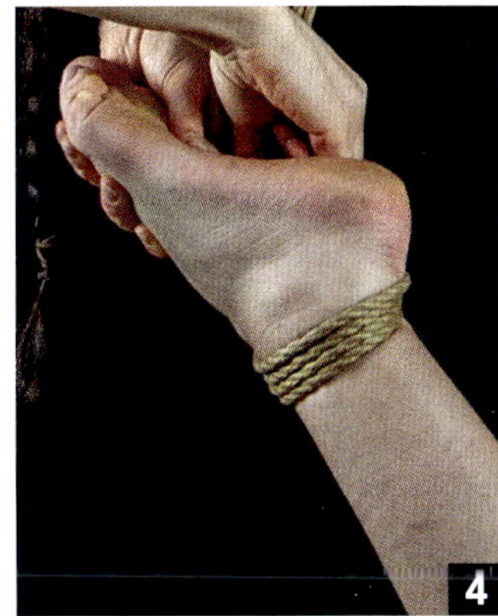

4

[2] Attach a new suspension line on one ankle using a 'V' shaped single column and pull upwards just enough that the foot is pointing towards the ceiling.

[3, 4] Temporarily secure the line by locking at the bottom (pg. 115). Hold the foot in one hand to take the weight, and with the other, slide the suspension line around to the model's preferred placement (see 'notes for models' on pg. 164).

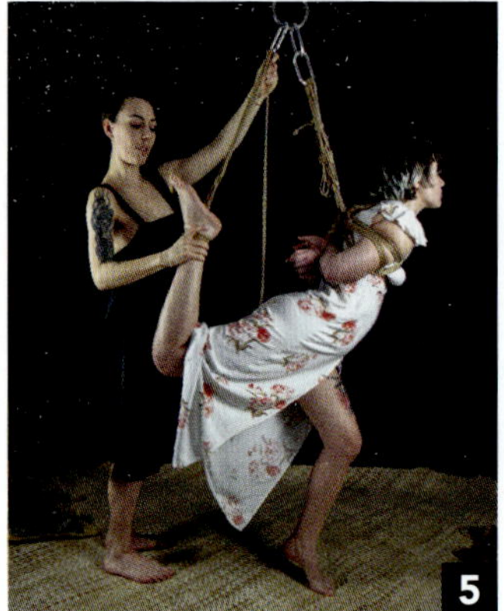
5

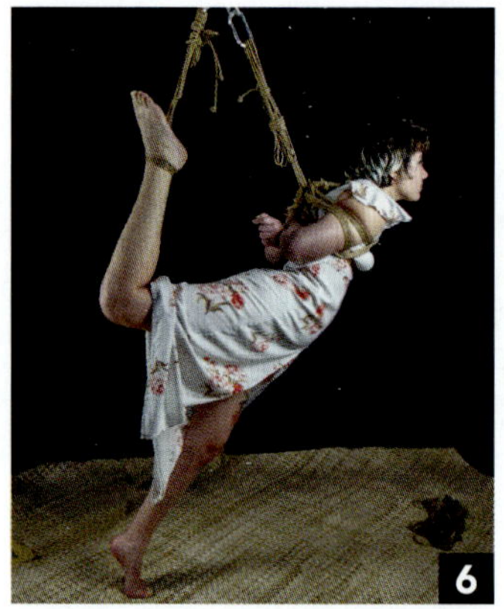
6

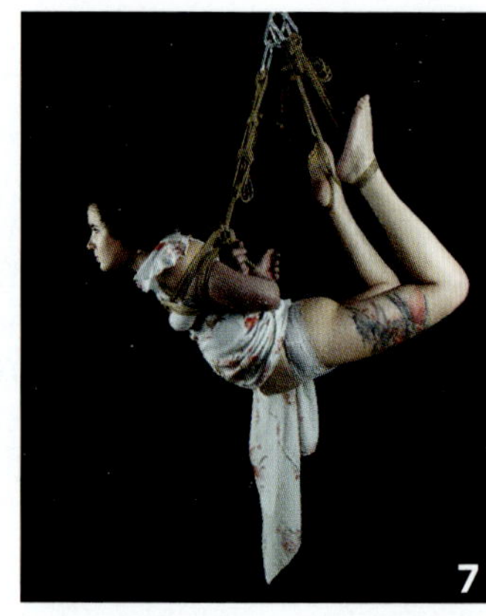
7

[5] Take the working end back up to the point and, holding the foot in one hand, gently push upwards whilst simultaneously pulling down on the suspension line in the other hand.

[6] Once you have the ankle rope to a good height (without pulling up so far that the model can't keep their foot on the ground) lock the line. It's usually best to bundle up the excess rope (pg. 119) in this case for the sake of speed.

[7] Repeat steps 2-6 on the other ankle.

Adding Support: Hips

It's very common to struggle with the pressure this kind of tie can place on the lower back – but there are various ways to add support.

[1] Instead of bundling the excess rope after you have locked the ankle line, lift up the hip with one hand **[2]** and once it's in position place this rope around the upper thigh or if you have enough rope left over, the whole hip area*.

[3] Secure this by creating a hojo cuff (with one rather than two wraps), taking the working end back to the point and locking the line.

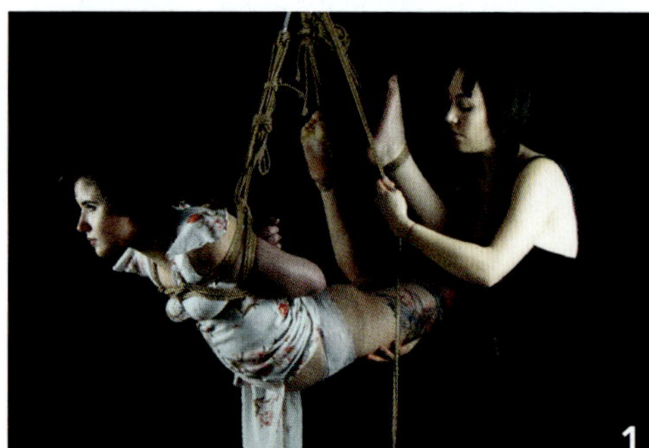
1

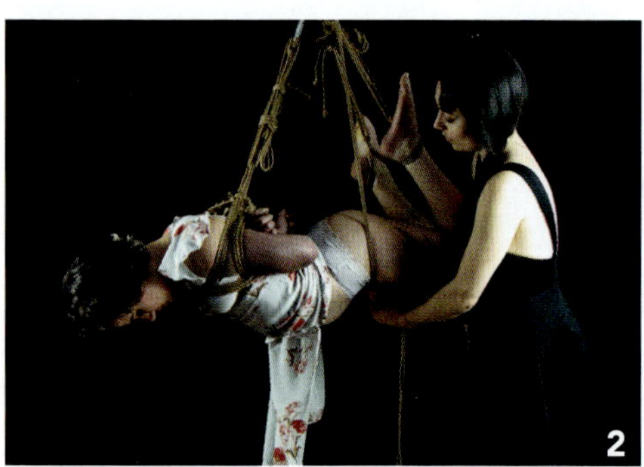
2

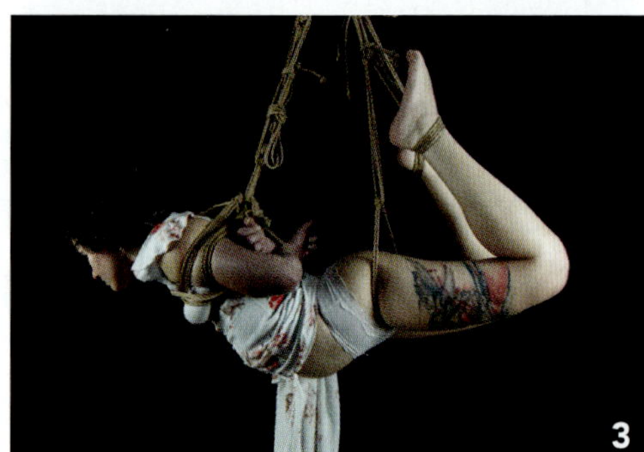
3

* Be aware that this supporting rope, whether placed around the thigh or the hip, has the potential to cross the path of the ilioinguinal or femoral nerves at a vulnerable point (pg. 74)

Adding Support: Futomomo

You can also replace one of the ankle ties with a futomomo which brings support closer in to the model's centre of gravity.

[1] I have used a futomomo with the stem on the outside, and the suspension line attached with a tight single column tie around the stem.

[2] Raise the futomomo until it is roughly level with the model's chest, and lock the line.

[3, 4] Raise the other ankle (exactly as you did in steps 2-6 of the basic tie) until you get to a point where the hips are level and balanced. If you wish, you can use the excess ankle rope to add the thigh support in the same way as before.

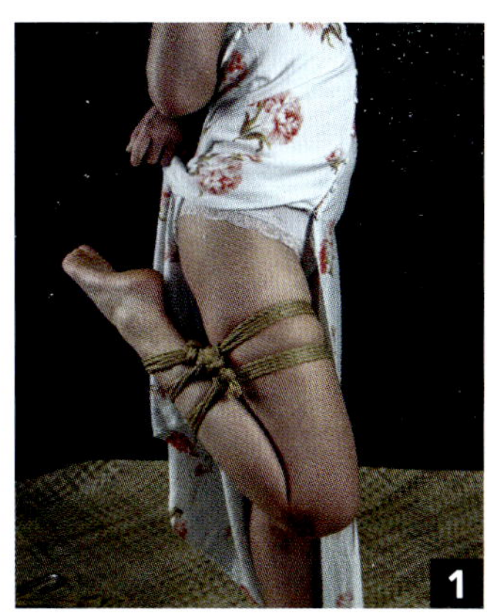
1

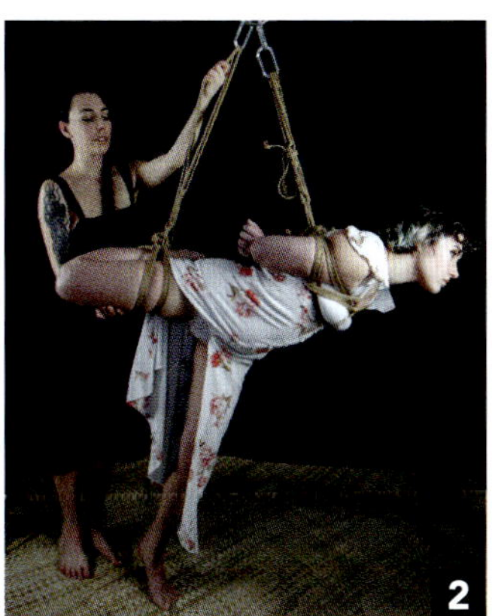
2

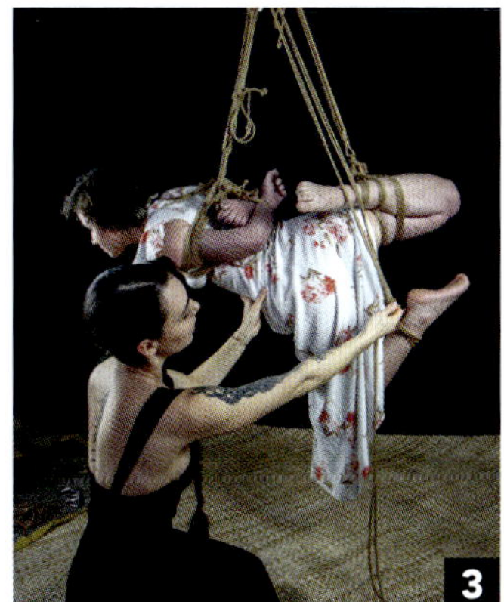
3

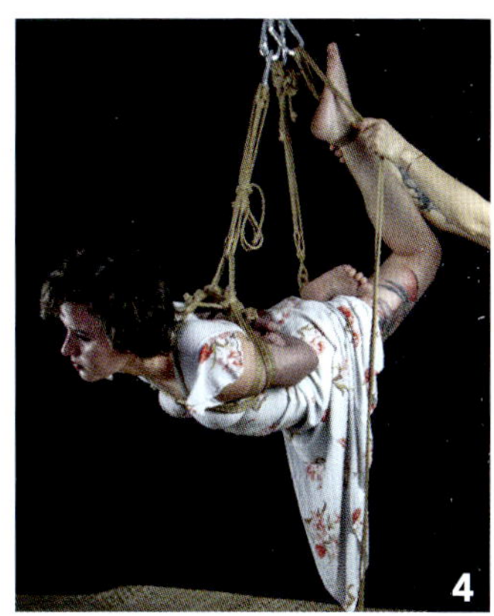
4

[E, F] Here the futomomo support has been used, but rather than using the excess rope from the ankle for further support I have wrapped it around the legs and suspension lines to create more of an extreme backbend shape. I have also placed the model a little closer to the suspension point than in the demo tie so you can see how the body is compressed as it gets closer to the point.

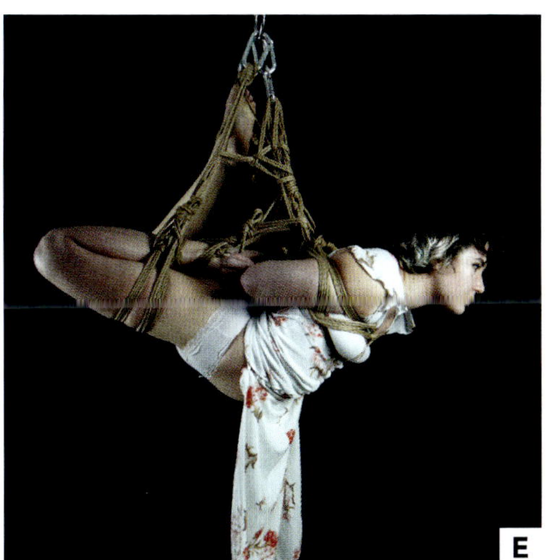
E

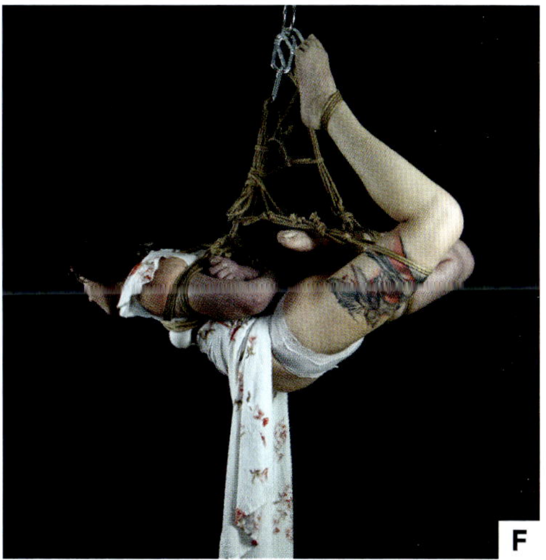
F

Notes for Models

This is often a very challenging tie for models as there are so many common issues that, whilst manageable individually, can build up together to create something overwhelming.

Take some time to experiment to find the most comfortable placement for your ankle wraps before you attempt this suspension by lying on the floor with one leg attached to the point, and gently pulling a little weight on the wrap. Some people prefer the knot on the outside, some on the inside – some people prefer the wrap tied a little looser, some a little tighter – some people prefer the wrap above the protruding ankle bone, and some below.

Many factors will influence how difficult you find the backbend in this tie, including your level of flexibility, the strength of your the muscles in your lower back and shoulders, and your weight distribution. Note that more flexibility does not necessarily make things easier; models with hyper-flexible backs can struggle just as much as those with inflexible backs if they don't have enough muscle to support that flexibility. Models who have very bottom heavy weight distribution can find it more difficult to support the weight of their hips and so might be in more need of hip support, whereas models with top heavy weight distribution might find that they struggle more with breathing as a result.

If you are struggling with the bend in your lower back you can pull down on the ankle wraps, bring your knees in closer to each other, and lift up your hips yourself. This will help to temporarily alleviate the problem but isn't sustainable for very long. It also puts a lot of additional pressure on the shoulders so it's generally better to use a hip support.

Many people find breathing difficult in this position because of the pressure from the takatekote. To help with this problem keep your neck level – with the head neither falling forwards nor tilted too far back – as this will keep your airways open. Rather than trying to take big deep breaths from the chest, concentrate on relatively small movements from the diaphragm and letting a steady stream of air flow in. Another issue sometimes found with the takatekote is the lower wrap pressing on the sternum can cause a feeling of nausea. A solution for some people might be to tie the lower wrap much looser that then top wrap – and also to consider making additional wraps around the shoulders (three of four instead of just two) so that the weight is better taken there. This latter solution might also help models with broader shoulders or top heavy weight distribution.

If you are someone who is comfortable with sinking into backbends it can sometimes be helpful to utilise this by having the chest a little higher as this can help take the pressure off of the shoulders and allow you to breathe more naturally. Regardless of how comfortable you are with backbends feel free to experiment with the relative height of the legs and chest to see which positions are most comfortable for you.

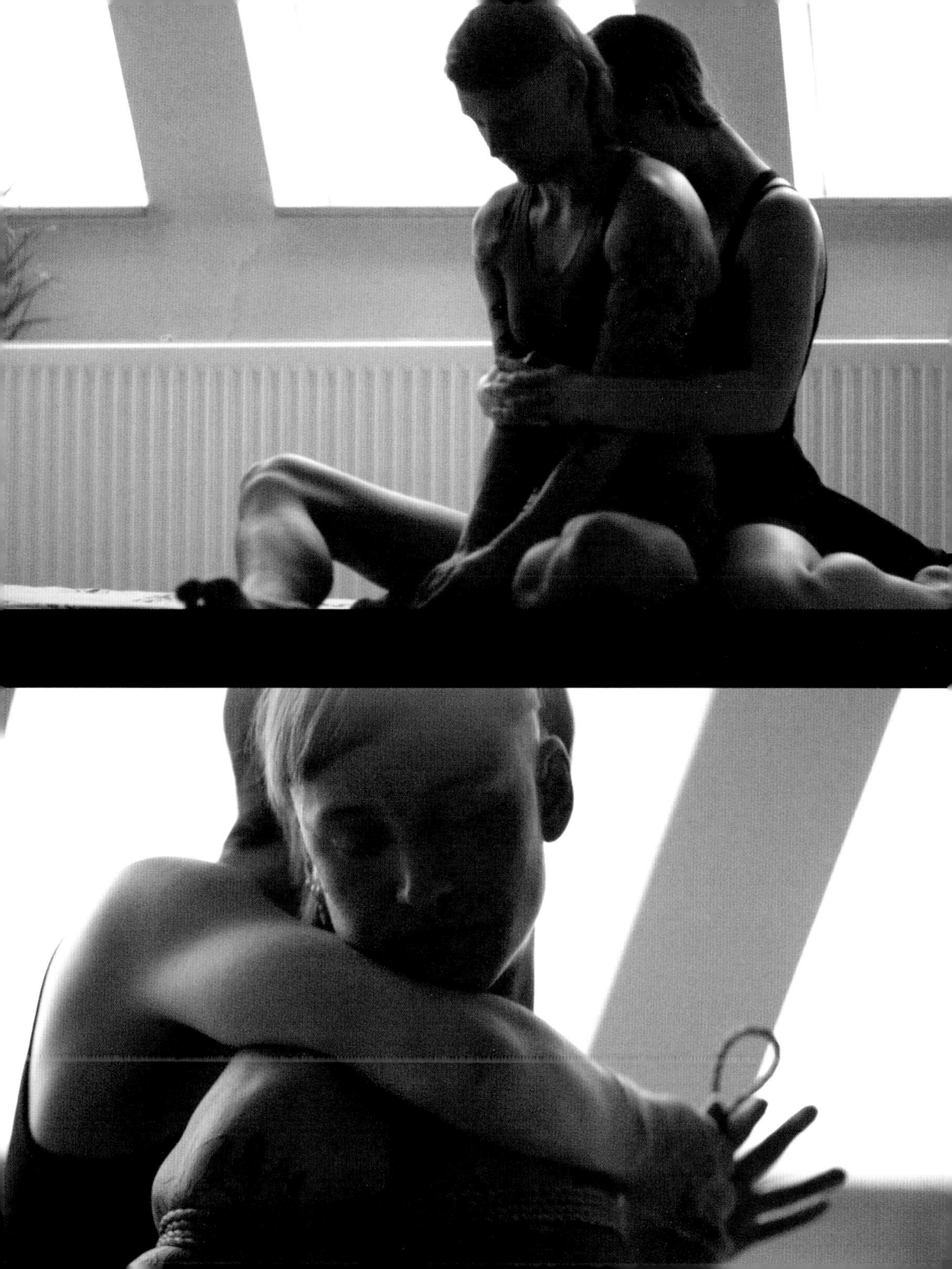

Glossary

Bight – The mid-point of a rope. In shibari, this is normally the part of the rope at which you begin a tie.

Double Bight – A yuki-knot used to reinforce the bight of the rope when performing suspensions.

Dressing the wraps – Evening out any twists, gaps, or uneven tensions in wraps, often by running a finger underneath them.

Dynamic load – The force exerted (on a hardpoint) by acceleration or deceleration, such as lifting, lowering, swinging, dropping, or spinning motions. This will be considerably more than the force exerted by static load.

Floor work – Any shibari that does not include suspension techniques.

Full turn – To take the working end and wrap it 360° around another piece of rope.

Gunslinger – A type of hip harness that loads from the side of the body.

Half hitch – A friction where the working end is wrapped around another rope and then passed back underneath itself. This can be used to lock off a tie, or to change the direction in which the working end is travelling.

Hip Harness – Any harness tied around the waist/hips.

Hogtie – A tie where the model's feet are pulled backwards, stretching out the front of the body – similar to a gyaku-ebi.

Hojo Cuff – A technique for creating a single column tie in the middle of a rope, rather than at the bight.

L-friction – A friction generally used to secure wraps to a central stem.

Main Line – Whichever suspension line(s) are giving the most critical support in a suspension.

Model – The person who is tied.

Overhand knot/lock – a knot formed by making a loop in a piece of rope and drawing one end through it. Often used to attach new ropes, lock off ropes, or prevent the end of the rope from fraying.

Partial Suspension – a suspension where at least one part of the body remains touching the floor at all times.

Reef knot – a knot consisting of two overhand knots tied in opposite ways.

Rigger – The person who is tying.

Secondary line – Any suspension line that is not the main line.

Single Column Tie – A wrap that goes around a single part of the body, locked in such a way that the size/tension is maintained.

Static Load – The force exerted (on a hardpoint) when the load is hanging completely still. Generally this will be equivalent to the actual weight of the person.

Stem – The line of rope connecting two or more wraps. This could, for example, be the link between two hojo cuffs (pg. 31) – but practically it is most often used to refer to a solid central point of a harness for example the back of a TK (pg. 52) or a futomomo.

Transition – To move the body between two different positions whilst tied.

Working End – The part of the rope that you are still working with. Generally the remainder of the rope from the last knot or friction you made, up to the rope ends

Yuki knot – A versatile variation of the half hitch named after Japanese rope artist Yukimura Haruki.

Aomuke-zuri 仰向け吊り – 'Face-up suspension' (pg. 156).

Ebi 海老 – 'Prawn' / **Ebizeme** 海老責め – 'Prawn torture'. A tie where the model's body is bent forwards (pg. 21).

Futomomo 太もも – 'Thigh'. Usually refers to a tie where the leg is bent at the knee (pg. 78).

Gote 後手 / also: **Gote-shibari** 後手縛り – 'Hands behind the back tie'. An alternative way of referring to the takatekote (pg. 50).

Gyaku-ebi-zuri 逆海老吊り – 'Reverse prawn suspension'. A suspension where the model's body is bent backwards. This usually refers to a face down position. (pg. 161).

Han'yuka-zuri 半床吊り – 'Half floor suspension'. One possible way of referring to partial suspensions in Japanese (pg 125).

Hikyaku-zuri 飛脚吊り – 'running postman suspension'. Hikyaku is the traditional Japanese name for messengers/couriers who ran long distances to make deliveries. (pg. 151).

Hashigata 橋形 – 'Bridge shape' (pg. 134).

Hishi 菱 / **Hishigata** 菱形 – 'Diamond shape' (pg. 89).

Honmusubi 本結び – 'true knot'. Reef knot (pg. 27).

Kannuki 閂 – 'Gate/door lock'. It is also referred to as a 'cinch' in English (pg. 32).

Kata-ashi kaikyaku 片足開脚 – 'one leg open'. (pg. 138).

Kata-ashikubi 片足首 – 'one ankle' (pg. 130).

Kinbaku 緊縛 – 'Tight binding'. This can be used interchangeably with the term 'shibari'. Although shibari seems to be the more common term in the west, in Japan Kinbaku is more likely to be immediately associated with rope bondage, whereas shibari could refer to any kind of tying.

Koshinawa 腰縄 – 'Waist/hip rope'. Can also be used when talking about a hip harness (pg. 134).

Munenawa 胸縄 – 'Chest rope'. Generally used to refer to a chest harness including (but not limited to) the takatekote (pg. 50).

Nawa 縄 – 'Rope'.

Nawagashira 縄頭 – 'Rope head'. The mid-point / bight of the rope (pg. 23).

Nawajiri 縄尻 – 'Rope ass'. The ends of the rope (pg. 23).

No-dome の止め – '"No" stop'. A friction or stop (dome) shaped like the hiragana character 'no' (の). This can be used to isolate tension in a particular part of the tie, or to change the direction in which the working end is travelling (pg. 36).

Semenawa 責め縄 – 'torment rope'. Often translated as 'torture rope' in English (pg. 14).

Shibari 縛り – 'Tying'. In Japan, this could refer to any kind of tying, not necessarily just rope bondage.

Takatekote 高手小手 – 'High hands, forearm' or 'upper arm, forearm'. Any tie where the model's hands are secured in a folded position behind their back (pg. 50).

Tsuri 吊り – 'Suspension' or 'hanging'. Pronounced as 'zuri' when it appears in the middle of a word/compound.

Ushiro-takatekote-shibari 後ろ高手小手縛り – '(high) hands behind the back tie'. Another way of referring to the takatekote (pg. 50).

Yokozuri 横吊り – 'Side suspension' (pg. 146).

Zuri 吊り – See 'Tsuri'.

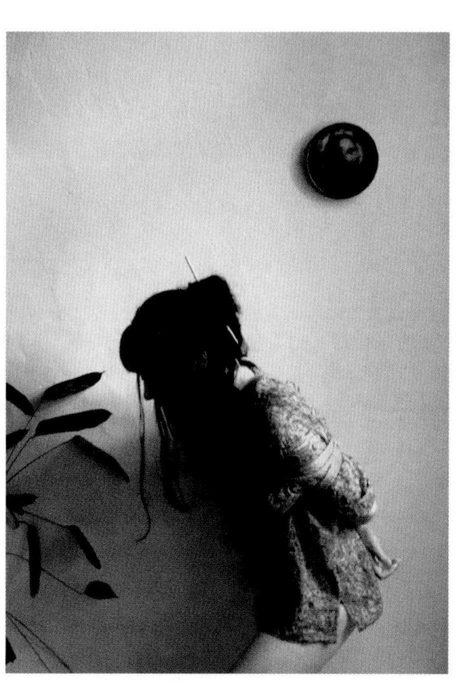

ABOUT THE AUTHOR

For information about Gestalta, please visit their website.

www.gestalta.co.uk

www.shibaristudio.com

ACKNOWLEDGEMENTS

Special thanks to Scarlot Rose and Evitrii – the models who appear in the majority of the demonstration photos – for making this book possible with their patience and endurance during those shoots.

Other models (in order of first appearance): Clementine Poulain, Ro Hardaker, Hassliebe, Bishop Black, Miss Hokusai, Aleks, Consuelosometimes, PotheadPixie, Sonya Lynn, Carlo Palermo, PlaisirDesPendus, Lahtnor, Anea Capaken, Tamandua, Aviana, Prettodekadens.

Photographer credits: Aleksander Stojanov (pg. 26, 42, 43, 57, 88, 103, 144), Shantel Liao (pg. 13, 35, 73, 77, 95, 117), Tentesion (pg. 17), Mista (pg. 94), Tamandua (pg. 126, 168), Simon Gentry (pg. 165). All remaining photography, editing, and/or photographic assistance by Philip, Gestalta, and Dan.

All ropework by Gestalta except pages 126 and 168 by Tamandua.

Illustration on page 102 by Evitrii.

Proofreader: Cad / Editor: Gestalta / Layout and design: Gestalta

Thanks to the people who gave technical consultation and/or feedback on the book: Green Gorilla, Mark DeViate (dv8), Gishinawa, Julia Merle, Nana777, Shantel Liao, Alex Young, Kimmii, and Rod Macdonald.

Thanks to everyone else who supported the process of making this book, in many different ways, both big and small, including: everyone at Rope Lab Leeds, Russell Dunphy, Ro Hardaker, Ellie Neptune, MMH, Cheshire, www.logicversusreason.xyz, Pedro, Nawakai Heilbronn, Fairydance, Aja, Olivia, Puk, Rebecca Tun, Molly Lee, and John.

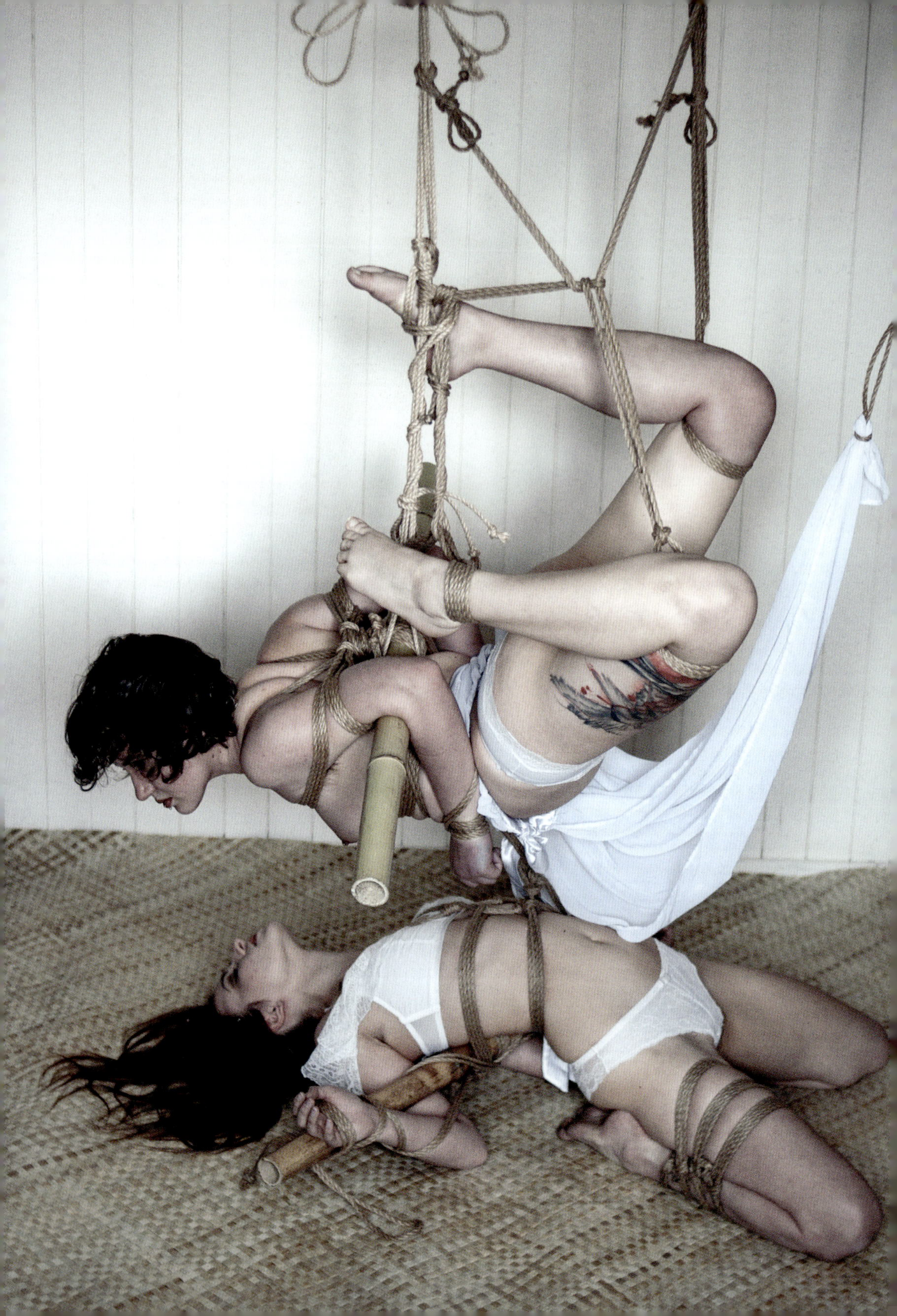

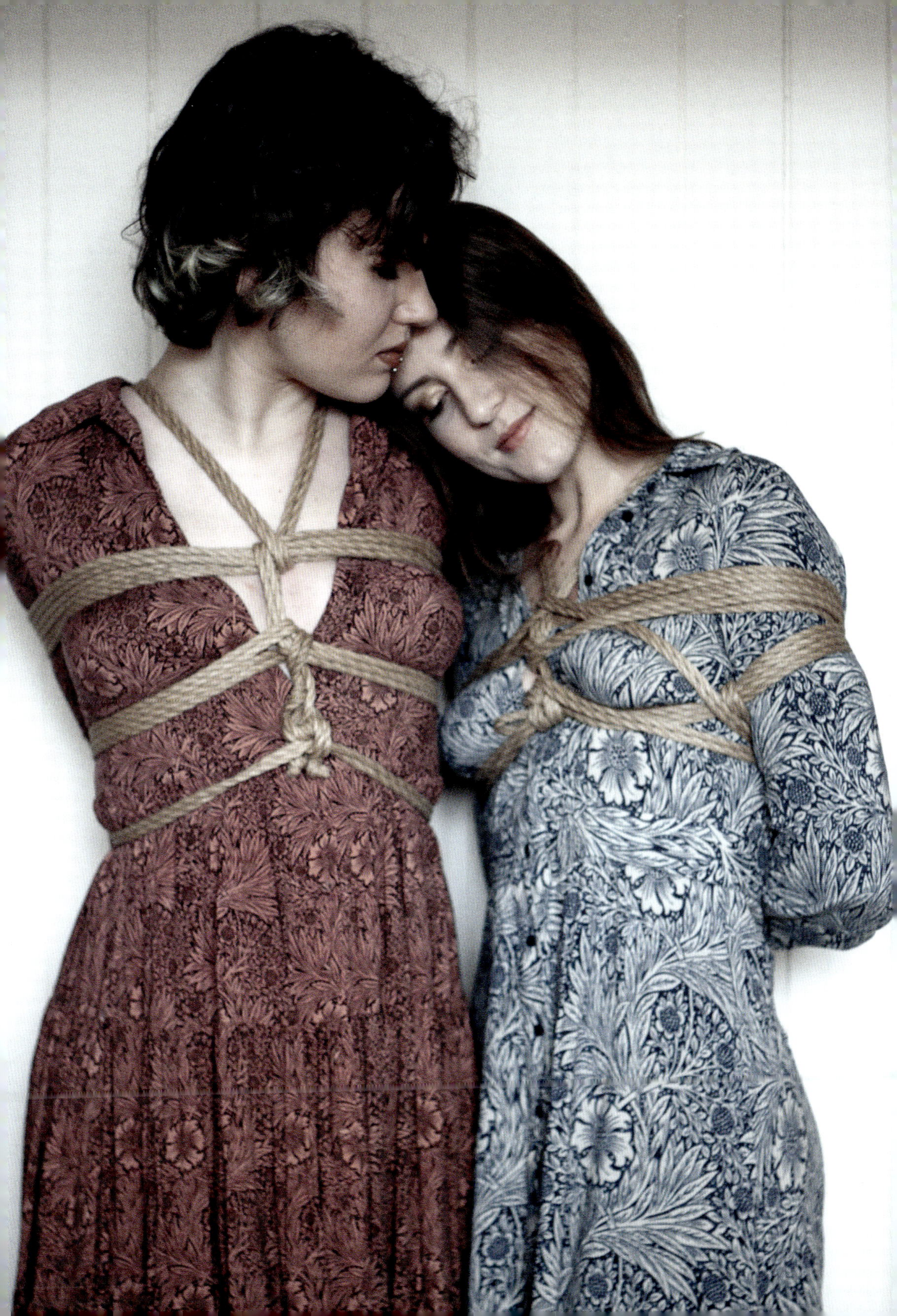

OTHER TITLES FROM KAHBOOM

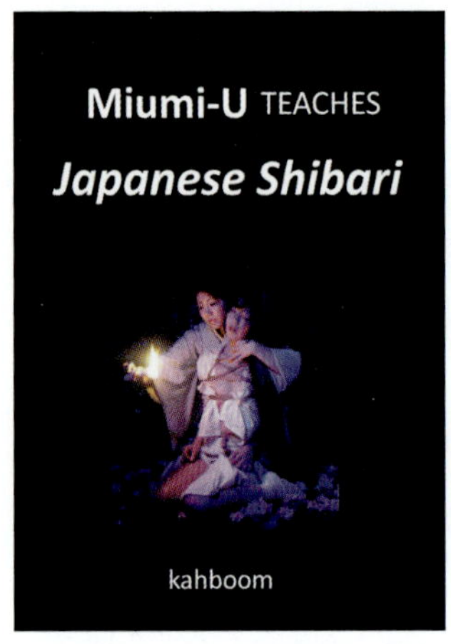

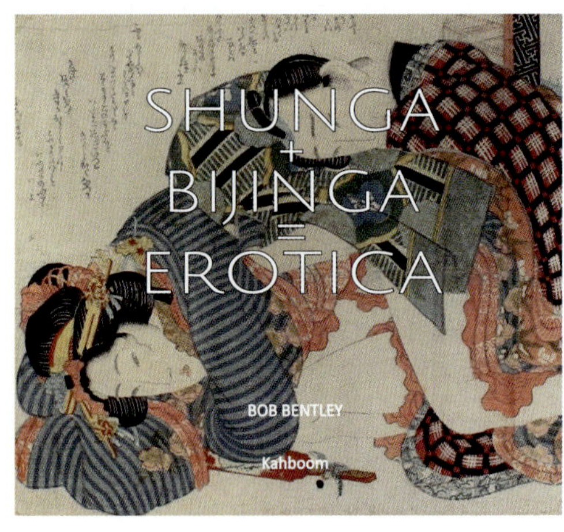

MIUMI-U TEACHES JAPANESE SHIBARI
ISBN: 978-0-9576275-1-2

SHUNGA + BIJINGA = EROTICA
ISBN: 978-0-9576275-5-0

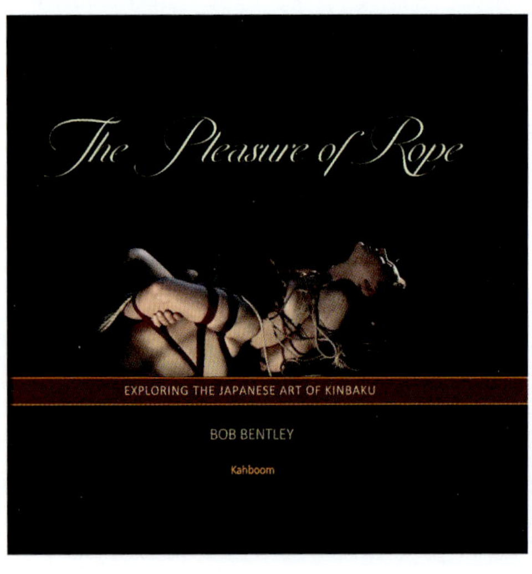

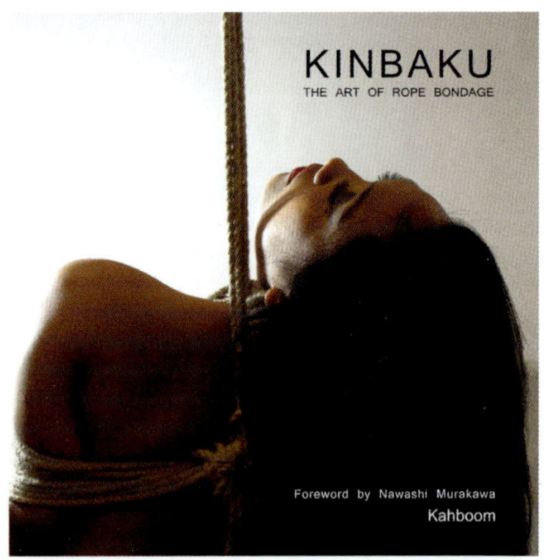

THE PLEASURE OF ROPE
ISBN: 978-0-9576275-3-6

KINBAKU
ISBN: 978-0-9576275-0-5